AMERICAN FOREIGN POLICY SINCE THE VIETNAM WAR

AMERICAN FOREIGN POLICY SINCE THE VIETNAM WAR

Second Edition

The Search for Consensus from Nixon to Clinton

Richard A. Melanson

M.E. Sharpe
Armonk, New York
London, England

Library of Congress Cataloging-in-Publication Data

Melanson, Richard A.
American foreign policy since the Vietnam War : the search for consensus
from Nixon to Clinton / Richard A. Melanson. — 2nd ed.
p.   cm.
Rev. ed. of: Reconstructing consensus. © 1991.
Includes bibliographical references (p.   ) and index.
ISBN 1-56324-521-3 (hardcover : alk. paper). — ISBN 1-56324-522-1 (pbk. : alk. paper)
1. United States—Foreign relations—1945–1989.
2. United States—Foreign relations—1989–   .
I. Melanson, Richard A.   Reconstructing consensus.
II. Title.
E840.M43   1996
327.73—dc20
95-32053
CIP

Printed in the United States of America

The paper used in this publication meets the minimum requirements of
American National Standard for Information Sciences—
Permanence of Paper for Printed Library Materials,
ANSI Z 39.48-1984.

BM (c)   10   9   8   7   6   5   4   3   2   1
BM (p)   10   9   8   7   6   5   4   3   2   1

Contents

Preface

The Vietnam War seriously damaged the domestic foreign policy consensus so painstakingly constructed by Presidents Truman, Eisenhower, and Kennedy and largely discredited America's Cold War strategy of global containment. It shattered the Democratic Party's former foreign policy unity and played an important role in helping to elect a series of Republican presidents, beginning with Richard Nixon. The sudden ending of the Cold War in the late 1980s completed the destruction of this national consensus by removing the Soviet Union as America's primary external enemy (and strategic lodestar) and by exposing some serious foreign policy disagreements within the Republican Party, especially about immigration, protectionism, and the United Nations.

In view of the frequently difficult domestic political circumstances in which U.S. foreign policy has been formulated since the late 1960s, this book has two aims: (1) to describe and evaluate the grand designs, foreign policy strategies, and tactics of presidents since Richard Nixon; and (2) to examine the efforts of these post-Vietnam and post–Cold War presidents to sell their foreign policies to an often skeptical Congress and public.[1]

Because of the divisive impact and long-term legacy of Vietnam, every president since Richard Nixon believed that the reconstruction of a domestic consensus constituted a fundamental foreign policy challenge. Indeed, immediately after the Persian Gulf War in 1991 President Bush proclaimed that the "Vietnam syndrome" lay buried in the sands of Iraq. But the termination of the Cold War did not really erase the collective public memory of Vietnam as events in Bosnia and Somalia soon made clear. Instead, it served to complicate further the efforts of George Bush and Bill Clinton to build a domestic foreign policy consensus.

This book pays a great deal of attention to the rhetoric used by these presidents to mobilize mass and elite support for their foreign policy grand designs, strategies, and tactics. I argue that this blizzard of presidential words, while not a wholly new phenomenon, is nevertheless intimately connected to the systematic "packaging" and "selling" of the president and the "image" of the presidency that began in earnest during the Nixon administration.[2]

To structure and focus the comparisons[3] of these administrations' foreign policies, I have posed the same six questions to all of them:

1. What were the domestic priorities of each president?
2. How did each perceive the problem of governance?
3. What were the relationships of questions 1 and 2 to each administration's foreign policy?
4. What were the grand designs, strategic objectives, and tactics of the Nixon (Ford), Carter, Reagan, Bush, and early Clinton foreign policies?
5. How did these presidents attempt to legitimate their foreign policies to the bureaucracy and the public?
6. Did any president succeed in reconstructing a domestic foreign policy consensus comparable to that of the pre-Vietnam era?

The book is divided into four parts. Part One, which is also chapter 1, discusses the elusive yet important concept of domestic foreign policy consensus and disaggregates it into policy, cultural, and procedural components. It then reviews the main axioms and conditions of the Cold War consensus and shows how first the Vietnam War and then the ending of the Cold War dramatically altered them. Next it argues that presidents since World War II have tried to construct and sustain consensus by seeking to legitimate the grand designs, strategic objectives, and tactics of their foreign policies to the public and political elites. Finally, it reviews some of the legitimation techniques used by Cold War, post-Vietnam, and post–Cold War presidents.

Part Two, which includes chapters 2 through 4, focuses on the post-Vietnam presidencies of Nixon, Carter, and Reagan with Gerald Ford treated briefly in the Nixon chapter.[4] Each chapter answers the six questions posed above, although there are a few variations in the format of each. Chapter 2 supplements discussion of the grand design, strategy, and tactics of the Nixon foreign policy with an examination of his attempts to legitimate his Vietnam policy. It does so because Nixon perceived a close link between the attainment of "peace with honor" and the development of superpower détente. Because of the dramatic shifts in Jimmy Carter's foreign policy between the first two years and the last two years of his presidency, chapter 3 argues that distinct grand designs, strategies, and tactics in effect separated the earlier period from the later one. Thus it compares and contrasts these "world order" and "neocontainment" approaches. Chapter 4 looks at two minicase studies, as well as the overall design, strategy, and tactics of the Reagan foreign policy. Two specific legitimation efforts are highlighted, one successful and one that largely failed, the Grenada "rescue mission" and aid for the Nicaraguan "democratic resistance."

Part Three, composed of chapters 5 and 6, considers America's first two post–Cold War administrations, those of George Bush and Bill Clinton. Chapter 5 tries to understand Bush's foreign policy approach by analyzing his administration's efforts to make sense of the collapse of the Soviet Union and the revolutions in Eastern Europe as well as to chart a "new world order" after the Persian Gulf War. Chapter 6 analyzes the early years of Bill Clinton's foreign policy by focusing on the confused handling of Bosnia, Somalia, and Haiti; his "backlash" state concept; his approach to Russia; and, most important, his "big, emerging markets" foreign economic strategy. But because of the necessarily tentative nature of this analysis, I do not discuss whether or not Clinton has thus far been successful in resurrecting a domestic foreign policy consensus. Chapters 5 and 6 also try to show how the post–Cold War world confronted both Bush and Clinton with very similar issues and dilemmas.

On the basis of the structured, focused comparisons undertaken in chapters 2 through 6, Part Four (chapter 7) offers a summary of their major conclusions and several tables to juxtapose them more easily.

My research strategy has been to rely on unclassified documents, particularly presidential speeches. These have proven very useful to a study partly focused on presidential rhetoric. I have supplemented these materials with secondary sources, the memoirs of leading participants, and a large number of personal interviews conducted with Nixon, Carter, Reagan, Bush, and Clinton officials over a period of several years.

This book constitutes a revision and expansion of my *Reconstructing Consensus: American Foreign Policy since the Vietnam War* (New York: St. Martin's Press, 1991). I have rewritten large sections of chapter 1 to account for some of the changes in the domestic politics of American foreign policy brought about by the end of the Cold War. Moreover, I have significantly expanded the chapter on the Bush administration and have added a new chapter on the early years of the Clinton presidency.

I would like to thank several people who assisted in various ways to enhance the quality of this new book. Several of my friends and colleagues at the National War College deserve mention: Hugh DeSantis, Ambassador

David Mack, Roy Stafford, Ron Tammen, Cynthia Watson, and Howard Wiarda. Special appreciation should be extended to Anna Roque, my superb research assistant for the Bush and Clinton chapters. I also wish to thank several other scholars who helped sharpen the argument along the way: Andrew Z. Katz, David Mayers, Charles Neu, Frank Ninkovich, and Robert W. Tucker.

The views expressed here are those of the author exclusively and do not represent the views of the National Defense University, the Department of Defense, or the U.S. government.

Notes

1. Alexander M. George, "Domestic Constraints on Regime Change in U.S. Foreign Policy: The Need for Policy Legitimacy," in *Change in the International System*, ed. Ole R. Holsti, Randolph M. Siverson, and Alexander M. George, 233–62. The literature dealing explicitly with the domestic legitimacy of American foreign policy remains meager. See, for example, two essays by B. Thomas Trout: "Rhetoric Revisited: Political Legitimation and the Cold War," *International Studies Quarterly* 19 (1975); and "Legitimating Containment and Détente: A Comparative Analysis," paper prepared for the annual meeting of the Midwest Political Science Association, Chicago, April 1979; and Dan Caldwell, *American-Soviet Relations: From 1947 to the Nixon-Kissinger Grand Design* (Westport, CT: Greenwood Press, 1981).

2. See Theodore J. Lowi, *The Personal President: Power Invested, Promise Unfulfilled,* and Jeffrey K. Tulis, *The Rhetorical Presidency.* These concepts are discussed in chapter 1 of the present study.

3. Alexander M. George, "Case Studies and Theory Development: The Method of Structured, Focused Comparison," in *Diplomacy: New Approaches in History, Theory, and Policy,* ed. Paul Gordon Lauren. Among the more noteworthy examples of works employing this method are John Lewis Gaddis, *Strategies of Containment: A Critical Appraisal of Postwar American National Security Policy;* Alexander M. George and Richard Smoke, *Deterrence in American Foreign Policy: Theory and Practice;* Richard Smoke, *War: Controlling Escalation;* Barry R. Posen, *The Sources of Military Doctrine: France, Britain, and Germany between the World Wars;* and Stephen M. Walt, *The Origins of Alliances.*

4. Because Gerald Ford relied heavily on the advice of Henry Kissinger, pursued the grand design and strategic objectives (if not the tactics) of Nixon's foreign policy, and was compelled to begin his fight for the 1976 Republican nomination barely a year after becoming president, this study does not give his presidency a separate chapter. Instead, it treats Ford's foreign policy as essentially an extension of Nixon's and thus discusses it in the course of chapter 2.

Part One

The Rise and Fall of the Cold War Consensus

1

In Search of Consensus

Consensus, like *balance of power, national interest,* and *bipartisanship,* is a frequently used and much abused term. More than twenty-five years ago, the sociologist Edward Shils offered a now classic definition:

> Consensus is a particular state of the belief system of a society. It exists when a large proportion of the adult members of a society, more particularly a large proportion of those concerned with decisions regarding the allocations of authority, status, rights, wealth and income, and other important and scarce values about which conflict might occur, are in approximate agreement in their beliefs about what decisions should be made and have some feeling of unity with each other and with the society as a whole.[1]

To claim that consensus exists whenever interested adults are in approximate agreement about what decisions should be made implies that consensus describes social agreement along a wide spectrum ranging from the general to the specific and from the lofty to the mundane. Even the more narrow notion of *political consensus* embraces a near-universe of activity. In short, because the word *consensus* has been used to describe agreement about almost anything, its utility might be suspect.

Yet investigating the domestic dimensions of American foreign policy virtually compels discussion of *consensus,* if only because presidents, their advisers, members of Congress, and the media routinely do. The term must be taken seriously because of its central role in contemporary American political discourse. And, indeed, if carefully defined and applied, it can provide useful insights into the domestic landscape of American foreign policy.

A brief review of U.S. foreign policy in the twentieth century should illustrate this point. Serious foreign policy disagreements abounded in the decades before World War II. The bitter debates over overseas annexations, entry into the Great War, the Treaty of Versailles, and interwar neutrality legislation represent important episodes in the internal politics of American foreign policy. Some of these struggles involved vital constitutional issues about executive and legislative powers in foreign affairs. Thus Henry Cabot Lodge opposed the Treaty of Versailles, not as an isolationist, but as a senator convinced that the League Covenant would enable presidents to make commitments and wage wars without congressional approval. The Neutrality Acts of the 1930s, Lend Lease, and Franklin Roosevelt's unde- clared naval war against Germany in 1941 provoked similarly important constitutional questions about presidential-congressional procedures. These serious policy and procedural disputes reflected profound disagreements about the requirements of American security. What kinds of international conditions promoted or weakened U.S. security? Should the United States seek merely to protect its physical security, or must it also act to preserve or export its political and economic values and institutions? How best could either of these goals be achieved? These questions yielded a variety of harshly discor- dant answers in the decades preceding World War II.

From the late 1940s to the mid-1960s, however, presidents offered for- eign policies that enjoyed substantial public and elite support.[2] The apparent demands of the Cold War largely overcame the often paralyzing divisive- ness of the interwar period and lent a certain coherence, purpose, and pre- dictability to American foreign policy. Some critics, however, have plausibly argued that Cold War presidents, by baldly and simplistically inflating the communist "threat," manufactured an artificial consensus that stifled domestic dissent, rigidified U.S. foreign policy, and ultimately trapped them in their own rhetoric.[3] In short, the desperate search for con- sensus encouraged Cold War presidents to present platitudinous, highly symbolic foreign policies embodying vague national, but supposedly uni- versal, values.

But to ask if presidents *should* try to create domestic foreign policy consensus seems largely irrelevant inasmuch as most presidents—Nixon was a partial exception—have acted on the premise that consensus is both possible and desirable, have worked hard to achieve it, and have done so despite the fact that there exists no generally accepted definition of consensus!

Cold War presidents from Harry S. Truman to Lyndon Johnson shared the conviction that public and elite support for foreign policy could be most effectively built on a framework of global anticommunism. From the late 1960s to the late 1980s, U.S. presidents, haunted and constrained by the legacy of Vietnam, tried to sustain America's international "relevance" in the face of widespread domestic fears about the costs of military intervention and global activism. These post-Vietnam presidents confronted a public increasingly preoccupied with domestic economic interests but simultaneously demanding that the United States remain a world leader. Presidents Richard Nixon, Jimmy Carter, and Ronald Reagan attempted to grapple with this post-Vietnam world by unveiling grand designs and foreign policy strategies in conflict with those of their immediate predecessors. These, in turn, provoked vigorous reactions from divided domestic elites now arrayed along ideologically adversarial lines. These presidents, in reaction to such difficult and often contradictory domestic realities, relied heavily on rhetoric, theater, and public relations to mobilize support for their foreign policies, with Ronald Reagan and his "handlers" merely continuing a trend begun by Nixon in 1968. The result was that by the late 1980s, "rhetorical" presidents had further widened the frequently prominent gap between words and deeds in American foreign policy.

There were, of course, several reasons for this disturbing development. The availability of instantaneous communications, congressional insistence on a central role in foreign policymaking, and the growing cultural diversity of American society since the 1960s conspired to tempt presidents to portray all decisions as "simple and stark choices between good and evil."[4] These rhetorical excesses could perhaps be defended as necessary while the Cold War raged, for behind the overheated words lay a reasonable geopolitical analysis that focused on the reality of the Soviet threat. But with the demise of the Soviet Union, and with it the central organizing concept of forty plus years of American strategy, post–Cold War presidents have often reached back to the old rhetoric in order to mobilize public support for international undertakings whose strategic rationale has been very difficult to define. Did George Bush really think that Saddam Hussein was "worse than Hitler"? Does Bill Clinton really believe that the United States is the "conscience of the international community"? Or should such statements be dismissed as rhetorical flourishes designed to achieve that elusive public consensus about the U.S. role in the post–Cold War world? The answers are not at all clear.

In sum, the quest for foreign policy consensus has been both an understandable presidential response to a fragmented, sometimes stalemated domestic political system and a dangerous temptation for them to misrepresent their foreign policies. The absence of consensus risks turning every foreign policy issue into a highly politicized domestic dispute, yet the search for consensus has often entailed the articulation of doctrinal, moralistic foreign policies ill suited to serve the interests of the United States. If anything, the geopolitical uncertainties unleashed by the ending of the Cold War have exacerbated this tendency.

The Elements of Consensus

To help clarify the inevitably slippery yet important concept of domestic foreign policy consensus I disaggregate it into three components: *policy, cultural,* and *procedural. Policy* consensus involves substantial public and elite agreement about the grand design, strategy, and tactics of foreign policy. *Cultural* consensus entails broad, grassroots agreement about an appropriate set of private and public values linked to America's international role. *Procedural* consensus refers to presidential-congressional understandings about the respective tasks to be performed by each governmental branch. The meaning of each is made clearer as concrete examples are given. Here I suggest that for about twenty years, beginning shortly after World War II, American foreign policy was characterized by a relatively stable policy, cultural, and procedural domestic consensus.

Policy Consensus

During the two decades following World War II, political elites, most notably the so-called foreign policy establishment, and the wider public, especially the better informed or attentive part of it, subscribed to a set of fundamental propositions about the nature of the international system, the requirements of American security, and the nation's proper orientation to the world. Chief among them were the following:

1. Alone among the nations of the free world the United States has both the material power and the moral responsibility to create a just and stable international order. While isolationism lingered for a time, after 1945, most prominently within parts of the Republican Party, Senator Arthur Vandenberg's well-known conversion to internationalism and Dwight Eisenhower's victory over Robert Taft at the 1952 national convention signified important triumphs for the emerging activist consensus. To be sure, there remained a residue of "Asialationist" sentiment among some Republicans, while Democratic leaders inclined toward a Eurocentric orientation, but these divergent tendencies largely subsided after the termination of the Korean War. Public opinion data on this issue of global involvement repeatedly revealed wide support for the proposition that it was better for the United States "to take an active role in," rather than "stay out of," world affairs. Typically, support hovered around 70 percent, dipping a bit in 1946 and 1947 and again immediately after the Korean cease-fire and soaring to 79 percent in June 1965.[5] No comparable surveys were done on elite attitudes until 1974, but most analysts believe that until at least the early 1960s, political leaders led the public into accepting a greater U.S. role in the world.

2. *In view of the interdependent nature of the world, U.S. security interests must be necessarily global.* As John L. Gaddis and others have shown, George F. Kennan and other Truman administration officials initially wished to limit America's interests to Western Europe, Japan, and the Western Hemisphere because of both the perceived nature of the Soviet threat and the finite resources available to the United States. But the psychological difficulties of drawing and sustaining distinctions between vital and peripheral interests, the reluctance of Congress to provide aid to Greece and Turkey, the frightening events of 1949 (such as the Soviet atomic test and the Communist takeover of China), and the outbreak of the Korean War combined to compel the Truman administration, first rhetorically and then in actuality, to embrace a dramatically more expansive definition of the nature of the Soviet threat and the requirements of American security.[6] The operative metaphors became Dean Acheson's infectious rotten apple and Eisenhower's row of failing dominoes, for they expressed the widely held conviction that the United States could not afford to "pick and choose" its overseas commitments. Nevertheless, opinion surveys from these years indicated that the public retained a certain sense of geographical priorities. For example, whereas opinion supported the Marshall Plan 57 percent to 21 percent in July 1947 and 65 percent to 13 percent in November 1948, the public was considerably more divided in July 1950 about sending military supplies to Chiang Kai-shek, with 48 percent in favor and 35 percent opposed. And while 74 percent approved of NATO in May 1950, only 55 percent wished to back this commitment with U.S. ground forces in January 1951. Support for sending American troops to Indochina ranged from 8 percent in August 1953 to 20 percent in May 1954, though approval increased rapidly—to 59 percent in March 1966—once the action was taken. And on the issue of dispatching U.S. armed forces to the Middle East to stop a hypothetical Russian invasion, opinion was divided in January 1957 with 50 percent in favor and 34 percent opposed. In contrast, a March 1959 poll showed that fully 81 percent favored retention of U.S. troops in West Berlin even if it risked war.7 We should be wary of reading too much into these results, but in general it appears that the commitment to Western Europe received a somewhat higher priority among the public, and that support inevitably grew in the immediate aftermath of all actual commitments.

3. *Soviet and Soviet-inspired aggression and subversion constitutes the primary threat to world peace.* Here again Gallup poll results help to illuminate the public's attitude. As late as January 1947, 43 percent thought that Russia would cooperate with the United States in world affairs, but by June 1949 only 20 percent continued to believe so.[8] The opinion that "Russia is trying to build herself up to be the ruling power of the world" reached

76 percent in October 1947 and remained at comparably high levels for most of the next two decades. This apparently pervasive consensus, however, largely masked two complicating elements. First, even among the elites there remained disagreement about the sources of Soviet expansion, with some analysts stressing Marxist-Leninist ideology, others emphasizing the long-standing aims of Russian nationalism, and still others focusing on the peculiarities of Stalin's personality. While these divergent perceptions implied *policy* differences over whether or not Soviet-American cooperation would *ever* be possible, they remained dormant, for the most part, until at least the 1960s. The Soviet threat appeared so serious and immediate that speculation about its roots seemed abstract and irrelevant to most political leaders and almost all of the public. Second, U.S. policymakers, especially after the outbreak of the Korean War, repeatedly warned of an international communist conspiracy, a monolithic threat to the free world, an alien way of life dedicated to the extinction of American values, an unholy alliance cemented by an evil ideology. The American public shared this view, yet it was not one actually held by most Truman and Eisenhower officials. Recent scholarship has shown that foreign policy specialists as otherwise different as George F. Kennan and John Foster Dulles believed that real opportunities existed for fragmenting the Soviet bloc, though they disagreed about the appropriate tactics to pursue.[9] For them, the Soviet empire was surprisingly fragile, probably overextended, and vulnerable to fissures. The anti-communist public consensus of these years, in fact, resulted in part from the rhetorical exaggerations of presidents and their advisers, exaggerations that involved a wide range of foreign policy issues.[10]

4. *The policy of containment represents the best way to stop further Soviet and Soviet-sponsored expansion.* Containment, though originally designed to deny Western Europe and Japan to the Soviet Union, was gradually universalized, first, rhetorically, in the Truman Doctrine, and later, in deed, during the Korean War. Yet even in its most exuberant form, containment remained a bounded crusade, more tolerated than loved by a public and elite consensus that preferred it to the alternatives of isolationism, rollback, and preventive war. Some commentators, such as Kennan and Walter Lippmann, worried about the cohesiveness of far-flung "collective security" pacts, and many more people (particularly within the Eisenhower administration) doubted America's ability to pay for global containment without incurring severe domestic costs; but, on balance, this policy seemed a responsible mixture of idealism and pragmatism. While some prominent Republicans in the early 1950s paid rhetorical homage to a "liberation theology" that preached against the Yalta "surrender" and the China sellout, its hollowness became evident as early as June 1953 when rollback enthusi-

asts remained generally silent during worker unrest in East Berlin and was fully discredited by similar behavior during the Hungarian Revolution in 1956. What little opinion data exist suggests a public unwilling to risk war in order to recapture lost territory but equally opposed to accepting additional communist triumphs. For example, in September 1962, at a time of severe U.S.–Cuban tension, only 24 percent of those polled by Gallup countenanced the use of American troops to overthrow Castro, while 63 percent were opposed.[11] In sum, despite the psychological frustrations and financial expense of containment, most Americans saw it as a prudent alternative that promised to keep the peace by demonstrating strength, resolve, and restraint to adversaries.

5. *The United States must possess nuclear weapons in order to help deter a Soviet attack on it and its allies.* Much of the public certainly worried about the risks of nuclear war during these years, and this nervousness dramatically increased during episodes such as the Berlin and Cuban Missile crises, but most Americans believed that nuclear weapons enhanced U.S. security and wished to preserve nuclear superiority. Interestingly, a 1955 Gallup poll indicated that only 27 percent thought that humankind would be destroyed in a full-scale Soviet–American nuclear war,[12] though large majorities opposed a United States preemptive nuclear attack. Indeed, this "deterrence through superiority" tenet so thoroughly dominated discourse that policy alternatives—for example, equivalence, freeze builddown, mutual elimination—were not even posed to the public by polling organizations until the issue of atmospheric testing emerged in the late 1950s.

6. *A stable, open world economy required American leadership.* While the public typically focused attention more on personal issues such as unemployment, recession, and inflation, political leaders shared the grander conviction that adherence to the Bretton Woods arrangements would lessen the likelihood of a new world depression. Some protectionist sentiment lingered and occasionally proved politically potent as, for example, when the International Trade Organization treaty failed to win Senate approval; but on balance the presumed lessons of the 1930s convinced most in Congress and almost everyone in the executive that the trade wars, competitive devaluations, and currency blocs of that decade had directly contributed to the outbreak of World War II. A powerful U.S. economy tied to multilateral institutions like the General Agreement on Tariffs and Trade (GATT), the World Bank, and the International Monetary Fund (IMF) would encourage growth and inoculate the free world against instability that could be exploited by communists. Nevertheless, international economic issues were clearly subordinate in these years to themes of political and military security.

7. The United States must assume leadership in such organizations as the United Nations. Public support for the United Nations remained remarkably high during these decades, despite misgivings about how well the organization performed. In a 1947 Gallup survey 85 percent favored the United Nations, and 77 percent did a decade later. In 1947, when asked if the United States should stay in the organization even if Russia continued to block the will of the majority of members, 73 percent said yes. Four years later, 75 percent approved of U.S. membership, and in 1962, 90 percent favored membership. At the same time, far fewer Americans expressed satisfaction with the work performance of the United Nations. Thus in 1947 only 39 percent were pleased with the progress made by the United Nations, and in 1951, 24 percent rated its performance as good, 30 percent fair, and 36 percent poor, in large part, no doubt, because of the frustrations brought on by the Korean War.[13] This high and sustained level of support for U.S. membership (and leadership) brings us back, in fact, to the first tenet of the Cold War consensus—that the United States must play an active role in world affairs. During the early postwar decades, large majorities of the public and the political elites believed that this active role could best be served as the leader of a free world military and economic alliance. Taken together, these fundamental propositions formed a foreign policy ethos for twenty-odd years that lay at the heart of the policy consensus.

Cultural Consensus

The Cold War cultural consensus was firmly grounded in a set of values that one recent study has called "cosmopolitan liberalism."[14] According to this definition of national identity, to be an American a person had only to subscribe to such values as liberty, individualism, popular sovereignty, and equality of opportunity. One's ethnic origin was much less important in defining "Americanness" than allegiance to these liberal ideals. In reality, of course, this definition discriminated against African Americans, Native Americans, and women.

Particularly in the 1950s, social analysts such as David Riesman, Vance Packard, William H. Whyte, and Paul Goodman ridiculed the conformity, materialism, and banality of American life and warned that large organizations, suburbia, the public education system, and other contemporary atrocities threatened to transform the population into herds of exceptionally well-behaved sheep. Others noted the growing intolerance of Cold War America and pointed to McCarthyism, loyalty oaths, security checks, the intrusiveness of the House Un-American Activities Committee, and a renewed focus on the symbols of civil religion (e.g., "under God" in the Pledge of Allegiance and "In God We Trust" on the currency) as trends that would eventuate in the imposition of a repressive "garrison state."[15] Eisenhower himself worried that the economic and political costs of the Cold War, expressed most vividly in the military-industrial complex, would destroy fundamental individual liberties.

Yet if some commentators emphasized the stultifying conformity of American society, many more celebrated the "American way of life." Much of the popular media, from *Life* magazine to the television show "Father Knows Best," projected widely shared symbols of normalcy and respectability: a stable family life, homeownership, rising prosperity, and community status.[16] In the academic community Talcott Parsons and Walt W. Rostow disseminated strongly positive views of "Americanism." Parsons contended that American society retained a "moral mission" rooted in family life and religious values wherein the individual sacrificed for the good of community and nation.[17] And Rostow celebrated a unique "American style" whose enduring strength had withstood the insecurities produced by the Cold War. For him, family, religion, and social stability demonstrated strong evidence of the fundamental health and character of the American identity.[18] Nothing better captured the cultural core of this era than the Nixon–Khrushchev kitchen debate of the opening of the American National Exhibition in Moscow during the summer of 1959. The vice-president's performance received an extraordinarily enthusiastic reception at home, all the more remarkable because instead of discussing weapons, geopolitics, or ideology, the two leaders carried on a lengthy, often heated, exchange about the relative merits of American and Soviet appliances. For Nixon, the essence of the good life lay within the walls of the suburban house, and he "proclaimed that the 'model home,' with a male breadwinner and a full-time female homemaker, and adorned with a wide array of consumer goods, represented the essence of American freedom."[19] Under the shadow of the bomb and the communist threat the "nuclear" family had emerged as a dramatically private statement of stability.

All these analysts, whether critical or admiring, saw an America during these decades that evinced a strong measure of cultural consensus. Moreover, there appeared to be a solid symbiotic relationship between this consensus and those broadly shared propositions about U.S. foreign policy. Indeed, more than one policymaker welcomed the "communist challenge" as a catalyst that could reinvigorate Americans' sense of duty and mission. Dwight Eisenhower and John Foster Dulles repeatedly sounded this theme, and even George Kennan seemed momentarily captured by its allure, for he concluded "The Sources of Soviet Conduct" by asking Americans to be grateful to a Providence that, by "providing this . . . implacable challenge, has made their entire security as a nation dependent on their pulling themselves together and accepting the responsibilities of moral and political leadership that history plainly intended them to bear."[20] And, indeed, this cultural consensus was characterized by an ethic of national sacrifice. No doubt the often bemoaned rampant consumerism of this period seemed to clash with the exigencies of the "struggle against communism," but these consumers nevertheless tolerated a peacetime draft and a defense spending burden that represented 9 percent of the gross national product and almost half of the federal budget.[21]

Procedural Consensus

Central to the procedural Cold War consensus was a series of votes in the Congress from 1945 to 1964 highly supportive of major presidential initiatives. U.S. membership in the United Nations, NATO, the Organization of American States (OAS), and the South East Asian Treaty Organization (SEATO); aid to Greece and Turkey; the Marshall Plan; ratification of the Japan Peace Treaty, the Korea Defense Pact, the Formosa Security Pact and the Nuclear Test Ban Treaty; and regional resolutions covering Formosa, the Middle East, Berlin, Cuba, and Indochina all received at least 70 percent of the vote with several claiming virtually unanimous support. Yet these overwhelming majorities pointed as well to a procedural consensus in executive-congressional relations that had been fostered by Roosevelt, partly threatened by Truman, revived by Eisenhower, and sustained by Kennedy. At the same time, the strength of this consensus can easily be exaggerated. For example, Congress prevented the State Department from administering Marshall Plan aid despite Truman's vehement protests; the Nuclear Test Ban Treaty was ratified only after many false starts and a great deal of compromise; and the Eisenhower Doctrine (Middle East Resolution) was delayed several months by a Congress that ultimately diluted its contents.

The experience of the interwar period played a major role in defining the nature of this procedural consensus. After the bitterness produced by the League of Nations debate and sharp divisions evident in the 1930s on the neutrality issue, Roosevelt began a serious effort in 1942 to make planning more coherent and unified for postwar international organizations. It involved, in essence, a three-step process that would be utilized in regard to a broad range of foreign policy themes during the next quarter century. First, FDR included key members of Congress—senators in particular—and leaders of prominent public organizations in the postwar planning process. This direct involvement helped win their approval for the outline of an internationalist foreign policy that featured U.S. leadership in a host of multilateral institutions. Second, FDR, in concert with these members of Congress and private citizens, launched a public relations campaign to win the support of the broader public and the remainder of Congress. The final step involved obtaining congressional approval for a joint resolution endorsing the proposed course of action.[22]

But this procedure did not always work. Roosevelt himself seriously compromised it by his refusal to involve members of Congress or the leaders of influential private associations in another aspect of postwar planning—the future of Eastern Europe and East Asia as embodied in the Yalta agreements. Some would later call these accords treasonous; for others, they were merely unconstitutional, but their legacy would haunt the Democratic Party for the next twenty years.

Truman's decision not to ask Congress for a declaration of war or some other legislative action during the Korean conflict did not directly violate the procedural consensus, for senior congressional Democrats had warned that such an authorization was both constitutionally unnecessary and politically risky. Nevertheless, as the costs of the war mounted, many in Congress (some of them Democrats) criticized Truman's decision, and after the president announced the dispatch of troops for NATO in early 1951, the Senate passed a nonbinding resolution directing the executive to seek congressional approval for additional deployments.

The process functioned most smoothly during the Eisenhower years, but even Ike was compelled to fend off the Bricker amendment in its various manifestations. This amendment, which received surprisingly strong (though primarily Republican) Senate support in an era of supposed unchallenged presidential supremacy in foreign affairs, would have made executive agreements more difficult to conclude and treaties harder to ratify. Some proponents did view it as a means to prevent future Yaltas and Koreas, but Senator Bricker and his chief ally, the American Bar Association, proposed these amendments primarily because of their belief that treaties such as the UN Charter and the proposed international agreements on human rights violated the U.S. Constitution. And many southerners who backed these amendments specifically hoped that they would prevent courts from ruling that the UN Charter invalidated state segregation laws. President Eisenhower and his advisers, in order to try and defeat the Bricker amendment, portrayed it as a dangerous threat to executive prerogatives in foreign affairs, but, in fact, its primary appeal was to states' rights and racial politics.[23]

Notwithstanding this rather peculiar episode, it was during the Eisenhower administration that the procedural Cold War consensus flourished.

The congressional joint resolution became an effective policy device—an element in the containment strategy—whereby presidents sought to win public and congressional support for proposed actions in order to deter would-be adversaries from doubting the genuineness of U.S. commitments. Some members of Congress objected to these predated declarations of war on the grounds that they constituted presidential blank checks to deploy troops and spend money without restriction, but most felt that they strengthened U.S. foreign policy and deterred war.[24] Interestingly, even these constitutional reservations largely vanished during the Kennedy and early Johnson administrations as the Cuba, Berlin (concurrent rather than joint), and Gulf of Tonkin resolutions swept through Congress with enormous majorities.

In sum, the procedural consensus rested on the widely shared assumption that the executive was the ultimate authority in making foreign policy commitments and in deciding if threats to them required the use of force.

But the strength of bipartisanship during this era should not be exaggerated. As James McCormick and Eugene Wittkopf have shown, it was most pronounced during the Eisenhower years when a majority of both parties supported the president's foreign policy positions almost 70 percent of the time in the House and the Senate. Lyndon Johnson received comparable levels of bipartisan support in the Senate but fared much worse in the House, where bipartisan levels reached only 40 percent.[25] Perhaps not surprisingly, the Korean War profoundly damaged President Truman's ability to win bipartisan backing for his foreign policy initiatives. In the Republican-controlled 80th Congress (1947 and 1948) bipartisanship was only slightly lower than Eisenhower's levels but sank to a mere 29 percent in Democratic Congresses after the North Korean attack in June 1950.[26]

Moreover, even during this "golden age" of procedural consensus, ideology remained a "primary determinant of congressional foreign policy voting, . . . often more important than partisanship"[27] in determining support for the president. In general, Eisenhower and Truman received their strongest backing from House liberals, somewhat less support from moderates, and the least from conservatives. Senate patterns varied only slightly.

The Foreign Policy Establishment

The so-called foreign policy establishment constituted the most important parainstitutional expression of the Cold War consensus. Indeed, so invisible did the establishment seem that few observers even noted its existence until it had begun to disintegrate in the late 1960s. Not until 1973 did it receive serious analytical attention, and then, quite tellingly, it fell to a left-leaning

British journalist, Godfrey Hodgson, to write its obituary.[28] In part, this general neglect stemmed from a reluctance to acknowledge the reality of a foreign policy establishment functioning at the center of a democratic polity. To do so would have challenged some cherished national myths. Moreover, the concept itself suffered from ambiguity. While the foreign policy establishment may have played a role in Cold War U.S. foreign policy comparable to that of the permanent government at Whitehall or the Quai d'Orsay, its lack of a clear institutional base made it more difficult to identify its members and chart its activities. Yet surely this relatively small group of foreign policy "amateurs," who frequently "went down" to Washington from New York and Boston in these years—men such as John McCloy, Robert Lovett, W. Averell Harriman, John McCone, Robert Bowie, Dean Acheson, C. Douglas Dillon, and Paul Nitze—formed an identifiable elite sharing some fairly obvious characteristics. Although a disproportionate number of its members (particularly among the older generation) came from privileged northeastern backgrounds featuring prep school and Ivy League educations, it ultimately depended less on sociology and genealogy than on "a common history, a shared approach, a preferred policy, an aspiration, an instinct, and a technique."[29]

Though this foreign policy elite did not emerge as a powerful force until after World War II, its origins can be traced back to the small group of advisers that gathered around Colonel Edwin House at Versailles to help lay plans for a democratic postwar world under American leadership. When the treaty was defeated in 1920, these businessmen and academics, now joined by a handful of international bankers and corporate lawyers, continued to press for an internationalist foreign policy. Through meetings and seminars at the Council on Foreign Relations and articles published in *Foreign Affairs* this group was able to survive the "normalcy" of the 1920s and the economic nationalism of the 1930s, even if it was unable to convert many to its cause. World War II provided the opportunity to implement its vision, and many of its members gained valuable governmental experience, particularly in the Office of Strategic Services (OSS). The war imparted a sense of power, accomplishment, destiny, and political involvement that gave them the confidence and stature to seek key roles in postwar American foreign policy.

Seeing themselves as bipartisan counterweights to the anticipated isolationist resurgence (especially in Congress), members of this influential group were convinced that America's reluctance to rearm and exert its power during the interwar years had helped trigger World War II and were determined to employ the presidency to build an internationalist consensus at home. Certain that the United States possessed the material resources to achieve world leadership, the establishment believed that it had to supply the missing moral and spiritual ingredients necessary to transform crude power into international authority. Though they themselves rarely stood for election, these men had an instinct for the political center—an instinct that buttressed their aspirations to serve as educators to an America whose alleged traditional tendency had been to vacillate dangerously between self-righteous withdrawal and evangelical activism. And while members of the establishment feared international communism as a mortal threat to Western values and institutions, they were unsympathetic to those who wished to ferret out subversives at home. They were, moreover, animated by a passionate devotion to public service, seeing it not as a career opportunity or a chance to make contacts for a lucrative, postgovernment life, but as a calling, a moral obligation to serve the president and the nation.

In short, the establishment both embodied and helped to construct the Cold War consensus. Substantively its members embraced that widely shared set of Cold War propositions about the nature of the international system and America's role in it. Procedurally they desired a strong presidency willing to enlist congressional support for its foreign policy initiatives but determined to assert its broad constitutional prerogatives. And culturally these unusual Americans, while far from typical in their backgrounds and positions, nevertheless thought they reflected those spiritual and civic values optimistically identified by Parsons and Rostow as central to the "American way of life."

The Cold War consensus was frequently idealized in the years after Vietnam and the Cold War. This nostalgia has overlooked the fact that U.S. policy successes during the Cold War largely resulted from its enjoyment of a unique—and temporary—hegemony produced by the outcome of World War II. It has also forgotten that the old consensus supported a foreign policy sometimes characterized by ideological rigidity and geopolitical imprudence. On the other hand, contemporary observers and participants tended simultaneously to underrate the solidity of the domestic consensus and exaggerate the permanence and inevitability of America's extraordinary global position.

Embroiled as they were in the demands and frustrations of daily duties, Cold War policymakers understandably focused on immediate problems, and these issues often did seem to pulsate with those "partisan, utterly consensus-free foreign policy debates" noted by Richard Neustadt and Ernest May.[30] Easily overlooked was the widespread public adherence to fundamental tenets about the proper U.S. approach to the world, the generalized deference to a wise and powerful presidency, and the broadly held conviction that sacrifice was necessary to preserve the superiority of the

American way of life. Yet these elements did contribute significantly to a relatively stable and orderly policymaking environment.

At the same time, both the public and the political elites tended to assume that America's extraordinary international position was natural and permanent, providential evidence of moral superiority. The highly unusual circumstances that had produced this happy situation were largely ignored, though much later it seemed clearer that U.S. global dominance had, in fact, facilitated the creation of the domestic foreign consensus. America could afford the luxury of the essentially superficial squabbles that passed for foreign policy debates in these early Cold War years, for it enjoyed a significant margin of power. This margin proved less sustainable than many at the time believed, and with its erosion this largely unappreciated domestic consensus reemerged, in retrospect, as a central feature of the early postwar era.

After Vietnam

Changes in Public Opinion

The domestic divisiveness spawned by the Vietnam War deeply eroded, but did not completely destroy, the Cold War consensus. A substantial majority of the American people continued to believe that containing communism remained an important foreign policy goal. But the public grew notably more skeptical after Vietnam about the desirability of using military force and economic assistance to stop communism.[31]

Foreign policy issues had dominated public opinion polls for more than twenty years after World War II. The public consistently named such issues as the containment of communism or the danger of war as being of primary importance to the nation. By the 1964, 1968, and 1972 elections, however, surveys indicated a fairly even split between domestic and international concerns. But after 1976 the economy—usually concerns about inflation and unemployment—was perceived by the public as the most urgent priority, and in the late 1980s drugs briefly emerged as the chief national concern. In 1976, for example, 78 percent mentioned economic problems and only 6 percent cited international issues as important; even in 1980, in the wake of Afghanistan and with U.S. hostages still in Iran, 77 percent listed economic problems as of primary importance and only 15 percent mentioned foreign policy.[32] In 1988 the budget deficit and drug trafficking topped the list. Compared with their Cold War counterparts, post-Vietnam presidents faced a public more concerned with the quality of domestic life than with more traditional national security issues. In sum, the *salience* of foreign policy issues for the public declined in the wake of Vietnam.

Moreover, the *structure* of public opinion changed. A "followership" model had best captured its essence from the late 1940s to the late 1960s. This model featured a layer of political leadership that in large measure agreed on the ends and means of U.S. foreign policy, an attentive public that followed this leadership, and a mostly inert, mass public generally uninterested and uninvolved in foreign affairs, but nevertheless hostile to communism. The prevalent foreign policy values of the Cold War reflected the fundamental propositions enumerated earlier in this chapter and shared by leaders and the attentive public alike. The mass public—less educated and largely ignorant of world affairs—was somewhat more suspicious of an active U.S. global role and inclined to oppose lengthy, costly military involvements not obviously related to U.S. security, but simultaneously wished America to remain strong and secure in its struggle against communism.[33]

The simple elegance of the followership model, however, was replaced after Vietnam by a complex and ideological structure of opinion. Four distinct attitude clusters about foreign policy emerged among both political elites and the broader public. Isolationism remained, of course, one outlook and found considerably more support with the mass public than the elites. For example, in the quadrennial polls of the Chicago Council on Foreign Relations (CCFR) done between 1974 and 1986, isolationism attracted about one quarter of the mass public but only between 2 and 7 percent of the opinion leaders. But internationists had divided according to their attitudes about communism, the use of force abroad, and relations with the Soviet Union. There were now two identifiable groups of *selective internationists:* hardliners and accommodationists.[34] Hardliners, believing that the Cold War still raged, supported the continued containment of the Soviet Union, overt and covert aid to antileftists in the Third World, and a well-funded defense establishment. They saw considerable validity in the domino theory, believed the Soviet Union to be expansionist, and were convinced that the United States must be willing and able to employ its military power unilaterally in pursuit of its interests. Not surprisingly, this group portrayed the international system in East-West terms: totalitarianism versus democracy, communism versus capitalism, repression versus freedom.

Accommodationists argued that for a variety of reasons—the Sino-Soviet split, the Vietnam quagmire, the diffusion of global military and economic power, Third World nationalism, the emergence of complex, transnational interdependence—the world of the 1970s had fundamentally changed from that of the 1940s and 1950s. They rejected the domino theory as a dangerous, self-fulfilling prophecy, viewed the Soviet Union as primarily defensive in its goals, and were deeply skeptical about the utility (and morality) of U.S. military force in peripheral areas. They viewed the international system more as a global unity beset by common problems and in need of multilateral solutions than as the arena of zero-sum superpower competition. Thus the arms race, natural resource depletion, environmental degradation, and international economic inequality were perceived as the most pressing problems. For the accommodationists, the Cold War was all but over. Yet both hardliners and accommodationists bestowed on the United States primary responsibility for implementing their respective agendas, and both approached foreign policy in highly moralistic terms. Those who held the fourth foreign policy outlook—the *traditional internationists*—supported active American involvement in world affairs and favored that combination of militant and cooperative, unilateral and multilateral approaches reminiscent of the pre-Vietnam internationist paradigm.[35]

In the CCFR surveys from 1974 to 1986 the mass public divided quite evenly and consistently into each of these four attitude clusters. In contrast, almost all the opinion leaders were internationalists of one stripe or another, though relatively few held hardliner outlooks (5 to 13 percent). For example, in 1974 about 54 percent had accommodationist attitudes, while just under 40 percent evinced traditional internationist beliefs. In the ensuing surveys the proportions gradually reversed so that by 1986 traditional internationalists accounted for almost 60 percent of the elites, whereas the accommodationists had fallen to about one-quarter.[36]

To win elite support for their foreign policies post-Vietnam presidents were obliged to construct coalitions composed of at least two of the three internationalist groupings. Although a traditionalist-accommodationist coalition was in theory the most readily available alliance, the rising visibility and influence of hardliners among opinion leaders in the late 1970s and early 1980s made it difficult for presidents to ignore this group. Indeed, the backbone of Ronald Reagan's support came from it. Furthermore, the much higher proportions of hardliners and isolationists among the mass public meant that post-Vietnam presidents, in fact, risked the loss of broader support if they overlooked these constituencies. Jimmy Carter's difficulties stemmed, in part, from accommodationist policies that repeatedly alienated hardliners and even some traditional internationalists.

This unstable coalition pattern was made even more volatile by the growing impact of television news on foreign policy attitudes. By exposing the mass public to information about foreign affairs that could earlier have been easily ignored in newspapers and magazines, television news created a "vast *inadvertent* audience" for foreign policy issues.[37] The impact of this information, frequently conveyed through vividly dramatic images, was significant in helping form new, though shallow and unstable, opinions. Moreover, this relentless bombardment of bad news tended to make the public even more impatient for quick results from U.S. foreign policy.[38]

In sum, a complex four-celled model replaced Cold War followership as the most accurate depiction of foreign policy attitudes in post-Vietnam America, and its emergence surely complicated the efforts of Richard Nixon, Gerald Ford, Jimmy Carter, and Ronald Reagan to win and keep elite and public support for their foreign policies.

Institutional Changes after Vietnam

Several institutional changes further added to the increased complexity of the foreign policymaking environment and altered the conditions that had formerly helped facilitate the executive-congressional procedural consensus. In part, these changes resulted from the fragmentation of the Cold War internationalist consensus and, in part, they made it more difficult to heal these ideological splits.

While Congress was never quite as docile and deferential in the early postwar decades as critics of the "Imperial Presidency" later claimed, executive-legislative relations in that era did embody more order and harmony than those in the aftermath of Vietnam. Important structural reforms in Congress made it much more difficult for presidents to strike and enforce deals by working with a handful of senior legislative leaders. Stripped of many of their old privileges and prerogatives by the reform movement of the early 1970s, these leaders found it difficult to deliver votes on presidential foreign policy initiatives. Moreover, the proliferation of committees and subcommittees dealing with various aspects of foreign policy vastly increased the number of legislators whose support needed to be curried.[39] Congress as a body, largely because of Vietnam and Watergate, no longer automatically trusted presidents and their advisers to provide accurate information, one major result being a dramatic increase in the size of Capitol Hill staffs. From 1947 to 1976, the number of personal staffers rose from 2,030 to 10,190, and whereas it was a rare senator before Vietnam who had a foreign policy specialist, now almost all did, as did a growing number of House members. By 1979 the 539 senators, representatives, and nonvoting delegates employed approximately 24,000 people working in fifteen different buildings around Washington. The size of committee staffs similarly grew. For example, the Senate Foreign Relations staff went from twenty-five in 1960 to thirty-one in 1970 to sixty-two in 1975, and the House Foreign Affairs Committee staff jumped from fourteen to twenty-one and then to fifty-four over the same period.[40] Far from simply providing foreign policy information to legislators, who in earlier days had been wholly dependent on executive sources, these staffers frequently functioned as powerful advocates of positions opposed by the White House. Staff experts such as Carl Marcy, Richard Moose, Robert Dockery, William Miller, John Ford, Jerry Christianson, Michael Van Dusen, and Peter Galbraith played crucial roles in contentious issues ranging from the Jackson–Vanik amendment and SALT II to the Turkish arms embargo and the Panama Canal treaties. And, again in contrast to the Cold War era when many members of Congress seemed to relish their ignorance of foreign policy as a reflection of their trust in presidential judgment, during the next two decades many became avid consumers of congressional foreign policy expertise. One result was the emergence of a new type of legislator—the bona fide foreign policy expert—who, by total immersion in a necessarily narrow range of issues (or subissues), could often mount damaging challenges to executive positions or, occasionally, provide useful support.

Members interested in foreign policy but unable to obtain a seat on one of the relevant committees were instrumental in fostering a new kind of institution, the legislative service organization. This forum allowed junior legislators to exert greater influence on issues such as arms control than their regular committee assignments would have allowed. Indeed, the best known of these organizations—the Arms Control and Foreign Policy Caucus (originally called Members of Congress for Peace Through Law—eventually counted among its membership fully one-quarter of the House and one-quarter of the Senate.

The preferred Cold War era device of the joint congressional resolution was replaced by an extended, yet fitful, series of efforts by Congress to limit the foreign affairs prerogatives of the president. Beginning with senatorial attempts in the early 1970s to restrict Nixon's ability to wage war in Southeast Asia, they soon came to involve both houses of Congress in issues that included arms control, human rights, arms sales, covert operations, and the deployment of U.S. armed forces abroad. The legislative veto, at least until the *Chadha* decision by the Supreme Court in 1983, functioned as a favored instrument of congressional assertiveness in foreign affairs. The House, citing its constitutionally mandated power of the purse, relied on several creative devices to intrude into foreign affairs and defense issues. In short, the procedural consensus of the early postwar decades largely evaporated and in its place emerged a protracted, inconclusive struggle between presidents who resented this so-called legislative micromanagement and a Congress that had grown deeply suspicious of alleged presidential attempts to subvert the Constitution. The results often bordered on chaos.

The explosion of television news coupled with advances in telecommunications technology made it much easier for members of Congress to gain wide audiences for their views. The proliferation of such television shows as ABC's "This Week with David Brinkley," CNN's "Crossfire," and "The MacNeil-Lehrer News Hour" on PBS, which purported to examine current issues in depth, almost guaranteed access to senators and House members who might oppose the foreign policy initiatives of the president. The resulting "point-counterpoint" format provided legislators with enormous incentives to dissent from executive positions and thus made policy consensus ever more elusive. Moreover, developments in satellite technology allowed members of Congress to appear daily on local television shows in their districts through video feeds using equipment provided by the Republican and Democratic parties. If local outlets were willing to accept these feeds, it became a simple matter for members to explain the independence of their foreign policy positions directly to the folks back home.[41]

Finally, lobbying, while hardly a new phenomenon in American politics, became an integral part of the foreign policy process as domestic pressure groups, foreign governments, and the executive found the post-Vietnam environment particularly conducive to these activities. The lack of a domestic foreign policy consensus, the decline of party discipline on Capitol Hill, the emergence of single-issue politics, the growing importance of "intermestic" issues (e.g., foreign trade), and the dramatic diffusion of power in Congress all contributed to this environment.[42] By 1987 there were 23,011 lobbyists registered with the secretary of the Senate—compared with 365 in 1961—or 43 for every member of Congress.[43] The president became but one lobbyist, though an exceptionally influential one, in a continual bidding war for congressional support. Obviously such an atmosphere drastically diminished the chances of establishing and sustaining a workable executive-legislative foreign policy procedural consensus.

In general, congressional bipartisanship eroded significantly from pre-Vietnam levels and continued to do so throughout the 1980s. Richard Nixon received the most backing from majorities of both parties—about 50 percent in both houses—and Ronald Reagan the least—averaging around 30 percent. Gerald Ford did the best of the post-Vietnam presidents in the Senate with a 52 percent backing but the worst in the House, where his former colleagues gave him bipartisan support less than one-quarter of the time.[44]

Not surprisingly, as the major parties became more ideologically distinct during the 1970s and 1980s, foreign policy voting in the House and Senate reflected this growing polarity. A majority of conservative internationalists in the House supported Jimmy Carter less than 40 percent of the time but backed President Reagan on fully 80 percent of foreign policy votes, whereas a majority of House liberal internationalists supported Reagan only 40 percent of the time but voted with Carter on over 70 percent of all occasions.[45]

The post-Vietnam presidency also changed in important ways. Since the early 1950s, the locus of foreign policymaking power had shifted back and forth between the national security assistant and the secretary of state, and this pattern continued in the post-Vietnam era. On balance, the result was a relative increase in the power of the National Security Council (and the White House staff) at the expense of the State Department, yet these perturbations, while inevitably well publicized, remained superficial, for they occurred within the context of a much more fundamental institutional reality: the modern presidency.

Franklin Roosevelt's creation of the "plebiscitory presidency" vastly increased centralized political power and stimulated ultimately unreasonable demands by the public on whomever occupied the White House. These "personal presidents," though apparently invested with enormous power, inevitably failed to fulfill popular expectations.[46] By slavishly following the dictum "He who can mobilize the masses may also mobilize the elite," modern presidents, at least until Reagan, have frequently ended by alienating almost everybody.[47]

Theodore Roosevelt began and Woodrow Wilson completed the institutionalization of a "rhetorical presidency" that, in its quest for effective, popular leadership spawned several serious dilemmas of governance.[48] Oratorical skill became a sine qua non of presidential leadership, and presidents were expected to make direct appeals to the people for support. Presidents had once reserved this tool for genuine crises—world war or severe economic depression—but since FDR they have often relied on popular, rhetorical leadership to *create* crises, real and spurious.[49] According to one presidential scholar,

> This surfeit of speech by politicians constitutes a decay of political discourse. It replaces discussion structured by the contestability of opinion inherent to issues with a competition to please or manipulate the public. It is increasingly the case that presidential speeches themselves have become the issues and events of modern politics rather than the medium through which issues and events are discussed and assessed.[50]

Post-Vietnam presidents did not reverse this trend. Indeed, beginning with Richard Nixon, the "personal president" model rapidly transmuted into a "stage-managed presidency" in which the allegedly hostile news media were systematically countered by presidential staffs obsessed with the *image* of their chief executive. According to this model,

> What a President or (Presidential candidate) says or does must always be calculated for its effect on his image, plotted as points along the arc of his ideal persona, a construct largely determined by what the pollsters say the people regard as the ideal at the moment.[51]

Confronted with presumably cynical reporters and media superstars eager to find flaws and inconsistencies in this carefully manufactured presidential image, White House "handlers" relentlessly marketed the president and his policies directly to the public through staged television events and urgent rhetorical appeals.

After Vietnam, presidents delivered their foreign policy messages in a domestic environment of relative dissensus. They often tried to restore direction and determination to American foreign policy "by subsuming all policy discourse within any one of several incommensurable set of beliefs."[52] Some of these presidents also headed "political factions committed to distinct, even ideological, policy positions," which they sought to implement once they were in office.[53] As a result, rhetorical, personal appeals by presidents frequently proved divisive and, in turn, stimulated rhetorical, personal appeals by political opponents. Furthermore, in contrast to Cold War presidents, who could ground their foreign policy initiatives in the set of core axioms that enjoyed broad public support, their post-Vietnam successors, largely lacking that ready-made base apart from a continuing public hostility toward communism, were compelled to construct working coalitions on an issue-by-issue basis, often at a considerable price. The difficult task of building these alliances, in turn, intensified the pressure on presidents to engage in direct, rhetorical, and frequently inflated appeals to the public.

Parainstitutional Changes

Not only did post-Vietnam presidents confront a Congress that bore scant resemblance to its Cold War counterpart, but the old foreign policy establishment had been similarly fragmented. In place of the remarkable group of gifted, privileged, foreign policy amateurs that shared a common outlook, the unifying experience of World War II, and a passion for public service, there arose ambitious, professional, highly visible counterelites vying for influence over American foreign policy. In part, this rather dramatic change resulted from a gradual but inevitable generational turnover. Aging members of the old establishment were replaced by a successor

generation different in several respects from its Cold War elders. The diffusion of political power away from the Northeast, the growing democratization of American culture, the emergence of strong, professional graduate
training in international relations at several universities, the divisive experience of Vietnam, and the increased importance of "intermestic" issues all
undermined the authority of the old establishment. Foreign policy advice in
the post-Vietnam decades was dominated by full-time foreign policy professionals—prolific, seemingly ubiquitous experts who waged ink wars, air
wars, and partisan battles in the hope of catching the attention of powerful
politicians.[54] Frequently housed in highly ideological think tanks and writing for openly partisan journals, many of these experts eschewed the proper
decorum of disagreement that had characterized the old establishment in
favor of shibboleths and caricature:

> Professional politicians might have been able to shrug off such things as just
> business, but not intellectuals. Thus, personal animosities added a bitter edge
> to everything else! Motives were always being questioned, and no one in the
> opposing camps was to be given the benefit of the doubt. For those out of
> power, it meant getting back in. It meant not giving the President an inch.[55]

Whatever the flaws of the old establishment, it did function as a reasonably
reliable anchor for Cold War presidents—a reservoir of steady, centrist
advice. Post-Vietnam presidents lacked this important resource, for warring
counterelites had replaced the cohesive old establishment. In this atmosphere the achievement of elite consensus for foreign policy initiatives became an exceedingly rare event.

The Erosion of the Cultural Consensus

The stable, white, middle-class, nuclear family composed of working father
and housewife mother and cemented by such values as patriotism, anticommunism, and civic-mindedness provided the Cold War consensus with
cultural stability, if only as a unifying myth. No doubt this model remained
compelling for millions of Americans in the post-Vietnam era. But it should
be obvious that the old cultural consensus was deeply shaken by successive
challenges to its domination. Racial conflict, the civil rights movement, and
the youthful counterculture of the 1960s; the sexual revolution and the
women's movement; large-scale immigration from Asia, Central America, and the Caribbean; the emergence of a drug culture; growing public
fears of violent crime; and the aging of the American population constituted but a few of the phenomena that in many ways transformed Cold
War America. At least, they muddied the notion of a single, preferred

American "way of life" by forging alternative lifestyles and emergent, competing social structures.

The foreign policy consequences of this cultural fragmentation were less clear. No doubt African Americans played a major role in elevating the importance of South Africa in the public consciousness. Likewise, Latin and Asian immigrants attached less importance to Soviet and European issues than had their European predecessors. And by the late 1980s stemming the flow of illegal drugs had surfaced as a major *national security* concern of the American people. On balance, these social changes probably made foreign policy issues less dominant and increased the importance of newer concerns such as child day care, the homeless, crime, education, and the environment. At the same time, military conscription, which had been widely accepted by Americans in the 1950s and early 1960s as a necessary sacrifice in the struggle against communism, became an extraordinarily divisive issue. Furthermore, and particularly during the late 1960s and early 1970s, the legitimacy of existing political processes was seriously questioned, especially among the well educated of the Vietnam generation.[56]

After the Cold War

Changes in Public Opinion

The public greeted the end of the Cold War with a combination of weariness and relief. Neither the fall of the Berlin Wall nor the disintegration of the Soviet Union elicited much interest and certainly no celebratory outpourings in the United States. Indeed, except for the remarkably short-lived euphoria that followed the victory in the Persian Gulf War, the public generally appeared to be angry, impatient, and distracted by domestic economic worries. But the relatively low importance the American people attached to foreign policy issues after the Cold War continued a trend that had been evident since the U.S. withdrawal from Vietnam. In the early 1990s the public considered the economy, health care, crime, the budget deficit, and education far more significant than foreign policy and defense. When a *Times Mirror* poll in late 1993 asked respondents to rank their *foreign policy* goals, "protecting the jobs of American workers" (85 percent a "top priority") easily topped the list. Next in importance were "preventing the spread of weapons of mass destruction" (69 percent) and "ensuring adequate energy supplies for the U.S." (60 percent). At the bottom of the public's foreign policy priorities were "promoting human rights abroad" (22 percent), fostering democracy overseas (18 percent), and aiding developing countries (18 percent).[57] In other words, issues of economic security dominated both the public's global and domestic priorities after the Cold War as they had in the years following Vietnam.

If the *salience* the public attached to foreign policy issues remained largely unchanged for the post-Vietnam era, so too did the *structure* of its attitudes. In the early 1990s internationalist sentiment continued at the same levels as the 1980s—roughly 70 percent, which was higher than the 1970s, with about one-quarter of the American people resisting an active world role for the United States. Thus the evaporation of the Soviet threat—only 8 percent perceived Russia as the "greatest danger" in 1993—did not translate into an increase in isolationist attitudes after the Cold War.[58] Furthermore, the three varieties of internationalism—accommodationist (liberal), hardliner (conservative), and traditionalist (moderate)—were evident in the post–Cold War era as well.

But the ending of the Cold War forced this internationally inclined public to confront a series of difficult issues that frequently involved the potential overseas deployment of U.S. combat troops. Civil wars, politically caused famine, ethnic strife, and massive human rights violations in areas of questionable importance to the world's "sole, remaining superpower" presented the public with complex choices quite unlike those of the Cold War of even the post-Vietnam era.

Despite the disappearance of the Soviet Union, and thus the possibility that local crises could escalate into global, nuclear confrontation, the American people remained extremely wary of committing U.S. forces abroad. The end of the Cold War did not erase the legacy of Vietnam from public consciousness, and its survival explains much about the continuing caution regarding the expenditure of resources on foreign adventures. On the other hand, as we discover in chapter 6, the Persian Gulf War offered a much more positive, alternative "model" that could assist the public in forming opinions about the advisability of future military operations. The public ultimately came to support the Gulf War in 1991 because a clear act of aggression had occurred, the security of a resource (oil) vital to the West's economic survival was perceived to be at risk, the United States fought the war as part of a broad international coalition, and, most important, the war was won cheaply and quickly. None of these conditions, the public believed retrospectively, had been present in Vietnam. Nor were many of them likely to be found in such places as Somalia, Bosnia, Rwanda, Haiti, and the Russian "near abroad." Thus any post–Cold War president contemplating putting U.S. troops in harm's way would first be obliged to convince the public that the experience would more closely resemble the Persian Gulf than Vietnam.

Institutional Changes

The "national security state" institutionalized during the Cold War had conferred unusual authority on presidents to help them meet the clear and present danger allegedly posed by the Soviet Union and international communism. Post-Vietnam presidents, newly constrained by a resurgent Congress less deferential to executive prerogatives, and confronted by a public demanding the avoidance of future foreign quagmires, could nevertheless still rather effectively raise the specter of Soviet global expansion to mobilize public and congressional support. But the sudden termination of the Soviet threat in the late 1980s removed a durable presidential trump card and threatened the foundations of national security institutions.[59] Furthermore, a feeling emerged across the political spectrum that the demands of the Cold War had greatly weakened America's domestic infrastructure and thus its ability to compete successfully in a new world of economic competition. Bill Clinton's creation of a National Economic Council constituted a rather obvious effort to redefine "national security" after the Cold War and to meld the domestic and international dimensions of economic issues such as trade and national competitiveness. These "intermestic issues," plus those relating to U.S. participation in UN peacekeeping, peacemaking, and peace enforcement operations, dominated the early post–Cold War agenda and necessarily compelled presidential attention to congressional requests for a significant role in refining, if not defining, foreign policy.

Overall, then, the diminution of presidential authority in foreign affairs that followed Vietnam (and Watergate) intensified after the Cold War even as presidencies continued to be "rhetorical" and "stage-managed." The disappearance of the Soviet Union—and with it a coherent U.S. global strategy—further strengthened the desire of Congress to help influence policy.[60] Moreover, the dramatic takeover of both houses of Congress by Republicans in 1994 for the first time in forty years portended heightened tension with the White House, at least as long as its occupant was a Democrat. Many of those newly elected to Congress owed their victories to the growing public cynicism about politics and seemed to share their constituents' concerns about the deterioration of American society. Unlike the professional reformers who came to Congress in the wake of Vietnam and Watergate, this newer crop of legislators appeared much more inclined to define their congressional roles more like the citizen-legislators of the nineteenth century.[61] The new Republican majority's dismantling of the caucus system, its desire to return power and programs to the states, and its deep suspicion of the United Nations may, in retrospect, represent a sea change in American politics.

In an important sense the Balkanization of the post–Cold War world—after the simple elegance of superpower competition—created a policy vacuum that some members of Congress sought to fill even before the "revolution of 1994." For example, hearings were held on a variety of emerging issues such as nuclear waste in the former Soviet Union, migration, religious fundamentalism, and peacekeeping in order to prod the executive into offering guidance on these subjects. The Republican 104th Congress threatened to disembowel foreign assistance programs, place significant restrictions on the president's power to commit American troops to UN operations, and even derail President Clinton's efforts to save the Mexican economy from collapse.

Parainstitutional Changes

The end of the Cold War had several important parainstitutional consequences. First, it threatened to marginalize those national security experts whose credibility depended heavily on the permanence of a Soviet threat and who failed notably to predict the imminent demise of the Soviet Union. Members of this traditional "politico-military" elite scrambled in different ways to cope with this new international environment. A few, among them Lawrence Eagleburger, openly mourned the passing of the Cold War.[62] Edward Luttwak saw an unfolding geoeconomic struggle of mercantilist proportions,[63] while Samuel Huntington discovered a world of clashing civilizations potentially dangerous to the West.[64] Henry Kissinger argued that a new, more mature multipolar balance had emerged and was subject to the same forces present in previous equilibria.[65] Frank Gaffney and Charles Krauthammer warned of the clear and present dangers posed by outlaw terrorist states whose behavior made the conduct of the Soviet Union appear almost benign in retrospect.[66] Similarly, research and advocacy organizations such as the American Enterprise Institute, the Heritage Foundation, and the Hudson Institute, whose agendas were intertwined with the Cold War, found themselves trying to remain relevant in a world bereft of old verities.

In contrast, the end of the Cold War significantly improved the fortunes of those members of the old foreign policy establishment (and their disciples) who, after Vietnam, had argued for new global U.S. priorities focused on transnational themes such as economic interdependence, the environment, population, and migration. After facing the ridicule of the politico-military elite as Soviet-American relations again worsened by the late 1970s, these experts reemerged after the Cold War as part of a nascent politico-economic elite eager to exert primary influence over American foreign policy.[67] Indeed, as we discover in chapter 6, members of this new elite—advisers such as Ron Brown and Jeffrey Garten—were to be found at the center of the Clinton administration's foreign economic policy team. At the same time, economics-oriented organizations such as the Economic Strategy Institute and the Institute for International Economics threatened to eclipse the influence of traditional national security groups. Whether this new elite will constitute the core of a new foreign policy establishment— comparable in unity and authority to its Cold War predecessor—depends in large measure on whether its agenda—trade, open markets, national economic competitiveness—remains relevant in the post–Cold War world or whether more traditional security issues again emerge.[68]

Finally, the end of the Cold War helped give to the national media additional power to help set the U.S. foreign policy agenda. This development was, of course, not wholly new, for leading print and broadcast journalists had played a major role in shaping foreign policy since at least Vietnam, but the strategic vacuum created by the demise of the containment policy gave to the media an increased opportunity to define American interests. According to one observer,

> by focusing on particular crises around the world [the media are in a better position] to pressure government to act. . . . Humanitarianism has taken on new dimensions as a component of American foreign policy, and the media are largely responsible.[69]

Furthermore, since the late 1960s media figures had gained considerable access to the bastions of the foreign policy establishment, most notably the Council on Foreign Relations. By the early 1990s they accounted for fully 10 percent of the council's membership; the editor of its flagship publication, *Foreign Affairs,* James Hoge, was the former publisher of the *New York Daily News;* and the council's president was former *New York Times* editor Leslie Gelb. The resultant blurring of the heretofore rather distinct identities of policymakers and policy reporters constituted a significant feature on the post–Cold War parainstitutional landscape.

The Further Erosion of the Cultural Consensus

The ending of the Cold War coincided with, but did not cause, the further erosion of the cultural consensus. That consensus had been most evident in the 1950s and early 1960s when a relatively unified America led the "free world" (i.e., liberal and capitalist) against revolutionary communism. But the divisiveness spawned by the Vietnam War and accompanied by social challenges like the civil rights and women's movements undermined the notion of a rigid "American way of life." By the 1990s an evolving, loosely connected set of beliefs that some commentators called "multiculturalism" had emerged to weaken further the dominance of the old liberal cosmopolitan consensus.[70]

At multiculturalism's core lies "an insistence of the primacy of ethnicity over the individual's *shared and equal status as a citizen* in shaping . . . identity and . . . interests." Thus racial group identity constitutes "the *preferred* choice of self-definition and validates the ongoing affirmation of ethnic distinctiveness." The apparent purpose of multiculturalism is "to justify the claims of subordinate ethnic groups to a larger share of society's" tangible and intangible goods and to make "communal representation" the ordering principle of public policymaking. Multicultural nationalism, by replacing the symbolic melting pot with a permanent mosaic, conceives of the United States "as a confederation of groups rather than a community of autonomous individuals . . . and implies that no national creed does, can, or should exist. . . . "[71] And it carries the potential to challenge settled policy on such issues as the role of religious values in public life, the content of school and university curriculums, cultural assimilation, and the symbolic hegemony of the English language.

Thus far, multiculturalism's appeal has been largely confined to some college and university campuses, though it has also become an increasingly central part of the political discourse in major urban areas. Yet it has probably helped contribute to a "nativist" backlash demonstrated by widespread anxiety about immigration from non-European regions and efforts to make English the official national language.[72] At the least, multiculturalism threatens to open a national debate about the meaning of "Americanness," and, by implication, complicates the achievement of a durable consensus about national interests. It also raises intriguing questions about how multicultural advocates in the United States might respond to the demands of overseas ethnic groups for rights and territory in such places as Bosnia, the former Soviet Union, and Rwanda. In the words of Citron, Haas, and Muste, "the domestic underpinnings for the long post–World War II hegemony of cosmopolitan liberalism and internationalism have frayed, apart from the fact that the United States no longer confronts a powerful military adversary."[73] Post–Cold War presidents thus may be hard pressed to build domestic foreign policy coalitions from an increasingly disintegrated social structure, one that by the mid-1990s featured the disturbing phenomenon of armed, angry "citizen militias" presumably at war with the U.S. government.

Foreign Policy Legitimation

At a minimum, domestic consensus describes the condition produced by broad agreement among members of the executive and Congress, political elites, the attentive public, and the mass public about the basic purposes of American foreign policy. Exactly *how much* agreement must exist before a consensus results remains debatable. I have argued that major foreign policy initiatives in the first two postwar decades received more overall support than those undertaken since the Vietnam War and that since the Cold War, the public has largely lost interest in noneconomic foreign policy issues. Moreover, I have suggested that for a pluralistic polity such as the United States to sustain a coherent, consistent, and reasonably effective long-term foreign policy, a relatively broad and stable domestic consensus is essential, though it hardly guarantees success and can, in fact, prove dangerous. A democratic consensus can impart authority to foreign policy by sharing and supporting its premises, purposes, and values. While consensus can hardly assure steady diplomacy, an effective foreign policy may be impossible without it. Furthermore, in a political system grounded in popular sovereignty consensus usually implies *legitimacy*. Different kinds of regimes can draw legitimacy from a variety of sources—religion, tradition, the soil, lineage, ethnic identity, revolution, laws, and so on—but in the United States foreign policy legitimacy primarily depends on whether that policy is generally construed to be valued and proper within the overall domestic political context.[74]

At those times when a consensus did exist, it did not "just happen." Cold War presidents worked diligently to achieve domestic legitimacy for their foreign policies. I have reviewed the role that historical, political, institutional, parainstitutional, and cultural factors have played in facilitating or hampering the achievement of consensus. Equally significant, however, have been the self-conscious efforts of presidents to *legitimate*—or "sell"— their foreign policies. Indeed, this process of policy legitimation constitutes the primary means presidents employ to construct consensus. Presidents and their foreign policy advisers try to provide interpretive images of the international situation that are compatible with domestic experience to justify the necessity, urgency, and character of their actions. Legitimation establishes the broad purposes of policy by translating its objectives into an understandable and compelling reflection of the domestic society's dominant norms. As such, it represents a political act within the context of national politics and characteristically relies on politically potent symbols to link foreign policy and these internal norms.[75]

Though all these activities are important, presidents cannot expect to achieve and maintain foreign policy legitimacy merely by adhering scrupulously to constitutional requirements, by duly consulting with Congress, by avoiding unreasonable secrecy and deception, or by brokering the demands of domestic interest groups.[76] On the other hand, those who oppose the *substance* of a foreign policy frequently disguise their opposition by claims that the president violated accepted *procedures* in making that policy. For example, early congressional opponents of the Vietnam War usually did not charge that America had no vital interests in Vietnam but that Lyndon Johnson and Richard Nixon had exceeded their constitutional authority in making commitments or had deceived Congress and the public about the nature and cost of their military strategies. Later, as antiwar dissent mushroomed, direct assaults on the *content* of America's Vietnam policy became common in Congress, but the collapse of the procedural consensus antedated and anticipated the decline of the substantive consensus. Policy legitimation, then, involves more than following legitimate procedures, although a president who flagrantly ignores or grossly violates them risks opposition, especially if the substance of his foreign policy proves controversial.

A president can achieve foreign policy legitimacy only if he can convince enough members of the executive, Congress, and the electorate that his policy objectives are desirable and feasible. The desirability of foreign policy legitimacy depends on the degree to which the policy appears to embody and enhance basic national values and interests, while its feasibility reflects the president's success in convincing people that he knows *how* to achieve these appealing long-range goals.[77] Alexander M. George separates these two components of policy legitimacy into what he calls the *normative* and *cognitive*. He suggests that foreign policies aiming to establish a new international system or regime—such as the grand departures of Wilson, Franklin Roosevelt, Truman, and Nixon—possessed an internal architecture comprising (1) the design-objective of the policy; (2) the strategy used to achieve it; and (3) the tactics employed to implement that strategy; and that presidents, to be successful, must obtain cognitive legitimacy for all three components. That is, "a president must be able to plausibly claim that he and his advisers possess the relevant knowledge and competence needed to choose correct policies and carry them out effectively."[78] In fact, the foreign policies of *all* presidents since FDR—whether or not advertised as "grand departures"—have featured the sort of internal architecture that George describes. For example, critics who charged that Jimmy Carter and Bill Clinton lacked the *competence* to make foreign policy were, in effect, arguing that their policies lacked "cognitive legitimacy." But foreign policy must also be seen as proper and desirable insofar as it reflects—in design-objectives, strategy, and tactics—core national interests, values, and purposes. Certain critics, for example, claimed that the Nixon–Kissinger strategy of détente lacked a moral compass because it ignored human rights issues. In short, there was no "normative legitimacy."

To achieve both kinds of legitimacy a foreign policy must involve in some manner a variety of individuals and groups ranging from the president and his senior advisers to the level of the mass public. Not surprisingly, as one moves from the highest levels of policymaking, through the bureaucracy, the political elites, the attentive public, and the mass public, the beliefs and assertions offered in support of the foreign policy's legitimacy become increasingly simplified.[79]

Legitimation can be divided into three analytical phases. During the *developmental* phase policymakers identify the structure and symbols of legitimation. In the case of Cold War containment this phase emphasized the ideological gulf emerging between the "free world" and the communist camp. The second, or *assertive,* phase occurs when these potentially legitimate symbols are introduced into political discourse by senior policymakers in order to describe the international environment. Thus in 1947 the Truman Doctrine asserted that the dichotomous world situation required the United States to support free people who were resisting subjugation by armed minorities or outside pressures. During the *operational* phase policy actions are advanced within the general framework previously developed and asserted. The policy and instruments of global, anticommunist containment followed logically from Truman's earlier rhetoric.[80] Such a sequential understanding of policy legitimation can help to illuminate this process by distinguishing an initial phase in which policymakers develop a compelling international image, a second phase where they tentatively test the waters of public opinion, and a third stage in which the new policy, appropriately adjusted, is unveiled.

At the same time, foreign policymaking and legitimation, especially in a pluralistic polity such as the United States, can often be distinctly improvisational. For example, even that most dramatic of postwar foreign policy departures—containment—only gradually and haltingly emerged as a coherent policy over a period of some years, and during that time senior American officials were quite able simultaneously to accommodate remarkably inconsistent images of the international system and Soviet intentions.[81] Nevertheless, the perceived requirements of domestic politics have repeatedly encouraged presidents to explain publicly their foreign policies through heavy rhetorical reliance on emotional symbols and metaphors that misleadingly suggest simple truths about the nature of world politics. To that extent Nixon's "generation of peace," Reagan's "era of democratic revolutions," and Bush's "new world order" followed in the tradition of Truman's "free world" crusade and Wilson's "war to end all wars."

Cold War presidents typically employed four primary legitimation techniques: (1) reducing policies to comprehensive doctrines that articulated generally accepted principles; (2) offering simple, declaratory explanations of policies that appeared to be required by these doctrines; (3) relying on symbols—historical and otherwise—to connect foreign policies to widely shared public values; and (4) overstating threats to national security while exaggerating the potential possessed by the recommended policy solution. Post-Vietnam and post–Cold War presidents, as we later see, altered but hardly abandoned these older devices.

Because the success or failure of legitimation affects the relative levels of domestic foreign policy support, this requirement creates significant political constraints on foreign policy. The inevitable thrusting of foreign policy into the public arena can lead to distortion and oversimplification.[82] Harry Truman, for example, in his well-known determination to "scare hell out of the American people," relied on New York advertising executives to craft the Truman Doctrine. Some early Cold War observers understood the dilemmas that presidents faced in "selling" their foreign policies domestically. For Hans J. Morgenthau,

> the conditions under which popular support can be obtained for foreign policy are not necessarily identical with the conditions under which a foreign policy can be successfully pursued. A tragic choice often confronts those responsible for the conduct of foreign affairs. They must either sacrifice what they consider good policy on the altar of public opinion, or by devious means gain popular support for policies whose true nature they conceal from the public.[83]

Moreover, the need to legitimate foreign policy frequently has encouraged presidents to unveil comprehensive frameworks that purported to explain the entire universe of international political behavior. Thus George F. Kennan recognized that

> [Americans] . . . seek universal formulae or doctrines in which to clothe or justify particular actions. We obviously dislike to discriminate. We like to find some general governing norm to which, in each instance, appeal can be taken, so that individual decisions may be made not on their political merits but automatically, depending on whether the circumstances do or do not fit the norm. We like, by the same token, to attribute a universal significance to decisions we have already found it necessary, for limited and paradoxical reasons, to take.[84]

The Vietnam War, with its consensus-eroding consequences, complicated the tasks of Presidents Nixon, Ford, Carter, and Reagan to legitimate their foreign policies publicly and bureaucratically, and they responded with sales strategies that frequently emphasized the personal and the rhetorical, even more than had their Cold War counterparts. Post–Cold War presidents, further deprived of ready-made domestic unity by the demise of the lodestar of anticommunism, have found it difficult to identify potential symbols of legitimation on which to base their grand designs.[85] Neither George Bush's "new world order" nor Bill Clinton's strategy of "engagement and enlargement" resonated strongly with the public.

Curiously, students of American foreign policy have often overlooked the key but subtle role played by *declaratory history* in presidential legitimation efforts. Sharing the conviction that their foreign policies require historical justification as well as contemporary rationales, they have laced their public utterances with a variety of historical references, including background contexts, trends, anecdotes, analogies, parallels, and lessons. Together these pronouncements constitute an official or "declaratory" history of American foreign relations and international politics designed to legitimate their policies. Cold War presidents relied heavily on the presumed "lessons" of the 1930s and the early postwar era to lend additional credence to the policy of global containment. In defending his actions in Korea, for example, Truman told a nationwide audience:

> If they had followed the right policies in the 1930s—if the free countries had acted together, to crush the aggression of the dictators, and if they had acted in the beginning, when the aggression was small—there probably would have been no World War II.[86]

Or, in explaining the reasons for U.S. opposition to Soviet missiles in Cuba, John F. Kennedy recalled:

> The 1930s taught us a clear lesson: Aggressive conduct, if allowed to grow unchecked and unchallenged, eventually leads to war. This nation is opposed to war. We are also true to our word. Our unswerving objective, therefore, must be to . . . secure the withdrawal or elimination of these missiles from the Western Hemisphere.[87]

Or, finally, to cite an example from the 1960s, Lyndon Johnson evoked similar memories in justifying the growing presence of U.S. troops in Vietnam by asserting that

> the central lesson of our time is that the appetite for aggression is never satisfied. To withdraw from one battlefield means only to prepare for the next. We must say in Southeast Asia—as we did in Europe—in the words of the Bible: "Hitherto shalt thou come, but no further."[88]

Sometimes presidential candidates used the 1930s to belittle the accomplishments of incumbent administrations. Thus, Senator John Kennedy compared the Eisenhower presidency to the cabinet of Neville Chamberlain:

Twenty-three years ago, in a bitter debate in the House of Commons, Winston Churchill charged the British Government with acute blindness to the menace of Nazi Germany, with gross negligence in the maintenance of the island's defenses, and with indifferent, indecisive leadership of British foreign policy and British public opinion. The preceding years of drift and impotency, he said, were "the years the locusts have eaten." Since January 1953 this nation has passed through a similar period.[89]

In sum, Cold War presidents attempted to create and sustain a historical consensus to buttress their foreign policy actions. In so doing they offered a publicly persuasive declaratory history that, in contrast to its academic counterpart, did not aspire to comprehensiveness, complexity, or controversy.

Post-Vietnam presidents hardly abandoned this legitimation technique, but because fewer and fewer people could remember the 1930s and 1940s, and because in an environment of domestic dissensus virtually all historical references could prove divisive, declaratory history lost a good deal of its former effectiveness. These presidents tended to emphasize the many ways in which the world had changed since these earlier decades. But when in the late 1970s and early 1980s the Soviet Union appeared bent on a new program of global expansion, Jimmy Carter, and especially Ronald Reagan, rediscovered the relevance of the "lessons" of the 1930s. The result was a declaratory history appropriate to wage a new Cold War.[90]

Then, by the late 1980s, Soviet-American relations had become more cordial, and these "lessons" were returned to the shelf, only to be pulled out again by George Bush after Iraq invaded Kuwait in 1990. But when Bush, and then Bill Clinton, proved extremely reluctant to become directly involved in Bosnia, critics manipulated other historical symbols—those of the Holocaust and the Spanish Civil War—to mobilize public pressure against U.S. policy. Defenders, in turn, relied heavily on Vietnam analogies to rebut these critics. In sum, the flux created by the ending of the Cold War created a bulging grab bag of potentially conflicting historical analogies available to both policymakers and their critics. In such an atmosphere declaratory histories were bound to be challenged.

Notes

1. Edward Shils, "The Concept of Consensus," p. 260.
2. Not everyone would agree with this argument. Ernest R. May and Richard E. Neustadt, for example, discovered "bitter, partisan, and utterly consensus-free" congressional debate about the loss of China, the long-term stationing of American troops in Europe, the limiting of warfare in Korea by Truman, and whether war should be risked for Dien Bien Phu, Quemoy, or the Matsus (*Thinking in Time: The Uses of History for*

Decision Makers, pp. 258–59). Thomas R. Hughes identified a "working dissent" composed of two distinct policy cultures—"security" and"equity"—that "disguised a real
division in the American body politic over what constituted the American national
interest" ("The Crack Up," pp. 52 and 53). Jerel A. Rosati and John Creed found six
important "schools of thought" among elites about U.S. foreign policy always present in
the postwar decades ("Clarifying Concepts of Consensus and Dissensus: Evolution of
Public Beliefs in United States Foreign Policy"). After trying to determine if there had
ever been a bipartisan foreign policy consensus in Congress during the Cold War,
Eugene R. Wittkopf and James M. McCormick admitted that their data and analyses
were inconclusive ("Was There Ever a Foreign Policy Consensus?"), I.M. Destler, Leslie Gelb, and Anthony Lake), while subscribing to the idea of a Cold War, anticommunist consensus, nevertheless disparaged the view that all politics had stopped at the
water's edge in those years (*Our Own Worst Enemy: The Unmaking of American Foreign Policy*).

3. See, for example, Michael Leigh, *Mobilizing Consent: Public Opinion and
American Foreign Policy* and Richard A. Falk, "Lifting the Curse of Bipartisanship," pp.
127–57.

4. Jonathan Clarke, "America, Know Thyself," p. 24.

5. Ole R. Holsti and James N. Rosenau, *American Leadership in World Affairs:
Vietnam and the Breakdown of Consensus,* p. 218.

6. Ole R. Holsti, "Public Opinion and Containment," p. 73.

7. John Lewis Gaddis, *Strategies of Containment,* ch. 3.

8. Holsti, "Public Opinion and Containment," pp. 76–78.

9. See, for example, John Lewis Gaddis, "Dividing Adversaries," in *The Long
Peace: Inquiries into the History of the Cold War;* and David A. Mayers, *Cracking the
Monolith: United States Policy Against the Sino-Soviet Alliance.*

10. Ernest R. May, "The Cold War," pp. 224–25.

11. Holsti, "Public Opinion and Containment," p. 78.

12. Daniel Yankelovich and Sidney Harmon, *Starting with the People,* pp. 23–24.

13. George H. Gallup, *The Gallup Poll, Public Opinion 1935–1971,* vol. 1, pp. 617,
672, and 681; vol. 2, pp. 1028 and 1519; vol. 3, p. 1754.

14. Jack Citrin, Ernst B. Haas, and Christopher Muste, "Is American Nationalism
Changing? Implications for Foreign Policy," p. 6.

15. Allan C. Carlson, "Foreign Policy and 'the American Way': The Rise and Fall of
the Post-World War II Consensus," p. 25.

16. Ibid.

17. Ibid., p. 27.

18. Ibid., pp. 29–30.

19. Elaine Tyler May, "Cold War—Warm Hearth: Politics and the Family in Postwar America," p. 158.

20. George F. Kennan, "The Sources of Soviet Conduct," p. 76.

21. Gaddis, *Strategies of Containment,* p. 359.

22. William C. Gibbons, "Vietnam and the Breakdown of Consensus," pp. 97–98.

23. Duane L. Tannanbaum, "The Bricker Amendment Controversy: Its Origins and
Eisenhower's Role," p. 79.

24. Gibbons, "Vietnam,' pp. 101 and 102.

25. James M. McCormick and Eugene R. Wittkopf, "Bush and Bipartisanship: The
Past as Prologue?" p. 9.

26. "Bush," p. 8.

27. Ibid., p. 11.

28. Godfrey Hodgson, "The Establishment," pp. 3–40.

29. Ibid., p. 8.

30. Personal interviews with Eisenhower advisers, 1983.

31. William Schneider, "Public Opinion," pp. 12 and 11.

32. Ralph B. Levering, "Public Opinion, Foreign Policy, and American Politics Since the 1960s," p. 12.

33. Schneider, "Public Opinion," p. 12.

34. Eugene R. Wittkopf, *Faces of Internationalism: Public Opinion and American Foreign Policy,* pp. 25–26.

35. Wittkopf identifies two dimensions of opinion—involvement versus noninvolvement and cooperation versus militancy. Some analysts, however, have suggested that a third dimension—unilateralism versus multilateralism—is needed to capture the actual profile of public opinion. See, for example, William O. Chittick, Keith R. Billingsley, and Rick Travis, "Discovering the Structure of Foreign Policy Beliefs: From Flatland to Spaceland." My reading of Wittkopf's data leads to the conclusion that his accommodationists have multilateral inclinations, while his hardliners are more comfortable with a unilateralist foreign policy. But none of this parsing should obscure the main point: the Vietnam War contributed to the erosion of the Cold War consensus by fragmenting internationalists into two or three identifiable attitude groups.

36. Wittkopf, *Faces of Internationalism,* p. 140.

37. Schneider, "Public Opinion," p. 19.

38. Ibid., pp. 19 and 20.

39. See, for example, Cecil V. Crabb Jr. and Pat M. Holt, *Invitation to Struggle: Congress, the President, and Foreign Policy,* p. 39.

40. Destler, Gelb, and Lake, *Our Own Worst Enemy,* p. 137.

41. Hedrick Smith, *The Power Game: How Washington Works,* pp. 131–35.

42. Crabb and Holt, *Invitation to Struggle,* p. 224.

43. Smith, *The Power Game,* p. 29.

44. McCormick and Wittkopf, "Bush," p. 9.

45. Ibid., p. 13.

46. Theodore J. Lowi, *The Personal President.*

47. Ibid., p. 153.

48. Jeffrey K. Tulis, *The Rhetorical Presidency.*

49. Ibid., p. 181.

50. Ibid., pp. 178–79.

51. Michael Kelly, "The Game," p. 67.

52. "Of Rifts and Drifts: A Symposium on Beliefs, Opinions, and American Foreign Policy," p. 373.

53. Destler, Gelb, and Lake, *Our Own Worst Enemy,* p. 237.

54. Ibid., pp. 124 and 125.

55. Ibid., p. 125.

56. Citrin, Haas, and Muste, "American Nationalism," p. 3.

57. "America's Place in the World: An Investigation of the Attitudes of American Opinion Leaders and the American Public about International Affairs."

58. As late as 1990, fully 32 percent of the public continued to rank the Soviet Union as America's greatest danger.

59. On the other hand, presidents no longer need fear the domestic political consequences of "losing" friendly states to communism. That fear put enormous pressure on Cold War and post-Vietnam presidents.

60. By 1993, 37,000 people worked on Capitol Hill, an increase of more than 15,000 since the late 1970s. The new Republican leadership in 1994, however, vowed to cut staff by at least one-third.

61. Hugh DeSantis, "The Domestication of American Foreign Policy," p.19.

62. Remarks at Georgetown University, Washington, D.C., September 15, 1989.

63. Edward Luttwak, *The Endangered American Dream.*

64. Samuel P. Huntington, "The Clash of Civilizations."

65. Henry Kissinger, *Diplomacy.*

66. Charles Krauthammer, "The Unipolar Moment."

67. For a fuller discussion of this issue, see A.F.K. Organski and Ronald Tammen, "The New Open Door Policy: U.S. Strategy in the Post Cold War World."

68. For a discussion of the centrist political instincts of political elites after the Cold War, see Nelson W. Polsby, "Foreign Policy Establishment: Toward Professionalism and Centrist."

69. Jon Vanden Heuvel, "For the Media, A Brave (and Scary) New World," quoted in Richard Harwood, "Ruling Class Journalists."

70. Citron, Haas, and Muste, "American Nationalism," p. 9.

71. Ibid., p. 10. Emphasis in the original.

72. A particularly striking example occurred in an Orlando, Florida suburb where in May 1994 the Tavares school board voted to require its teachers to instruct students that American culture, values, and institutions were inherently "superior to other foreign or historic cultures." *New York Times,* May 15, 1994, p. 22A.

73. Citrin, Haas, and Muste, "American Nationalism," p. 27.

74. B. Thomas Trout, "Legitimating Containment and détente," p. 2.

75. Ibid., pp. 3, 2, and 4.

76. Alexander M. George, "Domestic Constraints," in *Change in the International System,* ed. Holsti, Siverson, and George, p. 234.

77. Trout, "Legitimating Containment and Détente," p. 4.

78. George, "Domestic Constraints," p. 236.

79. Ibid., p. 236.

80. Trout, "Legitimating Containment and Détente," p. 5.

81. Deborah Welch Larson, *Origins of Containment: A Psychological Explanation.*

82. Trout, "Legitimating Containment and Détente," pp. 5–6.

83. Ibid.

84. George F. Kennan, *Memoirs, 1925–1950,* p. 322.

85. B. Thomas Trout, "Legitimating Post Cold War Foreign Policy."

86. Kennan, *Memoirs,* p. 322.

87. Ibid.

88. "Lyndon B. Johnson Explains Why Americans Fight in Vietnam."

89. Quoted in Michael Roskin, "From Pearl Harbor to Vietnam: Shifting Generational Paradigms and Foreign Policy," p. 572.

90. For a fuller discussion of this concept, see Richard A. Melanson, "Action History, Declaratory History, and the Reagan Years."

Part Two

American Foreign Policy After Vietnam

2

The Nixon Administration

On January 20, 1969, Richard Nixon became only the second Republican to serve as president since 1933. He had been elected with 43 percent of the popular vote—the barest of pluralities—and was the first new president since Zachary Taylor to face opposition-party control in both houses of Congress. Moreover, the country seemed to be coming apart, with urban riots and campus unrest dramatically symbolizing the apparent failure of Lyndon Johnson's simultaneous pursuit of the War on Poverty and the war in Vietnam. The twin pillars of post–World War II America—the elaboration of the New Deal at home and the pursuit of global anti-communism abroad—appeared, at the least, to be tottering. For Henry Kissinger,

> the new Nixon Administration was the first of the postwar generation that had to conduct foreign policy without the national consensus that had sustained its predecessors largely since 1947. And our task was if anything more complex. We faced not only the dislocations of a war but the need to articulate a new foreign policy for a new era.[1]

Nixon, like Eisenhower, had inherited a stalemated, unpopular, Asian land war from the Democrats and, like Ike, had pledged to end it. Moreover, the Nixon Doctrine bore some resemblance to the "new look" (Eisenhower's defense strategy), for both intended to prevent future military interventions in peripheral areas. But Nixon's inheritance was infinitely more troublesome than Eisenhower's, and the resources available to him were much more limited. The nation in 1969 seemed more divided than at any time since the Civil War. The prestige of public institutions, including the presidency, had plummeted. According to Kissinger, "the internationalist establishment . . . collapsed before the onslaught of its children who questioned all its values."[2] Eisenhower had been able to reknit the foreign policy consensus in large measure because of his unusual national stature: a war hero who appeared to be above party, a unifier who could afford to be above politics. Yet in 1969, in much more difficult circumstances, Richard Nixon became president—a man whose background, behavior, and temperament hardly seemed equipped to reconstruct a domestic foreign policy consensus.

Unlike Eisenhower, who before 1952 had trouble deciding whether he was a Republican or a Democrat, Nixon had built his career on party and partisanship. With the instincts of a street fighter he had demolished Jerry Voorhis, Helen Gahagan Douglas, and Alger Hiss and had been skillfully used by Eisenhower to do the sort of political dirty work that would have tarnished the general's image. After his decisive defeat by Pat Brown in the 1962 California gubernatorial race, Nixon remained active in Republican Party affairs, loyally supporting Barry Goldwater in 1964 and traveling widely to speak on behalf of Republican candidates. The remarkable Republican comeback in 1966 added to his reputation as an effective, gritty campaigner and strengthened his position for the presidential nomination two years later.

He brought to the White House impressive foreign policy experience. Although as a rule Eisenhower excluded his vice-president from the most sensitive national security decisions, he frequently sent Nixon on fact-finding and goodwill trips abroad, and Nixon took full advantage of these opportunities to curry personal relationships with foreign leaders, as well as to learn a good deal about world political issues. These travels brought Nixon much publicity as, for example, the stoning incident in Caracas in 1958 and the kitchen debate with Khrushchev the following year. Later, as a private citizen, he continued to travel widely, sustaining relationships with foreign leaders and writing about international issues, most notably a 1967 article in *Foreign Affairs* entitled "Asia after Vietnam."

Notwithstanding these calculated efforts to depict himself as a mature, worldly wise, and realistic statesman, many Democrats and journalists could not forgive his earlier excesses, including an apparently comfortable relationship with Joseph McCarthy and his vilification of Dean Acheson as "the dean of the college of cowardly communist containment." Nevertheless, Nixon's foreign policy views seemed to fit easily within the prevailing consensus, and he supported every major U.S. international initiative from the Marshall Plan to Vietnam. Indeed, if he had received a few more votes and defeated John Kennedy in 1960 there is every reason to believe that Nixon would have continued to pursue the main outline of Eisenhower's foreign policy. Consolidation and continuity would doubtless have been the guiding concepts of such a presidency.

But, as it turned out, Nixon, who viewed life as a series of crises to be surmounted through personal discipline and will, found himself president at a time of genuine national crisis. Moreover, Nixon was by temperament a riverboat gambler and, given the simultaneous breakdown of the domestic and foreign policy consensus by 1968, Nixon had a great opportunity to take risks both at home and abroad.[3] Unlike Eisenhower, whose natural proclivity had been to chart a safe "middle way" designed to protect the "American way of life," Nixon was instinctively a "chance taker" who perceived reality in terms of the "big picture" and who was "not necessarily a respecter of the status quo."[4] Then, too, until January 1973 Nixon served, in effect, as a wartime president, and this unusual circumstance, which temporarily expanded the executive's extralegal powers, further tempted Nixon to achieve dramatic policy changes through presidential decree.[5]

The New Majority

Richard Nixon knew that the Cold War consensus had been shattered. A number of academic commentators in the late 1960s argued that its passing was inevitable, the result of inexorable impersonal forces that had eroded the bases of public support for containment. Nixon did not deny that significant international changes had occurred, but he believed that the breakdown of the foreign policy consensus had been precipitated by the cowardly behavior of America's "leader class." This class, a concept fundamental to Nixon's political outlook, was an amalgam of the eastern establishment, the national press, senior federal bureaucrats, educational leaders, and other opinion makers that had provided political and moral leadership for the United States since World War II. During the Korean War, for example, when the military stalemate had soured many Americans on the conflict, Nixon remembered that the leader class had largely remained supportive of Truman's foreign policy and that this loyalty had helped Eisenhower end the war in an honorable way.

But Nixon had grown contemptuous of the leader class, particularly for its alleged pusillanimity over Vietnam. Instead of rallying to President Johnson's support, he believed that many of its members had been converted by the simpleminded slogans of the antiwar protesters. Despite his opposition to many Great Society programs, Nixon was genuinely distressed by the destruction of the Johnson presidency, hastened by the wholesale abandonment of its erstwhile supporters.[6]

Although middle America had slowly grown weary and disillusioned because of the endlessness of the Vietnam War, Nixon did not believe that the newfound "isolationism" of the leader class accurately reflected the American heartland's values. Nor did Nixon, the poor boy and self-made man from Whittier, believe that its interests were being served by a centralized bureaucracy dispensing social welfare liberalism from Washington. In short, Nixon detected among lower- and middle-class whites a growing anger and resentment toward federal social engineers preaching the virtues of school busing, racial quotas, abortion, gun control, and bans on school prayer. Reflecting on the 1968 election, Theodore H. White told journalist David Broder that America's leading cultural media, university thinkers, and influence makers, in their unprecedented fascination with experiment and change, had completely separated themselves from the "mute masses." For Broder, "Mr. Nixon's problem" was "to interpret what the silent people think and govern the country against the grain of what its more important thinkers think."[7]

For Nixon, then, the simultaneous breakdown of the domestic New Deal consensus and the Cold War foreign policy consensus shared a common root: the failure of the leader class to stay in touch with middle America. In the first instance it had transformed the federal government from an economic friend of the "little man" into an intrusive social enemy. And in the second case the leader class's loss of will in the midst of the Vietnam War had led it to retreat into a sentimental isolationism at odds with the real majority's inclinations. In response, Nixon attempted to fashion a new majority that, besides breaking the back of the old Democratic economic coalition, would provide crucial support for his Vietnam policy and, later, his policy of détente.

It took some time for Nixon to articulate fully his "new majority" strategy. He had only rather hazy notions about it at first, though his so-called southern strategy of 1968 had aimed to take advantage of regional dissatisfactions with Johnson's racial and economic policies. Moreover, as he made clear in his memoirs, Nixon recognized that he and George Wallace together had polled more than 58 percent of the popular vote. Nevertheless, Nixon's early presidential speeches emphasized unity. In the first Inaugural Address he suggested that "we are torn by division wanting unity" and that "we cannot learn from one another until we stop shouting at one another."[8] On May 14, 1969, he made his first nationwide speech on Vietnam conciliatory in tone, and he planned to announce the first troop withdrawal in early June.

But, according to speechwriter William Safire, Nixon did not want this initial withdrawal announcement to be misinterpreted as weakness:

> He felt he needed to show that Richard Nixon was not going soft. Troop withdrawal, a part of orderly Vietnamization, must not be taken as "cut and run. . . . " And he was convinced that only tough-minded men with the power to command would achieve . . . a peace in Vietnam that guaranteed self-determination. He sensed that this was the time for a tough speech, for a reassertion of pride and confidence that would appall many liberals.[9]

Thus, on June 4, 1969, before the graduating class at the Air Force Academy, Nixon abandoned the rhetoric of unity in favor of a much more provocative approach. Targeting domestic critics of a strong national defense for attack he claimed that "in some of the so-called best circles in America . . . patriotism is considered by some to be a backward fetish of the uneducated and unsophisticated. Nationalism is hailed and applauded as a panacea for the ills of every nation—except the United States of America." "These isolationists," the president asserted, argue that "the United States is blocking the road to peace by maintaining its military strength at home and its defenses abroad" and offer simple and powerful slogans that touch "a responsive chord with many an overburdened taxpayer." Nixon admitted that he could easily "buy some popularity by going along with the new isolationists" but added that such a course would result in national and global disaster. He held "a totally different view of the world" and was convinced that "if America were to become a dropout in assuming the responsibility for defending peace and freedom in the world . . . the rest of the world would live in terror" and would experience "the kind of peace that suffocated freedom in Czechoslovakia." Nixon claimed that "the skeptics and isolationists" had "lost the vision indispensable to great leadership. They observe the problems that confront us; they measure our resources and then they despair." Their timidity stood in direct contrast to the courageous astronauts who "inspire us," and who will allow "every American" to "stand taller" when they land on the moon. "When a nation believes in itself," the president concluded, "that nation can perform miracles," and "that is why I believe a resurgence of American idealism can bring a modern miracle, and that modern miracle is a world of peace and justice."[10]

By insinuating that anti-Vietnam critics were, in essence, hypocritical elitists, who, like countercultural dropouts, had allowed despair and selfishness to replace courage and vision, Nixon implied that there was another, better America made up of decent, proud patriots who felt a moral responsibility for building a better world. This sort of "us versus them" rhetoric, so characteristic of the old Nixon, was harshly attacked in editorials in major newspapers across the country, but, according to Safire, the president believed that he had succeeded in putting his war critics on the defensive by making them vulnerable to the charge of isolationism.[11] In addition, he laid the groundwork for an even more memorable address—the so-called silent majority speech of November 3, 1969.

Nixon scheduled this speech between two massive antiwar demonstrations in Washington and plainly intended to rob these protests of their anticipated impact. Even more than in the Air Force Academy address he wanted to draw the battle lines clearly between the "folks" and the "elitists," the "mute masses" and the "noisy minority." To underscore the importance he attached to the speech, Nixon wrote it himself.[12] After reporting that negotiations with North Vietnam remained stalemated, Nixon reiterated his commitment to Vietnamization and a phased U.S. withdrawal, but reserved the right to take "strong and effective measures" if Hanoi jeopardized "our remaining forces." He then focused on those who urged "an immediate precipitate withdrawal . . . without regard to the effects of that action." Branding this course "easy but wrong" the president predicted that, if followed, "our allies would lose confidence in America" and "far more dangerous, we would lose confidence in ourselves" as "inevitable remorse and divisive recrimination would scar our spirit as a people." Thus Nixon refused to allow "the policy of this Nation to be dictated by the minority who hold that point of view and who try to impose it on the nation by mounting demonstrations in the streets." To follow this "vocal minority," he warned, would bring an end to America as a "free society" and would ultimately lead to the suffocation of millions around the world by the "forces of totalitarianism" as America turned inward. Nixon then asked for support from "the great silent majority of my fellow Americans" to enable him more quickly to achieve a "just and lasting peace" in Vietnam. A divided America, he argued, would only prolong the war and provide encouragement to the enemy.[13]

Public response to the address was strongly favorable. Polls indicated that the public's approval of Nixon's Vietnam policy increased.[14] Supportive telephone calls and telegrams poured into the White House. The television networks, as was their custom in 1969, immediately scrutinized the speech but were thrown on the defensive a few days later when Vice-President Spiro T. Agnew excoriated them for indulging in "instant analysis." More than 300 members of the House of Representatives sponsored a resolution supportive of Nixon's Vietnam policy and more than 60 senators expressed their approval in letters to Ambassador Henry Cabot Lodge.[15] In response President Nixon on November 13, 1969, in separate speeches to the House and Senate, thanked those members for their loyalty. Nixon and Kissinger believed that the silent majority address had given them an additional six months of time to settle the war.

The speech was tactically brilliant because it allowed President Nixon to isolate and temporarily delegitimate a noisy minority allegedly clamoring for a precipitate withdrawal from Vietnam regardless of the consequences, while providing the silent majority with a concrete plan for an orderly pullout designed to protect national credibility and self-respect. He would juxtapose these so-called options again and again. And the public response to the speech further convinced Nixon that the silent majority was real and could be mobilized into a durable new majority.

According to Charles W. Colson, special assistant to the president from 1969 to 1973, as the "buckets of telegrams" supporting Nixon's November speech arrived at the White House, it began to strike the staff that they were hitting a responsive chord in Main Street, USA, about "standing firm in Vietnam." Colson and others also detected a growing frustration with the "big government excesses of the Great Society." Then in the spring of 1970, after the Cambodian incursion and the Kent State killings, a large group of "hard-hats" led a counterdemonstration of more than 100,000 people to New York City's Gracie Mansion. Nixon telephoned the leaders that evening and invited them to the White House to offer thanks. Ostentatiously piling their construction hats in the Roosevelt Room, these labor leaders' public support of Nixon constituted for Colson "a seminal event" and an "important symbol of an emerging political coalition."[16]

Yet in stumping for Republican candidates in the 1970 elections Nixon hardly mentioned the social and cultural issues of such apparent concern to middle America. He did, to be sure, bemoan the breakdown of "law and order," particularly on certain "elitist" college campuses, but more important, he claimed that he needed a Republican majority in Congress to help achieve his goal of a "generation of peace."

The election results disappointed the White House, though staff members took satisfaction in James Buckley's success in defeating—though barely—two liberal opponents in the New York senatorial race by appealing to white, traditionally Democratic, ethnic voters. Soon thereafter, Nixon, Robert Haldeman, John Ehrlichman, John Mitchell, Colson, and other senior officials met at Key Biscayne in Florida to discuss the formation of a new Republican majority in 1972 by incorporating the increasingly conservative Catholic, ethnic, labor vote into the party's more traditional constituencies. This goal seemed within reach.

These men had been impressed with the analyses recently offered by Kevin Phillips's *The Emerging Republican Majority*[17] and particularly, *The Real Majority* of Richard Scammon and Ben Wattenberg.[18] Noting that most Americans were not poor, young, or black, *The Real Majority* argued that the "economic issue," which had provided grist for the Democratic Party since the Great Depression, was being overtaken by the "social issue," a revolt by the middle and lower middle classes against the programs and permissiveness of 1960s liberalism. Ironically, the authors of *The Real Majority,* who were Democrats, found a very receptive audience in the Nixon White House. Colson and other staff strategists frequently held discussions with them. The president himself was "profoundly impressed" when Scammon suggested to him that busing was an elitist program that would disrupt traditional neighborhoods without achieving its educational goals.[19]

Intrigued by the electoral implications of these arguments, the Nixon administration made a determined effort to reach out to these traditional Democratic voters. Michael P. Balzano, himself a Democrat, played a central role in this strategy. Brought to the White House from the Office of Economic Opportunity by Colson, Balzano's constituency was blue-collar middle America. He met continually with such ethnic organizations as the Sons of Italy, the Polish-American League, and the Latvian League, community groups built around specific issues such as gun ownership and neighborhood preservation, a variety of Catholic organizations, and labor union representatives. Time and again, Balzano heard the same message: These people perceived themselves to be the targets of social policies dictated by federal government bureaucrats, of changing rules in the Democratic Party, and of the antiwar protest movement. They seemed especially annoyed by what they saw as Washington's assault on the "achievement ethic" in the form of waived entrance exams, racial quotas, and forced busing. But they also felt increasingly alienated from a social climate that encouraged abortion, "free love," and permissiveness, and they interpreted many Health, Education, and Welfare (HEW) guidelines as attempts to destroy the family. Yet when they complained to Washington about these policies, "they were mocked as 'Archie Bunkers' by the liberal establishment."[20] These groups also felt abandoned by a Democratic Party that appeared contemptuous of their concerns. Finally, Balzano believed that many of them had come to oppose the Vietnam War in large measure because the United States appeared unwilling to win it, but that they opposed a unilateral withdrawal, particularly if U.S. prisoners of war (POWs) remained in captivity. Furthermore, they were horrified by the tactics of some of the antiwar demonstrators. Indeed, according to Donald F. Rodgers, a Nixon labor adviser, the labor march in New York had been precipitated by construction workers angered when protesters burned the American flag, raised the North Vietnamese banner, and urinated on a statue of George Washington.[21] Balzano and Safire agreed that the protest movement's "stridency and violence did more than anything [else] to help Nixon crystallize his new majority."[22]

George McGovern's nomination in 1972 delighted the Nixon White House, for he proved the perfect foil for the new majority strategy. McGovern, a former college professor claiming to embody a "new politics," could easily be portrayed as an isolationist elitist hopelessly insensitive to the needs of middle America. George Wallace had been removed as a rival to Nixon for these votes by his serious wounding while campaigning in Maryland, and the economy in 1972 appeared prosperous and sound. According to Alonzo L. Hamby, "no American political leader was better equipped by temperament and outlook than was Nixon to engage in a politics of cultural confrontation designed to build a new majority of the resentful."[23]

Interestingly, however, Nixon increasingly saw this new coalition less as a Republican majority and more as *his* majority. In order to bring about a national political realignment he believed that liberal Republicans had to be purged and conservative and disillusioned Democrats welcomed. Nixon's new majority required a new *minority* to pummel and provoke. He rejected the consensual texture of Eisenhower's "middle way" or Johnson's "president of all the people" in favor of a confrontational "two-ideology system"[24] grounded in apparently irreconcilable social and cultural divisions.

Nixon quite characteristically felt that his own intentions were noble and that his New Class opponents—intellectuals, the national media, bureaucrats, ultraliberal Hollywood celebrities, nonbusiness professionals—wished to destroy him and the values of his heartland supporters. No doubt these suspicions were far from unfounded, but Nixon exacerbated the situation by depicting himself as a stern, righteous moralist who steadfastly chose the right way over the easy way of his critics. The most extreme kinds of hardball politics could be rationalized by the ultimate goals they promoted: a generation of peace in the world and the re-creation of a spirit of self-reliance in the American character.[25]

In essence, Richard Nixon attempted to coopt many of the old New Deal constituencies by binding them together with the glue of social and cultural politics. But in so doing he accepted the bulk of the New Deal's economic legacy. Professing to be a Keynesian, Nixon imposed wage-and-price controls to fight inflation, embraced the goal of the full-employment economy, favored a guaranteed annual income, and tried to limit the states' involvement in the welfare system. His New Federalism did not intend to cut federal spending programs but tried to distinguish between "activities requiring large cash transactions and those primarily involving services.[26] Thus Nixon wanted to restore to the states some control over such functions as education, job training, and public health, while reserving to the federal government such issues as welfare, energy, and the environment. According to Otis L. Graham, Nixon presided "over a more rapid evolution toward planning than any other President since FDR."[27]

What distinguished Nixon's new majority was its social and cultural attributes, rather than its economic character. Unlike the New Deal coalition, its membership depended primarily on shared values. Unless all Americans could be converted to its outlook, it would be inevitably more ideological and more divisive than its predecessor. Nixon responded, then, to the breakdown of the domestic policy consensus in the 1960s, not with a new consensus but with a new majority whose health depended on the existence of a domestic enemy—the new minority.

Nixon neatly captured these themes in an important but largely ignored radio address delivered shortly before the 1972 election. He began with an acknowledgment that "in the past generation there were cases in which power concentrated in Washington did much to help our people live in greater fairness and security and to enable our Nation to speak and act strongly in world affairs." But in the 1960s, he recalled, people had grown resentful and alienated because they felt frustrated "in dealing with a faceless machine called the Federal bureaucracy." Those who operated this bureaucracy frequently forgot that "government derives its power from 'the consent of the governed' and instead dismissed 'the will of the people' as 'the prejudice of the masses.' " Indeed, "a great many people in politics and elsewhere," in order to achieve "what they consider social justice," want to change America "by attacking [its] basic values." But, Nixon assured:

> There is no reason to feel guilty about wanting to enjoy what you get and what you earn, in wanting your children in good schools close to home, or about wanting to be judged fairly on your ability. Those are not values to be ashamed of, those are values to be proud of. Those are values that I shall always stand up for when they come under attack.[28]

He also reminded his audience that a democratic leader "must be willing to take unpopular stands when they are necessary," but in those cases, "he has an obligation to explain it to the people, solicit their support, and win their approval." Nixon remembered that "one of those moments came" in late 1969 after his declaration that "we were going to end our involvement in the war in Vietnam with honor." He "understood the difference between settlement and surrender," yet "the organized wrath of thousands of vocal demonstrators who opposed that policy descended on Washington," and "commentators and columnists" speculated about " 'the breaking of the president.' " In response Nixon, on November 3, had delivered a nationwide address "to summon up the strength of our national character," and "the great silent majority of Americans—good people with good judgment who stand ready to do what they believe to be right—immediately responded." Their support "made it possible for the Government to govern successfully."[29]

Having thus "seen the will of the majority in action, responding to a call to responsibility, to honor, and to sacrifice," Nixon noted, "that is also why I speak with pride of the 'new majority' that is forming not around a man or a party, but around a set of principles that is deep in the American spirit":

These are not the beliefs of selfish people. On the contrary, they are the beliefs of a generous and self-reliant people, a people of intellect and character whose values deserve respect in every segment of our population.

So, he concluded: "On matters affecting basic human values—on the way Americans live their lives and bring up their children—I am going to respect and reflect the opinion of the people themselves. That is what democracy is all about."[30]

By rhetorically transforming what some commentators were terming "the politics of resentment" into a set of positive values, President Nixon also, as we later see, attempted to enlist the new majority in his two major foreign policy goals: "peace with honor" in Vietnam and a "generation of peace" in the world.

Peace with Honor

There can be little doubt that if Richard Nixon had been elected President in 1960, he would have deepened America's commitment to South Vietnam. Certainly Nixon had shared the conviction held by almost every American leader of his generation that in order to preserve American security and global stability the right of the South Vietnamese people to national self-determination had to be guaranteed by the United States. But would Nixon have pursued the war strategy of Kennedy and Johnson? Probably not. As a private citizen, Nixon had criticized the Laotian neutralization agreement of 1962, Washington's inconsistent treatment of President Diem, the gradual pace of the American military buildup, and Johnson's reluctance to attack enemy sanctuaries. But these were tactical disputes; Nixon agreed that America's credibility as a superpower and alliance leader rested on its willingness to defend South Vietnam.

But by 1969 the United States "had been riven by protest and anguish," some of it "violent and ugly."[31] The psychological defeat of the Tet offensive, the assassinations of Dr. Martin Luther King Jr. and Robert Kennedy, urban riots, the tumult of the 1968 Democratic convention, and serious campus unrest had confused and demoralized "the leadership groups that had sustained the great American postwar initiatives in foreign policy."[32] Public opinion had begun to swing toward withdrawal from Vietnam, though a substantial plurality continued to favor military victory. Yet the Johnson administration had seemed utterly paralyzed: a bombing halt of the North had resulted in stalemated peace talks, while U.S. ground forces were still being increased. As Kissinger put it:

> Richard Nixon inherited this cauldron. Of all choices he was probably the least suited for the act of grace that might have achieved reconciliation with the responsible members of the [domestic] opposition. Seeing himself in any case the target of a liberal conspiracy to destroy him, he could never bring himself to regard the upheaval caused by the Vietnam war as anything other than a continuation of the long-lived assault on his political existence. . . . He accepted [the protesters'] premises that we faced a mortal domestic struggle; in the process he accelerated and compounded its bitterness.[33]

As was true of his efforts to build a post–New Deal new majority, Nixon's attempts to extricate the United States from Vietnam required the existence of domestic enemies that he could flay in order to mobilize support for "peace with honor."

Nixon never renounced his conviction that American credibility could be maintained only if the United States provided South Vietnam with a reasonable chance to determine its future, but he faced an American public whose weariness and frustration with the war severely narrowed his options. Nevertheless, Nixon set for himself an excruciatingly difficult task: to accomplish through the withdrawal of U.S. ground forces what had not been achieved with their presence.

On May 14, 1969, President Nixon delivered his first speech on Vietnam. In it he explicitly rejected what he described as two unacceptable alternatives: the imposition of a "purely military solution on the battlefield" and "a one-sided withdrawal from Vietnam or the acceptance in Paris of terms that would amount to a disguised American defeat."[34] He dismissed the latter course for several reasons. First, millions of South Vietnamese had placed their trust in America's commitment to help them, and "to abandon them now would risk a massacre that would shock and dismay everyone in the world who values human life." Second, a failure to meet these obligations would lower America's prestige by damaging the confidence that other nations had in its reliability. Third, a unilateral withdrawal would reward those in the communist world "who scorn negotiation, who advocate aggression, who minimize the risks of confrontations with the United States." Thus "to move successfully from an era of confrontation to an era of negotiation . . . we have to demonstrate . . . that confrontation with the United States is costly and unrewarding." And fourth, the security of the noncommunist nations of Asia would be threatened by a unilateral American withdrawal from Vietnam.

With the partial exception of the third reason, which implied that the communist world was no longer monolithic and that some elements might favor negotiations with the United States, Nixon's arguments against a precipitate withdrawal had already been made by both Kennedy and Johnson. Moreover, Nixon's basic goal sounded thoroughly familiar: "What we want is very little, but very fundamental. We seek the opportunity for the South Vietnamese people to determine their own future without outside interference."[35]

In contrast to the detailed arguments that he advanced against a "one-sided withdrawal" or a "disguised defeat" at the Paris talks, Nixon said little about why the United States would not seek "to impose a purely military solution on the battlefield." But Nixon knew that American public opinion would not tolerate the actions necessary to pursue such a course. In his memoirs Nixon recounted that during the presidential transition meetings at the Hotel Pierre he had weighed the costs of employing tactical nuclear weapons or bombing the Red River irrigation dikes and concluded that "the domestic and international uproar that would have accompanied the use of either of these knockout blows would have got my administration off to the worst start possible." And because it would take at least six months of dramatic conventional escalation to achieve victory, "there was no way I could hold the country together for that period of time in view of the number of casualties we would be suffering."[36] Publicly, however, Nixon merely reported that he and his advisers had "made a systematic, serious examination of all the alternatives open to us."[37]

Yet Nixon did not claim that it had been wise to intervene in Vietnam in the first place. In this speech he suggested that "repeating the old formulas and the tired rhetoric of the past is not enough."[38] Whatever may have been the situation a decade ago, "we no longer have the choice of not intervening. We have crossed that bridge." And while we can honestly debate the advisability of our entry into the war and its subsequent conduct, "the urgent question today is what to do now that we are there."[39] Nixon, then, even in this initial attempt to explain his Vietnam policy, argued that the issue was not whether the United States should have intervened but how the United States would withdraw. The *nature* of the withdrawal, Nixon would repeatedly contend during the next four years, would determine the character of post-Vietnam America and the post-Vietnam world. Thus, although public pressure had narrowed Nixon's real policy options to but one—withdrawal—Nixon's task was to convince the public that *his* pace of withdrawal was superior to those of his critics.

In chapter 1 I suggested that in order to help legitimate current policy, presidents frequently offer a "declaratory history" of past policy. Richard Nixon used the opening section of his crucial silent majority speech to unveil a declaratory history of the U.S. involvement in the Vietnam War. According to this account "fifteen years ago North Vietnam, with the logistical support of Communist China and the Soviet Union, launched a campaign to impose a Communist government on South Vietnam by instigating and supporting a revolution."[40] The government of South Vietnam requested help from the United States, and President Eisenhower "sent economic aid and military equipment to assist the people of South Vietnam in their effort to prevent a Communist takeover." In 1962 President Kennedy sent 16,000 military personnel to Vietnam as combat advisers. Three years later, President Johnson sent American combat forces to South Vietnam. Nixon recalled that Eisenhower, Kennedy, and Johnson all claimed that a U.S. withdrawal would "mean a collapse not only of South Vietnam, but Southeast Asia." Nixon agreed by arguing that "for the future of peace, precipitate withdrawal would be a disaster of immense magnitude." He vividly described how the North Vietnamese had massacred more than 50,000 people in 1954 and had unleashed a "bloody reign of terror" in the city of Hue in 1968. In sum, Nixon embraced the essence of the official Kennedy–Johnson account of the U.S. entry into Vietnam—an account that was, at the least, simplistic.

But Nixon broke with Johnson on the conduct of the war by reminding his audience that when he took office the war had been going on for four years; 31,000 Americans had been killed in action; the training program for South Vietnam was behind schedule; 540,000 Americans were in Vietnam with no plans to reduce the number; the United States had not put forth a comprehensive peace proposal at the Paris talks; and the conflict had caused domestic division and international criticism. Since becoming president, however, Nixon had begun to undertake "long overdue change" in American policy.[41] A series of diplomatic initiatives had been launched in Paris and elsewhere that, unfortunately, because of Hanoi's absolute intransigence, had not borne fruit. But Nixon claimed that his policy of Vietnamization had already strengthened the South Vietnamese to the point where over 60,000 American combat troops would soon be home, and United States casualties had "declined to the lowest point in three years."[42]

Nixon concluded, as we have seen, with a plea to the silent majority to support his policy of diplomacy, Vietnamization, and gradual, orderly withdrawal. If that majority rallied, then Nixon's plan would "end this war in a way that will bring us closer to that great goal to which Woodrow Wilson and every American President in our history has been dedicated—the goal of a just and lasting peace."[43]

This speech clearly revealed that President Nixon's perception of the stakes involved in Vietnam mirrored those of his immediate predecessors: American global credibility and South Vietnamese self-determination. Yet by 1969 a majority of Americans was demanding a U.S. withdrawal from Vietnam. Nixon responded by arguing that his kind of withdrawal would satisfy the public's yearning for peace and simultaneously preserve U.S. credibility and provide South Vietnam with a reasonable chance for survival.

Nixon realized that in order to maintain public support for his Vietnam policy, troop withdrawals, once begun, had to continue. The pace of the pullout could be geared to public toleration, but it could not stop or be reversed. That recognition led Nixon, particularly in the early years of his administration, to look for ways to achieve a battlefield resolution of the war without alienating public opinion. For example, in September 1969 Kissinger established a special National Security Council (NSC) task force to explore new military options, including a "savage blow" approach, designed to defeat North Vietnam. Secretary of Defense Melvin Laird, the chief champion of Vietnamization, learned of the project and argued against it and against Nixon's position.[44] Consequently, no savage blows were unleashed, though Kissinger continued to agitate for them. Nevertheless, the secret bombing of Cambodia and an expanded bombing campaign in South Vietnam were designed and clearly aimed at putting additional military pressure on Hanoi. Nixon and Kissinger also repeatedly tried to enlist Moscow's good offices in obtaining a North Vietnamese reciprocal withdrawal, which was one of the president's initial conditions for an American pullout. That demand, along with the attempt to achieve a military victory, was subsequently dropped by Nixon, though available evidence docs not indicate when these decisions were made. A. James Reichley, who conducted extensive interviews of administration officials in the late 1970s, believed that the widespread uproar following the Cambodian incursion in the spring of 1970 convinced Nixon that a mutual withdrawal had become impossible.[45]

But while quietly searching for ways to end the war on favorable military terms, publicly Nixon responded to the widespread demand for "no more Vietnams" with his Guam Doctrine of July 1969. Floated as a trial balloon in an off-the-cuff session with journalists during his around-the-world trip, the Guam (later Nixon) Doctrine rapidly emerged as a key element in both the administration's Vietnam policy and its developing détente strategy. In his rather rambling remarks Nixon predicted that just as the Pacific had brought war to the United States in World War II, Korea, and Vietnam, so the region would continue to constitute "the greatest threat" to world peace. But how can the United States "avoid becoming involved in another war in Asia?" Nixon asked. Not by withdrawal, "because whether we like it or not, geography makes us a Pacific power," but by continuing to play a "significant role."[46] Nixon then noted that in framing a post-Vietnam Asian policy the United States had to take account of "two great, new factors"—national and regional pride. The second factor, Nixon added, will have "a major impact on the future of Asia," and "Asians will say in every country that we visit [on the current trip] that they do not want to be dictated to from the outside. Asia for the Asians."[47] And, said Nixon, "that is the role we want. . . . We should assist, but we should not dictate. . . . We will give assistance to those [political and economic] plans. We will, of course, keep the treaty commitments we have. But . . . we must avoid that kind of policy that will make countries in Asia so dependent upon us that we are dragged into conflicts such as . . . Vietnam."[48]

From these inelegant sentences sprang a Nixon Doctrine that would subsequently be intoned in formulaic fashion in more than twenty presidential speeches. Thus, in the silent majority address of November 1969 Nixon's Guam remarks had already been codified as "principles" guiding future American policy toward Asia. According to Nixon, they consisted of three elements:

- First, the United States will keep all of its treaty commitments.
- Second, America shall provide a shield if a nuclear power threatens the freedom of a nation allied with us or of a nation whose survival we consider vital to our security.
- Third, in cases involving other types of aggression, the United States will furnish military and economic assistance when requested in accordance with our treaty commitments. But it will look to the nation directly threatened to assume the primary responsibility of providing the manpower for its defense.[49]

In an important sense, the Nixon Doctrine could trace its lineage to Eisenhower's "New Look." The New Look had attempted to find instruments that would credibly enable the United States to protect its global interests without risking additional, costly, direct military interventions on the "periphery," such as Korea. Eisenhower's answer had been to threaten the Soviet Union and China—the "center"—with nuclear weapons. The Nixon Doctrine also constituted an *instrumental* policy adjustment in the wake of an even more repugnant Asian war. Existing treaty commitments would be kept, though the doctrine failed to specify the reasons for doing so, but the United States would reduce the risks of future Vietnams by serving as a supply source, not a labor pool, for threatened allies. The New Look had been criticized as reckless and lacking in credibility, particularly after the Soviets enlarged their nuclear arsenal and developed strategic delivery and air defense systems.

The response to the Nixon Doctrine was more confused. Some commentators saw in it reassuring evidence that the old "test case" mentality that had led to indiscriminate U.S. involvement was to be replaced by a new flexibility of *selective* engagement. Others feared that the doctrine tied the United States to a defense of the Asian status quo in an age that Nixon himself described as one of change and flux. Still others claimed that the doctrine provided no criteria for future interventions, for it failed to specify the nature of American interests or to define the character of the threat to them. Moreover, what would the United States do if its assistance proved inadequate to save a threatened ally? In regard to this last criticism Nixon and Kissinger apparently "hoped that the rhetoric of commitment . . . could continue, because the reality of détente would allow the commitments to remain unimplemented."[50] Indeed, after Soviet-American relations had begun to worsen again in the mid-1970s, President Gerald Ford and Henry Kissinger used the doctrine to justify military aid to the Angolan rebels. Ironically, and as a measure of the confusion surrounding the Nixon Doctrine, some senators maintained that Ford's policy toward Angola violated the doctrine, just as some had earlier argued that the 1970 Cambodian incursion had done so.

But most of the public did not care if the Nixon Doctrine reflected an instrumental adjustment or a fundamental policy shift. It saw the doctrine as a promise that there would be "no more Vietnams." The public supported Nixon on Vietnam as long as regular troop withdrawals continued and American casualties kept decreasing, and it was those incessant demands that consistently narrowed Nixon's options.

Nixon himself did not at first fully grasp this reality, and according to H.R. Haldeman, Kissinger never did.[51] The president's tough rhetoric of the silent majority speech had apparently enabled him to mobilize public opinion behind his "just and lasting peace" strategy. Six months later, Nixon gave another speech on Vietnam, laced with even harsher rhetoric, but this time the tactic backfired as public divisiveness and anger exploded. Opinion polls did not fully capture this contrast. Before the November 1969 speech, 58 percent supported Nixon's handling of the war; afterward, 64 percent did. Similarly, his April 30, 1970, address increased his Vietnam support seven points, from 46 percent to 53 percent.[52] But whereas a majority in Congress had lined up behind Nixon's announced policy in November, the Kent State and Jackson State killings in May stole the headlines, and Congress moved to halt funding for the Cambodian operation.

As an effort in foreign policy legitimation, the April 30 speech was a disaster. Ten days earlier, President Nixon had announced a decision to withdraw an additional 150,000 Americans from Vietnam during the next year. That announcement had been something of a bow to public opinion because the size of the withdrawal was unprecedentedly large and involved a longer time period. It seemed to respond partly to those critics who had been urging a definite timetable for complete withdrawal on the president, but it had also been tempered by Nixon's warning that increased enemy activity in South Vietnam, Cambodia, and Laos that endangered the remaining U.S. troops would require "strong and effective measures."[53] Nixon began his April 30 address by claiming that North Vietnam had ignored his warning by increasing its "military aggression" throughout Southeast Asia. Hence, "to protect our men who are in Vietnam and to guarantee our withdrawal and Vietnamization programs," he announced that U.S.–South Vietnam "attacks are being launched this week to clean out major enemy sanctuaries on the Cambodian-Vietnam border."[54] Nixon quickly added that "this is not an invasion of Cambodia" and promised to withdraw as soon as North Vietnamese forces had been driven out of two areas along the border. In short, he sought to portray the operation as necessary to continue the phased withdrawal and to protect the remaining U.S. troops.

Nixon, it will be recalled, had concluded his November speech with some pointed references to noisy demonstrators and short-sighted isolationists. In April he ended with remarkably incendiary language that made the Cambodian incursion take on the appearance of a major military escalation. He described an age of international and domestic anarchy in which "great institutions which have been created by free civilizations in the last 500 years" are being "mindlessly attacked." At home "great universities are being systematically destroyed," while abroad "small nations all over the world find themselves under attack from within and from without." Nixon predicted, "If, when the chips are down, the world's most powerful nation . . . acts like a pitiful, helpless giant, the forces of totalitarianism and anarchy will threaten free nations and free institutions throughout the world."[55] Claiming that "it is not our power but our will that is being tested," he mentioned great decisions made by previous presidents and noted that "in those decisions, the American people were not assailed by counsels of doubt and defeat from some of the most widely known opinion leaders of the Nation." Rejecting the advice of those who had allegedly urged him to "take the easy path," and "blame this war on previous administrations . . . and . . . bring all of our men home immediately," Nixon contended that he "would rather be a one-term president and do what I believe is right than to be a two-term president at the cost of seeing America become a second-rate power and to see this Nation accept the first defeat in its proud 190-year history."[56] The history and future of Western civilization now apparently depended on whether U.S. armed forces moved a few miles inside the Cambodian border!

No doubt President Nixon had calculatedly employed this burning rhetoric to quell the anticipated screams from the antiwar movement and remobilize the silent majority. But in his zeal to practice again the politics of cultural confrontation, Nixon had parodied the technique that had worked so well in the Air Force Academy and silent majority speeches. A bare majority continued to back his handling of the war, but domestic divisions deepened, and Nixon, who normally relished the combat of cultural politics, pointedly softened his words at his first news conference after the April 30 address. In response to a question about student demonstrators, he suggested that he agreed "with everything they are trying to accomplish" and characterized the Cambodian decision as "terribly difficult." Later he expressed regret that his "use of the word 'bums' was interpreted to apply to those who dissent" and even appeared willing to receive some of the protesters in the White House.[57]

Nixon wrote in his memoirs that the success of the Cambodian incursion had enabled him to drop one of his key negotiating conditions: that all North Vietnamese troops must be withdrawn from the south before a cease-fire could occur. To the contrary, the domestic repercussions following the April 30 speech convinced Nixon that he could no longer afford to press that condition, even though it reduced the chances for South Vietnamese self-determination.[58] During the Cambodian episode and during operations such as Saigon's invasion of southern Laos in February 1971, the American mining of Haiphong harbor on the eve of the Moscow summit, and the Christmas 1972 bombing of Hanoi, public opinion proved somewhat more supportive of increased airpower than the expansion of the ground war. The latter seemed to set back the schedule for U.S. withdrawal from South Vietnam, while the former evidently entailed fewer risks of heavy American casualties.

After Nixon, in effect, abandoned the principle of mutual withdrawal in October 1970, only one major obstacle to peace with honor remained: the issue of President Thieu's resignation, which Nixon adamantly opposed. On this point he never yielded, though Hanoi refused to concede it for more than two years. But by allowing the continued presence of almost 150,000 North Vietnamese troops south of the demilitarized zone, Nixon, if he remained dedicated to the goal of a noncommunist South Vietnam, had also risked committing the United States to a policy of *reintervention.*

Nevertheless, by clinging to his objective of gradual, orderly withdrawal Nixon eventually led America out of Vietnam. The draft was terminated, the POWs came home, and the poisonous atmosphere that had dominated American politics for almost a decade slowly began to dissipate. But as Alonzo L. Hamby has noted, "a policy initiated to heal the divisions in American life was presented in a confrontational style that perpetuated them."[59] In large measure, of course, this pugnaciousness symbolized the divisive cultural politics that Nixon had exploited to help build his "new majority." It permeated virtually all of his public and privately taped remarks. At his first news conference after the conclusion of the Paris Accords, Nixon's vindictiveness soured what should have been a gratifying moment. When asked what he might do to help heal the internal wounds caused by the war, Nixon snapped,

> Well, it takes two to heal wounds, and I must say that when I see that the most vigorous criticism, or shall we say, the least pleasure out of the peace agreement comes from those that were the most outspoken advocates of peace at any price, it makes one realize [sic] whether some want the wounds healed. We do.[60]

After claiming that his administration, against very great obstacles, had finally achieved a peace with honor, Nixon added that "I know it gags some of you to write that phrase, but it is true, and most Americans realize it is true, because it would be peace with dishonor had we ... 'bugged out'!"[61] And in rejecting amnesty calls for draft evaders and war deserters, the elite/majority theme surfaced yet again. Those who served in Vietnam, he said, realized they

> had very little support among the so-called better people, in the media and the intellectual circles and the rest, ... certainly among some elements of the Congress—particularly the United States Senate—but which did have support among the majority of the American people ... despite the fact that they were hammered night after night and day after day with the fact that this was an immoral war, that America should not be there, that they should not serve their country, that ... they should ... desert their country.[62]

"Peace with honor," Nixon inferred, the goal of the silent majority, had been accomplished despite the best efforts of a noisy minority, and he was not prepared to forgive and forget.

What, then, had President Nixon legitimated through his Vietnam policy? At the least, he had convinced a slender domestic majority that his way out of Vietnam promised an honorable and durable peace and that the so-called other way—"bugging out"—amounted to surrender and would inevitably necessitate future American interventions. In making this argument Nixon repeatedly suggested that the Vietnam War could be America's last war, but only if peace with honor was achieved. Moreover, as we soon discover, he also claimed that improved relations with the Soviet Union and China depended on American perseverance in Vietnam. Needless to say, these represented bold, even extravagant, promises, yet they appealed to a war-weary public, eager for a relaxation of world tensions but reluctant to surrender in Vietnam.

Neither the policy of phased withdrawal from Vietnam nor the Nixon Doctrine, however, laid the basis for a new national consensus about U.S. military interventions on the periphery. This fact became obvious when first Nixon, and then Ford, asked Congress for the funds allegedly required to prevent the conquest of South Vietnam in the wake of the Paris Accords. Nixon himself contended afterward that Watergate played a decisive role in emboldening Congress to lose the peace that he had won. No doubt it did constitute a very important factor in Congress's reluctance to authorize additional funds for Saigon from 1973 to 1975. But even a politically robust president would have been hard-pressed to persuade Congress to provide massive assistance to the Thieu government after the peace settlement. A Gallup poll conducted on January 25, 1973, showed that an enormous majority—80 percent—favored the terms of the Paris Accords and that 58 percent considered it peace with honor. Moreover, 57 percent thought that the Christmas bombing had helped persuade Hanoi to sign the agreement. At the same time, only 35 percent thought that the settlement would prove durable, 54 percent doubted that South Vietnam could withstand communist pressures after the U.S. withdrawal, and fully 70 percent believed that North Vietnam would try in the next few years to conquer the South. Nevertheless, only 38 percent supported U.S. military assistance to Saigon—as presumably required by the Nixon Doctrine and the President's promises to Thieu. Even more astonishing was the fact that a mere 17 percent favored renewed bombing of the North in case of an invasion, and only 13 percent counseled the sending of U.S. troops to prevent a communist victory.[63] There was, in short, clear and overwhelming public opposition to reintervention of any sort well before Watergate began to damage Nixon.

Perhaps an untarnished Nixon could have roused the silent majority again to support large-scale military aid to South Vietnam. He had already proven an exceedingly adept player of cultural politics. On the other hand, Nixon staffers, such as Michael Balzano, who worked closely with many grassroots organizations that represented elements of the so-called new majority, believed that these groups desired essentially three things: an "honorable" withdrawal, the unconditional return of all POWs, and no amnesty for war evaders and deserters.[64] Nixon had already delivered on all these demands. Similarly, in Congress, even among such conservative Republicans as Senator Norris Cotton of New Hampshire, there was little sentiment for continued U.S. involvement. In opposing the bombing of Cambodia in the spring of 1973 Cotton said, "As far as I am concerned, I want to get the hell out of there just as quick as possible, and I don't want to fool around to the point that they might take more prisoners."[65] On the other hand, perhaps a Nixon without Watergate could have persuaded Congress to provide "assistance from a distance," thus precluding the possibility of a direct U.S. reintervention. And it is possible, though by no means certain, that such aid would have saved the Thieu government.

Notwithstanding such speculative ruminations, we can suggest with some confidence that when Nixon and then Ford left office there existed deep dissensus among the public and the elites about the issue of U.S. military intervention abroad. These disagreements have continued to plague U.S. foreign policy ever since, from Central America to Bosnia to Haiti.

A Full Generation of Peace

Richard Nixon in 1969 had not only inherited a stalemated war in Vietnam from an administration apparently imprisoned in a "more of the same" mentality, but he also felt himself burdened by a foreign policy that had seriously ossified during the previous decade. In part, this paralysis stemmed from the obsessive attention that President Johnson had paid to Vietnam, while such critical issues as Soviet-American relations and the Arab-Israeli conflict were largely submerged. But there remained a deeper problem. Both Nixon and Kissinger believed that the *structure* of international relations had changed significantly since the political bulwarks of American foreign policy had been established in the late 1940s. Because of the outcome of World War II, the United States had briefly exerted inordinate international influence. That unique moment had inevitably given way to an environment characterized by the growth of Soviet military power to parity, the remarkable economic recovery of Western Europe and Japan, and the fragmentation of monolithic communism. The United States had failed to devise a strategy to deal effectively with this new international landscape. A crude anticommunism remained the wellspring of an American foreign policy that had become lost in an obsession with crisis management.[66] The results had been drift and incoherence in place of strategy and design.

Neither Nixon nor Kissinger celebrated the relative decline of American power. Had they been in office at an earlier time, both surely would have eagerly pursued global containment. As it was, they thought these changing systemic circumstances required the United States to adapt. Complicating this difficult task was the evaporation of the domestic consensus that had sustained U.S. international commitments and achievements. According to Kissinger, many Americans, demoralized by Vietnam, yearned for a return to isolationism.[67] The Nixon administration, then, faced a dual challenge: to devise a foreign policy not only appropriate to altered external circumstances but also able to command domestic support.

The Nixon–Kissinger grand design entailed the creation of a stable, ultimately multipolar international structure cemented by a shared sense of Great Power legitimacy.[68] Most essentially, this structure would maintain and stabilize the nuclear peace by making the status quo palatable to the major powers. Soviet-American rivalry would be muted, though not eliminated, by regulating the nuclear arms race and by preventing regional disputes from escalating into dangerous direct confrontations. The Soviet Union, which, according to the old Cold War paradigm, constituted an implacable, world-revolutionary foe, would now be viewed more traditionally as an ambitious, opportunistic rival that shared certain interests with the United States. This conservative, largely nonideological design additionally insisted that the United States refrain from imposing its domestic order on the international framework. That is, the United States had to construct an unbreachable barrier between the universal claims of its internal political values and the sense of limits required by the new international equilibrium. Ideology would no longer constitute the litmus test of foreign policy. The United States, according to this vision, could continue to assert its global primacy by adroitly manipulating the balance. At the same time, Nixon and Kissinger at least partly realized that there was little in either the American domestic experience or its diplomatic record that had prepared it for such an eminently "European" role.

The Nixon–Kissinger strategy for realizing their grand design involved four main components. First, they recognized that little could be done as long as the Vietnam War sapped American power and poisoned the domestic political atmosphere. The war had to be terminated, but if not done correctly, a U.S. withdrawal could actually inhibit the emergence of a stable international equilibrium by raising serious questions about American resolve and credibility. Domestically, a precipitate pullout, besides rewarding the hated better circles, would trigger bitter recriminations, ugly insinuations about who lost Vietnam, and a public unwillingness to support further American global activism.

Second, it was imperative to establish more normal relations with the People's Republic of China and to begin to integrate it into the international system. Normalization possessed several potential benefits. Closer Sino-American ties would at the least obligate Moscow to devote greater military resources to its extremely lengthy border with China, thus reducing somewhat the Soviet threat to NATO. They would also heighten the diplomatic isolation of North Vietnam and encourage it to accept a compromise settlement of the war. In addition, a Sino-American rapprochement might encourage China to play a more constructive international role by replacing its rhetoric of world revolution with more traditional diplomatic behavior. Finally, both Nixon and Kissinger saw substantial domestic political benefits in normalization. Historically the American public had evinced an almost irrational sentimental attachment to China, and though largely dormant for two decades—except for conservatives who idolized Chiang—Nixon and Kissinger detected a reservoir of American goodwill toward the Chinese people. And Nixon particularly savored the thought of doing what liberal Democrats had only dreamed of doing.

Third, the central balance, that of Soviet-American relations, required additional stability. For the United States to flourish in a "posthegemonic" world, effective means had to be found to contain the expansionist tendencies of the Soviet Union. The most extreme, though least likely, threat, Nixon and Kissinger thought, came from the Soviet nuclear arsenal. With its achievement of nuclear parity, however, Moscow might now be willing to regulate the arms race and strengthen deterrence. And it was in the U.S. interest to prevent the Soviets from seeking to gain the credible perception of nuclear superiority. But Nixon and Kissinger fretted even more about the consequences of a highly armed Soviet Union engaged in provocative, bullying, erratic international behavior, whether in Berlin, the Middle East, Cuba, or some other area of tension. These actions could easily provoke a superpower confrontation that might escalate into a nuclear crisis. To reduce the likelihood of nuclear war Nixon and Kissinger wished to involve the Soviets in realistic negotiations designed, ultimately, to institutionalize deterrence. So critical was this issue that they were willing to detach it from other Soviet-American disputes. On the other hand, in order to persuade the Soviet Union to reduce regional tensions and to accept the legitimacy of the international order, they sought to enmesh Moscow in a complex web of incentives and punishments woven in Washington. As inducements to limit Soviet geopolitical ambitions, the United States could offer technology, grain, credits, and other desired economic benefits. In addition, recognition of the Soviet Union as a genuine superpower, and acquiescence in the legality of existing European boundaries, as well as Moscow's dominant position in Eastern Europe, could further diminish American-Soviet tensions. In exchange, Nixon and Kissinger had reasonable hopes for a Berlin settlement that guaranteed Western access to the city; Moscow's assistance in helping the United States to withdraw gracefully from Vietnam; and a Soviet willingness to manage Third World crises. But if the Kremlin reverted to its imperialist ways, the United States would move swiftly to withdraw economic favors, diminish Moscow's new international status through symbolic actions, and resist Soviet designs on the geopolitical periphery. Indeed, depending on the circumstances, these rewards and punishments might be meted out simultaneously. As Kissinger later noted, the basic issue was "whether we will use them or they will use us."[69]

Fourth, the implementation of the Nixon Doctrine would presumably enable the United States to avoid combat in future Asian wars. While it would be necessary to provide allies with substantial military and economic assistance, it would ultimately be their responsibility to defend themselves. But, of course, neither South Korea nor South Vietnam had earlier been able to do so. Were Nixon and Kissinger, consequently, more prepared to accept the loss of valued allies than Truman or Kennedy? In fact, they hoped the question would remain moot, for if Moscow and Beijing accepted the legitimacy of the new equilibrium, then they would have little incentive to sponsor aggressions by their Third World clients. And purely local conflict could be handled by the Nixon Doctrine or by regional allies such as Iran, who would enforce Washington's notion of stability. In this crucial sense events at the center and those on the periphery were mutually reinforcing. Superpower détente would help create more stable regional relations, and a superpower-managed stability along the periphery would, in turn, promote a political atmosphere conducive to the conclusion of additional functional agreements between the United States and the Soviet Union.[70]

The Nixon–Kissinger strategy of détente made global, anticommunist containment appear, in contrast, rather lumbering and unimaginative. Nevertheless, as we saw in chapter 1, Cold War presidents had argued vigorously and usually successfully that containment required broad executive powers in making foreign policy. But Nixon argued that the implementation of détente necessitated even more presidential freedom. Tactically, détente placed a premium on speed, dexterity, and manipulation. Moreover, because he was convinced that significant segments of the foreign affairs bureaucracy, especially at the State and Defense departments, wished to sabotage his strategy, Nixon imposed an extraordinary degree of secrecy and White House control on foreign policy formulation and implementation. No doubt Nixon's personality played a part in this process, but the strategy did, in fact, require tactics that only a highly centralized body could manage. At the least it demanded a certain ruthlessness to orchestrate adeptly an international equilibrium of ideologically diverse states. Regional stability, for example, might depend on the willingness to sell sophisticated arms to the autocratic shah of Iran or to tilt away from democratic India and toward the Pakistani dictatorship during the Bangladesh War. Or the stability of the central balance might require the United States to ignore what formerly would have constituted human rights violations in the Soviet Union and China. And, more extremely, the Nixon Doctrine might necessitate genuine *sangfroid* to place limits on the amount of assistance to be made available to endangered (and democratic) allies on the periphery.

Even under the best of circumstances such tactical maneuverability would have been difficult to obtain and sustain in the American political system. Nixon did, for a short while, largely succeed in gaining effective control over important aspects of foreign policy. It was his particular misfortune, however, to attempt to achieve this tactical freedom at the very moment that Congress, after years of de facto deference to executive initiative, began to reassert its constitutional prerogatives in foreign affairs and that the media, angered by a "credibility gap" that grew during the Vietnam War, started to subject American foreign policy to unprecedented scrutiny. But underlying these institutional changes was a more subtle issue. During the Cold War, presidential supremacy in foreign affairs could be justified by reference to the mortal threat of international communism. A policy of confrontation required a strong president. But in the early 1970s Nixon sought even more tactical freedom, despite the fragmentation of the communist bloc and the dawn of what he called an "era of negotiation." It seemed paradoxical, at best, that the president would need additional power to deal with a diminished threat.

In important respects, therefore, the Nixon–Kissinger reformulation departed from the Cold War policy of global anticommunist containment. Their grand design envisioned the emergence of a stable, multipolar balance chiefly managed by the United States and animated by a shared sense of international legitimacy; the strategy entailed a reduction of U.S.–Soviet tension by engagement on a variety of issues as well as a Sino-American rapprochement; and the tactics demanded that the United States be free to act swiftly and adroitly, and perhaps even with amorality and deceit. The Nixon–Kissinger approach, like its Cold War predecessor, identified the Soviet Union as the primary threat to international peace, but attempted to restrain it through a complex mix of incentives, rewards, and Soviet *self*-containment.

The public appeal of global containment from the late 1940s to the mid-1960s had in large measure rested on its simplicity. It appeared to be what was minimally required to "stop the spread of communism," without triggering World War III. Moreover, it divided the world into easily understandable moral categories: the free world and the communist bloc. In the context of U.S. public opinion this strategy successfully united the values of peace and strength. Yet global containment was conceptually flawed because the strategy became an end in itself, and the grand design—a pluralistic world inhabited by a mellowed Soviet Union or a noncommunist Russia—nearly disappeared. Containment, as it evolved, could promise only "more of the same."[71]

Nixon knew and Kissinger had written that "the acid test of a policy . . . is its ability to obtain domestic support" and that it involved two aspects: "the problem of legitimizing a policy *within* the governmental apparatus . . . and that of harmonizing it with the national experience."[72] In essence, Nixon and Kissinger attempted less to legitimate their policy within the bureaucracy than to circumvent existing structures by creating a tightly controlled, highly centralized, and loyal foreign policy apparatus. Nixon tried to wrest control of the most significant issues from State and Defense in order to implement his grand design. It would be difficult to overstate the resentments produced by these hardball tactics, and the so-called Pentagon spy ring that infiltrated the National Security Council staff in 1971 and 1972 was but an extreme manifestation of that outrage.[73] Nevertheless, Nixon and, to a large degree, Kissinger believed that their subtle, multifaceted, frequently audacious strategy would inevitably be sabotaged by timid, entrenched, bureaucratic interests. Nixon's response, somewhat ironically, was to construct a loyal new minority within the White House to outmaneuver his enemies in the governmental old majority.

Nixon's efforts to legitimate *publicly* his foreign policy—to "harmonize it with the national experience"—were critical to its success. "Scaring hell out of the American people" had been a favored tactic of Cold War presidents to mobilize public support for a rather simple policy, but Nixon's reformulation required a more sophisticated approach. His legitimation strategy involved six main elements: (1) a declaratory history of postwar American foreign policy that emphasized the remarkable success of that record; (2) an explanation of the ways in which the world had changed since 1947 and how his policies appropriately addressed those changes; (3) a relentless effort to castigate "isolationists" who would entrust the fate of the world to other nations; (4) a series of surprises and televised spectaculars designed to show the public that "only Nixon" could have accomplished these amazing diplomatic breakthroughs; (5) a clearly Wilsonian promise of a "full generation of peace"; and (6) a rather stern warning that the post-Vietnam world would challenge the character, will, and spiritual strength of the American people at least as much as the Cold War had in the 1950s.

Kissinger and, to a smaller degree, Nixon were aware that the Vietnam War had helped ignite a sweeping revisionist assault on the origins and development of the Cold War by a number of American diplomatic historians and journalists. This challenge to long-accepted interpretations of U.S.–Soviet relations constituted for Nixon and Kissinger further disturbing evidence of a breakdown of the old foreign policy consensus,[74] and Nixon's declaratory account of this history adhered closely to that of his Cold War predecessors. Indeed, he drew on his foreign affairs experience to personalize the historical record of postwar American diplomacy. For example, at every stop on his February 1969 tour of Western Europe, Nixon recalled how as a member of the Herter Commission in 1947 he had traveled to Europe, studied its economic needs, and helped lay the foundations of the Marshall Plan.[75] He also repeatedly stressed that American aid, combined with European efforts, had been crucial in creating a "strong, prosperous, free Europe."[76] Similarly, while visiting several Asian countries during his around-the-world trip in July and August 1969, timed to exploit the Apollo moon landing, President Nixon reminisced about touring those nations as vice-president in 1953 and noted that U.S. aid had helped them grow stronger.[77] These statements were designed to indicate a reassuring sense of continuity—as embodied by Nixon—in American foreign policy to both foreign and domestic audiences. Nixon's declaratory history also emphasized that despite America's overwhelming strength in 1945—its atomic monopoly and economic preeminence—it had merely sought to contain aggression. Never seeking anything for itself, the United States had fought in four twentieth-century wars so that others could live in freedom.[78] In short, he portrayed an American foreign policy record that brimmed with generosity, altruism, and self-restraint. The declaratory histories of Cold War presidents had focused on the "lessons" of the 1930s, but Nixon rarely invoked them. In view of his own age it would have been difficult to personalize them as he did the early postwar decades, yet he may also have sensed that these "lessons" had lost much of their previous grip on public opinion. Above all, however, the repeated references to the 1930s would have clashed with Nixon's primary historical challenge: to demonstrate the important ways that the world had changed since World War II. Thus Nixon conveyed a triple message: the American people should be proud of the U.S. foreign policy record, but significant international changes had occurred, and now the United States must fashion an appropriate diplomatic response.

It is interesting to note the manner in which Nixon characterized these changes. First, the "nuclear gap had been closed," and the United States would never again have superiority. Moreover, the Soviet Union had further enhanced its European offensive capability and had "closed the gap in military strength, particularly in the Mediterranean." But, Nixon added, "In describing this, this is no cause for fright. The United States is still infinitely strong and powerful."[79] Second, the great industrial nations of Europe, as well as Japan, had regained their economic strength. "Many of the policies that were necessary and right" at the conclusion of World War II "are obsolete today."[80] Third, "our adversaries no longer present a solidly united front; we can now differentiate in our dealings with them."[81] Fourth, the nations of Latin America, Asia, and Africa "have a new sense of pride and dignity and a determination to assume responsibility for their own defense."[82] And fifth, "we are moving with precision and purpose from an era of confrontation to an era of negotiation" in Soviet-American relations, "motivated by mutual self-interest rather than naive sentimentality."[83] In sum, nuclear parity, the economic resurgence of Western Europe and Japan, the fragmentation of the Soviet bloc, Third World nationalism, and new bases for U.S.–Soviet negotiations had brought about significant change. Nixon did not suggest that the Soviet internal system had or would soon be reformed, nor did he contend that its repressive nature posed an obstacle to a reduction in superpower tensions. Better relations, Nixon told the UN General Assembly in 1970, would be grounded in "a powerful common interest in avoiding nuclear confrontation," "the enormous cost of arms," "economic self-interest" in increasing "trade and contact," and "the global challenge of economic and social development" that "can give our competition a creative direction."[84] The general tone of President Nixon's public statements indicated that these changes, while making the world somewhat more complex, had also made it potentially less dangerous.

The real threat evidently came from within the United States—from those "isolationists" who, besides agitating for a dishonorable "bug out" in Vietnam, wished to compel America's withdrawal from the world. Here, of course, Nixon did borrow a term of opprobrium from the 1930s to tar his domestic enemies. As he had done to garner public support for his Vietnam policy, in legitimating his "stable structure of peace" Nixon claimed there were but two alternatives: his way and the approach of the isolationists. Drawn largely from the so-called better circles—the media and academe—these Cassandras were determined to betray America's rich international legacy by abandoning our allies to our adversaries. Nixon asserted that they sought to capitalize on the genuine "dangers of over-involvement . . . to withdraw from the world," and he repeatedly claimed that at the end of "a long and unpopular war" the American people were particularly susceptible to the isolationists' seductions. But he warned that the "deceptively smooth road of the new isolationism is surely the road to war." On the other hand, "our foreign policy today steers a steady course between the past danger of over-involvement and the new temptation of under-involvement."[85] This provocative, confrontational, and simplistic paradigm, in effect, internalized the Manichaean cosmos of the high Cold War. Nixon's rhetoric implied that as the world had grown more diverse the *domestic* environment had assumed the characteristics of bipolarity. And, unlike the Soviet Union, with which the United States shared certain interests, Nixon's differences with the isolationists apparently remained intractable. Once again he was less interested in a new domestic consensus than he was in fashioning a "new majority" by impugning the new minority.

President Nixon, as we have seen, repeatedly stressed the responsible and moderate nature of his efforts to inaugurate "an era of negotiation." It is not lacking in irony, then, that Nixon, Kissinger, and Robert Haldeman's White House staff came to depend on theatrics, surprises, and televised spectaculars designed to awe and entertain a vast domestic audience. Haldeman, who had been a successful advertising executive in Los Angeles, had no particular love for the détente policy, but he saw an enormous public relations potential in it. Highly visible summit meetings with the Chinese and the Soviets, particularly if carefully planned, were bound to enhance Nixon's reputation as a great statesman. And while Haldeman and other White House image makers resented Kissinger's alleged attempts to upstage Nixon or to share the credit, they were willing to pay that price as long as the public perceived that "only Nixon" could have accomplished these feats.[86] For his part, Nixon frequently told the press that he would only hold summits yielding concrete results and not merely produce illusory "spirits" of this or that meeting. And, of course, in April 1972 he risked cancellation of the Moscow summit by mining Haiphong harbor. Nevertheless, a policy that aimed at creating a new international structure was implemented through a series of well-staged tours de force. Nixon, in fact, cultivated the notion of his indispensability to détente. For instance, in a January 1972 interview with Dan Rather of CBS News Nixon claimed that his October 1967 article in *Foreign Affairs,* "raised the lid on what many think was the biggest surprise in history when I made the 90-second announcement that we were going to China."[87] In the long run these tactics whetted the public's appetite for more spectacles and additional agreements and damaged the chances to institutionalize détente domestically. This excessive personalization of foreign policy did not necessarily enhance its legitimacy but was fully consistent with Nixon's desire to time these events in order to maximize their impact on the 1972 presidential election.[88]

Televised pyrotechnics constituted but the end result of enormous amounts of diplomatic preparation, activity noteworthy for its extreme secrecy. Heavy reliance on so-called back channels permitted Nixon and Kissinger to dominate the foreign policymaking apparatus to a degree unmatched since Franklin D. Roosevelt. John Lewis Gaddis has suggested that notwithstanding this tactical secrecy the Nixon administration "set forth the broad methods of [its] strategy with . . . candor and clarity," primarily through the issuance of annual foreign policy reports from 1970 to 1973 that were quickly dubbed State of the World messages.[89] Divided into geographical and functional sections, each of which would typically begin with a relevant public statement by Nixon, followed by a few paragraphs of commentary, these reports were painstakingly drafted, largely by Kissinger and his staff. Kissinger considered them to be "a conceptual outline of the President's foreign policy . . . a status report, and . . . an agenda for action" that "could simultaneously guide our bureaucracy and inform foreign governments of our thinking."[90] Gaddis glowingly described them as "a serious and frank effort to explain the basic geopolitical assumptions behind the administration's approach to the world."[91] Interviews with several staffers who helped prepare these documents clearly indicated that Kissinger took them very seriously, frequently agonizing for days over individual words and phrases.[92] Immediately before the release of the initial report in February 1970, Nixon told William Safire that "it's a historic document, people will read it more and more as time goes by" and added, a "good theme to get across is that nobody else could have done this. Germ warfare, Okinawa, China—soon we'll have the genocide convention and I'll get it through Congress. But nobody else could."[93] These State of the World messages, then, were to be more (or less) than simply educative. They were also to be added evidence of Nixon's indispensability.

But Kissinger appears to have been disappointed in the reports' limited impact:

> To our sorrow we never managed to get across its basic purpose of raising fundamental questions and expressing a philosophy. Try as we might, the media would only cover the section on Vietnam, probing for hot news or credibility gaps, ignoring the remainder as not newsworthy.[94]

Running as each did to some 200 pages, these messages proved more useful as "rough guides for the bureaucracy,"[95] though Nixon attempted to convey their highlights to the public in short radio addresses delivered at the time of their release to Congress. Safire makes it clear that radio was chosen because Nixon and his advisers felt that a nationwide television audience would be numbed by such reports. The media were apparently not alone in "probing for hot news." But perhaps the reports themselves were not quite as "candid" as Gaddis and Kissinger have claimed. Stanley Hoffmann, writing as a contemporary critic in 1972, more accurately described them as messages that "oscillate from pious generalities to highly tactical and piecemeal accounts of recent decisions." No honest description of the kind of international system envisioned by the Nixon administration was offered, nor was there any indication of the "newly allegedly 'clear definition of our purpose.' " Instead, what Hoffmann found was "a set of moral attributes: moderation, fairness, compromise—which do not become more precise just because we proclaim that we no longer strike moralistic poses."[96]

In fact, Nixon's decision to describe his grand design to the public as a "full generation of peace" significantly magnified the disturbing tendency that Hoffmann noted in the State of the World messages, for, in his determination to harmonize his goals with the national experience, Nixon shrouded his *Realpolitik* vision in largely Wilsonian garb. It is true that he filled his public statements with caveats about the dangers and difficulties that lay on the road to peace and of the substantial differences of interest—not mere mutual misperceptions—that had divided the superpowers. Moreover, he refused to claim that either the world or the Soviet Union was growing more democratic. As Nixon told Eric Severeid of CBS News in January 1971, "We recognized the right of any country to have internal policies and an internal government different from what we might approve of. What we were interested in was their policy toward us in the foreign policy field."[97] And, of course, in his famous "pentagon of power" remarks in July 1971 President Nixon admitted that "the United States no longer is in the position of complete preeminence or predominance. That is not a bad thing. As a matter of fact, it can be a constructive thing."[98] Finally, Nixon repeatedly emphasized the crucial significance of U.S. military power in underwriting the new era of negotiation. As he told a joint session of Congress on his triumphant return from the first Moscow summit, "As we shape our policies for the period ahead, therefore, we must maintain our defenses at an adequate level until there is mutual agreement to limit forces. The time-tested policies of vigilance and firmness . . . are the only ones that can safely carry us forward to further progress."[99] It was the isolationists, according to Nixon, who in their antimilitarist zeal wished unilaterally to disarm the United States.

These and similar public statements do indicate a certain willingness to explain the grand design, in effect, as a multipolar, pluralistic, equilibrium maintained, in part, by American military strength. But much to the annoyance of Henry Kissinger, Nixon placed much more rhetorical emphasis on what he called a "full generation of peace."[100] Indeed, the words *balance and equilibrium* almost never appeared in Nixon's public discourse, no doubt because of his reluctance to employ these "un-American" terms to legitimate his foreign policy. Unfortunately, Nixon's constant references to a "full generation of peace," particularly in 1971 and 1972, far from candidly describing his grand design, ultimately became little more than a campaign slogan. Although he had occasionally used this phrase earlier, it did not play a central role in Nixon's speeches until the 1970 congressional elections campaign. Then, as part of a vigorous effort on behalf of Republican candidates, President Nixon began to assert that if the Vietnam War could be settled honorably, "we have in the world today an opportunity better than at any time since World War II . . . to have a generation of peace."[101] But this term, which was initially enlisted to win public support for Nixon's Vietnam policy, gradually became the centerpiece of his rhetorical vision for the postwar world. In dedicating the Woodrow Wilson International Center for Scholars, surely an act heavy with symbolism, Nixon noted that Wilson "was a man born ahead of his time. We have reason to hope that he was not born ahead of our time." Though he had "failed to stem the tide of postwar isolationism" and "died a broken man," Wilson's dream of ending the "terrible world habit of war" may be on the verge of realization. While Nixon, the self-proclaimed realist, did not speak of Vietnam as "the war to end wars," he did claim that "the strong likelihood exists that there will be no need for a war to end wars, that instead, by taking one careful step at a time, by making peace for one full generation, we will get this world into the habit of peace."[102] Similarly, in summarizing the 1971 State of the World message for a nationwide radio audience, President Nixon recalled that "our goal is something Americans have not enjoyed in this century: a full generation of peace" and added that its creation "depends on our ability to make certain that each nation has a share in its shaping and that every nation has a share in its lasting."[103] To build a "full generation of peace," Nixon told a "Salute to the President" dinner in November 1971, was, "in truth, a great goal."[104]

Yet while Nixon publicly promised that support for his foreign policy would produce, in effect, perpetual peace,[105] he also expressed great concern that the United States would misuse this peace by growing soft and complacent. With the Soviet threat more muted and with global containment no longer an appropriate way to mobilize the public, Nixon, as the end of the Vietnam War appeared increasingly imminent, sought to find a new international mission for America. Nixon repeatedly reminded his audiences that "the pages of history are strewn with the wreckage of great civilizations in the past who lost their leadership just at the time that they were the richest, and at a time when they had the capability of being the strongest." Nixon proclaimed that "the challenge of our time was to not turn away from greatness."[106] At a press conference in August 1972 he put it as follows: "What we need in this country is a new sense of mission, a new sense of confidence, a new sense of purpose as to where we are going."[107] But Nixon found it very difficult to articulate the essence of that mission beyond the predictable homilies about the importance of "staying number one" and "playing a world leadership role." The real "mission"—that of conservative, central balancer—could not be publicly mentioned. Instead, Nixon agreed with nineteenth-century American philosopher William James about the need to find "the moral equivalent of war: something heroic that will speak to men as universally as war does, and yet will be as compatible with their spiritual selves as war [is] incompatible."[108] Similarly, Nixon suggested that "America, in my view, will cease to be her true self when we cease to be engaged in an enterprise greater than ourselves"[109] He attempted to portray the post-Vietnam world as one that would test American "will and character," but aside from warning of the renewed danger of isolationism, he could not clarify the reasons for his concern.

In trying to harmonize his foreign policy with the national experience, Nixon spoke to the public with words drawn more from the political lexicon of Woodrow Wilson and Cordell Hull than that of George Kennan and Walter Lippmann. Perhaps Nixon had no choice but to rely on rather simple moral categories to describe his complex, necessarily expedient policies, for to do otherwise would have heightened public suspicions about Nixon's "tricky" tendencies and Kissinger's Central European background. Moreover, Nixon, despite an almost obsessive fascination with *Realpolitik,* could never wholly free himself from the grip of an essentially Wilsonian personal universe. It is important to reemphasize that the Nixon–Kissinger reformulation constituted an *adjustment* to new realities, realities that they thought might not prove permanent. In any case, despite occasionally candid statements about the real nature of his grand design, Nixon undertook no systematic effort at public education, relying instead on slogans and clichés to mobilize support. He spoke more openly about the strategy of détente and the Nixon Doctrine, but asked the public to accept on faith his assurances that the implementation of these concepts would somehow guarantee a "full generation of peace." In this sense Nixon's perceived need to make an expediential, balance-of-power policy publicly palatable resulted in rhetorical deceptions reminiscent of Cold War presidents.

A New Foreign Policy Consensus?

In chapter 1 we recalled that the Cold War consensus had possessed policy, procedural, and cultural components. Briefly stated, global containment, presidential supremacy in foreign affairs, and an ethic of national sacrifice in the service of anticommunism all received widespread domestic acquiescence for about twenty years after World War II. Richard Nixon attempted to reconstruct a consensus by reformulating American foreign policy, by modifying, but hardly abandoning, the old cultural dimensions, and by reasserting presidential prerogatives in foreign affairs.

In transmitting his fourth annual foreign policy report to Congress in May 1973, Nixon noted that "one of my basic goals is to build a new consensus of support in the Congress and among the American people for a responsible foreign policy for the 1970s."[110] Did he achieve that goal? Did Nixon successfully legitimate the grand design, strategy, and tactics of his foreign policy reformulation? If his grand design consisted of an emergent, multipolar, stable equilibrium managed by the United States, then Nixon, as we have seen, did little to win its public acceptance. To harmonize his vision with "the national experience" Nixon repeatedly spoke of a "full generation of peace"—subsequently extended to a "century of peace"—that his policies would allegedly guarantee. These words had undeniable appeal for a war-weary nation. What, after all, was the alternative? A "full generation of war," Nixon implied, would result from the rejection of his policies. Thus the fact that almost everyone could accept Nixon's goal of a "full generation of peace" proved largely irrelevant, for the phrase did not adequately describe the grand design.

It is, perhaps, not surprising that the strategy of détente, publicly discussed by Nixon with greater candor, became much more controversial and did so in large part because of its alleged failure to "harmonize with the national experience." More specifically, while the *process* of détente received widespread initial support, the concrete *results* of that process were quickly and quite effectively subjected to simultaneous liberal and conservative critiques.

The détente process, as publicly described by Nixon, held out the prospect for a less dangerous world. Heralding a new era of negotiation, it promised to end the paralysis that had gripped American foreign policy from Vietnam to the Middle East by exploiting the important international changes that were under way. At the least, this process would regulate the nuclear arms race by placing limits on superpower arsenals, reduce Soviet-American tension, allow the U.S. defense budget to shrink, normalize relations with the People's Republic of China, and avoid future Vietnams with the help of the Nixon Doctrine. Unfortunately, because of the lack of systematic public opinion data, it is difficult to assess popular support for these initiatives. Whereas Gallup closely tracked opinion about Nixon's Vietnam policy—a measure of this issue's persisting centrality—it did not ask the public to evaluate his overall foreign policy until June 1974, and in that poll 54 percent approved at a time when Nixon's presidential performance rating had tumbled to 24 percent.[111] On the basis of this admittedly fragmentary evidence it appears quite plausible to conclude that the détente process struck a positive chord with the public. Unlike George McGovern's foreign policy platform, which the Republicans successfully portrayed as dangerously irresponsible, Nixon's détente seemed to tap into the mass public's yearning for peace without unduly sacrificing strength. His landslide 1972 reelection, while primarily attributable to a prosperous economy and the likelihood of an imminent end to the Vietnam War, surely owed something to the popularity of détente.

In accounting for détente's subsequent domestic difficulties, as in explaining the congressional revolt against Nixon's post-Accords Vietnam policy, the importance of Watergate must be emphasized. The scandal gradually destroyed Nixon's ability to govern as it effectively replaced Vietnam as a national obsession. Détente thus passed from one shadow to another, and by late 1973 virtually all of Nixon's foreign policy actions were widely perceived as cynical efforts to bolster his sagging political fortunes. His pre-Watergate public claims that "only Nixon" could manage détente grew so blatantly insistent that at the June 1974 summit the Soviets openly sought to separate the president from the issue of improved superpower relations. In sum, Watergate certainly increased the domestic vulnerability of détente.

But Watergate alone did not create that vulnerability. It would have been exceedingly difficult for even an uninjured Nixon to make détente, as it was then understood, the foundation of a new domestic foreign policy consensus. By 1976 the policy had been rather tightly squeezed between a resurgent right alarmed by the unrestrained growth of Soviet military power and a dissatisfied left that found détente incapable of addressing a host of emerging global issues. President Ford, confronted with a shrinking domestic base, attempted to recapture the mass public by rechristening détente "peace through strength."

Nixon and Kissinger had been aware from the beginning that the right would find it difficult to accept the premises of détente, but felt that because of Nixon's own long-standing anticommunist reputation, it would have little choice but to support, or at least tolerate, this policy.[112] But as the process of détente unfolded and produced tangible superpower agreements, conservative critics, led at first by Senator Henry Jackson and then increasingly among Republicans by Ronald Reagan, Nixon and Kissinger were thrown on the defensive. In essence, they argued that the Soviet Union was unscrupulously exploiting détente in order to achieve global domination.[113] As early as the summer of 1972 Jackson had forcefully criticized the "asymmetries" of SALT that allowed the Soviet Union to maintain a larger ICBM force than the United States. Further, the Senate put Nixon on notice that any SALT II treaty would have to address these concerns about numerical imbalances. That autumn, Jackson introduced an amendment to an omnibus trade bill that made the granting of Most Favored Nation status to the Soviet Union contingent on the liberalization of its Jewish emigration policy. The amendment sought to link U.S. economic benefits to the reform of the Soviet domestic system. Kissinger strongly objected to this misapplication of linkage and argued that its passage would merely provoke Moscow without changing its policies. But Jackson was able to gain widespread congressional support for his amendment, not because these members doubted Kissinger's predictions, but because they feared the political ramifications of appearing to oppose Israel. Jackson and others also attacked another concrete result of détente: the Basic Principles of Relations document signed at the Moscow summit in June 1972. Though privately regarded by the administration as but the first step of translating a functional network of relations into a legitimate world order, Nixon nevertheless hailed it in an address to a joint session of Congress as a "landmark declaration ... that can provide a solid framework for the future development of better American-Soviet relations."[114] The agreement committed the superpowers to coexistence, an avoidance of direct military confrontation, the mutual disavowal of spheres of influence, and the exercise of leadership and restraint in regional conflicts. Conservative skeptics rather predictably put these principles in their own service to evaluate Soviet behavior in the Third World. Thus when Leonid Brezhnev threatened to send a military force to the Sinai during the October 1973 Middle East war, these critics argued that the Soviets had thereby violated the Moscow agreement. Soon Jackson and others began to argue that while détente had lulled America into a false sense of security, the Soviet Union had used it to achieve strategic superiority and to renew its determination to expand its global influence. Détente constituted appeasement— peace *without* strength.

Ford, fearing a Reagan nomination challenge in 1976 from the right, sought to accommodate some of these criticisms. His use of military force in the *Mayaguez* incident off Cambodia and his attempts to win congressional approval for "covert" aid to Angolan rebels fighting a new Marxist regime there were designed to restore American credibility after the fall of Saigon and to punish the Soviets for their African adventurism. His appointment of a very conservative "Team B" task force to estimate Soviet defense spending, in effect, acknowledged that earlier CIA figures had been misleadingly optimistic. His decision to postpone the completion of SALT II until after the 1976 election was based on a reasonable fear that Reagan would tellingly exploit any new treaty in the Republican primaries. And his acquiescence in a party plank highly critical of Kissinger further reflected Ford's fear of a conservative flight from his camp.

Yet while these attempts to refocus détente by emphasizing its competitive elements may have dampened some conservative criticism (though it scarcely eliminated them), they only provoked liberals in Congress, the media, and academe into launching a full-scale assault on both the substance and style of the Ford–Kissinger foreign policy. We defer discussion of the "style" issue until later in this chapter and here concentrate on the substantive objections raised by the mainstream left. By and large, liberals, while distressed by much of Nixon's Vietnam policy, applauded détente. Arms control, the opening to China, trade liberalization with the Soviet Union, a superpower code of conduct, the resolution of the Berlin issue, and reductions in regional tensions—the "carrots" of détente—were welcomed. Indeed, liberal Democrats in the Senate, worried that attacks on détente would escalate in the wake of Nixon's resignation, held hearings in 1974 designed to allow Henry Kissinger to defend détente in a largely friendly forum.[115] Some had reservations about the specific details of actual agreements—for example, the very high levels in offensive systems allowed by SALT—but, overall, liberals liked détente, and they accepted its major premises.

Nevertheless, particularly as the 1976 election drew closer, many began to question the adequacy and the direction of the Ford-Kissinger approach. At the root of their criticism lay the conviction that the world had changed even more than Ford and Kissinger were willing to admit. Thus they argued that American foreign policy, in its near obsession with the Soviet Union, had proven insensitive to a host of dramatic global developments. While liberal critics acknowledged the desirability of stable superpower relations, they contended that American foreign policy, with its focus on East-West relations, had become anachronistic. Impressed by the power of Third World nationalism, from North Vietnam's resiliency to OPEC's audacity, liberals claimed that U.S. foreign policy needed an agenda that reflected the growing importance of North-South relations. They criticized Kissinger's contemptuous dismissal of Third World demands for a New International Economic Order, his apparent satisfaction with the status quo in South Africa, and his very belated involvement in the Zimbabwe negotiations designed to end white rule in Rhodesia. Moreover, liberal critics, who at first had welcomed the Nixon Doctrine as a promise of "no more Vietnams," grew increasingly disenchanted with its emphasis on large-scale arms sales to "unsavory," yet friendly, regimes in Iran, Nicaragua, and the Philippines. Then, too, they discovered to their disappointment that Kissinger could invoke this doctrine to support CIA activities in Angola at a time when they, again impressed with the apparent "lessons" of Vietnam, perceived the "disutility" of military force in peripheral areas—or at least that employed by the superpowers. Liberal critics also charged that Kissinger's geopolitical machinations inevitably had neglected the emergence of significant international economic issues. The newly formed Trilateral Commission chastised Kissinger for ignoring economic relations with America's traditional allies (and major trading partners). Kissinger responded by proclaiming 1973 the "Year of Europe," only to later be forced to make it, in effect, the "Year of

OPEC," when the oil cartel dramatically raised prices after the Yom Kippur war. Critics suggested that resource shortages, global inflation, ecological damage, the energy "crisis," and similar "transnational phenomena" required that the United States learn to "manage interdependence."

Finally, there remained the more elusive theme of, for lack of a better term, the "national interest." Despite Nixon's occasional portrayal of Vietnam as an example of American overinvolvement, the Nixon Doctrine represented, as we have seen, an adjustment of means, not ends. Indeed, neither Nixon nor Kissinger ever publicly suggested that U.S. interests were less than global or indivisible, and their characterizations (and Ford's) of Vietnam, Angola, and the Middle East as "test cases" of American credibility strongly echoed earlier assertions of Cold War presidents. Yet liberal critics found it equally difficult to redefine the scope of U.S. interests. While some did envision a radical reduction in American commitments, particularly in the Third World, Nixon's rather obnoxious insistence that all liberal critics advocated "isolationism" grossly misrepresented the convictions of his critics. In fact, not only were most of them opposed to a "continental defense," but they found it difficult to counsel even a policy of "selective engagement." Instead, on the eve of Jimmy Carter's election, most liberal critics were searching for ways to make continued U.S. global involvement less militaristic and more reform-minded, less Machiavellian and more moral, less unilateral and more cooperative.

The tactics that Nixon and Kissinger claimed were necessary to implement the détente strategy received an emphatically mixed reception. Initially the public, doubtless encouraged by the media's infatuation with Kissinger, seemed awed by the clandestine trips and overt theatrics surrounding the opening to China. In contrast, many in Congress, already seething over the various deceptions hidden in Nixon's Vietnam policy, grew increasingly uncomfortable with the extreme secrecy, the back channeling, and the radical centralization of decision making in the White House that appeared integral to détente. Far from establishing a national consensus supportive of such tactics, they were instrumental in fueling a congressional revolt, in raising howls of protest about an "Imperial Presidency," and in triggering calls for a more open, democratic foreign policy. While conservatives seemed much less concerned about Nixon's tactics than congressional liberals, their criticisms began to increase in direct proportion to their growing disenchantment with the *strategy* of détente. (Because this issue of a tactical consensus also relates to congressional-executive procedures, we continue this discussion at the end of this chapter.)

This analysis leads to three conclusions: (1) Nixon achieved considerable success in publicly legitimating his grand design as a "full generation of peace" but in so doing he consistently misrepresented its true nature; (2) Nixon was initially able to legitimate the *process* of détente as an appropriate strategy but was unable to sustain a public consensus after the concrete results of détente proved increasingly controversial to the right and irrelevant to the left; and (3) the tactics developed by Nixon and Kissinger to implement détente alienated much of the bureaucracy, enraged many in Congress, and—in conjunction with Watergate—catalyzed public demands for a more moral, "American" foreign policy.

Nixon was less interested in reestablishing a cultural consensus in support of his foreign policy than he was determined to mold a new majority. Aware of the *Kulturkampf* unleashed by the divisive public and elite reactions to the Vietnam War and the Great Society, Nixon worked hard to exploit its political implications. In essence, he sought to build a post–New Deal electoral coalition held together by a set of widely shared social values. While certainly not unmindful of the crucial importance of a strong economy to electoral success, Nixon nevertheless wished to tap middle America's resentments toward big government, social engineering, countercultural excess, "crime in the streets," and similar phenomena. We suggested in chapter 1 that, though easily exaggerated in retrospect, an ethic of sacrifice in the service of anticommunism had characterized Cold War America. Nixon did not speak explicitly of an "American way of life," but he did repeatedly assert that the "challenges of peace" would sorely test the will and character of Americans, much as earlier presidents had described the threat of communism. In fact, Nixon transformed the old, external enemy of communism into the new, domestic enemy of the noisy minority—those who would presume to tell "real" Americans how to conduct their lives.

This provocative attempt to fashion a cultural majority only partly succeeded. Even as Nixon swept forty-nine states in the 1972 election, Democrats strengthened their hold on both houses of Congress, and his rough-and-tumble efforts to play cultural politics, while doubtless satisfying to millions who harbored social resentments, only deepened the gulf between Nixon's supporters and enemies.

Moreover, there was no clear relationship between the nature of Nixon's foreign policy—other than Vietnam—and the character of his cultural majority. During the Cold War it seemed appropriate that a policy of global, anticommunist containment was undergirded by an "American way of life." But détente would appear to have been at least as popular among Nixon's enemies as among his cultural supporters. Indeed, his descent into cultural politics diminished the likelihood of successfully legitimating the substance of his foreign policy by alienating those who might otherwise have applauded his efforts.

In chapter 1 I also recalled that the major initiatives in American foreign policy from the late 1940s to the mid-1960s had been supported by an unusual degree of executive-legislative harmony. Frequently referred to as "bipartisanship," these decades witnessed a rather solid procedural consensus characterized by presidential leadership and congressional acquiescence in foreign affairs. Though seriously challenged by Republican criticism of Truman's handling of the Korean War and by the series of Bricker amendments that caused the Eisenhower administration some annoyance, this Cold War procedural consensus was premised on the notion that the threat posed by international communism in a nuclear era required a strong presidency. As a result, Congress gave presidents very wide latitude in the conduct of American foreign policy. As long as they rather ritualistically "consulted" with the "bipartisan congressional leadership" (as it was always called), presidents during these years were paid an extraordinary amount of deference. Preferring ignorance to information in areas such as covert action, Congress would duly involve itself in foreign policy by passing, usually overwhelmingly, joint resolutions requested by the president.

Richard Nixon would have liked very much to have continued these procedures. Not only was he unable to restore the old procedural consensus that had begun to unravel by the late 1960s, but he also failed to establish the basis for any executive-congressional agreement on the conduct of foreign policy. Nixon, as we have seen, had emphasized the importance of international changes in his public efforts to legitimate détente. Similarly, he had sought to capitalize on the alleged negative changes triggered domestically by the Great Society to build his new majority. Curiously, however, Nixon never even tried to formulate new, mutually acceptable procedural arrangements with Congress. Doubtless the raw passions stirred by Vietnam would have greatly reduced the likelihood of an amiable outcome, yet Nixon exacerbated the situation through his confrontational tactics and his repeated insistence that his foreign policy absolutely required a strong president and an acquiescent Congress. In regard to Vietnam, he argued that congressional criticism reduced North Vietnam's incentive to negotiate, endangered Vietnamization, and prolonged the stationing of U.S. troops in Southeast Asia. Nixon taunted his congressional opponents to demonstrate their convictions by cutting off funding, and when Congress finally did so in 1973, he ordered the Defense Department to shift money from other accounts to cover the shortfall. Two years earlier, after Congress had repealed the Gulf of Tonkin resolution, he derided the action as superfluous and claimed that he, as commander-in-chief, would continue to prosecute the war as he saw fit. His periodic "consultations" were halfhearted exercises that merely informed Congress about decisions already reached—

often only minutes before they were made public. In effect, Nixon behaved as if "peace with honor" could be achieved if Congress would only "shut up."

Likewise, Nixon, as much through his actions as his words, conveyed the impression that only he could understand the complexities of global change and fashion an appropriately responsive American foreign policy. Ironically, the sophisticated mix of carrots and sticks that Nixon and Kissinger claimed were needed to modify Soviet behavior necessitated, if anything, increased congressional participation, for many of their initiatives required legislation. But Nixon claimed that a flexible, credible foreign policy depended on a president unburdened by a meddlesome Congress. As he told a White House reception for former POWs in May 1973, "Had we not had secrecy . . . , there would have been no China initiative, there would have been no limitation on arms with the Soviet Union and no summit," and American prisoners would still have been held in North Vietnam.[116] In sum, although Nixon argued that significant changes abroad and at home required new foreign and domestic policies, he insisted that Congress play essentially the same role that it had meekly fulfilled during the Cold War.

But a majority in Congress refused, and instead Nixon and Ford confronted a Capitol Hill revolt that eventually produced demands for executive-legislative "codetermination" in foreign policymaking. We need not recount here the details of specific congressional actions to legislate restraints on presidential power in foreign affairs. The Jackson–Vanik amendment, the Eagleton amendment cutting off funds for U.S. military operations in Cambodia, the War Powers Resolution, the Clark amendment banning the CIA from aiding Angolan rebels, the Turkish arms embargo, and the 1976 Foreign Assistance Act providing Congress with extensive oversight of human rights abroad represent but the best-known examples in a broad-ranging challenge to executive supremacy. By the mid-1970s a "new" Congress had begun to take shape: skeptical of presidential prerogatives, newly democratized, and armed with its own policymaking machinery. It could, in fact, be plausibly argued that the Nixon–Ford years witnessed a more fundamental change in the *procedures* than in the *substance* of American foreign policy. But as Jimmy Carter assumed the presidency in 1977 these executive-congressional procedures for conducting foreign policy, far from being consensual, threatened to produce institutional gridlock.

Notes

1. Henry Kissinger, *White House Years,* p. 65.
2. Ibid.
3. Joan Hoff-Wilson, "Richard M. Nixon: The Corporate Presidency," p. 165.
4. Ibid.
5. Ibid.

6. Helmut Sonnenfeldt, personal interview, November 4, 1988.

7. Quoted in William Safire, *Before the Fall: An Inside View of the Pre-Watergate White House,* p. 172.

8. Richard Nixon, "Inaugural Address," January 20, 1969.

9. Safire, *Before the Fall,* p. 136. Nixon also wanted to use the speech to build congressional support for an ABM system.

10. Richard Nixon, "Address at the Air Force Academy Commencement Exercises in Colorado Springs, Colorado," June 4, 1969.

11. Safire, *Before the Fall,* p. 141.

12. Ibid., p. 172.

13. Richard Nixon, "Address to the Nation on the War in Vietnam," November 3, 1969.

14. See Andrew Z. Katz, "Public Opinion, Congress, President Nixon and the Termination of the Vietnam War," p. 51.

15. *Weekly Compilation of Presidential Documents* (1969): 1589, 1590.

16. Charles W. Colson, "The Silent Majority: Support for the President," Retrospective. Jonathan Rieder correctly notes that "Middle America" did not really exist as a popular term before the 1960s. But out of this "maelstrom of defection" from the Democratic Party there emerged this new social formation that could be juxtaposed to "limousine liberalism" ("The Rise of the 'Silent Majority,' " p. 144).

17. Kevin Phillips, *The Emerging Republican Majority.*

18. Richard M. Scammon and Ben J. Wattenberg, *The Real Majority.*

19. Colson, "The Silent Majority."

20. Michael P. Balzano Jr., "The Silent Majority: Support for the President," *Nixon Retrospective.*

21. Donald F. Rodgers, "The Silent Majority: Support for the President," *Nixon Retrospective.*

22. Safire, *Before the Fall,* p. 172.

23. Alonzo L. Hamby, *Liberalism and Its Challengers: F.D.R. to Reagan,* p. 325.

24. Safire, *Before the Fall,* pp. 542–52.

25. Ibid., p. 551.

26. Hoff-Wilson, "The Corporate Presidency," p. 176.

27. Quoted in ibid., p. 176.

28. Richard Nixon, "Radio Address on the Philosophy of Government," October 21, 1972.

29. Ibid.

30. Ibid.

31. Kissinger, *White House Years,* p. 226.

32. Ibid., p. 227.

33. Ibid.

34. Richard Nixon, "Address to the Nation on Vietnam," May 14, 1969.

35. Ibid.

36. Richard M. Nixon, *RN: The Memoirs of Richard Nixon,* p. 371.

37. Nixon, "Vietnam Address," May 14, 1969.

38. Ibid.

39. Ibid.

40. Nixon, "Vietnam Address," November 3, 1969.

41. Ibid.

42. Ibid.

43. Ibid.

44. A. James Reichley, *Conservatives in an Age of Change: The Nixon and Ford Administrations,* p. 118.

45. Ibid., p. 45.

46. Richard Nixon, "Informal Remarks in Guam with Newsmen," July 25, 1969.

47. Nixon, "Guam Remarks," p. 548.

48. Ibid.

49. Nixon, "Vietnam Address," November 3, 1969. In the first State of the World message the phrase "and the security of the region as a whole" was appended to the second point.

50. Robert S. Litwak, *Détente and the Nixon Doctrine: American Foreign Policy and the Pursuit of Stability, 1969–1976*, p. 126.

51. H.R. Haldeman, *The Haldeman Diaries: Inside the Nixon White House.*

52. See Katz, "Public Opinion."

53. Richard Nixon, "Address to the Nation on Progress toward Peace in Vietnam," April 20, 1970.

54. Richard Nixon, "Address to the Nation on the Situation in Southeast Asia," April 30, 1970.

55. Ibid.

56. Ibid.

57. Richard Nixon, "The President's News Conference of May 8, 1970."

58. Reichley, *Conservatives in an Age of Change*, p. 119.

59. Hamby, *Liberalism and Its Challengers*, p. 307.

60. Richard Nixon, "The President's News Conference on January 31, 1973."

61. Ibid.

62. Ibid.

63. Gallup Opinion Index, no. 92 (February 1973): 5–7.

64. Balzano, "The Silent Majority."

65. Quoted in Thomas M. Franck and Edward Weisband, *Foreign Policy by Congress*, p. 15.

66. Kissinger, *White House Years*, p. 65.

67. Ibid., p. 56.

68. John Lewis Gaddis, *Strategies of Containment;* Litwak, *Détente and the Nixon Doctrine;* and Raymond L. Garthoff, *Détente and Confrontation: American-Soviet Relations from Nixon to Reagan.*

69. Gaddis, *Strategies of Containment*, p. 293.

70. Robert Litwak, *Détente and the Nixon Doctrine*, pp. 78–79.

71. Henry Kissinger, *A World Restored*, p. 326. Emphasis in original.

72. See, for example, Destler, *Our Own Worst Enemy;* and Roger Morris, *Uncertain Greatness: Henry Kissinger and American Foreign Policy.*

73. Roger Morris, "The Foreign Policy Process," *Nixon Retrospective.*

74. For a longer discussion of this theme, see Richard A. Melanson, *Writing History and Making Policy: The Cold War, Vietnam, and Revisionism.*

75. Richard Nixon, "Remarks to the North Atlantic Council in Brussels," February 24, 1969.

76. Richard Nixon, "The President's News Conference of March 4, 1969."

77. For a characteristic statement, see Richard Nixon, "Statement on the President's Visit to Thailand," July 28, 1969.

78. See, for example, Richard Nixon, "Remarks at the Veterans of Foreign Wars Annual Convention in Dallas, Texas," August 19, 1971.

79. Richard Nixon, "Remarks at the Convention of the National Association of Broadcasters," March 25, 1969.

80. Richard Nixon, "Annual Message to the Congress on the State of the Union," January 22, 1970.

81. Richard Nixon, "Radio Address about Second Annual Foreign Policy Report to the Congress," February 25, 1971.

82. Nixon, "1970 State of the Union Address."

83. Ibid.

84. Richard Nixon, "Address to the 25th Anniversary Session of the General Assembly of the United Nations," October 23, 1970.

85. See, for example, Nixon, "Radio Address on Second Foreign Policy Report."

86. Personal interviews, Autumn 1988; Safire, *Before the Fall,* pp. 388, 390–91.

87. Richard Nixon, " 'A Conversation with the President,' interview with Dan Rather of the Columbia Broadcasting System," January 2, 1972.

88. H.R. Haldeman, *The Haldeman Diaries.*

89. Gaddis, *Strategies of Containment,* p. 305.

90. Kissinger, *White House Years,* pp. 158–59.

91. Gaddis, *Strategies of Containment,* p. 305.

92. Personal interviews, Autumn 1988.

93. Safire, *Before the Fall,* p. 170.

94. Kissinger, *White House Years,* p. 159.

95. Ibid.

96. Stanley Hoffmann, "Will the Balance Balance at Home?" p. 73. Raymond Garthoff remarked on this theme several years later in this manner: This discrepancy between the private calculation and the public characterization, between the realistic management of power and the promise of "a new era" of "durable peace," ultimately came to haunt détente and undercut popular support as the excessive expectations it aroused were not realized. Nixon and Kissinger were reacting to what they saw as the conflicting imperatives of an external manipulation and wielding of power and an internal political dynamic that required a simple and confident avowal of peace, rather than education of the public in the complex ways of the world (Garthoff, *Détente and Confrontation,* p. 29).

97. Richard Nixon, " 'A Conversation with the President,' interview with Four Representatives of the Television Networks," January 4, 1971.

98. Richard Nixon, "Remarks to Midwestern News Media Executives Attending a Briefing on Domestic Policy in Kansas City, Missouri," July 6, 1971.

99. Richard Nixon, "Address to a Joint Session of the Congress on the Return from Austria, the Soviet Union, Iran, and Poland," June 1, 1972.

100. Personal interviews, Autumn 1988.

101. See, for example, Richard Nixon, "Remarks in Fort Wayne, Indiana," October 20, 1970.

102. Richard Nixon, "Remarks at the Dedication of the Woodrow Wilson International Center for Scholars," February 18, 1971.

103. Nixon, "Radio Address on the Second Annual Foreign Policy Report."

104. Richard Nixon, "Remarks at a 'Salute to the President' Dinner in New York City," November 9, 1971.,

105. In several 1973 speeches Nixon referred to a "century of peace and beyond."

106. Nixon, "New York Salute."

107. Richard Nixon, "The President's News Conference of August 29, 1972."

108. Nixon, "VFW Remarks."

109. Richard Nixon, "Remarks to Southern News Media Representatives Attending a Briefing on Domestic Policy in Birmingham, Alabama," May 25, 1971.

110. Richard Nixon, "Message to the Congress Transmitting Fourth Annual Report on United States Foreign Policy," May 3, 1973.

111. *Gallup Opinion Index* 108 (June 1974): 3.

112. Sonnenfeldt interview.

113. See, for example, Garthoff, *Détente and Confrontation.*

114. Nixon, "Address to a Joint Session."

115. U.S. Senate, *Hearings before the Committee on Foreign Relations,* "Détente." 93rd Cong., 2nd sess., August 15, 20, and 21, September 10, 12, 18, 19, 24, and 25, and October 1 and 8, 1974.

116. Richard Nixon, "Remarks at a Reception for Returned Prisoners of War," May 24, 1973.

$$3$$

The Carter Administration

Jimmy Carter's narrow victory over Gerald Ford in 1976 represented the culmination of one of the most unlikely journeys in the recent history of American national politics. Not since the Civil War had either major party given the presidential nomination to a nonincumbent southerner, and no one from the Deep South had been chosen since Zachary Taylor of Louisiana had run for the Whigs in 1848. Furthermore, Carter became the first nominee in twenty-four years to lack congressional experience. In 1979 he recalled at a news conference that "a week after I was an announced candidate for President [in 1974], Gallup ran a poll and listed 36 people . . . [including] Ralph Nader and Julian Bond. . . . My name was not on the list. But I became the President."[1] The first Gallup poll of Democratic voters in 1976 placed Carter in a last-place tie with Edmund Muskie and 4 percent behind Edward Kennedy, Hubert Humphrey, George Wallace, Henry Jackson, Birch Bayh, and George McGovern. Six months later he won the Democratic nomination on the first ballot in New York.

We will not retell the story of Jimmy Carter's "meteoric rise from obscurity,"[2] but a few points are worth emphasizing. His surprising primary electoral successes rested on his—and his Georgian staff's—ability to understand and exploit the new rules of the Democratic Party's nominating process. In particular, Carter, more than any of his rivals, recognized the significance of the Iowa caucuses, and his early organizational groundwork there made him an instantaneously "serious" candidate. Second, he took advantage of another circumstance: the notable increase in public cynicism about a range of institutions in American life, prominently including the federal government. Overall institutional confidence fell from 43 percent in 1966 to 20 percent a decade later, while confidence in the presidency and the Congress plummeted to 11 percent and 9 percent respectively.[3] Nixon's last approval rating bottomed at 24 percent, and Gerald Ford's dropped from 71 percent in August 1974 to less than 40 percent by January 1975. Hamilton Jordan, Carter's chief political strategist, wrote the governor of Georgia a remarkably prescient memorandum in November 1972, observing that "perhaps the strongest feeling in this country today is the general distrust of government and politicians at all levels. The desire and thirst for strong moral leadership in this nation was not satisfied with the election of Richard Nixon. It is my contention that this desire will grow in four more years of the Nixon administration."[4] Needless to say, the immense agony of Watergate, as well as the spectacular revelations of CIA misconduct, and a series of congressional peccadilloes featuring an Argentinian exotic dancer and a secretary who could not type,[5] further eroded the public trust in Washington. Here, of course, Carter as the quintessential outsider held an important edge over candidates saddled with Potomac baggage. Third, as Charles O. Jones correctly argues, policy circumstances in 1976 favored a Democratic candidate such as Carter, who was willing and able to turn from the expansionist themes of the Great Society to more managerial issues—governmental efficiency, budgetary reform, and decentralization."[6] Finally, the circumstances of the mid-1970s were such that Carter's total lack of foreign policy experience (or even demonstrable prior interest) did not disqualify him from seriously seeking the presidency. Whereas in every presidential election between 1948 and 1972 the public had cited foreign policy as the most important problem facing the nation, a Gallup poll of October 1976 showed that 78 percent indicated that inflation and unemployment were the most pressing issues, while only 6 percent mentioned foreign policy. Equally noteworthy, in the light of Carter's early identification with "good government" themes, was the fact that only 6 percent of those polled suggested that restoring public trust in government constituted America's biggest problem.[7] In sum, several rather unusual circumstances combined to favor the unknown, unblemished Jimmy Carter in 1976, yet the public's preoccupation with the health of the economy promised to make it the litmus test of his administration.[8]

The People's President

For Jimmy Carter, the fundamental task for his administration was the restoration of the faith of the American people in themselves, their government, and their government's foreign activities. This crisis of faith had produced a debilitating national disunity, which Carter believed had been exacerbated by Vietnam, Watergate, and the CIA revelations. But the core of the crisis went deeper than these disturbing recent events: "The root of the problem is not so much that the people have lost confidence in government, but that government has demonstrated time and again its lack of confidence in the people. For too long political leaders have been isolated from the public. They have made decisions from an ivory tower."[9] Carter's solution was straightforward: "There is a simple and effective way for public officials to regain the public trust—*be trustworthy!*"[10] And, not surprisingly, Carter sincerely and stubbornly believed that he was uniquely qualified to restore the public trust and to end the divisiveness of American life.

President Carter and his advisers early settled on a four-part strategy to achieve this goal. First, he attempted to personify the essential decency of the American people. As he put it in his Inaugural Address: "You have given me a great responsibility—to stay close to you, to be worthy of you, and to exemplify what you are. Let us create together a new national spirit of unity and trust. Your strength can compensate for my weakness, and your wisdom can help to minimize my mistakes."[11] He was an average American, no smarter than most, who like many of his fellows had served in the navy, tilled the soil, worshiped God, and raised a family. He, like them, was imperfect but was willing to learn, work hard, and do better. And, in contrast to his frequently disingenuous predecessors, Carter would "never lie" to the American people. Symbols, as well as rhetoric, were crucial to the strategy. Thus, by carrying his own bags, walking with Rosalynn down Pennsylvania Avenue, dispensing with "Hail to the Chief," donning a cardigan for a fireside chat, fishing in humble streams, playing softball in Plains, and enjoying Willie Nelson, Carter revealed himself as a man of the people. He, of course, was hardly the first president to play "log cabin" politics, yet in the wake of Watergate and the "Imperial Presidency" Carter believed that circumstances required this approach.

Second, President Carter attempted to stay close to the electorate by establishing a direct relationship with the public. Unlike Lyndon Johnson and Richard Nixon, who grew fatally isolated from the people, Jimmy Carter would listen, and by listening would convince Americans that they could trust the president to care about their well-being. Typical was this remark made in April 1977:

> I believe that many political . . . and news media figures underestimate the competence and intelligence and sound judgment of the American people. And when we've failed in the past number of years . . . it's been because the American people have been excluded from the process.
> . . . And I want the American people to be part of the process from now on so that when I do speak the American people are part of it.[12]

He invited them to debate openly issues such as the Middle East, energy, and arms control, and early in his term publicly announced negotiating positions before offering them to other nations. He held frequent press conferences with the Washington news corps—two a month through 1978. He met over sixty times in the White House with local editors. Even more unusual was Carter's participation in a couple of call-in radio shows designed to answer questions from the people. But it was the "town meeting" format that President Carter used on almost twenty occasions that demonstrated most dramatically his concern with the average citizen. Not only would these town meetings typically take place at a high school or civic auditorium, but he emphasized his "just folks" unpretentiousness by spending the night at someone's home and making his own bed as well. Taken together, these gestures were meant to convey the image of a decent, honest, accessible, and compassionate man who happened to be president.

Third, Carter, like Nixon, recognized that the old Democratic New Deal coalition had been greatly weakened by the perceived excesses of the Great Society and a growing resentment among many voters toward the alleged intrusiveness, arbitrariness, and inefficiency of the federal government. Carter, in fact, shared this resentment and was additionally distressed by what he saw as the pervasive tendency of politicians from both parties to do the bidding of narrow special interests. According to one of his inner circle of Georgians, "He doesn't like politicians. He really just doesn't like them. . . . He's not willing to risk his future on just the politicians. He knows that there are good ones and bad ones and so on, but he really does not like them. He's anti-politician."[13] And as a lifelong Democrat, Carter was particularly distressed by the tremendous power exerted by certain groups on the legislators of his own party.[14] Moreover, he was aware of the increasing vulnerability of the Democratic Party to the charge that it was the party of special interests and fiscal irresponsibility. On the basis of his own inclinations and his experiences in Georgia politics, Carter concluded that the public's faith in the federal government could be restored only if the presidency could serve as the repository of the public good. And he was convinced of his unique ability to discern and articulate the public good by circumventing established institutions and organizations. As Erwin C. Hargrove has suggested, Jimmy Carter considered "good policy"—comprehensive solutions to pressing national problems—to be the goal of enlightened political leadership.[15] At the same time he suspected that public policy, whether in Washington or Atlanta, had too often reflected political expediency and brokered interests. Carter and his advisers knew that such issues as energy, tax and budgetary reform, and the Panama Canal treaties lacked natural constituencies, but they conducted intensive programs of policy campaigning and issue-by-issue coalition building on their behalf. Indeed, President Carter particularly relished tackling those complex and difficult problems that had either cowed or defeated his predecessors. Good policy, he confidently believed, would inevitably be created after he had listened to conflicting views, personally mastered the issues through diligent homework, and applied his impressive analytic powers to the complexities of the problem. While he was certainly aware of the political benefits that the adoption of his policies could provide, Carter's primary aim was to formulate good policy to demonstrate that America's democratic system could constructively respond to challenges and restore popular faith in the integrity of government by showing that the public good could triumph over narrow self-interest.[16] Thus national unity would not be achieved through ideological appeals or by dividing the pie to "satisfice" politically potent groups, for Carter detested the Democratic Party's penchant for interest-group liberalism. Instead, Carter expected that the sheer good sense of wise policy, if carefully conceived and efficiently managed, would mobilize public support. And even if the White House were forced to retreat from its initial policy positions and compromise with Congress, Carter evidently believed that the public would nevertheless appreciate his courage in confronting complicated problems.

President Carter enjoyed substantial public popularity through the summer of 1977, but by the following spring his approval rating had fallen well below 50 percent. When the press asked him to explain this significant decline Carter repeatedly attributed it to the intractability of the issues that he had taken on, the difficulty of explaining their complexity to the public, and the disturbing reality that many citizens apparently doubted the very urgency of these problems. Carter's frustrations intensified during the summer of 1979 when he felt caught between a new energy crisis precipitated by the Iranian revolution and a public inclined to blame shortages on greedy oil companies. This situation provided the context for perhaps the most revealing speech of Carter's presidency, the so-called crisis of confidence or national malaise address of July 15, 1979. In it he highlighted the themes that had served as his *leitmotif* since the 1976 primary campaign. Characterizing the current condition of America as a "moral and spiritual crisis" Carter had "been reminded again that all the legislation in the world can't fix what is wrong with America," for it faced a nearly invisible threat that "strikes at the very heart and soul and meaning of our national will":

> We can see this crisis in the growing doubt about the meaning of our lives and in the loss of a unity of purpose for our nation.
> The erosion of our confidence in the future is threatening to destroy the social and political fabric of America. . . .
> Our people are losing that faith, not only in government itself, but in the ability as citizens to serve as the ultimate rulers and shapers of our democracy.[17]

This crisis, Carter insisted, had its roots in the traumas of the 1960s and early 1970s: the assassinations of John and Robert Kennedy and Dr. Martin Luther King Jr.; the "agony of Vietnam" that had "shown our armies to be not invincible"; the shock of Watergate that threw the presidency into disrepute; a decade of inflation that shrunk "our dollar and our savings;" and by a "growing dependence on foreign oil."[18] Moreover, Carter admitted, "these wounds are still very deep. They have never been healed."[19] What must be done?

> First of all, we must face the truth, and then we can change our course. We simply must have faith in each other, faith in our ability to govern ourselves, and faith in the future of this nation. Restoring that faith and that confidence to America is now the most important task we face.[20]

President Carter then claimed that America faced a turning point in its history with two paths to choose: one that led to "fragmentation and self-interest," the other that promised "common purpose and the restoration of American values" such as hard work, strong families, close-knit communities, and faith in God. "Energy," Carter argued, "will be the immediate test of our ability to unite this nation. . . . On the battlefield of energy we can win for our nation a new confidence." He concluded by reiterating his determination to act as a decisive leader and to listen even more intently to the American people.[21]

Carter, in this quite remarkable speech, admitted that good policy alone could not restore national unity and confidence but that strong presidential leadership in touch with the public was required. Immediately after the address, Carter did attempt to "be presidential" by firing a substantial portion of his cabinet, and he did listen anew to the people by staging a series of town meetings across the country. Nevertheless, by making energy the test of national will, he in effect once again implied that good policy would restore Americans' faith in themselves and their government. Yet, as Carter admitted several months later, it was not good policy but the national outrage caused by Iran's seizure of American hostages that "galvanized the American public toward unity" as nothing had "in the last decade."[22]

Finally, President Carter and his advisers sought to restore public trust by articulating a foreign policy that reflected the character, values, and experience of the American people. Whereas Nixon's foreign policy design and his efforts to fashion a domestic new majority were logically and substantively separable, Carter saw foreign policy largely as the external manifestation of American life. To that end he framed a foreign policy that would convey to the world the decency, honesty, and candor that he wished to project to the American public. We discuss Carter's foreign policy more fully in the chapter's remaining sections, but it should be emphasized that much of that policy was understood to be largely a continuation of domestic policy. In view of the tight connection that Carter drew between the internal and international realms, his appointment of Patricia Derian, a former Mississippi civil rights activist completely without foreign relations experience, to serve as assistant secretary of state for human rights affairs, becomes more comprehensible, for he viewed this issue, in particular, as one that inevitably bridged foreign and domestic policy.

In sum, President Carter believed that he had inherited a nation disillusioned and divided by a decade of war, scandal, and economic dislocation. He thought himself uniquely well qualified to restore public trust and unity by personifying the best features of the national character, by conducting an open and honest dialogue with the American people, by framing comprehensive policies that embodied the public good, and by offering a foreign policy reflective of enduring American values.

A Complex New World

Despite his own notable lack of foreign policy experience, Jimmy Carter made the Kissinger legacy a centerpiece of his 1976 campaign and leveled a series of substantive and stylistic charges against the secretary's stewardship. Most important, candidate Carter claimed that America's international image had been tainted by Kissinger's reliance on secret diplomacy, back channels, "Lone Ranger" decision making, and an amoral manipulation of power, and strongly implied that these proclivities were intimately related to the Watergate mentality that had gripped the Nixon White House. As a result, neither Congress nor the American people had been sufficiently involved in the formulation of U.S. foreign policy. Carter criticized as well the content of some of Kissinger's contributions, suggesting that (1) the United States had paid excessive attention to the Soviet Union and simultaneously signed a SALT agreement that had set unequal and overly high limits on ICBMs; (2) the United States in its obsessive pursuit of superpower condominium had been insensitive to the legitimate demands for change from Latin American and African nations; (3) human rights had been sacrificed to a policy that sold huge quantities of arms to unsavory friends; (4) there seemed to be little concern about the global threat of nuclear proliferation; and (5) the well-being of America's democratic allies—Japan and Western Europe—had been largely ignored. No doubt this grab bag of criticisms constituted, in part, an electoral strategy designed to separate Carter from what appeared to be the more unpopular aspects of the Kissinger record. James Fallows, an early Carter speechwriter who grew disenchanted with the administration, suggested as much in his contention that

> "history," for Carter and those closest to him, consisted of Vietnam and Watergate; if they could avoid the errors, as commonly understood, of those two episodes, they would score well. No military interventions, no dirty tricks, no tape recorders on the premises, and no "isolation" of the President.[23]

But while Fallows's uncharitable testimony captured an important dimension of the Carter presidency, it nevertheless underestimated the degree to which the administration's early initiatives embodied a worldview different in several respects from both American Cold War foreign policy and the Nixon–Kissinger reformulation.

At the core of that view lay the conviction shared to varying degrees by Carter and his senior advisers that the world had changed in decisive ways since 1945 and that America's failure to respond adequately threatened to condemn it to philosophical isolation. This critique had been developed with the help of the Trilateral Commission. Founded by David Rockefeller to express his concern about the Nixon–Kissinger alleged obsession with U.S.–Soviet relations, this group was to focus on U.S.–West European and U.S.–Japanese issues and to explore the economic dimensions of rapid global change. Carter joined the commission and was introduced to many of those whom he would later tap for senior administration posts. First, the era of unchallenged American economic and military global supremacy had ended and been replaced by a fluid, shifting configuration sometimes called "complex interdependence." Stanley Hoffmann, who often functioned as a friendly academic critic of the administration, likened this condition to a "vast omelet" in which "I may want my egg to contribute a larger part of the omelet's size and flavor than *your* egg—or I may want to break yours into it first, etc. . . . But we all end up in the same omelet."[24] In these circumstances no state could realistically expect to exert the sort of dominance characterized by the United States during the Cold War. Second, Third World demands for a New International Economic Order reflected this new global reality and, if unaddressed by the industrial democracies, would increase the likelihood of nuclear proliferation. In this regard Carter had been impressed with the seeming implacability of Third World nationalism, in Vietnam and Algeria in particular, and believed that it was imperative to improve North–South relations. Third, the overall level of armaments in the world had reached alarming proportions as power had been diffused among more and more nations. Superpower relations had been gripped by a spiraling nuclear arms race, while the developing world had been inundated with a flood of sophisticated conventional weapons. Both of these developments had made international relations less stable. Fourth, despite its recent arms buildup, the Soviet Union had been gradually transformed into a generally status quo power saddled with massive internal problems and an increasingly unattractive ideology. National Security Affairs Assistant Zbigniew Brzezinski, even early in the administration, demonstrated more skepticism about Moscow's intentions than Carter and some of his State Department advisers, but in general there was a belief that the Cold War, if not fully dead, had become comatose. Fifth, and closely related to the second point, Carter administration officials shared the conviction that military power—at least as employed by the superpowers to sustain their influence in the Third World—had lost much of its utility. Carter, of course, had appointed to top foreign policy positions many people who had helped conduct the Vietnam War and had been profoundly chastened by the experience. Indeed, only Brzezinski, among Carter's senior advisers, had remained away from Washington during these years, though he probably would have become NSC director if Hubert Humphrey had won the 1968 election. At the same time, however, these officials had also been impressed by the failure of the Soviet Union to preserve its influence through arms exports to countries such as Egypt and Syria. They concluded, therefore, that neither superpower could confidently employ military power against Third World nationalist movements without risking domestic repercussions or international embarrassment. Sixth, and finally, the Carter team identified several emerging "transnational" issues such as resource depletion, environmental degradation, and global inflation that posed insidious, long-term threats to the world community.

Contemporary critics frequently complained that the Carter administration lacked a grand design. Aware of the many public disagreements among his senior advisers that seemed to create inconsistency and indecisiveness, as well as Carter's inclination to describe his foreign policy with lists rather than an overall vision, these commentators were hard pressed to discover transcendent themes. In fact, Carter and his advisers did initially possess a grand design that, while poorly articulated, was nonetheless real. The administration's early foreign policy was animated by a vision that entailed the creation of a stable, just world order cemented by a mixed but increasingly cooperative superpower relationship; steadied by a serious, sustained "North–South dialogue" that would help accommodate the demands of the developing nations for greater participation in international political and economic decisions; and anchored by a relatively less powerful but more "mature" United States that would constructively exploit these massive global changes through good example and a willingness to cooperate with all nations.

Brzezinski, who knew of Carter's aversion to geopolitical thinking, attempted to translate this enormously ambitious, yet rather hazy, grand design into a list of strategic objectives. With the help of Samuel Huntington, a Harvard political scientist, and William Odom, an army officer and former Brzezinski student, he crafted a forty-three-page memorandum that formalized the themes of a 1976 paper Carter had relied on in his campaign speeches. In late April 1977 Brzezinski presented the new document to the president, who liked it and proceeded to use it as the basis for administration foreign policy.[25] In its preface Brzezinski wrote of the need for "a *broad architectural process* for an unstable world organized almost entirely on the principle of national sovereignty and yet increasingly interdependent socially and economically."[26] He then enumerated ten goals to be accomplished during the next four years that together constituted a set of "working blueprints":

> 1. To cooperate with the industrial democracies in promoting closer political and macroeconomic coordination in developing a stable and open monetary and trade system. Among specific targets were the reintegration of Greece into the NATO command structure, resolution of the Cyprus dispute, ratification of the Multilateral Trade Negotiations, and improved coordination of Western economic policies toward the Soviet Union and Eastern Europe.
> 2. To weave a worldwide web of relationships with new emerging regional "influentials" like Venezuela, Brazil, Nigeria, Saudi Arabia, Iran, India, and Indonesia, thereby widening, in keeping with historical circumstances, America's earlier reliance on the Atlantic community.
> 3. To develop more accommodating North-South relations in order to increase Third World economic stability and growth, diminish Soviet influence, decrease hostility toward the United States, and reward those developing nations eager to have good relations with the industrial democracies. The most specific target was to ratify a new Panama Canal Treaty by the end of 1978 as a symbol of America's understanding of change in the Third World and of its willingness to cooperate with these nations.
> 4. To push U.S.–Soviet strategic arms limitation talks into *reduction* talks and thereby lay the basis for a more stable relationship. At the same time the United States would rebuff Soviet incursions both by supporting friends and by ameliorating the sources of conflict which Moscow could exploit. Furthermore, the United States would counter Soviet ideological claims by assuming a more affirmative commitment to human rights. Finally, the administration would make détente more comprehensive and reciprocal. Specifically, the United States would work to complete SALT II by early 1978 and an arms reduction treaty (START) by 1980, achieve phased mutual and balanced force reductions by 1980, and begin discussing military restraints in the Indian Ocean.
> 5. To normalize Sino-American relations as a central stabilizing element in our global policy. The administration should try and establish full diplo-

matic ties by 1979 and thus lay the basis for a longterm cooperative relationship.

6. To obtain a comprehensive Middle East settlement in order to prevent the further radicalization of the Arab world and the reentry of the Soviet Union into the region's affairs.

7. To begin a peaceful transformation of South Africa toward biracial democracy, forge a coalition of moderate African leaders, and eliminate the Soviet-Cuban presence from the continent. Specifically, the United States should help achieve majority rule in Zimbabwe by 1978, pressure South Africa to begin dismantling apartheid by 1980, and reach agreement with Moscow for the joint cessation of arms sales to Africa by 1979.

8. To restrict the level of global conventional and nuclear armaments, the United States would reduce by 15 percent, with the exclusion of transfers to NATO, Australia, New Zealand, and Japan, the 1976 dollar value of transfers. It should also cooperate to restrain nuclear proliferation and sign a series of nuclear testing treaties early in the administration.

9. To enhance global sensitivity to human rights by highlighting U.S. observance of such rights and by undertaking initiatives designed to encourage other governments to give a high priority to them. Thus the administration should adhere to five major human rights treaties, push for a full review of these issues at the Belgrade conference, propose human rights criteria for the international Financial Institution loan program, and expand our refugee programs for those fleeing oppressive left-wing and right-wing regimes.

10. To maintain a defense posture capable of deterring the Soviet Union from undertaking hostile acts or applying political pressure. Such would require the modernization and reconceptualization of its defense posture reflective of broad changes in the world, NATO's needs and Soviet Third World interventions. Thus the administration should examine U.S. overseas commitments and bases, seek greater budgetary flexibility, and try to standardize NATO equipment.[27]

According to Brzezinski, President Carter was "quite taken" with this outline, referred to it regularly, and praised it as "an unusually useful document." Evidently Brzezinski agreed, because he cited it in his memoirs as convincing evidence that the Carter administration did indeed possess "a central strategy, a defined philosophical perspective, and certain basic priorities."[28] For Brzezinski, "a more accurate indictment . . . is that we were overly ambitious and that we failed in our efforts to project effectively to the public the degree to which we were motivated by a coherent and well-thought-out viewpoint."[29]

During the 1976 campaign Carter had also asked Cyrus Vance to formulate specific goals and priorities for a Carter administration foreign policy, and Vance complied with a long memorandum in late October that, like Brzezinski's, emphasized issues that all three men had helped develop at the Trilateral Commission. Vance's memo advanced five "persuasive general foreign policy themes," the last of which bore directly on the problem of domestic legitimation:

1. U.S.–Soviet issues, while of central importance, should not be allowed to so dominate our foreign policy that we neglect other important relationships and problems. In dealing with the Soviets we should stand resolutely firm to protect key interests while working to further reduce tensions.

2. There should be a new sensitivity, awareness, and priority to the vast complex of North-South issues and an emerging set of global issues like energy population, environment, and nuclear proliferation.

3. Without unrealistically inserting itself into the internal operations of other governments, the United States should give important weight to human rights considerations in selecting foreign policy positions while continuing in international forums its unwavering stand in favor of the rights of free people.

4. The administration's foreign policy should be marked by gravity, not flurry. It should not try to do everything at once or solve all of the world's problems, and it should focus on long-term general objectives.

5. The new administration must make the Congress and the American people joint partners in foreign policy matters. The president should assume major public leadership on foreign policy, and make a major investment in educating the public to perceive the difference between its long-term and short-term interests, and the difference between the national interest and the interests of particular domestic groups and subconstituencies.[30]

The first three items broadly reflected the priorities of Brzezinski's "working blueprint" while the fourth one would be repeatedly violated by a president who quickly launched an incredible number of domestic and foreign policy initiatives. Vance's last suggestion certainly captured Carter's deep commitment to use the presidency to serve the public good.

Neither Brzezinski's nor Vance's memorandum explicitly constituted an integrated strategy geared to implement a grand design. They were, instead, largely lists of objectives devoid of any self-evident connective tissue. But, in fact, Carter and his senior advisers were united in their determination for America to continue to play an active international role despite the Vietnam disaster. Moreover, they agreed that to do so the United States needed to adjust pragmatically to a "complex, new world," while finding ways to remain relevant to other nations. These shared convictions produced an approach that mixed managerialism, moralism, and retrenchment.

Interviews that I conducted with senior- and middle-level Carter foreign policy officials confirmed what many commentators had suspected: these policymakers had in varying measures been profoundly wounded by their Vietnam experiences, were extremely wary of making decisions that would suck the United States into other quagmires, but wished to carve out a constructive role for America in the post-Vietnam world that would mesh its unique strengths and experiences with new global realities.[31]

First, the United States, confronted by a newly diverse world of rapid change, would manage complex interdependence by encouraging the construction of what W. Anthony Lake, director of the State Department's Policy Planning Staff, described as new "global coalitions . . . which will be in constant motion, coming together on one issue, but moving apart on another. Any state will belong to many different coalitions, with loyalties and interests that cut across traditional lines." Fortunately, this multifaceted role was neatly tailored to America's domestic attributes, for "no other people have so well learned the workings of a pluralistic world and the political skills needed to keep it working. No other nation is composed of such diverse groups and shifting coalitions as the United States. Our domestic tradition is now our greatest international asset."[32] In this new world, where military power (at least among the strong) had lost much of its former utility, sophisticated managerial talents were now required to supervise the resolution of such complicated transnational issues as economic growth and inflation, energy, nuclear proliferation, and the environment. Such a world would resist American efforts to impose solutions or dominate outcomes, but the United States could influence events by adroitly working in cooperation with other states.

Second, members of the Carter administration feared that the American public—wearied, disillusioned, and disgusted after a decade of war, scandals, and assassinations—might well retreat into a bitter isolationism. At the same time they worried that the Vietnam War and Kissinger's unprincipled manipulation of power had led to the "philosophical isolation" of America in a hostile world. By emphasizing the role that human rights would begin to play in American foreign relations, both of these disturbing developments could be simultaneously addressed. Domestically, as I suggested earlier, a commitment to human rights would help restore the American people's faith and trust in their government. Human rights could help erase the collective memory of horrors like My Lai, the secret bombing of Cambodia, Agent Orange, and CIA misconduct. More specifically, it could provide common ground for conservatives who complained that Kissinger had ignored Soviet human rights violations and liberals who deplored his permissive attitude toward such brutal tyrants as the shah of Iran, Anastazio Somoza, and Ferdinand Marcos. Moreover, as Brzezinski put it, "by emphasizing human rights America could again make itself the carrier of human hope, the wave of the future," and "restore America's political appeal to the Third World."[33] President Carter, because of temperament and religious conviction, was particularly committed to this issue and seems to have been remarkably unconcerned about the potential geopolitical implications of this stance. There was, however, a general administration inclination to view human rights as a means to restore a domestic foreign policy consensus and to sustain U.S. international influence at a time of relatively declining American power.

Third, and perhaps most important, the Carter administration, like its Nixon-Ford-Kissinger predecessor, was searching for ways to restore a balance between diminishing resources and extensive international commitments. Carter's approach entailed a pragmatic, antidoctrinaire adjustment to this new reality through reducing commitments, shifting burdens, and accommodating rivals.[34] According to Leslie H. Gelb, director of the State Department's Bureau of Politico-Military Affairs from 1977 to 1979:

> The environment we are looking at is far too complex to be reduced to a doctrine in the tradition of post–World War II American foreign policy. Indeed, the Carter approach rests on a belief that not only is the world far too complex to be reduced to a doctrine, but that there is something inherently wrong with having a doctrine at all.[35]

Doctrine, then, would be eschewed in favor of an approach in which every issue and commitment would be carefully examined "on its merits." Commitments could be shrunk by reducing U.S. arms sales and military assistance, by withdrawing troops from South Korea, by diminishing CIA covert activities, and by avoiding situations that might become other Vietnams. Burdens could be shifted by urging NATO and Japan to intensify their own defense efforts, by strengthening ties with China, and by relying more on emerging regional powers. And rivals could be accommodated by making détente more comprehensive, normalizing relations with such erstwhile enemies as Vietnam and Cuba, and defusing regional conflicts that might exacerbate U.S.–Soviet tensions. The result was a foreign policy of geopolitical retrenchment that nonetheless reflected an optimism that an important American international role could be sustained through managerial competence and moral zeal.

The Carter strategy, with its stress on the management of shifting global coalitions and its focus on a long list of equally important policy objectives, surpassed in complexity not only the Cold War strategy of global containment but even the Nixon–Kissinger reformulation. On that basis alone one might have expected from the Carter administration the same emphasis on dexterity, flexibility, and speed that Nixon and Kissinger had claimed required extreme tactical secrecy and centralization. But, of course, since the very identity of the Carter presidency depended on its firm rejection of the Nixon–Kissinger style, it could hardly emulate the tactical approach of the previous administration. Thus the Carter administration emphasized openness, honesty, and participation in spite of the dizzying complexity of its foreign policy agenda. As we see in the next section, Carter repeatedly sought to win public support for his foreign policy by contrasting its democratic character to the deceptive tactics allegedly employed by recent presidents. Moreover, many of his early actions were clearly designed to demonstrate this difference as, for example, Carter's open letter to Andrei Sakharov, his public announcement of Cyrus Vance's SALT negotiating instructions prior to the March 1977 trip to Moscow, and the public unveiling of a Middle East peace strategy before discussing it with the relevant actors. The administration, by reinserting an "open covenant, openly arrived at" approach into U.S. foreign policy, predictably offended other governments but, initially at least, seemed ready to pay that price in order to prove its moral integrity to the American people.

Like Nixon and Kissinger, Carter and his senior advisers were keenly aware that American foreign policy had lacked a firm domestic consensus since the mid-1960s.[36] Yet in contrast to Nixon and Kissinger, who largely regretted the passing of the Cold War consensus, members of the Carter administration, with the partial exception of Brzezinski, tended to blame this consensus—and the policy of global containment it had supported—for leading the United States into Vietnam. Gelb exemplified this attitude in a book published very soon after he left the State Department. In *The Irony of Vietnam: The System Worked,*[37] Gelb argued that the Truman Doctrine and the policy of anticommunist containment it sanctioned lay at the root of America's involvement in Vietnam. Presidents had not been dragged into Vietnam against their wills, nor had they been deceived by the foreign policy bureaucracy. Instead, they had gone into Vietnam with their eyes wide open, because the doctrine and their convictions had demanded it. In short, Carter and most of his advisers wished to reconstruct a domestic foreign policy consensus but to do so with substantially different materials than those used to build the Cold War base.

Carter recognized the importance of legitimating his foreign policy within the bureaucracy. He had, as we have seen, as a presidential candidate severely criticized Nixon's and Kissinger's efforts to subvert the State and Defense departments by centralizing power within the staff of the National Security Council. Nevertheless, Carter accepted most of Brzezinski's recommendations to create a decision-making process that seemed to grant primacy to the national security assistant and his staff. In practice, however, at least until late in the administration, Carter employed a multiple advocacy system whereby the president, after listening to the arguments of Vance, Brzezinski, Harold Brown, and sometimes Andrew Young and others, would set policy. Because Carter found it useful to receive contradictory advice, he tended to underestimate the political damage caused by media accounts of policy disagreements.[38] Thus in an effort to infuse the policy process with openness, Carter risked creating a public perception of incoherence, which in turn complicated his efforts to garner broad support for his foreign policy.

Very early in his administration, President Carter attempted to explain his foreign policy to the bureaucracy by holding a rather unusual series of what were actually town meetings with large numbers of State, Defense, and CIA employees. After enumerating his objectives in exceedingly humble terms Carter then stood for questions from these bureaucratic audiences. Unlike his public town meetings, which continued throughout most of the administration, Carter did not repeat these forums, largely because he came to doubt their utility. Nevertheless, these exercises were designed to restore the morale of these agencies in the wake of their allegedly shoddy treatment by Nixon and Kissinger.

Similarly, Carter's efforts to legitimate *publicly* his foreign policy differed substantially from Nixon's. His consensus-building strategy in 1977 and 1978 involved six main elements: (1) a declaratory history of postwar American foreign policy that differed significantly from those of Truman, Eisenhower, Kennedy, Johnson, and Nixon; (2) an explanation of the ways in which the world had changed decisively since the end of World War II; (3) the repeated claim that his foreign policy reflected the character, values, experiences, and aspirations of the American people; (4) a portrayal of his foreign policy as courageously willing to deal comprehensively with extremely complicated issues in order to serve the long-term interests of the United States; (5) the assurance that America's strength allowed it to be generous and cooperative; and (6) the promise of an emergent world community characterized by greater justice and peaceful change. Nowhere in this public legitimation was there even a hint of retrenchment or retreat. Instead, at least during the administration's first two years, its rhetoric exuded optimism about the future.

The Carter administration's declaratory history constituted in several ways a revisionist account of post–World War II American foreign policy. In general, Carter said very little about that record and almost nothing about the historical themes emphasized by every president since Truman. Those presidents had repeatedly invoked the events of the 1930s and their presumed lessons, as well as such policy initiatives as the Marshall Plan, aid to Greece and Turkey, the North Atlantic Treaty, and the defense of West Berlin in order to celebrate America's firmness, prudence, and generosity. When on those very few occasions in 1977 and 1978 Carter did refer to the early postwar period, he contrasted its nature to the contemporary world. For example, in May 1977 he told the NATO Ministerial Meeting in London:

In the aftermath of World War II, the political imperatives were clear: to build the strength of the West and to deter Soviet aggression. Since then East-West relations have become far more complex. Managing them requires patience and skill.

Our sense of history teaches us that we and the Soviet Union will continue to compete. Yet if we manage this dual relationship properly, we can hope that cooperation will eventually overshadow competition.[39]

The use of a NATO forum to stress the management of complexity represented a significant departure from tradition, for presidents had routinely utilized these occasions to offer heroic accounts of the early Cold War.

But even more noteworthy was Carter's indictment of important parts of America's postwar record. In his first major foreign policy address, President Carter directly criticized U.S. policy *aims* in Vietnam and implied that global containment had driven the intervention:

For too many years we have been willing to adopt the flawed and erroneous principles of our adversaries, sometimes abandoning our own values for theirs. We have fought fire with fire, never thinking that fire is better quenched with water. This approach failed, with Vietnam the best example of its intellectual and moral poverty.

. . . [T]he unfortunate experience that we had in Vietnam has impressed on the American people deeply, and I hope permanently, the danger of our country resorting to military means in a distant place on Earth where our security is not being threatened.

Not since Franklin D. Roosevelt at Chautauqua in 1936 seemed to blame munitions makers and other profiteers for dragging the United States into Word War I had a president so thoroughly condemned an American military effort. Carter's additional assertion that an "inordinate fear of communism" had led the United States to "embrace any dictator who joined with us in that fear" threw the entire strategy of anticommunist containment into disrepute. He concluded this unorthodox account by arguing that America's traditional conviction that "Soviet expansion was almost inevitable" and "must be contained" had lost much of its validity in light of the "historical trends" that had "weakened its foundation."[40]

Finally, if Carter's declaratory history suggested that the U.S. inappropriate fear of communism and obsession with the Soviet Union had led it to abandon its principles and misdefine its security interests, it also claimed that American foreign policy had historically paid too little attention to Africa and Latin America. This neglect had allegedly damaged U.S. relations with these continents and had further threatened the United States with philosophical isolation. Thus in February 1978 Carter told a town meeting that "until just recently our country played no significant role at all in Africa. Since I've been in office, we have greatly increased our interest, involvement, and influence in Africa." He emphasized this point by recalling that Nigeria had refused to permit Henry Kissinger to visit that country and by crediting Andrew Young for changing that situation.[41] Carter expressed similar sentiments in regard to South America and suggested that the Panama Canal treaties symbolized a new U.S. appreciation of that continent's stature.

In sum, the Carter administration's early declaratory history contrasted dramatically with previous presidential accounts of postwar American foreign policy. By ignoring certain U.S. actions and indicting others, Carter sought to distance himself from the presumably discredited policy of global containment and its offspring, Vietnam, and simultaneously lay the foundation for his own foreign policy initiatives. We now lived in a complex new world, Carter repeatedly claimed, and historical analogies and lessons drawn from the 1930s and 1940s had lost their relevance as guides to the 1970s and 1980s.

Second, Carter sought to legitimate publicly his foreign policy by specifying the many ways in which the world had changed during the past three decades. In 1977 and 1978 President Carter and his advisers described this world as "new," "complex," and full of opportunities for the United States. In his Notre Dame speech Carter noted that "in less than a generation, we've seen the world change dramatically. . . . Colonialism is nearly gone. . . . Knowledge has become more widespread. Aspirations are higher." And although the world remained dangerously divided ideologically, economically, and racially, "America should not fear" this new world. "We should help to shape it" with "a new American foreign policy—a policy based on constant decency in its values and on optimism in our historical vision."[42] In October 1977 he told the UN General Assembly that "power is now widely shared among many nations with different cultures and different histories and different aspirations. . . . However wealthy and powerful the United States may be, however capable of leadership, this power is increasingly only relative. The leadership is in need of being shared."[43] In March 1978 Carter described a world that had "grown both more complex and more interdependent. There is now a division among the Communist powers. The old colonial empires have fallen. . . . Old ideological labels have lost some of their meaning. Over the past twenty years, the military forces of the Soviets have grown substantially, both in absolute numbers and relative to our own." Yet as he told a Nigerian audience the following month:

> Nothing can shake my faith that in every part of the world peaceful change can come and bless the lives of human beings. Nothing can make me doubt

that this continent will win its struggle for freedom . . . from racism and the denial of human rights . . . want and suffering . . . and the destruction of war and foreign intervention.[44]

Thus while Carter acknowledged that the world would never be "perfect," he assured the "citizens of the world" in a U.S. Information Agency (USIA) telecast on Inauguration Day that "our desire is to shape a world order that is more responsive to human aspirations."[45]

Third, Carter believed that a foreign policy that reflected the values and aspirations of the American people could serve as a powerful tool in achieving national unity. Again and again he asserted that recent American foreign policy, both in its formulation and its content, had largely ignored the wishes of the public. If the people had been involved in discussing policy options instead of being deceived and dismissed by their government, "some of the mistakes that were so devastating to our country in the past" could have been prevented.[46] A more democratically made foreign policy, Carter suggested, would result in a wiser, more responsible foreign policy. Furthermore, if the people could choose an appropriate foreign policy, they would infuse it with a deep commitment to human rights. The American people would not support "the intrusion of American military forces into the internal affairs of other nations" unless "our security was directly threatened."[47] At the same time, Carter frequently recalled:

> We've been through some sordid and embarrassing years recently with Vietnam and Cambodia and Watergate and the CIA revelations, and I felt like it was time for our country to hold a beacon light of something pure and decent and right and proper that would rally our citizens to a cause.[48]

And since "we are not trying to send in troops to make other nations conform to us, . . . there has to be some means . . . for a President to exemplify or to personify what the American people believe. And my opinion is that the American people believe very deeply in the concept of human rights." Carter admitted that it would be difficult to measure tangibly the success of such a foreign policy, but he repeatedly assured the public that the policy was helping to improve the world because "there's not a national leader on Earth who hasn't now in the forefront of his or her consciousness the question of human rights."[49]

Fourth, President Carter asked the public to support a foreign policy designed to tackle courageously a wide array of extremely complicated international problems. Issues such as nuclear proliferation, conventional arms transfers, southern Africa, the North-South dialogue, and international trade were presented as urgent matters, but, in practice, Carter's public rhetoric focused on the Panama Canal treaties, the Middle East, and SALT. According to Erwin C. Hargrove, Carter deliberately took on hard cases, hoping to achieve domestic political benefits, yet willing to accept domestic criticism.[50] Overall he wished to project an image of policy competence, the leader of an administration prudently implementing preventive diplomacy to bring about a safer and more just world. As in the domestic realm, Carter tried to build policy coalitions to support these "comprehensive" initiatives, not on the basis of ideology or party loyalty, but because of their allegedly inherent good sense. Thus Carter inferred that the Panama Canal treaties symbolized not retreat or surrender but the generosity of a strong, confident nation unwilling to use its power to bully the weak; the Camp David Accords represented the triumph of reason and compromise over hatred and distrust; and the "deep cuts" SALT proposal of March 1977 went far beyond that contemplated by previous administrations in order to halt the nuclear arms race.

When each of these issues proved more intractable than Carter initially anticipated, he publicly argued that such delays were inevitable in view of their innate difficulties. For example, in response to repeated press queries about the protracted SALT negotiations, Carter described them as "complicated," "very complicated," "extremely complicated," and "extraordinarily complicated" But he sought to reassure the electorate that his administration could competently manage these complexities despite the fact that "he had a lot to learn." The period of détente had not ended, Carter reiterated, but because "we are now trying to address some questions that in the past have been avoided . . . I think the period of debate, disagreement, probing, and negotiation was inevitable. And . . . I have no regrets about the issues that have been raised that have proven to be controversial."[51]

Fifth, President Carter claimed that America's strength allowed it to champion human rights, practice preventive diplomacy, and deal constructively with the opportunities created by this complex new world. There was, to be sure, some ambiguity in this message, for he repeatedly acknowledged that neither he nor the United States possessed the power or wisdom to solve all the world's problems. Indeed, it had been the wrong-headed desire of previous administrations to dominate others, to oppose change, and to intrude into the affairs of other nations that had presumably begotten Vietnam. But President Carter nevertheless sought to camouflage the retreatist elements of his foreign policy behind an optimistic rhetoric that emphasized the "improved" role that the United States could play by generously cooperating with others.

Sixth, on those rather infrequent occasions that Carter publicly articulated the outlines of his grand design, he described it as "a wider framework

of international cooperation suited to the new and rapidly changing historical circumstances."[52] Typically he would then list several issues that, if
successfully confronted, would help to build a genuine world community.
This reluctance to legitimate a comprehensive vision had multiple roots.
Secretary of State Vance, who throughout 1977 and much of 1978 functioned as the president's primary source of advice, was deeply committed to
a "case by case, step by step, stone by stone" approach and, like Gelb, Lake,
and other State Department officials, wished to avoid imposing simple slogans on a complex global reality. That sort of thinking had presumably led
directly to Vietnam. Carter, who had a genuine aversion to geopolitical
abstraction, found Vance's attitude very congenial. Moreover, the grand
design itself hardly suffered from an excess of conceptual clarity and would
have been difficult for any president to capture compellingly for the public.
At least some officials recognized the domestic liabilities of this incremental, nondoctrinaire approach. For example Paul Kreisberg, Vance's deputy
director of the Policy Planning Staff (PPS), noted that it was a

> very subtle policy, and subtlety is a characteristic that is very hard to sell
> politically. It's hard to make a speech about change . . . which says there are
> fourteen major problems in the world, and we have to deal with them all. . . .
> [People] kept asking "Where are the priorities?," and the argument that the
> priority was the East-West struggle began to appear . . . more attractive [to
> the administration] by the end of 1978.[53]

Finally, according to the testimony of several senior advisers, Carter lacked
deep and settled foreign policy convictions. He entered office committed to
human rights but had not thought through the foreign policy implications.
Instead, he viewed the issue primarily as a way to unite liberals and conservatives at home behind an appealing cause.[54] Carter possessed *inclinations*
but few convictions. Nevertheless, these officials also believed that

> the Carter Administration was trying, maybe imperfectly, but valiantly, to
> devise a new consensus. . . . [W]hat the Carter administration was trying to
> do at a minimum was to say, look, the world had changed dramatically, there
> are over a hundred new countries, there's economic interdependence, there's
> a whole series of problems that urgently need our attention . . . and our
> foreign policy has to be about a lot more things than it has been in the past.[55]

For PPS member John Holum, this new domestic consensus was to be
constructed on a "complex" foundation that included a "sensitivity" to
change, especially in the Third World, a renewed concern for human rights,
and arms control with the Soviet Union. But Holum admitted that no such
new consensus ever emerged: "It was a tragedy that those new directions in

foreign policy were so precariously based—they didn't have a popular foundation yet—that the whole thing could come unraveled over something like Iran."[56]

The Arc of Crisis

Indeed, the "shocks" of 1979—the fall of the shah and subsequent oil shortage, the Sandinista victory in Nicaragua, the discovery of the Soviet brigade in Cuba, the seizure of American diplomats in Teheran, and the Soviet invasion of Afghanistan—profoundly challenged the grand design and strategic objectives of the Carter foreign policy. Moreover, domestic shocks in the form of soaring inflation, rising unemployment, and a new energy crisis contributed to growing public and elite doubts about the ability of Carter to lead the nation. Polls showed approval ratings, especially for his handling of the economy and foreign policy, to be the lowest ever recorded.[57]

Although early in the administration Carter had been inclined to gravitate toward the advice offered by Vance—patience, prudence, and a step-by-step approach—these disturbing international events of 1979, as well as their astute political manipulation by domestic conservative critics such as the Committee on the Present Danger and *Commentary* magazine, accelerated Brzezinski's ascent in the foreign policy inner circle. That process had already begun the previous year, in part because of the continued Soviet arms buildup and its intensified "adventurism" in Africa, and in part because of Vance's reluctance to be a more forceful public advocate for the administration's foreign policy. In addition, beginning in mid-1978 Brzezinski began to replace several original NSC staffers, such as Jessica Tuchman Mathews, who had taken a "world order" approach, with more East–West orientated people such as Fritz Ermarth and F. Stephen Larrabee.[58] According to Ermarth, a former aide to Senator Henry M. Jackson,

> I was uncompromisingly of the view that the bear was coming out of his cage and was going to cause us no end of trouble. The United States was hourly falling behind in this challenge. My job was to cry alarm and mobilize resources, and that's what Brzezinski had me on the staff doing. There was no question about that.[59]

These personnel changes exacerbated the increasingly difficult State-NSC relationship. Gelb's replacement in April 1979 as director of politico-military affairs with Reginald Bartholomew, a career Foreign Service officer, was further evidence of the national security assistant's enhanced stature. The overall result was that Brzezinski seemed well placed to interpret the shocks of 1979 to a president who would soon face reelection.

Carter did not immediately nor wholly jettison the grand design and strategic objectives of 1977. Brzezinski, after all, had helped formulate them. The shift in foreign policy outlook occurred haltingly and incompletely, though it became more pronounced after Afghanistan. Some senior State officials—Hodding Carter III, for example—doubted whether the president was even aware that the *Weltanschauung* had changed. The same, however, cannot be said of Brzezinski, who by restoring an East-West focus to American foreign policy, tried to transform Jimmy Carter into another Harry Truman—in early 1948 an unpopular, but feisty, Democratic incumbent assailed by both left and right.

The "lessons of Vietnam" hovered like a mist around the Carter administration. Though rarely invoked explicitly, they informed many of its most important foreign policy statements. For example, on May 1, 1979, Secretary of State Vance delivered a speech in Chicago that, according to key aides, expressed his philosophy in an especially cogent manner. These officials further recalled that the wording of the following passage became the subject of a long and rather contentious discussion within the PPS. In the speech Vance asked:

> In seeking to help others meet the legitimate needs of their peoples, what are the best instruments at hand? Let me state first that the use of military force is not, and should not be, a desirable American policy response to the internal politics of other nations.[60]

In the words of one PPS member who participated in this debate:

> That word "desirable" was a compromise position between those who wanted to simply say that the use of military force is not an appropriate instrument, and those who felt that we could not rule that out in *every* circumstance. The great example that was given was. . . Saudi Arabia. The debate took place between the poles. And there was a lot of playing out of Vietnam in the course of that discussion both explicitly and implicitly.[61]

Vance himself apparently had difficulty in deciding the issue, and his indecisiveness highlighted a nagging problem for the administration: what *had* Vietnam "taught" America about military interventions? From the time of the Truman Doctrine's enunciation until the emergence of significant domestic opposition to Vietnam, presidents had reserved the right to intervene anywhere to "help free peoples" remain free. In essence, this meant that while the United States would abstain from military action in Eastern Europe (notwithstanding the rhetoric of rollback), it refused to rule out armed assistance for others, whether threatened from without or within.

But, although the Truman Doctrine had given equal rhetorical priority to combating external aggression and internal subversion, in practice, presidents invariably discovered evidence of outside support (usually Soviet) whenever they contemplated military intervention. Vietnam was no exception, and while the Johnson administration justified its policy in abstract, universalist terms, it consistently claimed that the war also represented an external (and illegal) aggression by Hanoi.

Vance sought to narrow the Truman Doctrine by explicitly reducing America's perceived stakes in *some* purely domestic upheavals. Military force would no longer be a desirable response to the internal politics of other nations, even, evidently, if free people were threatened by subversion. But if, for example, Islamic fundamentalists or Marxist revolutionaries toppled the Saudi monarchy and withheld petroleum, the United States, according to Vance's formulation, might nevertheless be required to intervene, not to uphold some imperial principle of world order, but to ensure the economic survival of the West. According to this view, American security had not been at stake in Vietnam—a domestic revolution. But what if Western economic survival was not directly endangered by either domestic subversion or external aggression? Until Vietnam, presidents had assumed that all external aggressions threatened American security, but Vance's formulation seemed to alter the old equation. How would the Carter administration view, for example, a pro-Soviet coup in a Third World nation? Paul Kreisberg described the State Department attitude in the following way:

> I think that the notion that the Soviets were making a gain and that we had to draw lines and say "here, and no further" was really, from the State Department's point of view, alien to our basic thinking about the world. It implied that specific places around the world were turning points, and that if the Soviets gained influence in, for example, Ethiopia or South Yemen, or in any other given place, that this (a) was irreversible and (b) would transform fundamentally the strategic balance. [Our] approach was basically to say that the world is a place that is in constant flux, things are never totally black or white, and, on balance, Soviet influence has been diminishing in recent years in a whole series of countries that seemed to be firmly in the Soviet camp.[62]

Pluralism would thus render Soviet gains temporary and reversible in certain instances, but pluralism frequently required time to work, and in the meantime a policy of patience and restraint was susceptible to domestic American pressures for bold action.

Brzezinski was acutely aware of this problem and was more impressed than his State Department's counterparts with an additional danger: the psychological impact that the loss of a marginally important country might have on nations of vital significance. Although choruses of "Who Lost

Iran?" and "Who Lost Nicaragua?" had not reached quite the crescendo of "Who Lost China?" in the late 1940s, they were proving to be very damaging to the administration's desire to be perceived publicly as a pragmatic problem solver.

Moreover, the national security adviser had little patience with the agonizing that Vance's May 1979 speech represented. He had concluded by 1978 that too many in the Carter administration had overlearned the lessons of Vietnam by seeming to rule out the use of military force in *all* circumstances.[63] Even a pluralistic world might require American intervention in areas of questionable strategic significance in order to counter Soviet efforts to exploit and exacerbate turbulent situations. Brzezinski, in contrast to Vance, believed that the rapid and judicious use of force in places such as South Yemen or Somalia could be justified in order to deny them to the Soviets or bolster the morale of regional friends. In the words of Madeleine Albright, a close aide,

> I think that's one of the legacies of Vietnam—we are afraid to use power. The tragedy of Vietnam is that there are a series of people that were in the government who felt that the use of power was something alien to America, because it had been misused. I think that what we needed to do was to get at the selective use of that power instead of saying, "we can't do that."[64]

Carter, who had been initially inclined to side with Vance on this issue, gradually grew more sympathetic to Brzezinski's views until evidently embracing them in the aftermath of Afghanistan.

President Carter also gravitated increasingly toward Brzezinski on what one senior NSC official saw as the most fundamentally divisive issue of all that plagued the administration: whether or not the Soviet Union was a status quo power.[65] Indeed, it heavily influenced judgments about a host of problems including SALT and its linkage to Soviet behavior in the Third World, Nicaragua, U.S. support for the shah, the meaning of the Soviet brigade in Cuba, the export of arms to China, and events in eastern Africa. On balance, Vance, whose top priority was superpower arms control, resisted placing regional and local issues in an East-West context, whereas Brzezinski showed a greater willingness to contain Soviet global pretensions through a variety of means including, if necessary, transforming SALT into a "carrot."[66]

By early 1980 the Carter administration, in reacting to the shocks of 1979 and the extremely damaging conservative attacks on it, unveiled what constituted a modified grand design and a new strategy that in important respects shared more with pre-Vietnam American foreign policy than with its own original world vision. Carter apparently continued to cling to the vision of an emerging cooperative global community but concluded that the Soviet invasion of Afghanistan, as well as Iran's seizure of the American diplomats, had severely damaged the likelihood that such a community would soon be realized. If the law-abiding and peace-loving nations of the world cooperated in punishing Moscow and Teheran for their transgressions, then the march toward global community could be resumed. The essence of the grand design remained valid, but its achievement would have to be postponed.

Carter's new strategy of containment was composed of five main elements designed to punish the Soviet Union for its Afghan aggression and deter it from launching additional invasions. First, the president pledged, in what the administration encouraged the press to call the Carter Doctrine, to take the necessary steps to protect the security of the Persian Gulf and Southwest Asia. Second, the United States undertook a broad diplomatic effort to mobilize a host of nations, including China and members of the Islamic Conference and Non-Aligned Movement (minus Cuba), into a loose, anti-Soviet coalition. Third, the administration initiated an across-the-board effort to expand and modernize strategic general-purpose forces, land, air, and sea capabilities, and the oft-delayed Rapid Deployment Force. Fourth, Carter canceled or suspended an array of ongoing negotiations with the Soviet Union involving, for example, the demilitarization of the Indian Ocean, the SALT II ratification, and the conventional arms talks. Indeed, the United States began to search for usable naval ports and arms recipients in eastern Africa, the Persian Gulf, and Southwest Asia. Finally, the administration attempted to coordinate with NATO and Japan, with mixed success at best, a series of punitive measures against the Soviets, including a grain embargo, a variety of additional trade sanctions, and the boycott of the Moscow Olympic Games.[67] In designing this list Carter had asked all of the relevant bureaucracies to send him inventories of possible sanctions, and on their receipt simply stapled them all together. Indeed, Carter's actions went beyond even the intentions of Brzezinski, who, unlike the president, appreciated the consequences of this massive shift in U.S. policy for Soviet-American relations. Whereas Carter fully expected to win quick Senate approval of SALT II early in his second term, Brzezinski suspected that some of the administration's symbolic measures would provoke and humiliate Moscow without necessarily containing it, with the consequence of destroying the remaining vestiges of détente.[68]

In view of this *volte face* it is somewhat surprising that the resulting turmoil in the foreign affairs bureaucracy was not more widespread. Secretary Vance, of course, angrily resigned in April 1980 and delivered a blistering public attack on the administration's apostasy at the Harvard commencement in June. In his memoirs he described Carter's response to Afghanistan as having tipped the scales toward those favoring confrontation, but Vance himself believed that the Soviet action had "threatened the very basis" of superpower relations.[69] Vance resigned primarily because of his profound objections to the Iranian hostage rescue mission, though he had felt increasingly excluded from Carter's inner circle for more than a year. Brzezinski, for his part, had preemptively moved to mute criticism of this new policy within the NSC staff by beginning a housecleaning operation in early 1979. Other would-be critics in the State Department, such as Gelb and Joseph S. Nye Jr., deputy undersecretary for security assistance, science, and technology, also left the government that year. But perhaps the most significant factor in encouraging the bureaucracy to acquiesce in the new Carter approach was the growing fear of Ronald Reagan's election. Carter's hard line was designed to appear eminently moderate in contrast to the Republican candidate's blusterings.[70]

President Carter's efforts to legitimate publicly his 1980 foreign policy involved six components: (1) a declaratory history of American foreign relations that emphasized the essential wisdom and continuity of that postwar record; (2) a predominately negative portrayal of international change; (3) a description of a complex, turbulent world that required a strong U.S. economy and military posture as the foundation for a truly cooperative global community; (4) the reassurance of American military superiority, after a period of neglect, due to his administration's far-sighted actions; (5) a plea for national unity at a time of unparalleled crisis; and (6) a series of theatrical exercises designed to underline the seriousness of the crisis and the administration's determination to confront it. On balance, this attempt to reconstruct a domestic foreign policy consensus bore a closer resemblance to the rhetoric of Cold War presidents than to Carter's own previous behavior.

In contrast to his earlier revisionist accounts of past American actions, Carter now recited a much more traditional history, which praised U.S. steadfastness in the face of Soviet aggressions. For example, in his 1980 State of the Union address (he had not even wanted to deliver one in 1978, believing the custom to be "imperial"), Carter treated the last thirty-five years as a coherent unity in which "America has led other nations in meeting the challenge of mounting Soviet power." He recalled U.S. leadership in founding NATO, in containing Soviet challenges in Korea, the Middle East, and Berlin, and in facing the Cuban missile crisis. While describing Soviet-American relations as a combination of cooperation, competition, and confrontation, the president claimed that in invading Afghanistan, Moscow had taken "a radical and an aggressive new step . . . that could pose the most serious threat to the peace since the Second World War."[71] In April 1980 he proudly remembered how "in 1946 the United States stood firm against Soviet occupation of northern Iran, against Soviet-sponsored subversion in Greece, against Soviet demands on Turkey" and asserted that the Soviet Union continued today "to exploit unrest to expand its own dominion and to satisfy its imperial ambitions."[72] Deeming its "aggressive military policy. . . unsettling to other peoples throughout the world," he condemned the invasion of Afghanistan as a "deliberate attempt of a powerful atheistic government to subjugate an independent Islamic people." Carter predicted that if the Soviets remained in Afghanistan and extended their control to adjacent countries "the stable, strategic, and peaceful balance of the entire world will be changed."[73] In April, for the first time in his presidency, Carter invoked the events of the 1930s:

> It is extremely important that we not in any way condone Soviet aggression. We must recall the experience of 1936, the year of the Berlin Olympic games. They were used to inflate the prestige of. . . Adolph Hitler, to show Germany's totalitarian strength to the world in the sports arena. . . .
> The parallel with the site and timing of the 1980 Olympics is striking.[74]

And in February 1980 Carter pointedly quoted Harry Truman to the American Legion: "It is not our nature to shirk obligations. We have a heritage that constitutes the greatest resource of this Nation. I call it the spirit and character of the American people."[75] In sum, Carter's linkage of the Soviets to the Nazis and President Truman to himself constituted a declaratory history that might have well been uttered in the 1950s.

Whereas the initial Carter rhetoric had welcomed international change and had emphasized the promising opportunities it provided the United States in helping to construct a better world, by 1980 President Carter usually portrayed it in largely negative terms. Thus in January he told Congress that his administration's policies had focused on three areas of change:

- The steady growth and increased projection abroad of Soviet military power
- The overwhelming dependence of Western nations on vital oil supplies from the Middle East
- The pressures of change in many nations of the developing world, including revolutionary Iran and a general uncertainty about the future.[76]

While he occasionally admitted that change could also bring benefits, Carter throughout the year stressed the centrality of global stability to his foreign policy objectives. Earlier optimistic references to "shifting coalitions" and getting on "the right side of change" ceased and were replaced by tones of concern appropriate to a world now described as in crisis.

By the last year of his administration Carter's complex world had grown turbulent and now required a strong U.S. economy and defense as its foundation. The vision of a truly cooperative global community remained, but the timetable for its achievement needed drastic revision. As he put it in February, "We must face the world as it is. We must be honest with ourselves, and we must be honest with others."[77] Two months later he described that world as "not one world, but many. It's a more complicated world— . . . uncertain, suspicious . . . searching for balance."[78] In May he called it a "complex . . . turbulent" place and admitted that transforming it into a "global mosaic . . . will not be an easy task." Carter then emphasized that in such a world the two preconditions for an effective American foreign policy were "a strong national economy and a strong national defense."[79]

Whereas candidate Carter in 1976 had pledged to cut at least $5 billion from the defense budget, in 1980, when running for reelection, he sought to take credit for reversing "a dangerous decline in defense spending" from 1969 to 1976, when "real defense outlays, that is constant dollars spent, declined every year." As he told the American Legion, "only since 1977 have outlays for defense been increased every year. Our five-year defense program through 1985 will continue this trend."[80] At a January press conference President Carter asserted that because he had "never doubted the long-range policy and long-range ambitions of the Soviet Union," his administration "had consistently strengthened the Nation's defense, after fifteen years of a decrease in commitment."[81] As a result of these efforts "we remain the world's most powerful force, and the American people and the Congress are now united as one in keeping the United States second to none in military strength."[82]

Beginning with his Inaugural Address, President Carter had repeatedly emphasized the importance of national unity to lay the foundation for a new American foreign policy and to formulate comprehensive solutions for urgent domestic and international problems. His crisis-of-confidence speech of July 1979 constituted an implicit admission of his failure to provide the leadership necessary to restore unity. The evidence suggests that Carter realized that the national outrage triggered by Iran and the Soviet Union in late 1979 had produced, at least in the short run, a "rally round the president" effect that might conceivably last through the election. Carter attempted to use these twin crises to build the unity that had previously eluded him. Thus in November 1979 he announced that "no act had so galvanized the American public toward unity in the last decade" as the taking of the American hostages. "We stand today as one people."[83] In early December Carter found the situation even more unprecedented, for "not since Pearl Harbor, some forty years ago, have we felt such a nationwide surge of determination and mutual purpose."[84] Two weeks later, in a truly remarkable statement, he suggested that "we must understand that not every instance of the firm application of the power of the United States is a potential Vietnam. The consensus for national strength and international involvement, already shaken and threatened, survived that divisive and tragic war."[85] Then, after the Soviet invasion of Afghanistan, Carter, in announcing a grain embargo, claimed that "I need the support of the American people. I believe that it's a matter of patriotism and . . . a matter of protecting our Nation's security."[86] On January 16, 1980, the president expressed pleasure "at the resolve and the courage and the unity of the American people."[87] Later that week, in dismissing the suggestion from columnist David Broder that his appearance on "Meet the Press" had been timed with the Iowa caucuses in mind, he insisted that "our country is in a state of crisis."[88] But by May, with the Soviets still in Afghanistan and the American hostages still in captivity, Carter called for public understanding and support for a foreign policy that could not promise "instant success." Instead, "we must expect prolonged management of seemingly intractable situations and often contradictory realities."[89] In short, the "rally round the president" phenomenon had largely disappeared six months after the onset of crisis.

Finally, President Carter, who in 1976 had criticized the flamboyant style of Kissinger, now undertook a series of theatrical exercises designed to heighten the sense of urgency provoked by Iranian and Soviet actions. Of course, a certain theatricality had never been wholly missing from the Carter foreign policy. Recall, for example, the open letter to Sakharov, Vance's early "mission to Moscow," the elaborate Panama Canal treaties signing ceremony, the Carter-Begin-Sadat White House lawn party, and Carter's Middle East shuttle of March 1979. But these efforts were more than rivaled by such administration atmospherics as the president's Rose Garden strategy, whereby Carter vowed to remain in the White House until the hostage crisis had been resolved;[90] the dispatch of Clark Clifford, a living relic of the Truman Doctrine era, to the Persian Gulf; and the spectacle of the national security adviser aiming an AK-47 through the Khyber Pass. Yet these efforts, though laden with heavy symbolism, seemed merely to emphasize Carter's immense frustration at failing to repatriate the hostages from Iran and dislodge the Soviets from Afghanistan.

A New Foreign Policy Consensus?

Did Jimmy Carter reconstruct the policy, procedural, and cultural components of a domestic foreign policy consensus? Did he successfully legitimate the grand design, strategy, and tactics of his foreign policy? To answer these questions we need to reemphasize the dramatic *policy* contrast, at least, between the "world order" initiatives of 1977 and "the neocontainment" actions of 1980. Did Carter rebuild a consensus around *either* of these policies?

Carter, like Nixon, remained exceedingly vague in his public statements about the nature of this grand design, but in contrast to his predecessor, who feared that the American people would not support an essentially *Realpolitik* vision, Carter's reticence stemmed from the genuine ambiguity of his design. What, after all, was a "truly cooperative global community," and what role would the United States play in it? President Carter did provide several clues to the American role: it would no longer rest on a rigid doctrinal foundation; it would tap its domestic experience to manage cooperatively shifting global coalitions; it would help resolve several nagging yet urgent regional and global problems; it would draw on its idealistic heritage to raise the global awareness of human rights; and it would not, of course, retreat into isolationism. But he failed to clarify exactly how this U.S. role would help realize a truly cooperative global community. Moreover, though many of his actions seemed designed to reduce or shift American commitments, he steadfastly refused to label them as such. Instead, the administration publicly claimed that by cooperating with others, instead of seeking to dominate them militarily, the United States would actually *increase* its global influence. And though Carter implied that American interests were no longer indiscriminately global—that is, Vietnam had not directly involved U.S. security—he refused to specify either their identity or their limits. Even worse, his public rhetoric about this crucial issue was sometimes dangerously confusing. Thus at a May 1978 news conference, after protesting that he was neither "preoccupied" with nor "fearful" of the Soviets, he claimed that "we have a major vested interest in Africa. Our trade relationships are there. It's a tremendous developing continent. . . . In the past, we've not had an adequate interest there."[91]

Did this enigmatic statement mean that Africa now constituted a vital U.S. interest? Perhaps, but not apparently because of a growing Soviet presence there. Yet were America's *economic* stakes in Africa sufficient to deem the continent vitally important? It would have been difficult to make that case. This sort of sloppy, hyperbolic rhetoric repeatedly plagued Carter's efforts to articulate the foundations of American foreign policy.

If the grand design remained obscure, the accompanying strategy also proved difficult to legitimate. Time and again, when asked to explain his administration's strategy, President Carter would offer a long list of objectives drawn directly from Brzezinski's memorandum of April 1977. But he had enormous difficulty in demonstrating the relationship among the items listed, even though some of them seemed to contradict others, as, for example, détente and human rights. In this regard, James Fallows indicated his astonishment that Carter told him several times that liberty and equality were perfectly compatible concepts that could be pursued simultaneously.[92] So, perhaps, Carter believed that Brzezinski's list did constitute an integrated strategy.

But more likely, Carter, suspicious of geopolitical abstractions in any case, simply found the notion of an integrated strategy to be largely irrelevant. In short, Carter attempted less to legitimate publicly a strategy than to win support for his managerial competence and his devotion to human rights. These were to serve as the bases for a reconstructed domestic foreign policy consensus. Neither, however, proved adequate to the task.

The "management of complex interdependence" had by the mid-1970s become a particularly fashionable phrase in the academic and foreign policy communities. Carter's tutelage at the Trilateral Commission had persuaded him of its desirability, and it gibed nicely with his own "problem-solving" inclinations. As president he surrounded himself with advisers similarly impressed with the phrase's import. These Trilateralists had been highly critical of Kissinger's reluctance to help manage the world economy, alliance relationships, and the North-South dialogue. The Carter administration believed that all these things, as well as the phenomenon of pervasive global change, needed to be managed competently by the United States working in concert with others. And Carter especially thought that good policy in the international arena, as in the domestic realm, would help restore the American people's faith in their government and thereby help rebuild a consensus. The Carter administration did achieve two notable "management" successes: the Panama Canal treaties and the Camp David Accords. The latter substantially boosted the president's standing before a public that now perceived him as a peacemaker. But a large majority of the electorate saw the Panama Canal treaties not as the symbol of American strength and generosity that Carter had portrayed them but as a dangerous act of weakness and appeasement. Carter, himself, on several occasions (before the hostage crisis and Afghanistan) called the ratification process the most unpleasant experience of his presidency. Moreover, as many analysts and participants noted, he was forced to spend so much political capital that little was left in Congress when other problems, like SALT, needed to be managed later.

Then, too, there seemed to be a nagging public perception about the administration's inability to deal competently with a host of foreign policy issues. An administration committed to the management of the world economy had immense trouble deciding on the fate of the dollar. An administration devoted to improving alliance relationships botched the neutron bomb issue, had difficulty persuading Western Europe and Japan to set meaning-ful energy import targets, and was openly ridiculed by West German Chan-cellor Helmut Schmidt. The North–South "dialogue," as Carter was surprised to discover, carried with it a substantial price tag, which the American people, beset by inflation, were unwilling to pay.[93] And when faced with two urgent examples of revolutionary change—in Iran and Nica-ragua—the administration appeared as unable to "get on the right side" of it as its predecessors had been in Cuba and Vietnam. But more than anything else, in view of the relatively low priority given to foreign policy by the public in these years, it was the Carter administration's widely perceived failure to manage the American economy with competence that lowered rather than restored the people's faith in government. Carter's "misery index" of 1976, used to such great effect against Gerald Ford, would be brilliantly exploited in 1980 by Ronald Reagan.

If managerialism proved to be a slender reed on which to construct a new foreign policy consensus, so too did moralism. There were several reasons for the failure of human rights to provide a powerful core value around which the public could rally. First, as early as 1975, Carter, impressed with the broad-based domestic assault on the alleged amoralism of Kissinger's foreign policy actions, believed that human rights could unite liberals and conservatives behind an appealing banner. During the Cold War, anti-communism had functioned in this manner, though liberals had insisted that, as the price for their membership in the coalition, U.S. economic development assistance be used to give anticommunism a more positive dimension. Cold War presidents had, of course, frequently raised the issue of human rights but had done so almost exclusively in regard to the trans-gressions of communist governments. Carter proposed to criticize the human rights behavior of all countries—including the United States, lest others claim him hypocritical—and to make U.S. aid and friendship contin-gent on that behavior. But after an initial flush of public and elite excite-ment about Carter's human rights rhetoric, the practical application of the policy provoked liberal and conservative ire as the administration attempted to deal "evenhandedly" with nations that differed in strategic significance and over which the U.S. possessed differing degrees of leverage. According to the 1979 Chicago Council on Foreign Relations (CCFR) Survey, whereas 67 percent of the public and 78 percent of the leaders thought that the United States ought to promote human rights abroad, only half of the public thought that Soviet treatment of its minorities was any "of our business," and only 40 percent agreed that the United States "should take an active role in opposing apartheid."[94] Among the elites, polls showed deep cleavages between "conservative internationalists," who criticized Carter for exerting excessive pressure on American "friends" in Manila, Managua, Santiago, Seoul, and Teheran, and for neglecting the human rights violations of communist totalitarian regimes, and "liberal internationalists," who expressed exactly the opposite sentiments. In summary, the attacks on Kissinger's amoralism had actually constituted a *negative* consensus, and Carter's efforts to transform such criticism into a human rights policy quickly revealed the deep ideological divisions that a common dislike of Kissinger had partly disguised.

Second, in contrast to Cold War anticommunism, whose power had derived from the perceived enormity of the Soviet threat, human rights bore no apparent relationship to U.S. national security, except in the rather tortured sense that a "philosophically isolated" America would eventually become an endangered America. But the Carter administration failed to make even this case persuasively. Moreover, whereas anticommunism had been used to justify a broad range of policies including nuclear deterrence, economic assistance, regional military alliances, and human rights, Carter's human rights approach lacked a compelling connection to many of his other initiatives and thus remained more an irritating anomaly than an integral part of a coordinated strategy.

Finally, despite Carter's conviction that this issue could help restore the public's faith in the U.S. government after Vietnam, Watergate, and the CIA revelations, support for an active human rights policy was "a mile wide, but only an inch deep."[95] For example, the same CCFR 1979 survey that indicated that 67 percent of the public and 78 percent of the elites believed that American foreign policy should promote human rights abroad also showed that, when asked to list the two or three biggest international problems, a mere 1 percent of the public and 7 percent of the leaders chose human rights! Human rights, by itself, remained a peripheral concern for the public and the elites.

It is more difficult to judge the success of the Carter administration's efforts to legitimate its foreign policy tactics. They represented, it will be recalled, President Carter's overall approach to governing in the aftermath of Watergate—a general attempt to breathe openness, honesty, and decency into the entire policymaking process, including foreign affairs. This populist theme—while ridiculed by many foreign policy professionals as naive and dangerous—seems to have been broadly popular. The Bert Lance affair during the late summer of 1977 surely raised questions about the administration's commitment to elevated ethical standards, yet opinion polls throughout his presidency showed consistently that well over 70 percent of the public deemed Carter to be personally moral and admirable. Yet these same surveys indicated widespread dissatisfaction with his leadership abilities. It seems, therefore, that these tactics proved both popular and largely irrelevant to the attempt to mobilize support for substantive policies.

The Carter administration, then, could not reconstruct a foreign policy consensus on the basis of its early outlook and initiatives, and its dramatic *volte face* of late 1979 and 1980 in part represented a tacit acknowledgment of its failure. Yet as significant as these international shocks undoubtedly were in compelling this turnaround, the administration's behavior had also been strongly affected by the growing domestic political power of conservative and neoconservative counterelites. Groups such as the Committee on the Present Danger (CPD) and the American Security Council, along with their congressional allies, had plagued the Carter administration from the beginning. Well funded and well connected, these organizations gained widespread media exposure for views that directly clashed with the administration's on a host of issues including SALT II, Africa, Central America, Soviet military strength and geopolitical intentions, the adequacy of the U.S. defense budget, and the advisability of the Panama Canal treaties. Moreover, Carter had seriously offended these groups by refusing to appoint a single member to his administration, preferring instead to surround himself with Trilateralists. He, in fact, came close to naming Paul H. Nitze to a top post, but after meeting with him in Plains, decided that his views were arrogant and inflexible.[96] The CPD had submitted fifty-three names to Carter and saw every one rejected, despite the group's heavily Democratic composition. When asked his opinion of Carter's foreign policy team, Eugene V. Rostow, cofounder of the CPD, acidly replied, "My views are unprintable." Nitze expressed similar sentiments, noting that "every softliner I can think of is in government."[97] In addition, publications such as *Commentary* and the editorial pages of the *Wall Street Journal* provided visibility for neoconservative intellectuals—many of whom had been liberal Democrats during the early Cold War—to undertake a merciless assault on the Carter agenda. As a result, Norman Podhoretz, Irving Kristol, Michael Novak, Peter Berger, and their confreres had begun to ridicule the administration's "world order" priorities well before the "shocks" of 1979. One particularly hostile statement by Carl Gershman, a Jeane Kirkpatrick protégé, neatly summarized the thrust of this dissent. Writing in *Commentary* in 1980, Gershman, apparently unimpressed by Carter's recent conversion, claimed that he had stocked the administration with a cabal of world order advocates, who, in their complete rejection of containment "had broken with thirty years of historical experience" and had repudiated the core of postwar American foreign policy. Furthermore, this new establishment

> had devalued the importance of national-security concerns . . . saturating American foreign policy with defeatism masquerading as optimism and "maturity" and "restraint,"cravenly following international political fashion even if this meant denigrating the interests and values of one's own country, and worrying less about American security than about Soviet insecurity, in the nature of which virtually any Soviet action could be condoned or blamed on the United States.[98]

This elite, according to Gershman, formed the core of a "liberal-populist" governing coalition "wherein a southern president who campaigned as a populist staffed his foreign-policy bureaucracy with members of . . . the new foreign-policy establishment."[99]

Ostensibly wracked by guilt and paralyzed by tendencies that bordered on isolationism and appeasement, at the heart of this group's outlook lay the conviction that military force was no longer a suitable foreign policy instrument for America to employ. Rejecting the bases of two generations of American foreign policy—the containment of communism and the "lessons of Munich"—this new elite embraced the "lessons of Vietnam" as the foundation of a new American diplomacy. And from the primary Vietnam lesson—that containment was counterproductive, unfeasible, and unnecessary—this establishment, Gershman claimed, drew several corollaries. First, "world order" must replace "national security" as the organizing concept of American diplomacy. Second, the United States should adopt an attitude of "equanimity" toward changes in the world that previously would have been considered injurious to its interests. Third, because the Soviet Union was essentially a status quo power, American foreign policy need not be preoccupied with relations with Moscow. Fourth, to avoid isolation in a world filled with revolutionary change, America had to learn to become more flexible and less ideological in its dealings with the Third World. Finally, our moral strength, rather than a primary reliance on military power, should be used to help alleviate such "global problems" as hunger, racial hatred, and the arms race. For Gershman and his colleagues, world order politics constituted a tragically naive departure in American foreign policy.

In place of such alleged wrong-headedness these angry counterelites argued for, in effect, the reembracing of Soviet containment as the foundation of U.S. foreign policy, and they demonstrated notable success in wresting control of the agenda from the Carter administration. Indeed, the back-and-fill behavior of Carter during the last year of his presidency constituted an effort to placate these critics and to assuage a public that had grown increasingly alarmed by Soviet transgressions and frustrated by America's evident lack of international leadership. In part, of course, this

public restiveness stemmed from the very success of the dissident counterelites in publicizing their message.

Yet Carter's rather frantic election-year attempt to run as a Harry Truman,
neocontainment underdog failed to impress the CPD and their allies. Unable to
forgive his past sins, they doubted the depth and sincerity of his conversion.
Moreover, these critics had found their own presidential candidate, someone
who, unlike the "flip-flopping" Carter, seemed to possess long-standing, unshakable, anticommunist convictions. With these conservative internationalists
unappeasable and with many liberal internationalists highly critical of his lurch
to the right, Jimmy Carter was unable to reconstruct a domestic foreign policy
consensus in the remaining months of his presidency. He tried to portray
Ronald Reagan as a trigger-happy, dangerous radical and himself as a responsible moderate who would stand up to the Soviets without unleashing World
War III. And, indeed, if foreign policy had been the sole issue in the 1980
election, Carter would have won. But only 15 percent of the voters ranked
foreign policy as the most important problem, whereas 77 percent chose the
economy. Double-digit inflation and rising unemployment, not foreign policy,
combined to defeat Jimmy Carter. In sum, he did not bequeath to his successor
a foreign policy consensus: détente was dead, the bear was prowling, a new
Cold War loomed, the public demanded billions more for defense. Yet neither
these conditions nor this mood constituted a policy consensus. Elites remained
deeply divided, and the public, while desiring a strong America, showed little
inclination to support military interventions, even in the Persian Gulf.[100]

In contrast to Nixon, President Carter strove to reestablish a cultural
consensus to undergird his foreign policy. Indeed, his intentions to relegiti-
mate an ethic of sacrifice informed both his domestic and world order
priorities of 1977 as well as his neocontainment efforts of 1980. Despite
the optimistic tenor of his early presidential rhetoric, Carter nevertheless
emphasized that the 1970s were a decade of limits: limits to what the
president and the federal government could do and limits to what the United
States could do unilaterally in the world. To live gracefully within these
limits, Carter intoned, Americans would need to restrict their appetites for
government services and, especially, for petroleum. As in wartime, all citizens would be called on to sacrifice for the common good. Yet Carter
realized that sacrifices would not be made if the public sensed that special
interests were receiving special privileges. He aimed, therefore, to devise
comprehensive policies that would spread the burden evenly throughout the
population. Similarly, his world order outlook implied a view that America
could no longer dictate to or dominate other nations. Both multilateralism
and nonintervention required restraint, maturity, and even a degree of sacrifice, for the wishes of other states would be respected to a far greater degree

than during the high Cold War. Carter's 1980 posture approximated more closely the pre-Vietnam ethic of sacrifice, for now Americans were asked to bear personal sacrifices in order to punish the Soviet Union, and some citizens—farmers, Olympic athletes, technology exporters, and nineteen-year-old males—were called on to perform special service for the nation.

Yet all these efforts must be judged failures. First, the energy issue pitted oil-producing states such as Texas and Oklahoma against oil-consuming states and collided with a public inclined to view the "crisis" as an oil industry conspiracy to raise prices. Carter proudly proclaimed that Congress's energy legislation had given him 65 to 70 percent of what he had asked and had thus far surpassed President Truman's accomplishments. But the compromises that Carter made in order to wage the "moral equivalent of war" appeared more like a meow than a roar and undercut the president's crisis rhetoric. Second, neoconservatives seized on the "retreatist" dimensions of Carter's world order agenda and lambasted him for succumbing to a "culture of appeasement." America, they agreed, was in decline and had been for well over a decade. The failure in Vietnam, the nonreciprocal nature of détente, Watergate and the subsequent crippling of the presidency, the pathetic responses to OPEC and Third World radicalism, and, most important, the inability and unwillingness to counter the massive Soviet arms buildup were but the most dramatic examples of a profound and pervasive erosion of American power. This decline had to be perceived as part of a more general rotting of traditional liberal values. These critics decried the alleged excesses of African Americans, women, gays, and other minorities, who sought more and more equality. The consequences of this "illiberal extremism" were supposedly obvious: the fragmentation of the family, the eclipse of traditional religions, reverse discrimination, pornography, drugs, the spawning of an amoral psychoanalytic elite, and the growth of a culture of appeasement. Moreover, they condemned Carter for contributing to this decline by proposing a foreign policy agenda that, in demanding self-restraint while forgiving totalitarian transgressions, recalled the cravenness of interwar Britain. For them, Carter's ethic of sacrifice constituted disguised surrender.

Finally, President Carter's belated reassertion of containment failed to resuscitate the old cultural consensus. Instead, his pleas for national unity at a time of crisis provoked the resentment of groups that felt unfairly victimized by the sanctions imposed on the Soviet Union. Farmers protested, athletes sulked, those nineteen-year-olds required to register for the draft fretted, and neoconservative critics waited for Reagan. Moreover, during a period of soaring inflation, even modest economic sacrifices appeared as terribly unfair burdens.

For someone who "just didn't like politicians" and who frowned on

Congress as the seat of special interests, Jimmy Carter, more than any other modern president, consulted, informed, and even negotiated with legislators about foreign policy. There were two major reasons for this unprecedented effort to involve Congress. First, as was true of so much of the administration's outlook, Carter and his advisers believed that after Vietnam, Watergate, and other examples of an Imperial Presidency run wild, it was necessary to rebuild popular and legislative trust in the executive. Vance, in his October 1976 memo had urged Carter "to make the Congress and the American people joint partners in foreign policy matters" and to use the presidency to educate both about the long-term interests of the United States. Carter, as we saw, sought to implement this advice by publicly announcing the secretary of state's negotiating instructions in advance of his ill-fated trip to Moscow in March 1977. On the other hand, the White House demonstrated extreme secrecy in negotiating the Panama Canal treaties and in formulating its initial energy proposals. In fact, the hostile Senate reception to the treaties compelled Carter to shift tactics dramatically in order to obtain ratification. The president, who early in 1977 had similarly provoked congressional ire by peremptorily cutting twenty-nine water projects from his budget request, reversed course and undertook an intense and prolonged campaign of "horse-trading," "schmoozing," and "stroking." Forty-two senators and several House members visited Panama, and some even conducted their own negotiations with General Omar Torijos after the treaties had been signed. Carter himself negotiated, often publicly, with Dennis DeConcini, a freshman Democrat from Arizona, about a reservation that could have eviscerated the treaties. Rosalynn Carter lobbied the wife of Edward Zorinsky, a Nebraska freshman senator, as well as his friend, the Catholic archbishop of Omaha. Yet despite Carter's enormous political investment, his appeals to the public failed to enhance the treaties' popularity; he could not marshal enough Senate votes; and the Senate leadership was forced to save him from disaster.[101] Moreover, the president's stature suffered serious damage as a result of these self-demeaning actions.

In a similar fashion, the Carter administration engaged Congress in the SALT II process. In contrast to Nixon's handling of SALT, when only a handful of legislators monitored the progress of the talks, Carter appointed a diverse group of thirty senators and fourteen representatives as SALT II advisers. Nearly all the senators traveled to Geneva, participated in discussions with both the American and Soviet delegations, and reviewed the draft text of the treaty. As an agreement with the Soviets became imminent, Carter, in order to placate potential opponents, replaced Paul Warnke, his chief negotiator, with a less controversial figure. Unlike the Panama Canal treaties, whose contents were sprung on unsuspecting senators, the administration maintained constant liaison with Congress on SALT II. Nevertheless, none of these gestures prevented Henry Jackson from comparing the June 1979 Vienna Summit with Neville Chamberlain's 1938 journey to Munich, and Carter's withdrawal of the treaty from the Senate in January 1980 surely prevented its defeat.

Second, Congress, quite apart from Carter's willingness to involve it in making foreign policy, demanded to play a major role. By insisting on its alleged prerogative to "codetermine" human rights policy, to oversee intelligence operations, to veto a wide array of executive initiatives, including conventional arms sales and nuclear technology transfers, and to compel the executive to negotiate treaties with it, Congress reasserted its foreign policy rights in a manner unseen since the 1930s. In contrast to Nixon, who responded viscerally and vengefully to this revolt, Carter demonstrated surprising patience in attempting to fashion workable procedural arrangements with Congress. On only a single occasion did he publicly chastise it for unwarranted interference in foreign policymaking, and then he submerged his criticism within a general assault on the device of the legislative veto.[102] Indeed, Carter showed much more concern with Congress's reluctance to deal with his domestic legislative program than with its repeated intrusion into the foreign policy process.

Yet the Carter administration nevertheless failed to construct a new procedural consensus. In part, the failure stemmed from the sweeping institutional changes that had recently occurred in Congress: the erosion of seniority, the multiplication of subcommittees often with overlapping jurisdictions, and the explosive growth of staffs. And, in part, it was rooted in more general developments: the accelerated decline of political parties and the proliferation of lobbies—some single issue and others with ties to ethnic groups and foreign governments. All these changes helped produce a dramatically more complex policymaking environment. In these circumstances the achievement of an executive-legislative foreign policy procedural consensus became more difficult.

But these institutional and parainstitutional obstacles, though undeniably important, masked a more fundamental problem—the absence during the Carter administration of a *policy* consensus about such issues as the requirements of U.S. security, the conditions in which American military power should be sanctioned, the strength and intentions of the Soviet Union, and the nature of change in the contemporary world. In those relatively rare instances of broad policy agreement, institutional impediments were easily surmounted. For example, Congress generously funded the Camp David Accords, despite their expense and despite a raging domestic inflation, because they were perceived as intrinsically valuable. Carter, moreover, had obtained the agreements through a combination of secret and shuttle diplomacy and had not involved legislators in the process, yet Congress seemed unconcerned. Similarly, the establishment of formal diplomatic relations with China proved domestically so popular that Barry Goldwater and a handful of senatorial conservatives, lacking the votes to wage a political battle against this action, retreated to federal court to protest the alleged unconstitutional abrogation of the Mutual Defense Treaty with Taiwan.[103] On the other hand, the security implications of Salt II and the Panama Canal treaties provoked deep disagreement in Congress, and Carter's endless attempts to find an acceptable *procedure,* especially with SALT, merely reflected the underlying *policy* dissensus.

Notes

1. "Remarks and a Question-and-Answer Session with Editors and Broadcasters," September 21, 1979.

2. Jules Witcover, *Marathon: The Pursuit of the Presidency, 1972–1976;* Martin Schram, *Running for President: A Journal of the Carter Campaign;* and Betty Glad, *Jimmy Carter: In Search of the Great White House,* ch. 11–20.

3. Warren E. Miller, "Misreading the Public Pulse," p. 11; idem., "Opinion Roundup," pp. 30–31.

4. Witcover, *Marathon,* p. 111.

5. Recall, for example, the widely publicized exploits of representatives Wilbur Mills (D-AK) and Wayne Hays (D-OH).

6. Charles O. Jones, *The Trusteeship Presidency: Jimmy Carter and the United States Congress,* p. 17.

7. *Gallup Opinion Index,* 71 (September 1980): 24.

8. Jones, *Trusteeship Presidency,* p. 18.

9. Jimmy Carter, *Why Not the Best?* p. 145.

10. Ibid., p. 146.

11. Jimmy Carter, "Inaugural Address of President Jimmy Carter," January 20, 1977.

12. Jimmy Carter, "Remarks at a Luncheon for Members of the Democratic National Committee's National Finance Council," April 28, 1977.

13. Jones, *Trusteeship Presidency,* p. 1.

14. For example, in May 1977, in a pointed criticism of George Meany of the AFL-CIO, Carter suggested that "it would be good for special interests of all kinds—labor, business, environment, and others—to cooperate and express a partnership in things that are accomplished for the [public] good." Jimmy Carter, "The President's News Conference of May 12, 1977."

15. Erwin C. Hargrove. *Jimmy Carter as President: Leadership and the Politics of the Public Good,* ch. 1 and 2.

16. James Sterling Young, "Foreword" in Hargrove, *Jimmy Carter,* p. xx.

17. Jimmy Carter, "Address to the Nation on Energy and National Goals," July 15, 1979, pp. 1236, 1237.

18. Ibid., pp. 1237–8.

19. Ibid., p. 1238.

20. Ibid.

21. Ibid., pp. 1238–40.

22. Jimmy Carter, "Remarks at the 13th Constitutional Convention of the AFL-CIO," November 15, 1979.

23. Austin Ranney, "The Carter Administration," in Ranney, ed., *The American Elections of 1980,* p. 5.

24. Stanley Hoffmann, *Primacy or World Order: American Foreign Policy Since the Cold War,* p. 111.

25. Hargrove, *Jimmy Carter,* p. 120.

26. Zbigniew Brzezinski, *Power and Principle: Memoirs of the National Security Adviser, 1977–1981,* p. 53.

27. Ibid., pp. 52–4.

28. Ibid., p. 56.

29. Ibid., p. 57.

30. Cyrus Vance, *Hard Choices: Critical Years in America's Foreign Policy,* pp. 441–42.

31. Background interviews, Washington, DC, 1981 and 1982.

32. W. Anthony Lake, "Pragmatism and Principle in U.S. Foreign Policy," Address to the Boston Council of World Affairs," June 13, 1977.

33. Brzezinski, *Power and Principle,* p. 3.

34. David G. Skidmore, "The Politics of Decline: International Adjustment versus Domestic Legitimacy during the Carter Administration," p. 10.

35. Ibid., p. 18.

36. Background interviews, 1981 and 1982. Hodding Carter III, personal interview, March 23, 1989.

37. Leslie H. Gelb, with Richard K. Betts, *The Irony of Vietnam: The System Worked.*

38. Hargrove, *Jimmy Carter,* p. 118.

39. Jimmy Carter, "Remarks at the First Session of the NATO Ministerial Meeting," London, May 10, 1977.

40. Jimmy Carter, "Address at the Commencement Exercises at the University of Notre Dame," May 22, 1977.

41. Jimmy Carter, "Remarks at a Question-and-Answer Session at a Town Meeting with New Hampshire High School Students," February 18, 1978.

42. Carter, "Notre Dame Address."

43. Jimmy Carter, "Address before the United Nations General Assembly," October 4, 1977.

44. Jimmy Carter, "Remarks at the National Arts Theatre," Lagos, Nigeria, April 1, 1978.

45. Carter, "Inaugural Address," 4.

46. Jimmy Carter, "Question-and-Answer Session with a Group of Publishers, Editors, and Broadcasters," June 24, 1977.

47. Carter, "Publishers, Editors, and Broadcasters," p. 1166.

48. Jimmy Carter, "Remarks and a Question-and-Answer Session with a Group of Editors and News Directors," July 15, 1977.

49. Jimmy Carter, "Remarks and a Question-and-Answer Session with Members of the Advertising Council, Inc.," June 22, 1977.

50. Hargrove, *Jimmy Carter,* p. 142.

51. Jimmy Carter, "The President's News Conference of July 12, 1977."

52. Carter, "Notre Dame Address."

53. Paul H. Kreisberg, personal interview, June 13, 1981.

54. Hodding Carter interview.

55. John Holum, personal interview, May 27,1981.
56. Ibid.
57. Miller, "Opinion Roundup," p. 29.
58. Brzezinski had appointed to the NSC staff several advisers of losing or would-be Democratic presidential candidates of 1976.
59. Fritz Ermarth, personal interview, May 22, 1981.
60. Cyrus Vance, "Meeting the Challenges of a Changing World," Address before the Chicago Council on Foreign Relations, June 1, 1979.
61. Background interview, 1981.
62. Kreisberg interview.
63. Three weeks after the 1980 election, Brzezinski publicly denounced "do-gooders" in the administration and the Democratic Party that had been "traumatized by the experience of Vietnam because their party was responsible for the policies that produced the debacle." *New York Times,* November 29, 1980, p. 1. Although critical of Ronald Reagan for his alleged desire to achieve military superiority, Brzezinski "asserted that his attempts to expand military strength had encountered 'a great deal of opposition within the administration' and within 'a party which was automatically fearful that any emphasis on competition meant you were wanting to revive the cold war.' "
64. Background interview, 1981.
65. Hargrove, *Jimmy Carter,* p. 153.
66. Yet, after Afghanistan, even Vance declared that "our relations with the Soviet Union have been and will be essentially competitive." Quoted in Raymond L. Garthoff, p. 968.
67. Ibid., pp. 972–4.
68. Ibid., p. 967. Background interview, 1989.
69. Vance, *Hard Choices,* p. 394.
70. Background interviews, 1981 and 1982.
71. Jimmy Carter, "The State of the Union Address before a Joint Session of the Congress," January 23, 1980. Two weeks earlier, he had stated flatly that the invasion was the greatest threat to world peace since World War II.
72. Jimmy Carter, "Remarks and a Question-and-Answer Session at the Annual Convention of the American Society of Newspaper Editors," April 10, 1980.
73. Jimmy Carter, "Address to the Nation on the Soviet Invasion of Afghanistan," January 4, 1980.
74. Carter, "American Society Remarks."
75. Jimmy Carter, "Remarks at the Annual Convention of the American Legion," February 19, 1980.
76. Jimmy Carter, "Annual Message to the Congress on the State of the Union," January 21, 1980.
77. Carter, "American Legion Remarks."
78. Ibid.
79. Jimmy Carter, "Address before the World Affairs Council of Philadelphia," May 9, 1980.
80. Carter, "American Legion Remarks."
81. Jimmy Carter, "Interview on 'Meet the Press,' " January 20, 1980.
82. Carter, "American Legion Remarks."
83. Carter, "AFL-CIO Remarks."
84. Jimmy Carter, "Remarks concerning Candidacy and Campaign Plans," December 2, 1979.
85. Jimmy Carter, "Remarks to Members of the Business Council," December 12, 1979.

86. Jimmy Carter, "Remarks at a White House Briefing for Members of Congress," January 8, 1980.

87. Jimmy Carter, "Remarks and a Question-and-Answer Session with Editors and News Directors," January 15, 1980.

88. Carter, "Meet the Press."

89. Carter, "Philadelphia Address."

90. And until Edward M. Kennedy (D-MA) had been defeated.

91. Jimmy Carter, "The President's News Conference of May 25, 1978."

92. James Fallows, "The Passionless Presidency," p. 36.

93. Background interview, 1982.

94. John E. Rielly, *American Public Opinion and U.S. Foreign Policy, 1979,* pp. 13–14.

95. Skidmore, "Politics of Decline," p. 27.

96. Strobe Talbott, *The Master of the Game: Paul Nitze and the Nuclear Peace,* p. 149.

97. Quoted in Jerry W. Sanders, "Empire at Bay: Containment Strategies and American Politics at the Crossroads," p. 7.

98. Carl Gershman, "The Rise and Fall of the New Foreign-Policy Establishment," p. 24.

99. Ibid., p. 20.

100. See, for example, William Schneider, "The Public and Foreign Policy," p. 26.

101. William L. Furlong, "Negotiations and Ratification of the Panama Canal Treaties" in Spanier and Nogee, ed., *Congress, the Presidency, and Foreign Policy,* p. 103.

102. Jimmy Carter, "Message to the Congress on Legislative Vetoes," June 21, 1978.

103. *Goldwater* v. *Carter,* 617 F. 2nd 697 (DC Cir. 1979), vacated with directions to dismiss, 100 Sup. Ct. 533 (1980).

4

The Reagan Administration

In contrast to Jimmy "Who?", an obscure former governor about whom little was known even after his election in 1976, Ronald Reagan entered the White House as the most recognizable president since Dwight Eisenhower. But unlike the general, whose fame rested on his military record and not on his largely mysterious political outlook, Reagan's long-standing notoriety derived from a distinctive political philosophy articulated and reiterated for over twenty years. Indeed, conservatives had dreamed of a Reagan presidency since the eve of the 1964 election, when he had delivered a memorable nationally televised speech in support of Barry Goldwater. Yet by 1980, after two failed bids for the Republican nomination and nearing his seventieth birthday, Reagan risked becoming another Harold Stassen. Political pundits, especially those who prognosticated "inside the Beltway," were confident that as an ex-actor and a rightwing ideologue, Reagan could never be elected president, and it was widely reported that he was Jimmy Carter's favorite potential opponent. Despite the warnings of Edmund "Pat" Brown, whom Reagan had thrashed in the 1966 California gubernatorial election, the Carter White House believed that once Reagan's "real," that is, "extremist," views on social security, foreign policy, the environment, and other issues were effectively publicized, the electorate would be frightened into voting for the incumbent. Moreover, Carter's advisers evidently anticipated a campaign in which Reagan's legendary "gaffes" would multiply and expose him as unqualified and irresponsible. They attempted, in short, to imitate Lyndon Johnson's successful 1964 strategy against Goldwater.

But, of course, 1980, for many reasons, was not 1964, and the most important difference was the woeful condition of the U.S. economy. With inflation, interest rates, unemployment, and gasoline prices soaring, the "misery index" that had served Carter so well against Ford was used to even greater effect by Reagan. To these seemingly intractable economic problems Governor Reagan offered a simple, "supply-side" solution: cut taxes and slash domestic social spending. If these actions were taken, the artificially shackled economy would respond with robust growth. George Bush, independent candidate John Anderson, and President Carter all pointed out the impossibility of doing these things, while drastically increasing defense spending, without incurring massive budget deficits. Reagan nevertheless insisted that his program could square the circle by stimulating savings, investment, and productivity. In 1976 Carter had suggested that an over-regulated economy and the runaway growth of the federal government needed to be checked. Four years later, Reagan much more loudly conveyed a similar message and blamed Carter and the Democrats for producing these very evils. Carter, who had run against Washington in 1976, now found himself portrayed as part of the problem by another anti-Washington candidate.

Jimmy Carter had the ignominious distinction to be the first elected incumbent since Herbert Hoover and the first Democratic president since Grover Cleveland to be defeated. And to be drubbed by someone commonly believed too "ideological" to win the presidency only magnified Carter's loss. Yet postelection surveys indicated that Reagan owed little, if any, of his victory to foreign policy issues. Despite his insistence that American foreign policy under Carter had been characterized by weakness, retreat, confusion, humiliation, and naiveté, Reagan was perceived by a plurality of voters as trigger-happy and potentially dangerous. That the electorate nonetheless presented Reagan with a landslide victory reflected its willingness to take a chance at a time of acute economic distress.

We the People

Notwithstanding the apparent gulf that separated Carter and Reagan during the 1980 campaign, the new president's priorities closely paralleled those pursued by his opponent since 1977: the restoration of the economy, national self-confidence, and America's standing in the world. But whereas Carter had sought to achieve these goals by offering a long list of "good" policies, by trying to embody the nobility of the national character, and by "speaking out" on human rights, Reagan relied on a simple, understandable, comprehensive, and unusually consistent political philosophy presented with the help of often dazzling rhetoric to mobilize support for his priorities. Far from disqualifying him from the presidency, his acting (and sports broadcasting) background provided a hugely valuable asset in communicating with the citizens of the "electronic commonwealth."[1] In contrast to

Carter, a plodding speaker with a singsong voice that "dropped like a wounded bird at the end of his phrases, frequently fading into total inaudibility,"[2] Reagan's mellifluous baritone, craggy good looks, and easy affability thrived behind microphone and camera. Though his improvised remarks and press conference performances often revealed a shocking lack of substantive knowledge, the mere prospect of a nationally televised presidential address invariably sent tremors of fear through congressional Democrats. Reagan's uncanny ability to deliver lines sincerely, narrate poignant stories, and publicly evince an impressive range of emotions—all firmly hitched to an unwavering public philosophy—combined to make him a formidable rhetorical president.

In a fundamental sense Ronald Reagan continued the domestic political project begun by Richard Nixon. Before Watergate, Nixon had begun to build a new coalition—the "real majority"—from groups that shared a common resentment of New Class liberals, Great Society excesses, federal social engineering, and creeping permissiveness. Reagan mined this populist vein throughout the 1970s, but did so more systemically, programmatically, and consistently than Nixon. By forging bonds among previously disconnected (or nonexistent) groups—the Moral Majority, working class "ethnics," neoconservative intellectuals, big and small business, "yuppies"—Reagan entered the presidency as the spearhead of a movement that seemed poised to replace the New Deal coalition as the dominant constellation in American politics. It was, to be sure, like its predecessor, a potentially unstable amalgam composed of people with partly clashing political, economic, and social agendas. Issues such as school prayer, abortion, and women's rights—immune to compromise—threatened to be especially disruptive. Yet in the short run, at least, this emerging coalition agreed with Reagan that "individual freedom is the touchstone of good government; government power, especially when it is centralized in Washington, is to be distrusted; free enterprise is the key to economic and personal liberty; the role of government is to assure equal opportunity, not to mandate particular results";[3] and it is the unique responsibility of the federal government to provide a strong national defense.

President Reagan's initial priorities simply and neatly captured these convictions. The insidious growth of governmental regulations would be reversed in order to liberate the "entrepreneurial spirit" for investment and productivity increases. Dramatically reduced tax rates would stimulate savings, investment, and growth. Federal social programs would be dismantled and their funds returned to state and local governments as block grants. Accelerated defense spending would enhance America's military capability and help restore national pride and international respect. Reagan paid lip service to divisively controversial issues such as school prayer, abortion, law and order, and "reverse discrimination," but almost always before carefully chosen conservative audiences and never to obscure his economic and defense priorities.

In Nixon's version of America the honest, hard-working, patriotic new majority had found itself constantly menaced by a privileged, selfish, effete, unscrupulous minority—an enemy who remained permanently outside the mainstream. Reagan's more ideological populism could certainly have been used to darken further this discordant portrait. On occasion, as we see in our discussion of Central America, Reagan did lash out at those who obstructed his policies, but as a general rule, in speech after speech throughout two terms, he sought support for his programs by rhetorically portraying an America brimming with love and kindness and populated with caring neighbors, eager to volunteer their help to the community, if only the government would unshackle them. One prescient commentator, a speech communication scholar, accurately dubbed this powerful rhetorical creation "Mister Reagan's Neighborhood," designed to unify the nation, impel action, and insulate the president from criticism.[4] Drawn from familiar themes rooted in the American "civil religion," Reagan's rhetoric wove a seamless tapestry of "morality, heritage, boldness, heroism, and fairness" that offered a compelling, if rather fanciful, vision of a genuine national community. Composed of "extraordinary 'ordinary' Americans who never make the headlines and will never be interviewed," Reagan's nation was fundamentally good and decent.[5] He characteristically defined the citizenry in terms of occupations as, for example, in the first Inaugural Address: "men and women who raise our food, patrol our streets, man our mines and factories, keep our homes, and heal us when we're sick—professionals, industrialists, shopkeepers, clerks, cabbies, and truckdrivers."[6] These constituted the everyday heroes of America, who, through teamwork and partnership, labored to construct a cooperative community.[7] Moreover, sick and tired as they had grown of excessive taxation, runaway inflation, and a burdensome, meddling federal government, these sturdy folk had in the 1980 election "sent a message" to Washington to lower taxes, curb federal spending, and return political power to "we the people." Time and again, like the narrator in an apocryphal Frank Capra film, Reagan told stories about Americans who, instead of passively awaiting governmental assistance, joyfully volunteered to build a better community. Thus economic and political freedom, far from unleashing greed and license, encouraged compassion and quiet heroism.

"We the people," a more inclusive and magnanimous notion than Nixon's new majority, allegedly faced a genuine economic crisis in the early 1980s, and Reagan, of course, blamed the federal government for causing it—"tax and spend" legislators who enacted expensive laws and regulations, and bureaucrats who implemented and administered them. At the same time, however, he sometimes acknowledged that government had grown, at least in part, in response to the people's demands. For example, in February 1981 President Reagan noted that "*we all* had a hand in looking to government for benefits, as if government had some source of revenue other than our earnings."[8] Even he, the former New Deal Democrat, "had for a time accepted government's claim that [taxing and spending] was sound economics."[9] Many "well-intentioned but misguided people" had persisted in their wrong-headedness. Yet, Reagan, whose domestic community required no permanent enemies, seemed confident that someday soon they too—like him and "the people"—would mend their ways. For "the problem isn't who to blame; it's what to blame," and the problem was government, with its built-in "tendency to grow."[10]

In bold contrast to Carter, who wondered publicly about the sources of the contemporary national "moral and spiritual crisis," Ronald Reagan repeatedly pointed to individual acts of heroism as convincing proof that America remained a good and vibrant society. Secret Service agent Tim McCarthy who helped save Reagan's life, airliner crash rescuer Lenny Slotnick, Space Shuttle astronauts, community volunteers, and the marines in Beirut were invoked to demonstrate that "America never was a sick society." Indeed, "the heart of America is strong; it's good and true. . . . We're seeing rededication to bedrock values of faith, family, work, neighborhood, peace, and freedom—values that bring us together as one people, from the youngest child to the most senior citizen."[11] For Reagan, America constituted a genuinely moral community of individuals with shared values and a common purpose, and his ability to convey this appealing vision in human and understandable terms greatly contributed to his personal popularity.

And, not surprisingly, this uniquely virtuous community—this "shining city on a hill"—had been providentially instructed to bring freedom and peace to the rest of the world. According to Reagan, American foreign policy reflected the selflessness, goodness, peacefulness, and generosity of the American people. In fact, virtually everyone in the world allegedly shared the same values and aspirations as the members of the American community, though many had been frustrated by the actions of oppressive governments. Evil still existed, particularly in the Soviet Union (at least before 1988), but Reagan evinced growing confidence that the rising tide of democratic revolutions would sweep away the remnants of totalitarianism.

Reagan's rhetorical vision reflected four underlying themes—antigovernment nationalism, communitarian individualism, free-market radicalism, and Wilsonian internationalism—which together formed a seamless web that purported to dip deeply into the American experience, but in fact constituted only one part of it.[12] First, in continually celebrating the American spirit, Reagan discovered a preexisting *nation* of individuals dedicated to the common interest and general welfare, waging a heroic struggle against a late-arriving, alien, corrupt national government held hostage by special interest groups. In March 1982 Reagan asked:

> Did we forget that government is the people's business, and [that] every man, woman, and child becomes a shareholder with the first penny of tax paid? . . . Did we forget that the function of government is not to confer happiness on us, but just to get out of the way and give us the opportunity to work out happiness for ourselves?[13]

In this manner, as Hugh Heclo correctly noted, Reagan revived "a rhetoric older than the Constitution itself—the country versus the court—the real nation perceived as morally superior to a corrupt government."[14] Furthermore, this concept of a nation of individuals pitted against overweening centralized powers in Washington gave voice to those "Main Street" Americans who had felt victimized by the Great Society, as well as the youthful dissenters of the 1960s who had urged the return of "power to the people." Second, with the theme of communitarian individualism Reagan sought to disarm liberal critics who claimed that his real goal was to reward the rich and brutalize the poor by crippling the federal government. But Reagan turned the tables by arguing that federal social engineers suffering from moral relativism and secular humanism were determined to impose their perverted form of community on a very reluctant citizenry. He contended that a genuine community rooted in the traditional values of family, God, self-help, free enterprise, and individual freedom constituted the real America: "a nation of neighbors and an economy of rugged individualists."[15] Third, in extolling the virtues of a free marketplace, Reagan attempted to sweep aside the flotsam of the 1970s—those "doubting Thomases," "doomsayers," "Malthusian pessimists," and "false prophets" who had ominously warned of a more straitened future. In place of this depressing collection of "handwringers," President Reagan offered an America of hard-working individuals, who asked only that the market be liberated from governmental interference. Allow the market to work its magic, Reagan implored, and the future will be filled with growth, not tradeoffs. Just as he had shown much success in banishing the *l* word—liberal—from the American political vocabulary, so did he remove the *d* word—decline—from all but academic discourse. Finally, as we see in greater detail in the next section, Ronald Reagan sought to make Wilsonian internationalism once again respectable. Notwithstanding his emphasis on the twin threats of totalitarianism and terrorism, Reagan's international rhetoric exuded the same remarkable optimism as his domestic oratory. In contrast to Carter, who seemed content to know that as a result of his public statements foreign leaders had been forced to think about human rights, President Reagan by June 1982 had proclaimed an era of democratic revolutions that would surely remove the dead hand of communism forever. Not merely an exemplar of freedom, America, Reagan suggested, had a sacred duty to defend the rights of others. Only after the march of freedom had created democratic governments, free markets, and individual liberty everywhere could Americans rest. And just as the tide of history had swung in favor of "we the people" at home, who had demanded an end to oppressive government, so too did it now favor people abroad who were fighting to destroy repressive states.

It cannot be gainsaid that Ronald Reagan's peculiar brand of "feel good," "pain free" conservatism struck an enormously respondent chord in the American body politic. His early tax and domestic spending cuts, coupled with the ensuing unprecedented budget deficits, relegated those who wished to expand significantly federal social programs to the political sidelines. The issue of the 1980s became, rhetorically at least, not whether, but how, to limit the size of the national government. In that sense Nancy Reagan's "Just Say No" antidrug campaign slogan typified Reaganism's general public posture toward nondefense expenditures. Moreover, in contrast to an older American conservatism, which had been traditionally vulnerable to charges of privilege and elitism, Reagan's was baldly populist in which "we the people" struggled against a Washington sodden with experts, special interests, social engineers, and secular humanists. Masterfully building on the accomplishments of Richard Nixon and George Wallace, but doing so with a "human face," Reagan claimed to speak for the millions who had for too long been patronized and coerced by an antidemocratic liberal establishment. And, again, unlike Tory conservatives who had dourly fretted about an unretrievable past and a dangerous future, Reagan dispensed with tragedy and offered a vision bubbling with optimism. Whereas Carter had soberly spoken of restraint, sacrifice, and complexity, Reagan promised Americans self-described "simple" solutions, unlimited economic growth, and technological salvation. Finally, his rhetoric of national assertiveness, particularly in regard to America's adversaries, neatly captured a public wearied by a decade of "bad news" from abroad. Thus, to offer but one colorful example, Reagan told the American Bar Association in July 1985 that "we're . . . not going to tolerate . . . attacks from outlaw States by the strangest collection of misfits, loony tunes, and squalid criminals since the advent of the Third Reich."[16] Whereas the "Blame-America-First Crowd" had allegedly been busy defending these unsavory types, Reagan (and "we the people") saw the truth and spoke it.

Notwithstanding the apparently pervasive political appeal of these themes, none was immune to difficulties that could eventually threaten Reaganism's agenda. First, as Heclo, Budget Director David Stockman, and others suggested, the Reagan administration failed to develop any principled basis for either cutting or decentralizing federal social programs. Despite Stockman's initial insistence that a consistent sense of equity govern policy, the administration, with the connivance of Congress, allowed political expediency to determine budget priorities. It soon became clear to Stockman that it was the poor and other unorganized groups that were particularly victimized, while middle-class "entitlement" programs remained sacrosanct.[17] And although Reagan's electoral triumphs seemed to vindicate the administration's understanding of political realities, the growing gap between rich and poor throughout the 1980s, the emergence of a permanent underclass, and the disturbing phenomenon of homelessness served as reminders of Reaganism's potential vulnerability on the "fairness issue." Of more immediate political significance was an issue that had begun to manifest itself as early as 1984—defense spending. On an abstract level, one would expect Reagan conservatives to find it increasingly difficult to argue simultaneously for a strictly limited national government and an enormous military establishment that, among other things, distorted the market and regulated important parts of the economy. More practically, the perpetuation of massive deficits and the remarkable diminution of the Soviet threat during Reagan's second term brought the long defense buildup to an abrupt halt.

Second, Reagan's sentimental vision of a national community of caring neighbors eager to volunteer, yet hamstrung by an arrogant, alien, corrupt federal government, was severely damaged by a series of private-sector abuses culminating in Wall Street insider-trading scandals and the savings and loan crisis. Not even Reagan could plausibly indict the federal government as the cause of those excesses or other instances of unbridled individual greed, nor could he easily blame Washington for provoking a national drug crisis that threatened the very "family" values so dear to the president. Furthermore, despite the apparent broad popularity of Reagan's limited government message, opinion polls throughout the 1980s indicated widespread support for public programs, particularly those perceived as personally relevant. At the same time, however, there remained a great reluctance to pay for these services with higher taxes. In this sense, the federal deficit constituted the "free lunch" that conservatives had traditionally dismissed as an oxymoron, but, in fact, the deficit enabled the public to fulfill its twin

wishes of federal services and lower taxes. Unlike inflation and unemployment, the deficit had an abstract, eschatological quality that made it politically tolerable in the short run.

Finally, Reagan's optimistic Wilsonian international vision, like his domestic outlook, obscured, as we later see, some important operational dilemmas. For example, under what conditions would the United States
employ military force to "expand freedom"? Would an American public,
told by Reagan that sacrifice at home was unnecessary, support prolonged
engagements abroad?

A Shining City on the Hill

As a former governor of California, presidential candidate Ronald Reagan
may have lacked foreign policy experience but he surely did not lack opinions about America's proper role in the world. He had been delivering these
opinions, as well as those on domestic issues, since his days on the "mashed
potato circuit" as a spokesman for General Electric, in "the speech" on
national television in October 1964, and in a long series of five-minute
weekly radio addresses after leaving Sacramento. In essence, Reagan's assault on the Carter foreign policy built on these earlier views, with an
adjusted focus to take advantage of the president's current predicament.
Like Carter in 1976, Reagan leveled a combination of stylistic and substantive charges against the incumbent designed to distance him from the recent
American foreign policy record. Once again the functioning of the National
Security Council staff emerged as a campaign issue with Reagan, who
pledged to end the policymaking confusion of the Carter administration by
ensuring the supremacy of the State Department. More tellingly, candidate
Reagan claimed that (1) while the United States had been "unilaterally
disarming" in the 1970s, the Soviet Union had undertaken history's most
massive arms buildup; (2) the Soviets had exploited the arms control process to threaten the United States with a window of vulnerability that would
soon put at risk its entire land-based ICBM force; (3) President Carter had
unwisely signed a "fatally flawed" SALT II agreement; (4) the Carter administration, in part because of its highly publicized human rights campaign, had abandoned many of America's traditional friends, while
apologizing for the misdeeds of its adversaries; (5) the United States had
placed excessive faith in multilateral organizations such as the United Nations, which had repeatedly abused and humiliated it; (6) for well over a
decade, America's standing in the world and the respect afforded it had
steadily fallen; and (7) an anemic, inflationary domestic economy had diminished America's ability to provide international leadership.

Upon its electoral victory in 1980 the Reagan administration faced a public that manifested several not wholly consistent foreign policy attitudes: a sense of vulnerability in the wake of the Soviet arms buildup; a preoccupation with Soviet military power; a disinclination for direct military involvement in conflicts abroad; and paradoxically a simultaneous desire for U.S. world leadership. The administration responded with a program that allegedly aimed to restore the domestic economy, end the era of Soviet military superiority, reward the anticommunist friends of the United States abroad, halt the spread of Soviet influence, and combat terrorism. Furthermore, it promised to accomplish these goals without triggering a nuclear war (some early statements notwithstanding), risking another Vietnam-type conflict, or incurring federal budget deficits.

Central to both Reagan's domestic and global grand design was the restoration of the American economy, and the administration focused its attention during 1981 on the federal budget and tax reductions. Indeed, apart from some rather heavy-handed declaratory signaling, which reflected the administration's ideological inclinations—for example, opposition to the Law of the Sea Treaty, withholding payments to the United Nations, and shooting down two Libyan jets in the Gulf of Sidra—the Reagan presidency appeared devoid of a foreign policy. Secretary of State Alexander Haig's early efforts to "go to the source" of Central American instability met with serious resistance from the White House *troika* of Edwin Meese, Michael Deaver, and James Baker, and the president's only important foray into foreign policy involved his rescue of the Advanced Warning Air Control (AWACs) sale to Saudi Arabia before a skeptical Congress—a deal initiated by the Carter administration. In contrast to his predecessor Reagan delivered no major foreign policy addresses until the Caribbean Basin Initiative in January 1982.

Yet Reagan's early foreign policy rhetorical quiescence hardly meant that he lacked strong beliefs. Indeed, the president and his senior advisers shared a set of overlapping convictions best termed "conservative internationalism" that collided with the world order outlook of the early Carter years. First, and most fundamentally, they believed that Soviet-American competition remained the defining characteristic of contemporary international relations, a struggle that the United States was losing through a lack of effort. Second, they were confident that the Soviet Union, despite its formidable, even preeminent, military power, suffered from grave economic and social woes and was vulnerable to external pressure. Third, previous U.S. efforts to achieve détente had been naive, one-sided disasters and would continue to be so until the internal nature of the Soviet regime had been decisively altered. Fourth, the world was not nearly as diverse or complex as liberal cant fashionably claimed, and thus regional conflicts in Africa, Central America, and the Middle East should best be viewed as part of the East-West struggle. Fifth, recent administrations, in misguided attempts to accommodate Third World Marxist states, had abandoned traditional, if authoritarian, friends and thus strengthened Moscow's hand. Sixth, the Soviet Union and its clients had exploited America's "Vietnam syndrome" to expand their influence. The United States, they believed, had to give renewed priority to military and paramilitary policy instruments—a sharp increase in the defense budget, covert action, military assistance and arms sales—instead of vainly attempting to win friends through agreements like the Law of the Sea and the Panama Canal treaties. And, finally, they were convinced that because America's wounds had been self-inflicted and were not the product of inexorable forces such as the diffusion of economic power and high technology, its decline could be reversed and its global preeminence restored. Much would depend on rebuilding domestic confidence in the strength, morality, and wisdom of the United States.

Together these convictions constituted a grand design reminiscent of a world much like that of the 1950s—only better. This world would resemble the earlier decade inasmuch as a respected, powerful America would again exert global leadership, but now, having lost the Cold War, the Soviet Union would no longer pose a serious threat. The United States could thus escape the security dilemmas that had traditionally bedeviled states. Surrounded by friends—some democratic, others authoritarian—the United States would not need to manipulate an international balance of power to survive, for, with the Cold War now history, international relations—traditional statecraft—would be largely obsolete. This enormously optimistic yet quintessentially Reaganesque vision went considerably beyond containment. George Kennan, it may be recalled, had argued that the patient application of pressure against the Soviet Union would eventually lead to its collapse or moderation, which in turn would usher in a multipolar world with the United States playing a major balancing role. Moreover, Reagan's initial design grew in time even more grandiose as he took advantage of favorable trends first in Latin America and later in Eastern Europe and the Soviet Union to proclaim a new age of democratic revolutions that would universalize the contagion of liberty. Reagan's address to the British Parliament in June 1982 asserted that "around the world today the democratic Revolution is gaining strength" at a time when "a great Revolutionary crisis . . . is happening . . . in the home of Marxism-Leninism—the Soviet Union." Reagan suggested that democracy "is not a fragile flower. Still it needs cultivating. . . . It is time that we committed ourselves as a nation—in both the public and private sectors—to assisting democratic development." For "freedom is not the sole prerogative of a lucky few, but the inalienable and universal right of all human beings."[18] Indeed, Reagan's grand design, while clearly indebted to Woodrow Wilson, some of the founders, and many nineteenth-century publicists, possessed certain advantages over earlier visions. During other revolutionary democratic ages—the 1790s and 1840s—the United States had the desire but not the power to assist fellow democrats, while after World War I the United States had enormous power but confronted a world beset by radical revolutionary change. Now this design stood a better chance of being realized, for U.S. power and favorable international trends were presumably converging. Thus Reagan's grand design entailed nothing less than a fully democratic world guided by a resurgent America in which peace and prosperity could flourish.

It proved difficult, however, to translate these overlapping convictions and this global vision into a coherent foreign policy strategy. Reagan's early immersion in winning public and congressional support for his economic recovery program, as well as a hands-off leadership style, left the White House *troika,* Secretary of Defense Caspar Weinberger, Director of the Central Intelligence Agency William Casey, and Haig vying for control over foreign policy, while a greatly weakened National Security Council provided very little coordination. As a result of this organizational confusion, the early Reagan foreign policy consisted primarily of a collection of departmental initiatives, whose sole common thread was an antipathy to anything that smacked of "Carterism." Neither a formal decision-making apparatus nor a basic national security document existed until after Reagan confidant William Clark moved from State to the NSC in early 1982. Three months after his arrival, a National Security Decision Directive, coordinated by former Secretary of the Air Force Thomas C. Reed, received the president's signature. This eight-page directive outlined the political, economic, diplomatic, informational, and military components of a comprehensive national strategy.[19] Its contents remained classified, though Clark and other senior advisers publicly offered a general description of what some of its architects dubbed "prevailing with pride." First, because the Soviet Union was an "economic basket case," the United Sates should exploit this situation by waging economic warfare. Détente had created powerful interests in the West whose well-being depended on expanding Soviet trade and investment. The Soviets, in turn, had manipulated those interests into helping prop up their faltering economy. In the future, the West had to ensure that its resources, credits, and technology could not be used in this manner. Instead, every effort should be made to deny the Soviet Union access to Western economic assets. Thus Weinberger took the lead in tightening controls over the Western export of critical goods, in ending

Soviet industrial espionage, in opposing the extension of credits to Poland, and in demanding that West Germany cancel a contract with Russia for a natural gas pipeline. Moreover, he recommended that weapons systems be built not only for their military utility but in order to maximize the economic burdens they would place on Soviet attempts to counter them.[20] As it turned out, not only did vigorous Western European and congressional resistance to the notion of economic warfare largely scuttle Weinberger's plans, but by the late 1980s Soviet-American trade had reached unprecedented levels as a "Détente II" was in full bloom.

Second, this document apparently endorsed an extremely skeptical approach to nuclear arms control. If not for the intrusion of domestic political considerations, first in the Federal Republic of Germany in 1981 and then in the United States the following year, the Reagan administration would probably have preferred to offer no arms control proposals at all. Moreover, as part of the "two-track" theater nuclear force agreement reached with NATO in December 1979, the administration was obliged to negotiate with the Soviets while making preparations to deploy Pershing II and Cruise missiles in Western Europe. Huge antideployment rallies in West Germany helped pressure the administration to unveil in November 1981 a "zero-zero" option that would have forced the Soviets to remove their theater nuclear forces in exchange for a U.S. pledge to forego deployment of its new weapons. In view of the administration's well-known doubts about reaching agreements with a Soviet Union that "had broken every treaty it had ever made," many interpreted this offer as a propaganda ploy. Nevertheless, it did succeed in defusing the West German protests and, of course, ultimately served as the basis for the 1987 Intermediate Nuclear Forces (INF) treaty. It remains unclear if the zero-zero option was taken seriously by the administration in 1981, for some Defense Department officials subsequently found it very difficult to tolerate Moscow's acceptance of the offer. In a somewhat similar fashion, Reagan's rejection of the SALT process in favor of the commencement of START, designed to reduce existing strategic arsenals, struck some observers as public relations hyperbole, especially his Eureka proposals of May 1982 that would have cut deeply into land-based missiles, but it stole the thunder from the nuclear freeze movement, which, Reagan claimed, wished merely to sanctify a dangerous status quo. In any case, "prevailing with pride" evidently urged that serious negotiations be postponed at least until the U.S. force modernization and expansion program was well under way, for positions of strength needed to be constructed first.

Third, according to Clark, "the modernization of our strategic nuclear forces" would "receive first priority in our efforts to rebuild the military capabilities of the United States."[21] Whereas the final Carter military budget had emphasized general-purpose forces—largely to help implement the new commitment to Persian Gulf security—Reagan's fiscal year 1983 increases focused on strategic forces. Specifically, the administration "accorded the highest priority to a survivable command, control, communications, and intelligence system."[22] This force modernization contained eleven major elements, eight of which were continuations of Carter initiatives, while the others—the B-1, air defenses, and sea launched Cruise missiles—were Reagan innovations."[23] Taken together, these programs represented a strategic force buildup comparable to those of the Korean War and Kennedy years. Yet, somewhat surprisingly in view of the 1980 campaign rhetoric, little was done to deal with the "window of vulnerability," other than undertaking a search for a feasible basing mode—a search that ended with the recommendation to deploy the MX in existing Minuteman silos. More innovative was the decision to substitute the threat of escalation in space and time for the threat of escalation in weapons. Rather than climb a vertical ladder to deter nuclear war, the administration proposed "horizontal escalation," whereby threats of conventional counterattacks against major Soviet interests held out the prospect of "prolonged war" in which Western economic superiority would prove decisive.[24] Weinberger's FY 1984–88 Defense Guidance singled out Cuba, Vietnam, and North Korea as likely targets for conventional retaliation.[25] Central to the strategy of horizontal escalation and prolonged conventional war was a naval expansion program aimed at achieving a 600-ship fleet. Equally essential, of course, was the development of a domestic industrial base that could sustain U.S. forces in a war of long duration. That, in turn, depended on the restoration of the American economy.

Fourth, the Reagan administration proposed to launch a comprehensive informational offensive strongly reminiscent of Eisenhower's psychological warfare efforts of the early 1950s. Concerned that the Soviets had been winning the propaganda struggle—"nuclear pacifism" in West Germany and widespread Western acceptance of the doctrine of "moral equivalence" were seen as evidence of Moscow's success—it was determined to seize the moral high ground and expose the Soviet Union and its friends as ruthless, aggressive totalitarians. Several steps were taken to implement this part of the strategy. Jeane Kirkpatrick, whose *Commentary* article "Dictatorships and Double Standards" had been admiringly read by Reagan during the campaign, was made ambassador to the United Nations, where she quickly earned a reputation as a formidable "Soviet basher."[26] Similarly, Michael Novak, a 1960s hippie-turned-conservative Catholic philosopher, became chief representative to the UN Commission on Human Rights—a post he used to promote a distinctly libertarian approach. President Reagan appointed Charles Wick, an old friend, to head the U.S. Information Agency with instructions to transform it into an active combatant in the struggle against communism. The State Department through its Bureau of Public Affairs published a long series of reports that accused the Soviets of promoting terrorism, causing "yellow rain" in Southeast Asia, abusing human rights, systematically violating treaties and other international agreements, and a host of other transgressions. President Reagan, as we later see, unleashed a rhetorical barrage against Moscow culminating in his March 1983 "evil empire" speech. The administration, in an effort to exert pressure on Fidel Castro, asked Congress to fund Radio Marti. Finally, plans were laid to create a National Endowment for Democracy (NED), an amalgam of American business, labor, academic institutions, and the two major political parties, which was to disperse government funds abroad in order to promote political pluralism. Loosely based on Cold War programs of the CIA, which had clandestinely channeled financial assistance to democratic (or at least anticommunist) groups, the NED was openly to strengthen pluralism both within and outside the Soviet bloc. It was, in fact, established in 1983 under the presidency of Carl Gershman, who oversaw such activities as training teachers, opening schools, publishing textbooks in Afghanistan, helping Solidarity print underground publications in Poland, providing printing supplies for the anti-Sandinista paper *La Prensa,* and helping the opposition in South Korea. It also, much more controversially, made a $575,000 grant to an ultraright French group, the National Inter-University Union.[27] All in all, these initiatives were designed to put the Soviet Union on the ideological defensive and to win the "war of ideas" with communism.

Finally, the Reagan administration gradually evolved a geopolitical project that at its core reflected the long-standing conservative aversion to containment. Ronald Reagan, in particular, a self-described admirer of James Burnham, had during the 1950s and 1960s spoken of the alleged moral bankruptcy of containment's reluctance to assist people struggling against communist governments. The Eisenhower administration, Dulles's rhetoric notwithstanding, had found it impossible to implement rollback in Eastern Europe for fear of triggering a war with the Soviet Union. But by the early 1980s the Soviet empire stretched far beyond its traditional security zone to places such as Ethiopia, Angola, South Yemen, Cambodia, Cuba, Nicaragua, and Afghanistan. As we have seen, most senior Carter officials initially suspected that the Soviet Union was overextended and that powerful indigenous nationalist forces would eventually loosen Moscow's grip on many of these areas. Moreover, because of their dread of another Vietnam quagmire, they opposed funding military assistance to anticommunist organizations until, of course, the Soviet invasion of Afghanistan. The Carter administration's decision to help arm the Afghan rebels constituted the genesis of what would become known as the Reagan Doctrine, a synthesis of rollback and the Nixon Doctrine, whereby the United States would provide modest funds for "freedom fighters" struggling to unseat Third World communist governments. The Reagan administration came to view this policy as a low-cost, low-risk effort to chip away at the periphery of the Soviet empire. At the least, it would greatly increase the price that Moscow would have to pay to retain its Third World clients, and it might even lead to the overthrow of these governments, which, among other things, would destroy the validity of the Brezhnev Doctrine and adjust the global "correlation of forces."

In sum, the Reagan administration by mid-1982 had formulated a reasonably comprehensive strategy designed to realize its grand design. Though it represented in large measure an extension and a systematization of programs begun by Carter, as well as the highly moralistic tone of its predecessor, Reagan's strategy rejected the managerial and retreatist dimensions of that approach. Instead, "prevailing with pride" involved the reassertion of American global leadership and the maintenance of all existing commitments. There was, to be sure, disagreement among senior officials about whether this reassertion should be primarily unilateral or the result of close allied cooperation, with Weinberger and NSC Director Richard Allen evincing acute impatience toward Western European "détenteniks" and believing that Carter's obsession with multilateral initiatives had needlessly paralyzed American foreign policy. Furthermore, these advisers dismissed the devolution strategies of Nixon and Carter as symptomatic of the post-Vietnam loss of will.

But how did the Reagan administration propose to underwrite these global commitments? After all, its predecessors had perceived a reality of shrinking resources and had adjusted accordingly. Cold War presidents had, as John Gaddis pointed out, faced similar dilemmas. In Truman's case, the vast defense expenditures required by NSC-68 (the 1950 study that recommended global containment) were to be financed through short-term deficits that would, his Keynesian advisers assured, be quickly eliminated by robust economic growth. Walter Heller delivered essentially the same message to Kennedy a dozen years later.[28] Neither president had seemed comfortable with the prospect of budget deficits and had been persuaded to accept them as temporary evils on the road to economic recovery and military expansion. Reagan, citing the theories of supply-side economists, reassured the electorate in 1980 that as long as federal social spending was controlled, tax rates could be slashed, defense expenditures significantly increased, and, in a few years, the budget brought into balance, as savings and investments acted to spur economic growth and increase tax revenues. Some critics, among them Senator Daniel Patrick Moynihan (D-NY) argued, in retrospect, that Reagan had known all along that huge deficits would be the inevitable result of this supply-side voodoo and that he planned to exploit the issue in order to reduce drastically the size of the welfare state. But the difficulty with Moynihan's conjecture is that it overlooked the pressures that these deficits ultimately exerted on defense spending as well. Thus, although the defense share of the budget rose from 22.7 percent in 1980 to 28.7 percent in 1987, the defense budget in constant dollars actually declined by more than 10 percent between its peak in fiscal 1985 and 1989.[29] Indeed, it appears likely that Reagan and his original inner circle genuinely believed that a growing U.S. economy could afford "prevailing with pride" without the necessity of long-term deficits. As it turned out, during the Reagan presidency the national debt tripled to $2.8 trillion. Massive borrowing, much of it from foreign sources, allowed the Reagan administration to pursue its ambitious national security strategy.[30] Put differently, other countries could, by lending money to the United States, in effect subsidize the cost of U.S. security protection and thus disguise any hint of American retrenchment.

The Reagan administration employed tactics that emphasized the centrality of declaratory signaling, frequently in the form of powerful rhetoric emanating from the president and his foreign policy advisers. It waged an unrelenting war of words against its adversaries designed to expose them as liars, oppressors, hollow failures, terrorists, and the like and to prove that the United States possessed the will to confront them. And yet, as Coral Bell correctly suggested, even before Gorbachev's accession to power in 1985, "all was actually quiet, *save on the rhetorical front,* in the central confrontation between the superpowers."[31] The result was a heavily stylized "second Cold War" in which words were chosen with the same care usually accorded military weapons in a real conflict. At home, as we have seen, the Carter tactic had been to welcome the participation of the American people in debating and formulating foreign policy. Reagan, despite a comparably populist rhetoric, did not speak of an open, honest foreign policy but one that expressed the innate strength of "we the people." And whereas Carter had sought to demonstrate his devotion to democratic participation through town meetings and call-in shows, Reagan surrounded himself with the more traditional trappings of presidential power. His majesty would presumably embody the grandeur of those "ordinary, extraordinary Americans."

As the leader of a self-described "revolution" determined to challenge the Washington status quo, Reagan undertook a rather systematic effort to assert presidential control over the entire federal executive bureaucracy, including the various foreign affairs and national security agencies. The central elements of this strategy involved (1) extensive use of the appointment power to infuse the federal establishment with loyalists; (2) development of a cabinet council system and other interagency devices to focus the attention of these political appointees on the Reagan agenda; (3) strengthening the ability of the Office of Management and Budget (OMB) to implement presidential wishes; and (4) repeated articulation of broad principles of acceptably "conservative" ways to manage the federal government.[32] The absence of a foreign policy consensus since the mid-1960s had been reflected in the widespread housecleaning of those relevant departments and agencies by Nixon and Carter. Reagan, initially at least, made ideological affinity even more critical, while extending this practice to the domestic bureaucracies in a manner that Nixon must have envied.

This largely successful "infiltration" strategy certainly eased the task of legitimating the Reagan foreign policy within the bureaucracy, for there were now loyal soldiers in key positions eager to receive their marching orders from the president. On the other hand, Reagan's radically detached management style required a team of foreign policy advisers that had access to the Oval Office and whom the president could trust to translate his instincts and convictions into policy. These requirements, as we know, were rarely met. Rancorous bureaucratic infighting, fully as bitter as that which had plagued the Carter administration, infected the Reagan White House until the last year of his presidency. Weinberger and Haig, and then Weinberger and George Shultz, opposed each other on a variety of issues including, most fundamentally, nuclear arms control and the conditions in which U.S. conventional arms should be employed. And when Weinberger and Shultz did agree that weapons ought not to be sold to Iranian "moderates," both were overridden and excluded by a renegade NSC in a truly bizarre attempt to free American hostages in Lebanon and illegally resupply the Nicaraguan "democratic resistance." Indeed, the internecine warfare between administration pragmatists and ideologues dragged on until Reagan, deeply shaken by public reaction to the Iran-*contra* debacle, allowed most of the remaining ideologues to be purged from the foreign policy apparatus.

But, particularly during his first term, when Reagan seemed more able to "be Reagan," his speechwriting office was remarkably effective in using presidential rhetoric to legitimate his foreign and domestic policies to both the federal bureaucracy and, as we later see, the wider public. Like theologians absorbing and interpreting a sacred text, Reagan's wordsmiths drew on "the speech" of 1964 for inspiration. Consisting of a central, simple claim—that powerful governments weakened the character of free people—

this text was memorized by the speechwriters and served as the foundation for the half-million words annually uttered by President Reagan. It was, for speechwriter Al Meyer, "the conscience of the presidency." According to chief writer Bentley Elliott, "What I personally did to sound like Reagan was to spend the three weeks before I went to work for him reading all his speeches and making . . . sheaves of notes—on war, on blacks, on rhetoric, on [the] economy." Reagan, in turn, employed the resulting rhetoric to transform his cabinet into "willing evangelicals who carried the word to the specialized bureaucracies and their clienteles."[33] While such foreign policy pragmatists as Shultz, Frank Carlucci, and Colin Powell may have ulti-mately steered a course inimical to Weinberger, Kirkpatrick, and other "evangelicals," they did so only after accepting the outlines of Reagan's original agenda.

We concluded the last chapter by suggesting that Carter largely failed to reconstruct the substantive procedural and cultural components of a domes-tic foreign policy consensus. How did President Reagan attempt to legiti-mate publicly the grand design, strategy, and tactics of his foreign policy in view of the fact that it bore a great resemblance to the post-Afghanistan approach of his predecessor?

Reagan's public legitimation efforts consisted of six elements: (1) an oft-repeated declaratory history of American foreign policy that likened the 1970s to the 1930s—as decades of economic decay at home and appease-ment of totalitarianism abroad; that extolled the period from 1947 through the mid-1960s as an era of strength, wisdom, generosity, prudence, firm-ness, and achievement; and that, as the administration gradually compiled its own record, portrayed the 1980s as a second golden age; (2) the reassur-ance that the setbacks of the 1970s were but aberrations that could be easily reversed with little pain or sacrifice from the American people; (3) the assertion that because the contemporary world bore a strong resemblance to that of the early postwar decades, its problems were thus susceptible to simple solutions; (4) a moralistic depiction of international relations that prominently featured a struggle between good and evil and a portrayal of Reagan's foreign policy as one committed to defending and promoting the universal value of individual liberty; (5) the claim that the American politi-cal community and the world community (or parts of it at least) were similar in structure and aspiration; and (6) the increasingly confident prom-ise of an emergent, fully democratic world.

In contrast to Carter's unusually ahistorical early rhetoric, Reagan's brimmed with powerful historical images and lessons. By comparing the 1970s to the 1930s, Reagan and his advisers were following a tradition of creating distance from one's immediate predecessors. Again and again administration officials portrayed the 1970s as a decade of doubt, defeat, deceit, and despair, comparable only to the 1930s as an era of embarrassment for the United States. Secretary of State Alexander Haig, for example, claimed that during the 1960s and 1970s "the cohesion of America's foreign, defense, and economic policies disintegrated" in the face of Vietnam, Watergate, and prolonged economic distress, and while the American people wasted their time debating the utility of military power, the Soviets embarked on a vigorous military modernization program.[34] In 1982 Haig described the 1970s as "a decade when negotiations often seemed to be a substitute for strength," for the United States had been "dominated by the psychology of Vietnam and rising domestic resistance to military programs."[35]

President Reagan peppered his speeches with the same sentiments. In 1983 he described to the American Legion the international situation that he had inherited as president as "truly alarming for all who cared about America and the cause of peace and freedom" and suggested that only a "truly bipartisan effort" could "make things right again."[36] The president spoke to a group of high school students in January 1983 with even fewer qualifications: ". . . what we're doing with our present buildup of the military is overcoming several years in which we virtually, unilaterally disarmed. We let our arms go. We canceled things like the B-1 bomber and so forth."[37]

Reminiscences about the "lessons" of the 1930s occurred repeatedly in the president's improvised responses to questions. Barely six weeks into his first term, in an interview with Walter Cronkite, he linked his situation to that of Franklin Roosevelt's on the eve of World War II:

> I remember when Hitler was arming and had built himself up—no one's created quite the same military power that the Soviet Union has, but comparatively he was in that way—Franklin Delano Roosevelt made a speech in Chicago. . . . And in the speech he called on the free world to quarantine Nazi Germany. . . . [B]ut the funny thing was that he was attacked so here in our own country for having said such a thing. Can we honestly look back now and say that World War II would have taken place if we had done what he wanted us to back in 1938 [*sic*]?"[38]

Reagan cited FDR's "quarantine the aggressors" speech again and again, particularly during the years of the large U.S. defense buildup. He also liked to tell a story about the state of America's war-readiness in the late 1930s. During war games in Louisiana, he recalled, "we had soldiers that were carrying wooden rifles, and we were simulating tank warfare with cardboard tanks." Compare that to another oft-told story about the alleged condition of U.S. armed forces in 1980: "We had aircraft that couldn't fly and ships that couldn't leave port. Many of our military was on food stamps because of meager earnings, and reenlistments were down. Ammunition was low, and spare parts were in short supply."[39] Sometimes the president explicitly connected the 1930s to those in Congress who opposed his defense spending requests:

> The calls for cutting the defense budget come in nice, simple arithmetic. They're the same kind of talk that led the democracies to neglect their defenses in the 1930s and invited the tragedy of World War II. We must not let that grim chapter of history repeat itself through apathy or neglect. This is why I'm speaking to you tonight—to urge you to tell your Senators and Congressmen that you know we must continue to restore our military strength."[40]

While not actually accusing his predecessors of appeasement, Reagan habitually identified himself with FDR—not the Roosevelt of Yalta to be sure, but the vigilant president who had warned the world of the Nazi threat while the West slept and thus insinuated that his critics were recommitting the mistakes of the 1930s.

The administration's characterization of the 1970s no doubt reflected widely shared popular perceptions. It outlined a declaratory history that was simplistic and tendentious. Moreover, to score rhetorical points with the public, Reagan and his advisers ignored significant, but less helpful, events of that decade. For example, whatever else may be said of the Carter foreign policy record, the Camp David Accords, formal diplomatic ties with the People's Republic of China, the Panama Canal treaties, and a rapprochement with much of southern Africa surely qualified as solid achievements. Yet Reagan's declaratory history of the 1970s conveniently omitted them. Note this telling exchange in May 1983 when Reagan was asked to evaluate these aspects of the Carter legacy:

> *Interviewer:* Four years ago when the Carter administration was in its third year, they had completed the Camp David agreement and the treaty from that; the SALT II treaty was about to be negotiated; normalization with China had taken place; and the Panama Canal treaty had been approved. Can you name several [tangible things] that you've achieved?
> *Reagan:* Well, in the first place, China relations had been normalized by the visits of a previous president. . . . And he carried on from there. And I'm not at all sure that I added to what had already been accomplished. With regard to the Camp David agreements, yes, they started, and we're proceeding within the framework of those agreements, because those agreements were simply to begin negotiations . . . but we're the ones who've gone a step beyond that with regard to trying to have an overall peace in the area. That had never been proposed.[41]

Its inaccuracies aside, this soliloquy underlined the purpose for which the administration used the history of the 1970s: to frighten and anger the public into supporting its foreign policy priorities.

Yet while Reagan officials indiscriminately condemned the U.S. diplomatic record of the 1970s, they enthusiastically praised the achievements of Truman, Eisenhower, and Kennedy. It was clear that the Reagan administration wished to identify with the feats of these presidents. For instance, in asking Congress to authorize aid to the *contras* in April 1983 Reagan quoted extensively from the Truman Doctrine and contended that "President Truman's words are as apt today as they were in 1947 when he, too, spoke to a joint session of the Congress."[42] The president also invoked the words of Eisenhower, repeatedly citing a letter in which Eisenhower argued that negotiations were the only alternative to nuclear destruction. Thus Cold War presidents were recalled for their restraint as well as their activism. In order to fend off congressional criticism of his dispatch of marines to the Beirut airport, Reagan compared his actions to those of Eisenhower, who in 1958 had "used a bipartisan congressional resolution to send 8,000 American soldiers and marines to Lebanon. When order was restored, our military came home."[43]

President Reagan and his advisers supplemented these largely anecdotal references to past leaders with a somewhat more systematic public account of the Cold War—an account that, in its unambiguous celebration of American achievements, stood in stark contrast to the more complex and critical analyses of contemporary diplomatic historians. Secretary of State Haig captured this approach fully when he recalled in April 1982 how the United States, after drifting into a disastrous isolationism in the 1920s and 1930s, had been determined to avoid this mistake after World War II by "eagerly" founding a new international order. "American resources, American perseverance, and American wisdom provided the crucial underpinnings of this international order," and "the successful application of American power" had brought 'economic health and political stability to Western Europe and Japan."[44] Moreover, as President Reagan suggested to the British Parliament in 1982, the Western democracies in the 1940s and early 1950s had shown unique restraint in refusing to use their nuclear monopoly for territorial gain.[45] A few months later he reiterated this theme in a national television address designed to mobilize public support for the MX missile. Reagan reminded his television audience that at the end of World War II, with the United States the only undamaged industrial power, with its military power at its peak, and with an atomic monopoly, "We didn't use this wealth and power to bully; we used it to rebuild. . . . We had deeply held moral values," and "Our strength deterred . . . aggression against us."[46] Just as American power had kept the peace in that earlier era, so the MX—now dubbed "Peacekeeper"—was to do likewise in the 1980s.

It was perhaps appropriate that Jeane Kirkpatrick, the administration's best-known professor, was the only official to admit even the slightest possibility of other historical interpretations. Yet she did so only to disparage them. Thus, in a speech to the knowledgeable National Committee on American Foreign Policy she observed that NATO was "forged as a direct response to the actual, imminent danger to Western Europe of Soviet subversion and aggression. *No amount of historical revisionism can explain away facts of Soviet expansion into Europe.*"[47] There was a certain irony here, for Ronald Reagan's declaratory history embraced policies that he had once vilified. While his administration articulated a history that fell well within the old containment consensus of the Cold War years, Reagan, for most of that era, had been a disciple of James Burnham and other conservative critics of U.S. foreign policy. What Reagan now called "restraint" and "generosity," Burnham had labeled "appeasement" and "naiveté." Both had called for an offensive strategy that went well beyond containment to overthrow Soviet client governments in Eastern Europe and ultimately the Soviet Union itself. Yet the administration's declaratory history did not aim to convert the electorate to Burnham's brand of "liberation theology." Curiously, despite his clear indebtedness to Burnham, the president did not defend the Reagan Doctrine by disparaging the accomplishments of containment. Despite early efforts of Reagan's NSC staff to develop a forward strategy, in 1981 and 1982 the administration was publicly attempting to mobilize support for a massive defense buildup without deepening popular perceptions of a trigger-happy president. By portraying the Cold War as an era of U.S. strength and world order, administration officials sought to allay public fears of a dangerous new arms race.

Yet the shadow of Vietnam intruded into this tidy history of U.S. foreign policy. In general, Reagan and his advisers tried to say as little as possible about the Vietnam War, usually lumping it with Watergate as an event that had produced national disillusionment and self-doubt. Occasionally, when speaking to especially friendly audiences, this circumspection yielded to more visceral sentiments. During the 1980 campaign Reagan had told the American Legion that it was "time to recognize that ours was in truth a noble cause."[48] Jeane Kirkpatrick proclaimed to the same group two years later that "I don't think that we were driven out of Vietnam—I think we left. I think that's an important distinction and one we should not lose sight of."[49] In February 1987 Reagan suggested that U.S. troops came home without a victory not because they had been defeated but because they "had been denied permission to win."[50] Overall, it was the press and not the administration that raised the issue. For example, a reporter asked Reagan only six weeks after his first inauguration to compare the situation in El Salvador to Vietnam in the early 1960s, and the president replied rather disjointedly,

> I don't believe it is a valid parallel. I know that many people have been suggesting that. The situation here is, you might say, our front yard; it just isn't El Salvador. What we're doing, in going to the aid of a government that asked that aid of a neighboring country and a friendly country in our hemisphere, is trying to halt the infiltration into the Americas by terrorists, by outside interference, and those who aren't just aiming at El Salvador, but, I think, are aiming at the whole of Central and possibly later South America and, I'm sure, eventually North America.[51]

Not until 1985, on the occasion of the tenth anniversary of Saigon's fall, did Reagan offer a more elaborate defense. He told a news conference in April,

> That was the great disgrace, to me, of Vietnam—that they were fed into this meatgrinder, and yet no one ever had any intention of allowing victory.
> Well, the truth of the matter is, we did have victory . . . .
> But what happened? We signed the peace accords, . . . and we made a pledge to [Saigon]. And when the North Vietnamese did violate the agreement and the blitz started . . . and then the administration in Washington asked the Congress for the appropriations to keep our word, the Congress refused. We broke our pledge . . .
> And so, we didn't lose the war. When the war was all over and we'd come home—that's when the war was lost.[52]

But the American public's overwhelmingly negative memory of Vietnam clashed with the administration's and certainly constrained President Reagan's foreign policy options, especially in Central America. Opinion polls showing huge majorities opposed to sending U.S. troops to El Salvador and Nicaragua no doubt helped convince the administration to aid the *contras* as an alternative to direct military involvement. It subsequently began to turn the Vietnam issue to its own advantage by arguing that only congressional support of the *contra* program would preclude the chances of another Vietnam. But this legislative tactic only partially succeeded, for public backing of *contra* aid remained around 30 percent, and congressional enthusiasm for it was divided at best.

By the late 1980s the Reagan administration had compiled a historical record that it eagerly incorporated into its declaratory statements. In October 1987 Reagan reminded a West Point audience that "from the beginning, our administration has insisted that this Country base its relations with the Soviet Union upon realism, not illusion. This may sound obvious. But when we took office the historical record needed restatement. So restate it we did."[53] In April 1988 the president recalled that

> at first, the experts said this kind of candor was dangerous, that it would lead to a worsening of Soviet-American relations. But far to the contrary this candor made clear to the Soviets the resilience and strength of the West. . . . And now this approach to the Soviets . . . has borne fruit.[54]

History had vindicated his strategy, as he told students at the University of Virginia in December 1988, for "as I suggested in 1982, if the West maintained its strength, we would see economic needs clash with the political order in the Soviet Union."[55] Or, as he put it in his Farewell Address,

> That's what it was to be an American in the 1980s. We stood, again, for freedom. I know we always have, but in the past few years the world again, and in a way, we ourselves rediscovered it. . . .
> The fact is, from Grenada to the Washington and Moscow summits, from the recession of '81 and '82, to the expansion that . . . continues to this day, we've made a difference.[56]

For Reagan, then, the events of the 1980s had legitimated his approach to both foreign and domestic policies and had ushered in a new "golden age" of American achievement.

President Reagan also sought to legitimate his foreign policy by reassuring the American people that its goals could be realized with little pain or sacrifice. The 1980 Republican platform neatly captured the apparent gap between the dire nature of the current crisis and the instruments available to confront it. After intoning that "the United States faces the most serious challenge to its survival in the last two centuries," this document then recommended a drastic tax reduction, ending the grain embargo against the Soviet Union, and the abolition of draft registration.[57] The massive increases in the defense budget between 1981 and 1985, apart from the resources that it *may* have drawn away from social spending, hardly constituted a national sacrifice because, as we have seen, it was largely financed with foreign funds. Moreover, as Reagan himself repeatedly argued, even with this significant defense buildup, the proportion of the federal budget and the gross national product devoted to the military remained well below that of the 1950s and 1960s. Increases in defense spending—in itself a declaratory signal of future intentions—coupled with the president's famous rhetorical "candor" about communism, the Soviet Union, and Third World adversaries, would together reverse the tide. Of course, as Coral Bell shrewdly observed, "since the image of U.S. military weakness was created chiefly by words (mostly from the Reagan camp . . .) it is logical that more words from the same sources should have been effective in readjusting that somewhat distorted image."[58] Surely that helps to explain how Reagan, a mere four months into his presidency, could announce that "the people of America have recovered from what can only be called a temporary aberration. There is a spiritual revival going on in this country, a hunger on the part of the people to once again be proud of America—all that it is and all that it can be."[59]

But, in fact, Reagan did not demand sacrifice because he knew that such rhetoric would inevitably provoke a public weary of twenty years of "bad news" and seriously disillusioned with the risks and burdens of global leadership. Certainly the public was tired of watching America get "pushed around," but it also dreaded the prospect of another Vietnam. It did not want to be frightened, as its reaction to Reagan's early loose talk about nuclear war made clear. It wanted, instead, to be praised, encouraged, and reassured, and Reagan skillfully responded to those needs, in part because he was, by temperament, uncomfortable with struggle and sacrifice.

Third, Reagan sought to legitimate the various elements of his foreign policy as "simple" responses to deceptively simple problems. In direct contrast to Carter, who had described a new world of dizzying complexity that grudgingly yielded complicated solutions, Reagan emphasized the essential continuity of the post-1945 era. The only significant disjunction had occurred in the 1970s, when America had been beset by guilt and self-doubt, but that period, Reagan claimed, had largely ended with his election. His postwar world had been characterized by three fundamental realities—an aggressive Soviet Union determined to expand its influence; a prudent, selfless America leading the West against oppression; and billions of people around the globe struggling for individual freedom. Here again, Reagan rhetorically identified himself with the American people who, unlike unnamed "experts" despairing of the world's intractability, understood these simple truths. The world, of course, Reagan admitted, was not entirely static—changes had occurred since 1945. But in contrast to Carter, who strived to "get on the right side" of changes largely uncontrollable by the United States, Reagan saw change in terms of democratic revolutions tailormade for American leadership. Even Reagan's legendary inability to keep his facts straight seemingly appealed to a public that wanted answers yet felt inundated by information overload.

President Reagan was particularly successful in employing this "simple-mindedness" to legitimate his nuclear arms control strategy. By the late 1970s the arms control "process" had begun to encounter formidable domestic obstacles. It had grown incredibly complex as the array of "sub-limits" written into the SALT II treaty demonstrated; it had become largely

detached from other aspects of Soviet-American relations; even its proponents appeared increasingly pessimistic that the process could defuse the
arms race; and the public seemed less willing to accept the logic of
Mutual Assured Destruction (MAD), which promised more of the same
perceived insecurity, and more interested in reducing the nuclear arsenals of the superpowers.[60] Carter had tried to respond to these difficulties but found his options narrowed by domestic critics eager to junk
SALT II and by a series of devastating international shocks. Several
Reagan officials, particularly in the Defense Department, were, in fact,
opposed in principle to any arms control agreements with the Soviets. In
short, by the early 1980s the domestic politics of arms control had produced a strategic stalemate,[61] and some of Reagan's early initiatives—
for example, the zero-zero option and the Eureka proposals—seemed to
invite Soviet rejection.

But, in fact, Reagan gradually unveiled an arms control approach that
addressed the concerns of the public and that ultimately broke the domestic
stalemate by, in effect, stating that his strategic modernization program
would send a signal of firmness and determination to Moscow that would
pressure the Soviets into concluding verifiable arms *reduction* agreements
with the West. Whether the Soviets signed the zero-zero INF treaty and
began to show great interest in drastic decrease, in nuclear weapons because
of Reagan's "simple" approach, or for their own reasons—after all, they
had responded to U.S. pressure in the early 1960s in a vastly different
way—cannot yet be determined. But the American public responded positively to a process that now promised to reverse the arms race and bring
greater security. Appropriately it was a Reagan slogan—"trust but ver-
ify"—that captured the public imagination by brilliantly blending idealism
and realism toward the Soviet Union. And though "experts" shuddered at
the destabilizing potential of the Strategic Defense Initiative (SDI), more
than two-thirds of the public supported Reagan's idea of a population defense against nuclear weapons because it confronted the moral ambiguity
and apparent illogic of MAD. While Reagan may not have viewed SDI as a
bargaining chip, subsequent negotiating behavior by the Soviets suggested
that their fear of it worked to soften their positions. Again, we cannot be
certain about the cause, but the result—the prospect of a START treaty—
won widespread public approval.

There were limits, however, to the effectiveness of Reagan's rhetoric of
simplicity. Its success in arms control resulted from its very appealing goal
and from its fidelity to Reagan's public persona as a firm man of peace.
Selling arms to Iran proved to be a very different matter. Characteristically,
Reagan attempted to offer a "simple" explanation for the policy:

> [The Iranian initiative] was undertaken for the simplest and best of reasons: to renew a relationship with the nation of Iran, to bring an honorable end to the bloody six-year war between Iran and Iraq, to eliminate state-sponsored terrorism and subversion, and to effect the safe return of all hostages.[62]

But much of the public found this far from simple explanation wholly incomprehensible. In the month following the revelations the president's approval rating tumbled dramatically from 67 percent to 46 percent.[63] Not even Reagan could legitimate a policy that, despite its noble intention of freeing American hostages, appeared both immoral—selling arms to a terrorist state—and illegal—siphoning the profits to the *contras*. Reagan's tortured efforts to distinguish the hated Iranian regime from unnamed moderates sounded unconvincing, for the president had never before engaged in these fine, lawyerly distinctions. The world, he had repeatedly claimed, was simple. And whereas Reagan's previous factual confusions had seemed almost charming—for his grand design remained clear—his professed inability to remember key aspects of the Iranian affair appeared to the public as either woeful incompetence or outright prevarication. In retrospect, his rather miraculous political recovery from this disaster was closely tied to the continuing improvement in Soviet-American relations. Some of his hard-line advisers even came to suspect that Reagan's eager rush to détente in 1987 reflected a desperate desire to save his presidency.[64]

Fourth, President Reagan portrayed the world in highly moralistic terms and sought to demonstrate that his administration's foreign policy embodied this reality. That much he shared with Carter—which distinguished them both from Nixon—but unlike Carter, who failed to integrate human rights into a coherent strategy, Reagan firmly harnessed moralism to his strategic purpose. At first, this moralism appeared little more than a warmed over anticommunism. For example, Reagan's original nominee for Assistant Secretary of State for Humanitarian Affairs, Ernest LeFevre, testified to Congress that he knew of not a single noncommunist violator of human rights, and Jeane Kirkpatrick's convenient distinction between totalitarian and authoritarian governments appeared to rationalize American support for right-wing military dictators. Reagan himself routinely contrasted the goodness of the American people to the evil of communist regimes and terrorist organizations.

These features never entirely disappeared from the administration's rhetoric—indeed, many of Reagan's supporters welcomed them—but over time they were supplemented with more positive statements that aligned American foreign policy with those struggling to create democratic, capitalist institutions. Many observers believed that the administration was the lucky beneficiary of a trend toward democracy in Latin America begun by Carter, and Reagan's initially pro-Marcos actions raised doubts about his commitment to Philippine democracy. But these suspicions were overshadowed, at least among the public, by Reagan's fierce democratic rhetoric that proclaimed America "a shining city on the hill," drenched with virtue, and possessed of universally sought values. As he put it in early 1985: "Our mission is to nourish and defend democracy, and to communicate these ideals everywhere we can."[65] "Freedom is the universal right of all God's children."[66] Simply by being itself, America could serve as a global inspiration.

But America would be more than an exemplar of liberty, it would help to vindicate the rights of others. In what quickly became known as the Reagan Doctrine, the president asserted that "we must not break faith with those who are risking their lives on every continent, from Afghanistan to Nicaragua to defy Soviet-supported aggression and secure rights which have been ours from birth, . . . [for] support for freedom is self-defense."[67] In the next section of this chapter we look more closely at administration efforts to legitimate its policies toward Grenada and Central America, but here it should be noted that the Reagan Doctrine, as described to the public, proclaimed both a moral obligation and a national security imperative—self-defense—to assist anti-Soviet "freedom fighters." This deft synthesis of principle and power distinguished the Reagan administration from the legitimation efforts of its immediate predecessors.

The Carter administration had sought to show that the American political experience would prove useful in helping the United States manage those shifting, global coalitions that constituted "complex interdependence." But this rhetorical effort was short-lived, perhaps because it seemed rather abstract and arid. Reagan too tried to forge a link between the domestic and the international realms. As we have seen, he repeatedly claimed that the United States exemplified universally shared values. In a less philosophical manner, he also argued that the democratic parts of the world constituted an enlarged American "neighborhood," composed of the same kinds of God-fearing, hard-working "ordinary, extraordinary" people that could be found on Main Street, USA. For example, in early 1982 he suggested that

> the people of the Caribbean and Central America are in a fundamental sense fellow Americans. Freedom is our common destiny. . . . We are brothers historically as well as geographically. . . . [Now], more than ever, the compassionate, creative peoples of the Americas have an opportunity to stand together . . . to build a better life for all the Americas.[68]

And in February 1985 Reagan identified the "freedom fighters" of Nicaragua as "peasants, farmers, shopkeepers, and students. . . . " In short, they were neighbors, the kinds of people "we've aided around the world struggling for freedom, democracy, independence, and liberation from tyranny."[69] This metaphor of an extended neighborhood, global in scope yet rooted in the American experience, had, of course, been used by other presidents. Not only had Franklin D. Roosevelt announced a Good Neighbor Policy, but during World War II had likened his Four Policemen idea to neighborhoods patrolled by friendly cops. To reduce the world to the familiar, whether done by Roosevelt or Reagan, seemed designed to make foreign policy personally relevant to the public. It could, of course, also encourage the unfortunate notion that the world was a replica of Main Street.

Finally, Reagan repeatedly asserted that his grand design—or "dream," as he called it—involved nothing less than the realization of a fully democratic world. This simple, appealing, and powerfully articulated vision sharply contrasted with the rather murky (or disguised) designs of Carter and Nixon. Carter claimed that he had made American foreign policy moral once again and that, as a result, other leaders had been compelled to weigh the human rights consequences of their actions. But Reagan implicitly denied that American foreign policy had ever been less than totally moral— except during the 1930s and 1970s—and predicted that a tidal wave of democratic revolutions would continue to flood the world. These grandiose assertions, if made by someone else, might have seemed absurdly hypocritical or utopian, yet when uttered by Reagan, they appeared to flow naturally and easily from deeply held convictions.

The "Rescue Mission" and the "Democratic Resistance"

At the root of the dissensus that had plagued American foreign policy since Vietnam lay a disagreement about the nation's security requirements. A central manifestation of that dispute concerned the issue of the use of force abroad. Where, for what purpose, and under what conditions should the United States deploy combat troops? And, as a related theme, which friendly groups and governments should receive American military assistance? In fact, this ongoing argument had focused much less on the central front in Europe and more on the so-called periphery, where U.S. interests appeared more ambiguous.

The Reagan administration's desire to roll back Soviet influence from its new outposts was bound to reopen these unresolved issues. In this section of the chapter we examine the administration's efforts to legitimate, bureaucratically and publicly, two specific applications of the Reagan Doctrine: the Grenadian "rescue mission" of October 1983 and its long-standing support for the Nicaraguan "democratic resistance." These examples neatly illustrate the ways in which the legacy of Vietnam shaped and constrained the Reagan administration's behavior.

If "prevailing with pride" initially functioned as its global strategic blueprint, the Committee of Santa Fe's July 1980 report foreshadowed the essence of the administration's approach to Latin America. Authored by several regional specialists such as Roger Fontaine, Lewis Tambs, David C. Jordan, and Lieutenant General Gordon Sumner Jr., all of whom would obtain posts in the new administration, this document bluntly rejected President Carter's Latin American policy as indecisive and naive. In addition, it charged that the effort "to socialize the Soviets and their Hispanic-American puppets" was "merely a camouflaged cover for accommodation to aggression."[70] The report claimed that Latin America was being "overrun by Soviet supported and supplied satellites and surrogates," and argued that "decisive action, such as the occupation of the Dominican Republic in 1965" had been "replaced by retrograde reaction, as exemplified by the Carter–Torrijos treaties of 1978, and by anxious accommodation," such as President Carter's cancellation of the sea–air exercise "Solid Shield '80" after the Panamanian president objected.[71] The Committee of Santa Fe urged instead that the United States "take the strategic and diplomatic initiative by revitalizing the Rio Treaty and the Organization of American States; reproclaiming the Monroe Doctrine; tightening ties with key countries; and aiding independent nations to survive subversion."[72] It concluded that "in war there is no substitute for victory; and the United States is engaged in World War III." Thus, "containment of the Soviet Union is not enough. . . . [O]nly the United States can, as a partner, protect the independent nations of Latin America from communist conquest and help preserve Hispanic-American culture from sterilization by international Marxist materialism."[73] The Reagan administration's desire to exert pressure on Cuba, Nicaragua, and Grenada flowed logically from this analysis.

The Carter administration had greeted with ambivalence the nearly bloodless coup d'état that ousted the Grenada government of Eric Gairy on March 13, 1979, and installed Maurice Bishop's New Jewel Movement. The State Department had been appalled by Gairy's human rights record, which featured the frequent use of the so-called Mongoose Gang to assault and sometimes murder his political opponents. According to one U.S. official he was "a blemish not only on the face of Grenada, but also on the Caribbean. [His] departure was probably a blessing for Grenada. It is unfortunate that his removal was by extraconstitutional means, but let's face it, this is probably the only way he would have gone."[74]

The new regime—ominously called the Peoples Revolutionary Government (PRG)—soon began to worry Washington, for in April it received two arms shipments from Cuba, and Bishop repeatedly accused the United States of plotting to assassinate him and return Gairy to Grenada. By the summer of 1979 the PRG had clearly become a problem for mid-level officials at State. Indeed, Brzezinski's first reaction to the coup had been to consider blockading the island, and he soon began to see the entire region as a "circle of crisis."[75] According to one Carter adviser, there was not "an island in the Caribbean that couldn't go the way of Grenada in five years." Beyond these geopolitical concerns the administration grew increasingly disturbed by serious PRG human rights violations and its refusal to hold elections. Bishop and other senior PRG officials frequently engaged in provocative anti-U.S. rhetoric, and Grenada's UN representative refused to support a resolution condemning the Soviet invasion of Afghanistan.

It was this last action that led the Carter administration to reduce official contact with Grenada. It had never accepted the credentials of Grenadian ambassador-designate Dessima Williams, but now it instructed the U.S. envoy, Sally Shelton, to cease visits to the island, though she met several more times with Bishop in Barbados. Yet the Carter administration never viewed Grenada as a major issue. Neither the president nor his secretaries of state ever mentioned it publicly; Grenada was handled at the level of assistant secretary.

The Reagan team, in contrast, entered office determined to isolate, punish, and perhaps even overthrow Bishop. Its multifaceted strategy was evidently coordinated at the most senior governmental levels. Soon after becoming secretary of state, Alexander Haig ordered officials at the Bureau of Inter-American Affairs to make sure that Grenada would not receive "one penny" from any international financial institution (IFI).[76] Accordingly, Grenada was added to an informal "hit list" of countries that the State Department tried to prevent for political reasons from receiving IFI loans. In the words of one analyst, "Whenever a loan for one of these countries comes under consideration at an IFI"—in 1981 the list reportedly included Vietnam, Cuba, Nicaragua, Afghanistan, and Grenada—experts prepared "a negative critique in the technical, economic language that IFI uses to evaluate proposals." Then U.S. officials relied on these critiques "to lobby against the loan with the . . . IFI and other countries' foreign ministers and representatives on [the] IFI's executive board."[77] Apparently the U.S. executive director to the International Monetary Fund (IMF) used these "technical" arguments to try to deny loans to Grenada in 1981 and 1983.

In November 1979 the PRG announced plans to construct an international airport at Point Salines to encourage tourism. The Carter administration, while skeptical, did nothing, but Reagan's advisers feared that the airport's 10,000-foot runway would be used by Cuban and Soviet military planes and tried vainly to persuade the European Economic Community (EEC) to refuse the PRG's request for assistance. Arguing that large loans to Grenada would add excessively to its external debt, U.S. officials evidently helped convince the IMF to reduce the loans from $9 million over three years to $3 million for one year. In August 1983 the United States again tried to stop or at least reduce a three-year IMF loan of $14.1 million to Grenada, but this time the other executive directors supported the staff's decision to offer the aid.[78] More than two years earlier, in June 1981, the State Department had put intense pressure on the Caribbean Development Bank to eliminate Grenada from a $4 million U.S. grant for basic human needs projects.[79] Moreover, the United States pressured the World Bank's International Development Agency to refuse a Grenadian request for a $3 million loan.[80] Yet, despite these vigorous efforts, the PRG was notably successful in obtaining international assistance. For example, the $23 million it received from Cuba, East Germany, the EEC, and Canada in 1982 was more than twice the amount that President Reagan proposed for the entire eastern Caribbean in his Caribbean Basin Initiative.

Covert operations against the Bishop government had been discussed by the Carter administration in the wake of Grenada's UN vote on Afghanistan, but after reviewing options the president apparently "rejected all but propaganda measures." In July 1981, however, the CIA approached the Senate Select Intelligence Committee with a plan to cause the PRG economic hardship. In February 1983 an unnamed CIA official denied that it sought to oust Bishop: "We may cause a little economic trouble, a little publicity, and [give] aid [to opposition groups], but we don't overthrow governments."[81] One member of the committee, however, characterized the proposal as economic destabilization affecting the political viability of the government." In any event, the scheme found little support among the senators. Lloyd Bentsen (D-TX), for example, exclaimed, "You've got to be kidding!" when told of the plan.

Military pressure, however, was exerted against Grenada. From August 1 to October 15, 1981, the United States staged Caribbean maneuvers. In large part, of course, they were designed to intimidate Cuba. On Vieques Island, a military installation near Puerto Rico, more than 200,000 U.S. and NATO personnel not only invaded "Red," described as "a mythical island interfering in the region and shipping arms to Central America," but also "Amber and the Amberdines," which, according to the Defense Department, was "our enemy in the Eastern Caribbean where U.S. hostages were in need of rescue." According to the fictional scenario, the U.S. troops, after rescuing the hostages, would remain on Amber to "install a regime favorable to the way of life we espouse."[82]

The administration applied rhetorical pressure too. In June 1982 Stephen D. Bosworth, principal deputy assistant secretary of state for inter-American affairs, told a House subcommittee that U.S.–Grenadian relations could not improve unless the Bishop government (1) halted its unrelenting stream of anti-American propaganda and false statements about U.S. policies and actions; (2) moved to "restore constitutional democracy, including prompt, free, and fair elections"; (3) returned to "the high standard of human rights observance that is typical" of the Caribbean Commonwealth (CARICOM) states; and (4) practiced "growing nonalignment rather than continuing its present role as a surrogate of Cuba."[83] President Reagan had made passing reference to "the tightening grip of the totalitarian left in Grenada" when announcing the Caribbean Basin Initiative in February 1982, but he lingered longer in remarks made in Barbados on April 8, 1982, while on a "working vacation": "El Salvador isn't the only country that's being threatened with Marxism, and I think all of us are concerned with the overturn of Westminster parliamentary democracy in Grenada. That country now bears the Soviet and Cuban trademark, which means that it will attempt to spread the virus among its neighbors."[84] Then, in a speech on Central America and El Salvador to the annual meeting of the National Association of Manufacturers in Washington on March 10, 1983, Reagan presented Grenada in the context of a geopolitical nightmare:

> Grenada, that tiny little island—with Cuba at the west end of the Caribbean, Grenada at the east end—that tiny little island is building now, or having built for it, on its soil and shores, a naval base, a superior air base, storage bases and facilities for the storage of munitions, barracks, and training ground for the military. I'm sure all of that is simply to encourage the export of nutmeg.
>
> People who make these arguments haven't taken a good look at a map lately or followed the extraordinary buildup of Soviet and Cuban military power in the region or read the Soviets' discussions about why the region is important to them and how they intend to use it.
>
> It isn't nutmeg that's at stake in the Caribbean and Central America; it is the United States national security.
>
> Soviet military theorists want to destroy our capacity to resupply Western Europe in case of an emergency. They want to tie down our attention and focus on our own southern border and so limit our capacity to act in more distant places, such as Europe, the Persian Gulf, the Indian Ocean, the Sea of Japan.
>
> Those Soviet theorists noticed what we failed to notice: that the Caribbean Sea and Central America constitute this nation's fourth border. If we must defend ourselves against [a] large, hostile military presence on our border, our freedom to act elsewhere to help others and to protect strategically vital sealanes and resources has been drastically diminished. They know this; they've written about this.

We've been slow to understand that the defense of the Caribbean and Central America against Marxist-Leninist takeover is vital to our national security in ways we're not accustomed to thinking about.[85]

Finally, and most spectacularly, in a nationwide address on national security on the evening of March 23, 1983, the President unveiled aerial reconnaissance photographs of Cuba, Nicaragua, and Grenada:

On the small island of Grenada, at the southern end of the Caribbean chain, the Cubans, with Soviet financing and backing, are in the process of building an airfield with a 10,000-foot runway. Grenada doesn't even have an air force. Who is it intended for? The Caribbean is a very important passageway for our international commerce and military lines of communication. More than half of all American oil imports now pass through the Caribbean. The rapid buildup of Grenada's military potential is unrelated to any conceivable threat to this island country of under 110,000 people and totally at odds with the pattern of other eastern Caribbean states, most of which are unarmed.

The Soviet-Cuban militarization of Grenada, in short, can only be seen as power projection into the region. And it is in this important economic and strategic area that we're trying to help the Governments of El Salvador, Costa Rica, Honduras, and others in their struggles for democracy against guerrillas supported through Cuba and Nicaragua.

These pictures only tell a small part of the story. I wish I could show you more without compromising our most sensitive intelligence sources and methods. But the Soviet Union is also supporting Cuban military forces in Angola and Ethiopia. They have bases in Ethiopia and South Yemen, near the Persian Gulf oil fields. They've taken over the port that we built at Cam Ranh Bay in Vietnam. And now for the first time in history, the Soviet Navy is a force to be reckoned with in the South Pacific.[86]

Thus, by the spring of 1983 the Reagan administration had elevated Grenada to the status of a serious security threat to the United States and its allies. Its strategic position in the eastern Caribbean allegedly formed the third point on a geopolitical triangle that stretched to Cuba and Nicaragua; its new airport would soon allow the Cubans and Soviets to threaten vital Caribbean sealanes; and Havana could use the island as a military bridge to Africa and as an ideological bridge to the eastern Caribbean. Finally, the administration even raised the spectre of another Cuban missile crisis. For example, Nestor D. Sanchez, deputy assistant secretary of state for inter-American affairs, claimed in February 1983 that Grenada's new military facilities "would provide air and naval bases . . . for the recovery of Soviet aircraft after strategic missions. It might also furnish missile sites for launching attacks against the United States with short and intermediate range missiles."[87]

The administration had virtually ended formal diplomatic relations with Grenada in 1981 by excluding it from the list of states to which the U.S. ambassador in Barbados was accredited. Occasionally, however, Grenadian Foreign Minister Unison Whiteman or an assistant was able to meet with mid-level U.S. embassy personnel in Bridgetown. Bishop wrote several letters to President Reagan asking for more normal diplomatic relations, but all went unanswered. Rumors about a U.S. or U.S.-supported invasion of Grenada, usually fueled by PRG statements, had routinely swept the island since the 1979 coup, but Reagan's March 23, 1983, speech seemed to have genuinely alarmed Bishop. Fidel Castro probably urged Bishop to try to talk to President Reagan. In any case, at the invitation of Transafrica, self-described as "the Black American Lobby for Africa and the Caribbean," and with the support of the congressional Black Caucus, Prime Minister Bishop came to Washington in early June 1983 to attempt to see the president. Not only was he prevented from doing so, but he was apparently rebuffed by the State Department as well until two senators, Claiborne Pell (D-RI), and Lowell Weicker (R-CT), intervened on his behalf. Soon thereafter, Bishop met for forty minutes with National Security Adviser William Clark and Deputy Secretary of State Kenneth Dam.[88] Bishop termed the meeting "a useful first step in the recommencement of dialogue between the governments" and evidently promised to hold elections within two years. He added that the talks had "delayed" an invasion but admitted that "we do not think the threat has been entirely removed."[89] U.S. officials declined to characterize the talks.

On October 19, after a serious split developed in the PRG leadership, Bishop was killed by troops loyal to his opponents. An entity calling itself the Revolutionary Military Council (RMC), apparently led by General Hudson Austin, declared a twenty-four-hour shoot-on-sight curfew. Six days later, 1,900 U.S. Marines and Army airborne troops, assisted by 300 men from a handful of Caribbean countries, landed on Grenada, the first time since 1965 that U.S. forces had participated in a Caribbean military action. President Reagan, accompanied by Prime Minister Eugenia Charles of Dominica, soon appeared on television to announce the operation and the reasons for it. Reagan explained that the United States had responded to an "urgent, formal request from the five-member Organization of Eastern Caribbean States (OECS)," plus Barbados and Jamaica, "to assist in a joint effort to restore order and democracy" on Grenada. He emphasized that "this collective action" had "been forced on us by events that have no precedent in the eastern Caribbean and no place in any civilized society." First, "a brutal gang of leftist thugs" had "violently seized power," thereby threatening the "personal safety" of between 800 and 1,000 U.S. citizens, including medical students and senior citizens. Second, the "rescue mission" had been carried out to forestall further chaos. Finally, Reagan proclaimed his wish "to assist in the restoration of conditions of law and order and of governmental institutions" to Grenada.[90]

We will not pass judgment on the factual accuracy of Reagan's statement, although it apparently contained several discrepancies,[91] but instead will examine the administration's efforts to legitimate its actions.

The primary impetus for the pressure campaign against Bishop came from the State Department, initially orchestrated by Haig, and later by Shultz and Assistant Secretary for Inter-American Affairs Langhorne Motley. It was strongly supported by a variety of mid-level political appointees, many of them Latin American specialists at State and the NSC, including Nestor D. Sanchez, Roger Fontaine, Otto Reich, and Constantine Menges. Weinberger and the Joint Chiefs of Staff (JCS) had no objections to staging Caribbean maneuvers to intimidate the PRG (and the Sandinistas).[92] But whereas the State Department and National Security Adviser Robert McFarlane strongly advocated the "rescue mission," representatives of the JCS resisted State's desire even to begin contingency planning for the evacuation of U.S. citizens. After Bishop's murder, they reluctantly agreed to do so, but Weinberger evinced little enthusiasm for the actual intervention, apparently fearing that it would whet the administration's appetite for riskier operations in Central America.[93]

In view of the psychological warfare that had been waged against the PRG for more than two years, the Reagan administration needed to allay the widespread suspicion that this operation was not simply a unilateral invasion by the "northern colossus." Thus Reagan and his spokespersons repeatedly emphasized that the United States had been "invited" to participate in a multinational humanitarian action. Secretary Shultz, Deputy Secretary of State Kenneth Dam, the U.S. ambassador to the Organization of American States, and others offered elaborate justifications, but Jeane Kirkpatrick and Ronald Reagan delivered the most comprehensive defenses. At the UN Security Council on October 27, Kirkpatrick began by challenging an alleged perspective about world politics that "treats the prohibition against the use of force as an absolute; and the injunction against intervention in the internal affairs of other states as the only obligation of states under the U.N. Charter." Instead, Kirkpatrick argued, "the prohibitions against the use of force in the U.N. Charter are contextual, not absolute. They provide ample justification for the use of force against force in pursuit of other values also inscribed in the Charter—freedom, democracy, peace." Thus, "the Charter does not require that peoples submit supinely to terror, nor that their neighbors be indifferent to their terrorization."

In evaluating the U.S. actions, one must begin, not with the October 25 landing, the ambassador suggested, but with the character of the Bishop government and the group that supplanted it. Bishop's government came to power in a coup, refused to hold elections, and "succumbed to superior force" when, "with the complicity of certain powers . . . it first arrested, then murdered Bishop and his ministers. Thus began what can only be called an authentic reign of terror in Grenada." Political violence thus had gripped the island well before the arrival of the task force on October 25.

Furthermore, the people of Grenada had been subjected to "foreign intervention" because Maurice Bishop had "freely offered his island as a base for the projection of Soviet military power in this hemisphere. The familiar pattern of militarization and Cubanization was already far advanced in Grenada." In effect, "Grenada's internal affairs had fallen under the permanent intervention of one neighboring and one remote tyranny. Its people were helpless in the grip of terror."

But why was the U.S. action different from other interventions that, under the guise of restoring self-determination, actually deny it? Because, she answered, "we in the task force intend . . . to leave Grenada just as soon as law is restored, and the instrumentalities of self-government—democratic government—have been put in place." But don't all contemporary governments claim to be democratic? What would ensure that this new Grenadian government will represent the authentic expression of the people any more than the "gang of thugs" from which the island was delivered? "There is," Kirkpatrick asserted, "a simple test," because free institutions—a free press, free trade unions, free elections, representative, responsible government—will be clearly in evidence.

Kirkpatrick then attempted to show that the "U.S. response was fully compatible with relevant international law and practice." Reagan's "brutal gang of leftist thugs" now became "madmen" and "terrorists," who, the United States reasonably concluded, could at any moment decide to hold 1,000 U.S. citizens hostage in a duplication of Iran. The ambassador admitted that in normal circumstances "concern for the safety of a state's nationals in a foreign country" does not justify military measures against that country. But in the Grenadian case no new government had replaced the old one; anarchy prevailed; and terrorists had wantonly endangered the lives of its own citizens, foreign nationals, and the security of neighboring states. In these circumstances, Kirkpatrick claimed, military action to protect endangered nationals was legally justified.

Second, the OECS concluded that the heavily armed "madmen" who had engineered the coup possessed an oversized army—one and one-half times the size of Jamaica's—supported by more than 600 armed Cubans and had ambitions for using Grenada as a center for subversion, sabotage, and infiltration. Lacking sufficient security forces, the OECS asked the United States to join the effort to restore order to Grenada and to remove it as a security threat.

Finally, Kirkpatrick vehemently denied that the U.S. action was somehow counterrevolutionary. "The issue was not revolution . . . nor was it the type of government Grenada possessed," for neither the OECS nor the United States had ever attempted "to affect the composition or character" of the Bishop government. Instead, the military power that Grenada had "amassed with Cuban and Soviet backing had fallen into the hands of individuals who could reasonably be expected to wield that awesome power against its neighbors." At the same time, however, "the coup leaders had no arguable claim to being the responsible government," as the failure of other states to recognize them, the governor-general's aid request, and their own declarations made clear. Kirkpatrick concluded that "in the context of these very particular, very unusual, perhaps unique circumstances, the United States decided to accede to the request of the OECS for aiding its collective efforts aimed at securing peace and stability in the Caribbean region."[94]

That same evening, President Reagan addressed the nation in an effort to defend his policies in Lebanon and Grenada. He claimed that the nation's will was being tested by Soviet-backed terrorism in both the Middle East and the Caribbean. After asserting that the United States as a global power had a variety of vital interests in the Middle East, the president warned that "if terrorism and intimidation succeed, it'll be a devastating blow to the peace process and to Israel's search for genuine security." Pointing to a massive Soviet military presence in Syria, he asked, "Can the United States, or the free world, for that matter, stand by and see the Middle East incorporated into the Soviet bloc?"

Then Reagan turned to Grenada and reminded his audience that Maurice Bishop, "a protégé of Fidel Castro," had overthrown a government elected under a "constitution left to the people by the British," sought Cuban help to build an airport, "which looks suspiciously suitable for military aircraft including Soviet-built long-range bombers," and alarmed his neighbors with a large army. Bishop, in turn, was ousted and subsequently killed by a group "even more radical and more devoted to Castro's Cuba than he had been." Now "Grenada was without a government, its only authority exercised by a self-proclaimed band of military men." Concerned that upward of 1,000 U.S. citizens on Grenada might "be harmed or held hostage," the president recounted how he had ordered a marine flotilla headed for Lebanon to be diverted to "the vicinity of Grenada in case there should be a need to evacuate our people." Then the OECS sent "an urgent request that we join them in a military operation to restore order and democracy to Grenada. These small peaceful nations needed our help." Hence Reagan acceded to their legitimate request and to his own concern for the U.S. citizens on the island. Resurrecting a theme from his Inaugural Address, he asserted that "the nightmare of our hostages in Iran must never be repeated."

President Reagan raised another issue connected with the landing, but did not quite offer it as a reason for the intervention: "We have discovered a complete base with weapons and communications equipment which makes it clear that Cuban occupation of the island had been planned." A warehouse of military equipment, stacked with enough weapons and ammunition to supply "thousands of terrorists," had been discovered. The president was unequivocal. Grenada "was a Soviet-Cuban colony being readied as a major military base to export terror and undermine democracy. We got there just in time."

Nor did Reagan leave any doubt about the relationship between Lebanon and Grenada: "Not only has Moscow assisted and encouraged the violence in both countries, but it provides direct support through a network of surrogates and terrorists. It is no coincidence that when the thugs tried to wrest control of Grenada, there were 30 Soviet advisers and hundreds of Cuban military and paramilitary forces on the island."[95]

Initial congressional reaction to the operation was largely negative. The Senate was not in session on October 25, but in the House several representatives voiced sharp criticism. For example, Don Bonker (D-WA) accused the administration of "a cavalier attitude about using military force to deal with diplomatic problems" and claimed that "it flies in the face of the president's condemnation of Soviet interference in other countries."[96] Howard Wolpe (D-MI) called the action an example of "gunboat diplomacy in direct contradiction to American ideals, traditions, and interests."[97] Edward J. Markey (D-MA) asked the president: "Where does all this military intervention end? Are the Marines going to become our new Foreign Service officers?" And George Miller (D-CA) maligned Reagan for refusing to meet with Maurice Bishop in June.

The next day, in the Senate, Gary Hart (D-CO) introduced a resolution to invoke the War Powers Resolution and "vowed to oppose any further extension of U.S. military involvement in this small island country."[98] The rest of the Senate, though, had virtually nothing to say about Grenada, and John Melcher (D-MT) warned that the intervention "should not distract us from the timely and urgently needed correction of a disastrous Lebanon policy."[99]

The Democrats continued the offensive in the House on October 26. Bob Edgar (D-PA) argued that American lives were not endangered in

Grenada, that the people of Grenada had not been consulted, and that the Congress had been circumvented. Noting that bloody coups d'état were a common occurrence in the world, he asked, "Are we to send in our marines and rangers every time there is an international disturbance?"[100] Major R. Owens (D-NY) called the invasion "illegal, immoral, and a wasteful expenditure of resources and human lives" and predicted that "the United States will now become a scapegoat" as the poor and unemployed throughout the Caribbean will blame this country for their condition."[101] Jim Leach (R-IA) reminded his colleagues that "our most loyal ally, Great Britain, strongly objects to our decision." Questioning the legality of the action, Leach complained that "we have reconstituted gunboat diplomacy in an era when the efficacy as well as the morality of great power intervention have come increasingly into question."[102] Gus Savage (D-IL) was even more blunt. He recalled Prime Minister Charles's briefing of the Black Caucus the previous day and terming her "this puppet of the president" who "represents 'Aunt Jemimaism' in geopolitics," claimed that the intervention had raised "to an international level Reagan's antebellum attitude towards blacks in this country."[103]

Most Republicans had immediately leaped to the president's defense, but by October 26 even some Democrats began to offer support. Most notable in this regard was Dante Fascell (D-FL), soon to become chairman of the House Foreign Affairs Committee. Although deploring the administration's failure to consult Congress prior to the invasion, be stated that "under the circumstances which existed in that region, which is virtually in our backyard, I believe the U.S. was justified."[104] Speaker Thomas P. ("Tip") O'Neill's (D-MA) first reaction was to urge national unity while the fighting was in progress, though he soon suggested that unless U.S. citizens had been in actual danger, the invasion would represent gunboat diplomacy.

As the medical students began returning from Grenada on October 26, however, and as U.S. forces began to uncover evidence of Cuban and Soviet weapons, criticism of Reagan diminished markedly. Tim Valentine (R-NC) exclaimed: "What a beautiful sight to see . . . our youthful countrymen kiss the soil of South Carolina with praise and thanks on their lips. Thank God for our Armed Forces."[105] And Dan Burton (R-IN) echoed: "We have heard the terms 'warmonger' and 'gunboat diplomacy' used. Well, last night we saw the results of that action. Students were getting off the plane. They were kissing the ground. They were saying 'God bless America.' They were thanking the president for sending in the marines and the rangers."[106] For William S. Broomfield (R-MI), the ranking Republican on the Foreign Affairs Committee: "It appears obvious . . . that the Soviets and Cubans had definite plans for turning Grenada into another Cuba. With yet another base in that area, the Soviets could continue to export revolution and terrorism to the small countries of the region.[107]

On October 28 the Senate voted 64–20 to invoke the War Powers Act in Grenada, but most of those who favored the resolution were careful to explain that their support did not imply criticism of the invasion. A few senators such as Gary Hart and Paul Sarbanes (D-MD) did use the resolution as the occasion to attack Reagan's action, but even Senator Hart tried to narrow its meaning: "This amendment . . . has nothing to do with whether the U.S. citizens were in danger. It does not question the authority of the president. . . . Whether we could have adopted some different remedy . . . is not an issue." The House also voted overwhelmingly (403–23) on November 1 to apply the War Powers Act to Grenada on these restricted legal grounds.

But when Steven D. Symms (R-ID) rose in the Senate to insert into a laudatory resolution a passage that would have described the rescue mission as "swift and effective action in enforcing the Monroe Doctrine," Majority Leader Howard Baker (R-TN) indicated that the White House preferred not to alter the resolution's language.[108] This extremely telling exchange provided an insight into the Reagan administration's dilemma. On the one hand, it wished to use the Grenada operation to help dissolve the "Vietnam syndrome" and to put other regional "undesirables" on notice, but it did not want to alienate friendly governments in the Caribbean and Central America. "Getting there just in time" to prevent the Sovietization of the Caribbean was one thing, invoking the Monroe Doctrine was something else again.

Despite the administration's elaborate efforts to portray the Grenada intervention as a humanitarian rescue mission, a compassionate response to an urgent request for help by small, friendly, democratic neighbors, and the successful foiling of a Soviet-Cuban colony, the American public supported the action because it was swift, conclusive, and relatively free of cost. Several polls conducted in the immediate aftermath of the operation affirmed the overwhelmingly pragmatic nature of the public's reactions. The November ABC–*Washington Post* survey, for example, showed 71 percent in favor and only 22 percent opposed to the Grenada landing. Yet although most people—50 to 35 percent in the *New York Times* poll taken after Reagan's October 27 speech—thought the United States had intervened to protect U.S. lives rather than overthrow a Marxist government, most people also believed that the U.S. citizens in Grenada had not been in a "great deal of danger." And in a *Newsweek*–Gallup canvass more respondents favored the withdrawal of U.S. troops as soon as the safety of the U.S. nationals was assured than those who wanted the troops to stay until Grenada was able to install a democratic government. Consistent with this finding was a *New York Times*–CBS survey that indicated that the public was opposed by a 60 to 21 percent margin to U.S. support for the Nicaraguan *contras*. Furthermore, at the same time that the public supported the president on Grenada, a plurality—47 to 43 percent—continued to believe that he was "too quick to employ U.S. forces," and another plurality—49 to 44 percent—felt more "uneasy" than "confident" about Reagan's ability to handle international crises. The public, in short, liked the Grenada invasion because it worked, but was unwilling to read broader lessons into the affair.

Nevertheless, despite this public assessment and despite the judgment of those such as Alexander Haig, who later claimed that Grenada could have been captured by the "Providence police force,"[109] Reagan repeatedly invoked the episode as one of his greatest achievements, a turning point in American foreign policy that had successfully challenged the Brezhnev Doctrine. But rhetoric aside, Reagan officials, as we later see, showed a curious reluctance to use the success in Grenada as a springboard to direct military action in Central America.

The Reagan administration, as it frequently reminded the public, had inherited from Carter a Central American situation marked by pervasive instability. In El Salvador leftist guerrillas had recently failed to topple the military government in a "final offensive" but seemed ready to try again. The Carter administration's efforts to encourage political reforms had not been notably successful, and right-wing death squads were suspected of murdering four American nuns in late 1980. In Nicaragua, Carter officials had watched Somoza fall in July 1979 to a revolutionary coalition subsequently dominated more and more by the Sandinistas.[110] Yet despite the avowed radicalism of this group, the Carter administration, recalling how Eisenhower's rough treatment of Castro had allegedly pushed Cuba toward Moscow, tried to establish normal relations with it. A leading Sandinista, Daniel Ortega, visited the White House, and Carter afterward asked Congress to authorize a $75 million loan to the new Nicaraguan government. A lengthy debate ensued, and though the administration eventually sent $118 million in direct aid and encouraged $262 million in multilateral assistance, it had to compete with a rapidly growing Cuban presence in Nicaragua. The CIA uncovered evidence of large arms shipments from the Sandinistas to the Salvadoran guerrillas, Farabundo Marti Liberacion Nacional (FMLN), thereby endangering the continuation of U.S. aid. By January 1981 it had become increasingly obvious that Nicaragua wished to reserve its closest relationships for Cuba and the Soviet Union, while rhetorically branding the United States as the "enemy."

The twin legacies of the Vietnam War and the Cuban Revolution would also help shape and constrain the Reagan administration's policies in Central America. Many of these officials agreed that Eisenhower had mishandled Castro by allowing him to consolidate his power before attempting to oust him in a "covert/overt," half-hearted invasion. Yet largely because of the limits imposed by fears of another Vietnam, the Reagan administration evolved a policy toward Nicaragua that in its bogus secrecy and limited support for proxies came to resemble an eight-year-long Bay of Pigs.

Secretary Haig had not desired such an outcome. From the beginning he had wanted to "go to the source" of Central American instability—Cuba—and in June 1981 had submitted to the NSC a specific proposal to bring "the overwhelming economic strength and political influence of the United States, together with the reality of its military power, to bear on Cuba by a naval blockade and other military actions." He "stood virtually alone," however, and the plan was rejected because (1) Weinberger feared another Vietnam quagmire, and the JCS feared a Soviet counteroffensive against a vulnerable U.S. asset; (2) the administration doubted that such actions could be publicly justified without prior Cuban provocation; (3) some State Department officials thought that Castro would continue to "export revolution" despite a blockade; and (4) the White House *troika* did not want to divert public attention from Reagan's economic priorities.[111]

Two months later, in a surprising move perhaps facilitated by the fact that Reagan had not yet filled key State positions with political appointees, Assistant Secretary of State for Inter-American Affairs Thomas Enders began a series of meetings with the Sandinistas to reach an agreement that would renew U.S. economic aid (halted in April) if Managua stopped arming the FMLN. Specifically, Enders proposed that (1) Nicaragua would cease its support of Central American insurgents; (2) Nicaragua would reduce its armed forces from 23,000 to 15,000; (3) the United States would promise to enforce its neutrality laws and to refrain from interfering in Nicaraguan internal affairs; (4) Washington would resume economic aid; and (5) both countries would expand cultural relations. Enders told the Sandinistas of U.S. concerns about political pluralism, a mixed economy, and their close ties with Moscow and Havana but, significantly, in the light of subsequent demands, did not include them in the proposal.[112] It appears unlikely, however, that Enders could have in any case persuaded the administration to support the scheme. He had already provoked resentment by excluding key officials from planning discussions and had travelled secretly and alone to Nicaragua.[113] Moreover, hardliners at the White House doubted that the Sandinistas would fulfill their promises, and these suspicions were fueled by reports that the *commandantes* "had continued to express support for the FMLN." In any case, the Nicaraguans, instead of directly responding to Enders's proposals, complained about U.S. naval exercises off the Honduran coast, the termination of aid, and Washington's reluctance to stop training exile groups. The Reagan administration, in search of a pretext to end negotiations, interpreted the Sandinista response as a final rejection. Yet Enders, in his eagerness for secrecy, had failed to leave a clear documentary trail, thereby complicating later administration attempts to demonstrate publicly that it had exhausted diplomacy before adopting stronger measures.[114]

Largely as a result of the persistence of John Carbaugh, an aide to Senator Jesse Helms (R-NC), the 1980 Republican convention had adopted a plank that supported "the efforts of the Nicaraguan people to establish a free and independent government." On March 9, 1981, Reagan signed a presidential finding, authorizing the CIA to help interdict arms flowing from Nicaragua to Central American guerrillas. CIA Director William Casey used this authority to begin organizing Nicaraguans opposed to the Sandinistas. Since late 1980 the Argentine military had been training some of Somoza's ex-Guardsmen in Honduras, and at an August 1981 meeting in Guatemala, U.S. officials persuaded these groups to unite and form the Nicaraguan Democratic Force (FDN).[115] Reagan's signing of National Security Decision Directive (NSDD) 17 on November 23, 1981, made support for the *contras* official U.S. policy by authorizing $19 million for a 500-member force to counter "the Cuban infrastructure in Nicaragua" that was "training and supplying arms to the Salvadoran guerrillas." Haig vehemently objected to the decision, arguing that it failed to address the larger problem of Soviet-Cuban intervention and correctly predicting that it would commit the administration to replacing the Sandinistas with a more congenial government."[116]

In March 1982 ex-Guardsmen trained by the CIA blew up two bridges in northern Nicaragua. This act not only had the effect of strengthening the administration's commitment to armed struggle but also caused the Sandinistas to intensify their repression of suspected sympathizers, thereby winning additional converts to the FDN. The House Permanent Select Intelligence Committee had voted to approve U.S. covert actions as long as their sole aim was arms interdiction. When news reports claimed that the *contras* wished to overthrow the Nicaraguan government, the House, in December 1982, adopted the first Boland amendment, 411–0, to prohibit expending U.S. funds for that purpose. Meanwhile, the Reagan administration, to its great annoyance, was also burdened with a regional initiative by Mexico, Panama, Colombia, and Venezuela—the "Contadora" countries—to negotiate a settlement with the Sandinistas.

During 1982 and 1983 it had become increasingly obvious to U.S. intelligence agencies that the flow of Nicaraguan arms to El Salvador had virtually stopped. But instead of moving to resuscitate the Enders proposals of 1981, Reagan signed another presidential finding in September 1983 that authorized support for the FDN in order to induce the Sandinistas to negotiate with its neighbors and to "pressure" them to cease assisting the FMLN. This open-ended goal paved the way for a greatly increased U.S. naval and military presence in Honduras and off the Nicaraguan coast, as well as a contingency plan for an invasion, if provoked. Yet, despite the heady atmosphere that prevailed at the White House in the aftermath of the Grenada "rescue mission," the administration refused to consider seriously directly intervening in Nicaragua, and it even discouraged the FDN from capturing Nicaraguan territory for the purpose of proclaiming a "Free Nicaragua" government. And it did so, at least in part, because of the vehement objections of Weinberger and the JCS. The secretary of defense repeatedly raised the specter of Vietnam in high-level policy discussions and "worried over the possibility that the president would be drawn into 'involuntary escalation.' "[117]

In October 1984 Weinberger took the extraordinary step of publicly laying down six "tests" that any proposed U.S. military action must meet prior to presidential approval. If followed, these tests would have effectively removed "limited war" as a foreign policy option. Yet the effectiveness of the Department of Defense's (DOD) preferred tactic—conducting provocative maneuvers in Honduras and along Nicaragua's coastlines—was seriously damaged by the White House decision to announce these operations, in advance and to issue assurances that they did not presage an invasion. This practice, of course, stemmed from the perceived need to avoid provoking a hostile domestic reaction.

During 1984 the House, partly in response to credible reports that the CIA had participated in mining Nicaraguan harbors and had helped the *contras* compile an "assassination manual," repeatedly voted to end funding of the "covert" war. It had first done so in September 1983 (H.R. 2760). Yet the Senate, controlled by the Republicans, refused to go along until late 1984. Finally, in March 1985 the House rejected Reagan's request for $14 million in military aid as well as two requests for "humanitarian assistance."[118] Soon thereafter, Daniel Ortega, in a politically obtuse move, visited Moscow, and the administration embarked on a fierce rhetorical campaign against him. Democrats, their ranks split and on the defensive, sought political cover in the form of "nonlethal, humanitarian" assistance for the *contras*. Reagan, for his part, sent a letter to Congress promising to "pursue political, not military solutions, in Central America." In June 1985 both houses voted to provide $27 million in humanitarian aid to the FDN as long as the *contras* stayed in their Honduran camps and observed a cease-fire. With this action Reagan had established the principle that the *contras* were a legitimate organization worthy of U.S. support, though it remained unclear exactly how humanitarian aid could do much more than feed them.

In February 1986 Reagan went back to Congress to ask for another $100 million, three-quarters of which was military. Once again the administration combined harsh rhetoric and symbolic concessions—the widely respected Philip Habib was appointed as special ambassador to Central America—to wear down congressional resistance. The administration, despite Reagan's pledge to seek a diplomatic resolution, tried its best to frustrate Contadora efforts while blaming Nicaragua for the failure to produce an acceptable treaty. In fact, neither nation wished to compromise, and Habib eventually resigned. When the World Court decided in June 1986 that the United States had violated international law by helping the *contras* mine Nicaraguan harbors and destroy transportation facilities, the Reagan administration rejected the judgment and reiterated its commitment to the FDN.

But the administration found it much more difficult to sustain its Nicaraguan policy in the wake of the sensational Iran-*contra* revelations. In its zeal to provide Nicaragua with a "democratic" alternative, Reagan officials had solicited *contra* funds from the Saudi royal family, the sultan of Brunei, and Taiwan. Moreover, in order to evade earlier congressional prohibitions against aiding the FDN, the NSC had helped to organize an "enterprise" to train and fund the *contras*. Thus Reagan's call for volunteerism and private-sector takeovers of previously public responsibilities reached their ultimate conclusion—a private foreign policy!

Nevertheless, Reagan survived politically and in the autumn of 1987 asked Congress to re-fund the FDN for yet another year. The administration skillfully exploited the public's infatuation with Lieutenant Colonel Oliver North, a mastermind of the Iran-*contra* scam, and the congressional testimony of a Sandinista defector, which, among other things, claimed that some of the *commandantes* maintained secret Swiss bank accounts. In late December Congress voted to keep the *contras* alive with $8 million in humanitarian aid and promised to vote again in February 1988.

By then, Costa Rican President Oscar Arias had developed a regional peace plan that seemed to meet almost all of the administration's professed goals, including internal democratization processes and verification procedures to ensure an end to arms trafficking. Reagan officials, however, while awkwardly welcoming the proposals in public, undertook a campaign to damage Arias's credibility and privately urged the FDN to harden its negotiating position. On March 23, 1988, the Sandinistas and the *contras* signed an agreement that Reagan officials feared would lead to the surrender of the FDN. One week later House Speaker Jim Wright (D-TX) succeeded in putting together $47 million in aid that included humanitarian assistance channeled through "neutral organizations," a fund to help children victimized by the war, and money for a verification commission. Both chambers overwhelmingly approved this package.

Yet many in the administration remained convinced that the Sandinistas would never allow "democracy" in Nicaragua and would interpret congressional action as an invitation to destroy the FDN. When, early in March, Congress refused to re-fund the *contras,* Reagan pounded his desk and exploded: "This is the same old thing by Congress. Look at all the countries that went down the tubes right after Vietnam because of congressional interference in foreign policy."[119]

Reagan's frustration should be measured against the administration's stubborn seven-year effort publicly to legitimate its Nicaraguan policy. From the beginning, its Central American initiatives had provoked controversy. Public hostility had greeted early efforts to shore up the Salvadoran junta with military aid and a few dozen U.S. advisers because it triggered widespread fears about another Vietnam in the making. Death squad atrocities, apparently carried out with the connivance of the Salvadoran government, outraged many members of Congress, as did Jeane Kirkpatrick's suggestion that the four murdered American nuns were partly responsible for their own deaths. But when the administration began to shift toward a policy of reform in El Salvador, primarily by encouraging legislative and presidential elections, congressional and public support notably increased. While a substantial number of congressional Democrats continued to question the Duarte government's commitment to land reform and human rights, by 1984 Reagan's Salvadoran policy had been substantially legitimated.

But Nicaragua soon replaced El Salvador as an object of domestic controversy and remained so despite the administration's unending verbal offensive designed to mobilize public support. Reagan literally tried everything to persuade Congress and the public of the wisdom of his Nicaraguan policy. At the core of this effort lay the multifaceted contention, coordinated by the Office of Public Diplomacy, that America's vital interests were at stake in Central America and that Nicaragua threatened U.S. security. In contrast to Vietnam, where Haig now claimed that national security had not been directly at issue after all, "in Central America we're talking about the strategic vulnerability of the Canal. . . . We are . . . at the core of United States hemispheric interests."[120] Unlike Southeast Asia, which was half a world away, Central America, the administration argued, was in "our backyard," and, with the Caribbean, formed "our fourth border," a "strategic basin" containing "vital" shipping lanes. Reagan recalled how Nazi submarines in 1942 had threatened these routes and had sunk several Allied ships. Other administration officials occasionally claimed that the Caribbean Basin possessed critical strategic materials. They even contended that the United States needed to preserve access to regional air and naval facilities in Puerto Rico, Cuba, and Honduras. More significant was the assertion that Nicaragua as a Soviet-Cuban outpost would pose a genuine threat to Central American stability and ultimately U.S. national security. Like Grenada, a Sovietized Nicaragua could be used as a missile and submarine base to launch attacks against the U.S. mainland. Administration spokespersons more frequently invoked a domino scenario, whereby other Central American states would be subverted, intimidated, or invaded by Nicaragua until Mexico itself crumbled. Moreover, they predicted that the resultant turmoil would unleash floods of refugees that would weaken—in unspecified ways—the social fabric of the United States.

But the administration implied that something more than American physical security was at stake—its credibility as a beacon of freedom and a world leader depended on its willingness to support the FDN. If the United States failed to act in Central America, where would it act? The line had to be drawn, or else our allies would doubt its reliability and its adversaries would be emboldened. Similar arguments had, of course, been used by Cold War presidents in a variety of contexts, but they had been rarely heard since Vietnam. After initially denying the validity of the Vietnam analogy to Central America, Reagan officials, as they scrambled for *contra* votes in Congress, began to encourage the comparison. In April 1985 Secretary Shultz noted that during the Vietnam War some Americans had made "an endless and shifting sequence of apologies for the Communists," had condemned "military solutions," and had then turned their attacks on the United States itself. He warned that "we should bear this past experience in mind in our contemporary debates," for "the litany of apology for Communists and condemnation for America and our friends is beginning again." In fact, "our goals in Central America *are* like those we had in Vietnam: democracy, economic progress, and security against aggression."[121] Reagan officials tread very carefully, however, and repeatedly claimed that U.S. support for the FDN constituted an *alternative* to direct intervention, not the prelude that congressional opponents feared. Indeed, Reagan argued that to oppose *contra* aid now made direct U.S. involvement in the future more likely.

He also tried to cast the Nicaraguan issue as a moral drama. What had the Sandinistas done to incur Reagan's wrath? After solemnly pledging to liberate Nicaragua from tyranny, they had instead "betrayed" their revolution by refusing to create a genuine democracy. By imprisoning their opponents, persecuting the Catholic church, forcibly relocating the Mesquito Indians, shutting down a free press, and building an enormous army, the

Sandinistas had transformed Nicaragua into a "totalitarian dungeon." Not only had they welcomed Cuban and Soviet military personnel and received vast quantities of offensive weapons, but they had invited "terrorists" to Nicaragua from Libya, Iran, and North Korea and had spearheaded a drive to export illegal drugs to the United States. Facing this unspeakable evil was the "democratic resistance," "our brothers, these freedom fighters of Nicaragua," "the moral equal of our Founding Fathers and the brave men and women of the French Resistance." For Reagan, "the struggle here is not right versus left; it is right versus wrong."[122] Rarely had a president used such words to describe the *U.S.* Army, let alone a five-year-old organization that critics claimed was dominated by Somozistas. Certainly no senior U.S. official had ever lavished such praise on the government of South Vietnam, for example. But that, of course, was the point.

Yet these efforts were damaged by claims that the administration was seeking to overthrow the Nicaraguan government. Reagan and his advisers at times halfheartedly denied these charges, but on other occasions implied that the Sandinistas had to be replaced or at least say "uncle." These congressional concerns compelled Reagan to legitimate his Nicaraguan policy as an effort to find a diplomatic solution. As a result, Reagan appointed a string of special ambassadors to Central America. They and Shultz engaged the Sandinistas in desultory bilateral discussions in Mexico and Nicaragua. But nothing was accomplished, for the Sandinistas demanded that the U.S. withdraw support from the *contras,* while the administration would accept nothing less than FDN participation in the Nicaraguan government. Nevertheless, diplomatic initiatives probably convinced twenty to thirty House Democrats to vote for *contra* aid.

Reagan also attempted to portray his policy as bipartisan and consensual and as part of a larger effort to bring democracy and stability to all of Central America. His Caribbean Basin Initiative, announced in early 1982 and passed by Congress in August 1983, provided economic and military assistance and investment and trade incentives to the entire region, except, of course, Cuba, Nicaragua, and Grenada. Turning to a favorite device, Reagan appointed the allegedly bipartisan Kissinger Commission, charged with developing additional policy recommendations for Central America. Composed of conservative to moderate Republicans and Democrats, it contended that the "roots of the crisis are both indigenous and foreign," but also claimed that "in the Central American–Caribbean region, our credibility world wide is engaged. The triumph of hostile forces in what the Soviets call the 'strategic rear' of the United States would be read as a sign of U.S. impotence."[123] Despite its endorsement of land reform, congressional liberals correctly saw the commission as a disguised attempt by the administration to create a center-right coalition supportive of aid to the *contras.*

Finally, Reagan officials portrayed non-Nicaraguan Central America as a hotbed of democratic vitality. The Sandinistas' totalitarian grip thus became ludicrously anachronistic as such states as Honduras and Guatemala allegedly became increasingly democratic. Yet Costa Rica, indisputably the region's foremost democracy, seemed equally critical of both Managua and Washington, and by 1988 the administration was even more seriously embarrassed by revelations tying the CIA to the drug trafficking Manuel Noriega of Panama. Reagan's presumably clear moral categories appeared to be blurring.

Until the blossoming of Soviet-American détente in 1987 and 1988 the tiny nation of Nicaragua had become *the* central preoccupation of American foreign policy and the focal point of presidential rhetoric. It was also partly responsible for creating the paramount crisis of the Reagan presidency. Yet the reasons for the administration's rather extraordinary exertions against it remained elusive. From the vantage point of the early 1980s, this policy seemed designed to implement the "prevailing with pride" strategy. At the least, it would have raised the cost that Moscow would be obliged to pay to retain a peripheral client, and a policy of unremitting pressure might have even succeeded in toppling the Sandinistas and thus punctured the Brezhnev Doctrine. Moreover, it would have provided an opportunity for the United States to atone in part for its mishandling of the Cuban Revolution in the late 1950s and early 1960s. Reagan, after all, had been disappointed when Kennedy had resolved the missile crisis without invading Cuba.[124] But the paltry sums that the administration requested from Congress to support the FDN undermined this explanation. While it was true that by the late 1980s the Nicaraguan economy lay in ruins, the reasons for its collapse had less to do with the *contras* than with governmental mismanagement, decreases in Soviet aid, and the U.S. trade embargo.[125] On the other hand, the administration could plausibly have claimed that its economic pressure had contributed to this situation. Yet the destruction of the Nicaraguan economy had never been publicly offered as a policy aim.

By the late 1980s there was a growing suspicion, however, that Reagan's Nicaragua policy had been a sop to pacify the hard right, while the administration built bridges to Gorbachev. John Carbaugh, the Helms aide who played an early role in bringing the *contras* to the administration's attention, suggested that "Haig and Enders realized they had to throw a bone to the right-wingers. They can't have the Soviet Union or the Middle East or Western Europe. All are too important."[126] But this explanation ignored Reagan's attitude. Was he part of this scheme, or had he been persuaded by Kirkpatrick, Casey, and other zealots to lead the charge against the

Sandinistas? Given the fact that Reagan remained committed to the "demo-cratic resistance" even after virtually all the original supporters had left the government, Carbaugh's thesis appeared rather dubious. But it did acknowl-edge the anomaly of a fiercely anti-Sandinista president strolling arm-in-arm through Red Square with his "friend," Mikhail Gorbachev, in May 1988.

A third, and somewhat more compelling, explanation would interpret Reagan's Nicaraguan policy as yet another example of the president's un-canny ability to know exactly how far to push a pet project in the face of public and congressional resistance. Recognizing from the beginning that his would inevitably be a Vietnam-traumatized administration, Reagan nev-ertheless saw in Central America the opportunity to defeat a Soviet proxy with relatively little risk. According to this view, the administration never had the slightest inclination to send U.S. troops to Nicaragua. At the least, Reagan's fierce rhetoric would have driven dissenting Democrats into a political tizzy by questioning their commitment to freedom and democracy. The Democratic Party could then be charged with "losing Nicaragua," and the Republicans could even more thoroughly dominate the national security issue.

But unlike Grenada, where Congress and the public applauded the suc-cess of the "rescue mission," the administration never obtained majority public backing for its Nicaraguan policy. By March 1986, those who be-lieved that Nicaragua posed a threat to the security of the United States had risen to 56 percent, though only 29 percent deemed it a "major" threat. Yet at no time between 1983 and 1987 did more than 28 percent believe that the United States should try secretly to overthrow the Sandinistas (March 1986), and by January 1987, immediately after Iran-*contra,* that figure had fallen to 16 percent. Opposition to a U.S. invasion of Nicaragua was com-parably high. Most of the public (57–59 percent) blamed the trouble in Central America on poverty and the lack of human rights, though about the same number opposed the spread of communism there. A large part of the public favored nonmilitary approaches to Nicaragua. For example, a May 1984 Harris poll revealed that 81 percent supported the Contadora process. And while public fears that the United States was headed for another Viet-nam in Central America fell from 68 percent in the early 1980s to 30 percent by 1986, support for the *contras* rarely rose above one-third. Most telling, perhaps, was that Reagan's overall approval rating consistently ran from 15 to 28 percent ahead of his Nicaraguan policy.[127]

Just before leaving office in January 1989, Lieutenant General Colin Powell, Reagan's sixth NSC adviser, admitted that the administration had failed to educate the public about the seriousness of the Nicaraguan prob-lem and blamed it on insufficient effort. Interviews that were conducted with NSC staffers confirmed that view.[128] It was certainly true that the public's understanding of the Central American situation remained very low. For example, an April 1986 CBS–*New York Times* poll showed that 50 percent of the public did not know anything about the Nicaraguan government and that among those who did, half believed it to be a right-wing dictatorship.[129] Nor did Reagan's rhetorical warfare change many people's minds. From mid-1983 to 1985 those who supported the overthrow of the Sandinistas rose from 23 to 32 percent, and from March 1985 to July 1986 approval of Reagan's handling of Nicaragua increased nine points to 35 percent.[130] Yet even this modest shift was erased by Iran-*contra*. What more could Reagan have done to "educate" the public?

But the Nicaragua issue did have a significant differential impact on the major political parties. A May 1986 *National Journal* poll indicated that 16 percent of Democrats and 36 percent of Republicans favored aid to the *contras,* while 75 percent of Democrats and 51 percent of GOP supporters opposed it. A 1985 poll showed that of the 38 percent of the public that knew of U.S. support for the *contras,* 67 percent of Republicans approved and 64 percent of Democrats opposed this policy.[131] In short, this issue seemed to divide the attentive public along party lines.

A New Foreign Policy Consensus?

President Reagan's rhetoric left little doubt about the answer to this question. As he put it in December 1988,

> In the decade of the eighties the cause of freedom and human rights has prospered and the spectre of nuclear war has been pushed back because the democracies have recovered their strength, their compass. Here at home a national consensus on the importance of strong national leadership is emerging. No legacy would make me more proud than leaving in place such a consensus for the cause of world freedom, a consensus that prevents a paralysis of American power from ever occurring again.[132]

Nor was he shy about claiming credit:

> And as I walk off into the city streets, a final word to the men and women of the Reagan revolution. . . . My friends: We did it. We weren't just marking time. We made a difference. We made the city stronger. We made the city freer, and we left her in good hands. All in all, not bad, not bad at all.[133]

And, in fact, a persuasive case could be made to support Reagan's claims. The United States did seem "more prosperous, more secure and happier"[134] than it had eight years before. An unprecedented period of recession-free, low-inflation economic growth had replaced the stagflationary rut of the

1970s. A resurgence of national self-confidence and pride, predicted by Reagan in 1981, had apparently swept away the guilt, doubt, and introspection of the previous decade. An ambitious program of military expansion and modernization, coupled with the administration's determination to deploy Pershing II and Cruise missiles, had frightened the Soviets into signing an asymmetrical arms control agreement and had paved the way for deep strategic cuts. The Reagan Doctrine, by deftly exploiting Soviet vulnerabilities on the periphery of its empire, had compelled a withdrawal from Afghanistan and had facilitated a settlement in Angola. The result was a new and infinitely better détente, based not on Soviet promises of domestic reform and international restraint but on deeds. And in contrast to the 1970s, when superpower détente had often haunted by the spectre of American decline and Russian ascendancy, the 1980s version featured a reenergized United States and an enervated, bankrupt Soviet Union. Finally, the Reagan foreign policy had evidently been instrumental in once again making America relevant to the rest of the world, for its message of freedom and democracy had found eager audiences everywhere. Now a democratic revolution was sweeping the globe from the Philippines and Latin America to Eastern Europe, China, and even the Soviet Union. Indeed, it was difficult to avoid the conclusion that the Cold War had ended (or nearly so), that the West had won, and that the old American dream of a world of liberal democratic states would soon be realized.

In the light of these achievements and prospects, was not Reagan also correct in claiming as his legacy the reemergence of a domestic foreign policy consensus? After all, signs of consensus abounded. At the elite level, scholars, pundits, and participants during the 1970s had emphasized the seemingly intractable divisions that hindered efforts to achieve a coherent, supportable foreign policy. The notion of consensus was rarely discussed. James Chace, in a 1978 *Foreign Affairs* essay, did so, but only to dismiss it as a remote possibility, and, as we have seen, neoconservatives waged a four-year war against the Carter foreign policy.[135] Yet by the mid-1980s this situation had begun to change. During the 1984 presidential campaign the Center for Security and International Studies sponsored a symposium on bipartisanship and consensus, and in early 1985 Richard Lugar (R-IN), the new chairman of the Senate Foreign Relations Committee, conducted hearings on "Commitments, Consensus, and U.S. Foreign Policy." And while neither exercise may have shown much interest in exposing a broad spectrum of opinion, more difficult to dismiss was a 1988 *Foreign Affairs* article by Henry Kissinger and Cyrus Vance, who buried old hatchets in order to formulate the outlines of a consensual foreign policy.[136] More pessimistically, the Foreign Policy Institute of Johns Hopkins University acknowledged that "during the past dozen years, the number and intensity of contentious issues in U.S. foreign and defense policy, already severe since the mid-1960s, have risen markedly and now threaten a serious breakdown in the policy process." But in early 1988 it launched a program designed to identify a "middle ground" where a bipartisan consensus could be built on significant issues of immediate relevance."[137] In short, on the eve of the 1988 presidential election, consensus, if not yet achieved, had once again become a prominent feature of elite discourse.

Moreover, by 1988 public attitudes about foreign policy, carefully measured in two extraordinarily detailed surveys—Americans Talk Security (ATS) and the Public Agenda Foundation (PAF)[138] project appeared to vindicate Reagan's claim of an emergent national consensus. Democratic pollster John Marttila, one of the principal ATS researchers, announced that "the president's success in negotiating with Mr. Gorbachev has . . . reestablished a national bipartisan consensus on U.S.-Soviet relations."[139] The twelve ATS reports demonstrated that about two-thirds of the public believed that the Reagan military buildup had been necessary, that about the same percentage counseled cautious negotiation with the Soviets from a position of U.S. strength, and that a strong majority thought that real opportunities existed for important breakthroughs in the superpower relationship.[140] The PAF project characterized these attitudes as a "rational, hard-headed stance on which a new national consensus can be firmly built."[141] Though voters remained suspicious of Soviet intentions, 57 percent believed that relations with the Soviets would continue to improve and lead to fundamental change.[142] In a May 1988 ATS survey 75 percent of the respondents gave excellent or good marks to Reagan for "standing up to the Soviets," 73 percent for "keeping America out of war," 73 percent for his arms control record, 71 percent for "developing a sound national defense," and 61 percent for using U.S. military power appropriately.[143] That same poll indicated that clear majorities credited Reagan with "promoting the spread of democracy," "preventing the spread of communism," and "winning respect for America." According to Mitchell E. Daniels, former chief political adviser to Reagan, "Right now, in at least its general outlines, Reagan's view of the world seems to be vindicated in the eyes of most people."[144] And these public perceptions provided the Republican Party with an important political edge, for most Americans had come to view it as the party of both strength *and* peace.

George Bush and Michael Dukakis conducted their fall 1988 campaigns as if convinced of an emergent foreign policy consensus. Bush skillfully portrayed himself as Reagan's rightful heir, willing and able to combine negotiations with national power, while dismissing the inexperienced governor of Massachusetts as a warmed-over Jimmy Carter who would bargain away American strength in order to cut imprudent deals with the Soviet Union. Dukakis, though suggesting that Gorbachev deserved much of the credit for improved superpower relations, pledged to pursue Reagan's Soviet policy, and applauded the window of opportunity opened by the president with an enthusiasm that even Bush found difficult to match.[145] Stung by Bush's charges of weakness on national security issues, Dukakis softened his earlier stand against modernizing the U.S. land-based nuclear deterrent, promised to continue SDI research, and took an unfortunate ride in a tank to demonstrate his toughness. Indeed, he did his best to avoid foreign policy issues except to implicate Bush in Iran-*contra* and sleazy dealings with General Noriega.

Had Ronald Reagan left America with its first genuine foreign policy consensus in twenty-five years? Had he, in the conceptual vocabulary of our study, legitimated his grand design, strategy, and tactics?

Certainly Reagan's grand design possessed enormous appeal, largely because it deftly employed powerful symbols to tap into important dimensions of America's civil religion. Reagan's articulation of a shining city on the hill—compassionate, moral, strong, and exceptional—constituted the secular equivalent of a stern yet loving Providence so ingrained in traditional American Protestantism. This city, dedicated to individual freedom and democratic government, had long served as a beacon of hope for all humanity. Reagan's "dream" was for the rest of the world to experience the exhilaration of a democratic revolution, and now that America was once again prosperous and strong, it could help others achieve freedom.

What gave this grand design significance was not its originality. Woodrow Wilson and early Cold War presidents had shared comparable visions. But Reagan was the first in a generation to invoke unabashedly these things without fueling firestorms of protests and derision. This "dream" resonated positively through much of the population in part because it captured the essence of the new patriotism and in part because, with the decline of communism and the retreat of the Soviet Union, it seemed both more plausible and less dangerous.

Furthermore, in contrast to the disguised and fuzzy designs of Nixon and Carter, which seemed retreatist and, in Nixon's case, amoral as well, Reagan's vision combined an unshakable faith in the future with moral fervor. In Reagan's America it became politically impermissible even to hint at national decline or to doubt the universal validity of the American dream. Not surprisingly, the president and other administration officials repeatedly scored points by portraying the Democratic Party as "doomsayers" and the "Blame-America-First crowd." The Democrats, including Dukakis, responded by protesting the genuineness of their optimism and patriotism. George Bush's pledge of allegiance ploy in the 1988 campaign should be viewed as a heavy-handed (and effective) effort to exploit this component of the Reagan legacy.

Reagan's resuscitation of a Wilsonian internationalist grand design—a world of free, democratic, and thus peaceful states—achieved both *normative* and *cognitive* legitimacy. But he proved less successful in legitimating his strategy, especially in regard to the critical issue of the use of U.S. military power abroad—the primary cause, after all, of the breakdown of the Cold War consensus.

As we have seen, the Reagan administration, on taking office, believed that a reconstituted domestic base—a revived economy, a vast rearmament program, and a renewed vision of and confidence in America and its role in the world—took priority over anything else. This strengthened domestic base could then be used to stop and gradually reverse the decline in America's international standing, to restore a willingness to employ national power, and to halt the expansion of Soviet influence as a prelude, perhaps, to putting Moscow on the defensive. In retrospect, as Robert W. Tucker correctly noted, President Reagan possessed an even grander strategic goal: the alteration of the essential conditions that had defined American security for most of the postwar era: nuclear deterrence and the Soviet threat.[146]

Reagan, to the utter disbelief of many observers, harbored deeply antinuclear sentiments. Though many of his advisers wished to transcend deterrence by achieving strategic superiority and war-fighting capabilities, Reagan embraced SDI primarily because he viewed nuclear weapons as intrinsically evil and threatening and only secondarily as an insurance policy against the possibility that an agreement eliminating all nuclear weapons might eventually be violated.[147] Moreover, while these advisers offered arms control proposals and verification demands that they knew the Soviet Union would reject, Reagan took these initiatives seriously. When Gorbachev surprisingly accepted many of them, Reagan, to the horror of Weinberger, Richard Perle, and others, moved to conclude agreements that eliminated intermediate-range nuclear forces and anticipated deep strategic reductions. A clear majority of the public supported SDI as a population shield and START as a way to reduce nuclear arms.[148] Though most experts continued to dismiss SDI as either technologically infeasible—at least its "leakproof" version—or strategically destabilizing or both, Reagan nevertheless played a major role in forging a nascent antinuclear national consensus. But if Reagan helped erode the public's faith in nuclear deterrence, it remained to be seen what, if anything, would replace it.

On the other hand, Reagan's antipathy toward containment had been more widely recognized—and feared. These long-standing moral and strategic doubts, which he shared with many American conservatives, dated at least from the 1950s. For Reagan, the U.S.'s failure in Vietnam demonstrated the moral and strategic bankruptcy of containment, not because it had produced indiscriminate intervention, as liberal critics had claimed, but because it was insufficiently ambitious. Hence the Johnson administration, in its half-hearted attempt to implement containment in Vietnam, refused to win the war by destroying the external source, of Vietcong support. That decision had produced a military stalemate, which in turn unleashed the antiwar movement at home. It and Congress then proceeded to prevent U.S. forces from winning in Vietnam. Moreover, the war's legacy left a deep national skepticism about the overall utility and legitimacy of American military power.

The Soviet Union, according to this view, had taken advantage of this post-Vietnam paralysis to expand its global influence vastly. The United States, Reagan and many of his advisers believed, might exploit the resulting imperial overstretch if it could move beyond containment to chip away at these new outposts and perhaps trigger a chain reaction throughout the Soviet empire. By 1985 this vague aspiration had been codified in the Reagan Doctrine, which proclaimed for the United States the right to intervene against Marxist-Leninist governments on the grounds that they had come to power through illegitimate means.

Yet in the absence of a new public consensus about the proper use of U.S. military power, which in turn required a drastically revised memory of the Vietnam War, the grand objectives of the Reagan Doctrine could not be fulfilled. Nevertheless, as we have seen, the administration in its otherwise assertive declaratory history of recent American foreign policy, tried to avoid even mentioning Vietnam. It certainly did not undertake a systematic revision of the prevailing understanding of the war. The very nature of the Reagan Doctrine—the support of "freedom fighters" as an alternative to direct intervention—implicitly acknowledged the administration's refusal to challenge the "Vietnam syndrome," despite occasional rhetoric about the "noble cause." It might disparage the "Solarz Doctrine" as the willingness to aid anti-Soviet guerrillas as long as they stayed "eight time zones away," but the eagerness of anti-*contra* Democrats to support Afghan and Angolan rebels went to the heart of the matter. There was, after all, absolutely no possibility that U.S. troops would be sent to rescue the *mujahadeen* or UNITA (National Union for the Total Independence of Angola), but both Congress and the nation fretted that Reagan would indeed directly intervene to save the FDN or facilitate their overthrow of the Sandinistas. And, as we have seen, the administration itself remained ambivalent about whether the *contras* would suck America into another Vietnam-type quagmire. The Grenada "rescue mission" and the April 1986 bombing of Libya demonstrated that the public would support low-risk, ends-specific, limited-cost military operations, but it would doubtless have also supported a successful "Desert One" outcome in the Carter years. After eight years of Reagan rhetoric about a fully democratic world, the nation remained deeply divided about the external conditions of American security. A January 1989 ATS poll indicated that a 49 to 45 percent plurality agreed that the failure in Vietnam showed that the United States should only fight a war to repel an invasion of the nation itself.[149] If, however, the Cold War had all but ended and the world was on the verge of universal democracy, then the continuing dissensus about U.S. military power would presumably be irrelevant, for there would no longer be any need to intervene anywhere.

Reagan's détente indeed attained a domestic legitimacy that far exceeded Nixon's. Unlike the early 1970s, when the so-called global correlation of forces appeared to tilt away from the West toward Moscow (and the Third World as well), Détente II crystallized at a time of perceived U.S. resurgence and growing Soviet weakness. On that basis alone, it became much more difficult for American skeptics to dismiss Reagan's détente as disguised appeasement. Those who tried did so largely from *within* the administration, but by late 1987 most of them had resigned. Second, whereas a politically insecure Nixon had promised much and delivered relatively little, Détente II's evident accomplishments came as a pleasant surprise in part because Reagan had not raised public expectations. When, with relatively little forewarning, the Soviets withdrew from Afghanistan, showed new interest in an Angolan compromise, signed an asymmetrical INF treaty with an intrusive inspection regime, and announced *glasnost* and *perestroika* at home, the American public grew increasingly optimistic about the prospects for superpower amity. Moreover, much of the public remembered the disillusionment produced by the disappointments of Détente I and was more inclined to proceed cautiously this time.[150]

Finally, and perhaps most important, in contrast to the Nixon–Kissinger strategy, which had insisted that Soviet domestic institutions be insulated from the issue of superpower relations, from the start Reagan had emphasized the moral shortcomings of the Soviet system. And while he never explicitly made internal reform a precondition for improved relations, the administration did put human rights on the agenda of every Reagan–Gorbachev summit and publicly applauded Soviet progress. Given this record, the public seemed understandably puzzled when Reagan during the 1988 Moscow summit blamed remaining Soviet domestic repression not on communism but on "bureaucracy." The Soviet Union had apparently become just another overcentralized state.

But if Nixon's détente lacked domestic legitimacy because it tried to ignore Moscow's moral turpitude, Détente II risked becoming hostage to ever expanding Soviet political reforms. During 1988 these reforms, as well as greatly moderated external behavior, were largely responsible for lowering by fifteen points (45 percent) the percentage of Americans who believed the Soviet Union constituted a serious threat to the United States. Nevertheless, 66 percent still believed that communism threatened American moral and religious values.[151] If Gorbachev's political reforms had been halted or reversed, Détente II would have been difficult to sustain in the United States even if Soviet foreign policy had failed to grow more provocative. In this sense, Reagan's domestically appealing dream of a democratic world inevitably endangered any détente that did not demand continued Soviet democratization.

At the same time, the rather drastic diminution of the perceived Soviet threat thrust to the surface a variety of less conventional security issues that hounded the Reagan administration during its final months in office. Thus, in the 1988 ATS surveys the public consistently indicated that international drug trafficking, terrorism, nuclear proliferation, and economic competition from Japan and West Germany would pose greater threats to the United States in the 1990s than Soviet expansionism.[152] Moreover, fewer than 50 percent believed that the administration had handled these issues well, while a mere 26 percent approved of its policy toward General Manuel Noriega.[153] Yet in view of the experience of the past forty-five years, it seemed likely that if Détente II had begun to unravel, public concerns about the Soviet Union would have pushed these newer issues to the background.

In sum, while Ronald Reagan did achieve more domestic legitimacy for his foreign policy strategy than any other post-Vietnam president, his accomplishments should not be exaggerated. He helped shake the public's faith in nuclear deterrence without necessarily providing a workable alternative. He argued that U.S. support for anti-Soviet "freedom fighters" constituted self-defense, but most of the public remained unmoved by the primary focus of the Reagan Doctrine. And although his Soviet policies were overwhelmingly popular with the American public, Reagan's détente—built on the public expectation of continuing Soviet democratization—could have proven to be evanescent.

Yet there can be little doubt that Reagan's rhetoric—central to his foreign policy tactics—captivated the American public like no president since Franklin D. Roosevelt or perhaps John F. Kennedy. Whether employed to send hostile or friendly signals to Moscow or to mobilize domestic support,

Reagan's words were paramount. And when his simple moral messages became uncharacteristically garbled, as during the Iran-*contra* affair, Reagan's public standing plummeted. Usually, however, Reagan (and his speechwriters) used words to spectacular effect to make his policies appear not only prudent but ethically superior. And that, ironically, was achieved by a president who presided over an administration marked by more scandal than any since Warren G. Harding.

Did Reagan reconstruct the *cultural* components of a domestic foreign policy consensus? At the conclusion of his first Inaugural Address the new president told a story about Martin Treptow, a doughboy killed in France. On his body was found a diary containing an entry entitled "My Pledge." It read: "America must win this war. Therefore I will work, I will save, I will sacrifice, I will endure, I will fight cheerfully and do my utmost, as if the issue of the whole struggle depended on me alone." But this tale did not foreshadow a "bear any burden, pay any price" message, for Reagan quickly assured the nation that the present crisis did not demand the sort of sacrifice made by Martin Treptow. Instead, it would require only "our best effort and our willingness to believe in ourselves and to believe in our capacity to perform great deeds. . . ."[154] Three years later, George Shultz, in a surprisingly frank statement, admitted that "We cannot pay *any price* or bear *any* burden. We must discriminate. We, must be prudent and careful. . . . " Yet while praising Kennedy's inspiring vision, Shultz ridiculed Jimmy Carter's emphasis on global complexity as "a counsel of helplessness," unworthy of an American president.[155]

Notwithstanding the secretary's reproof, Carter, as we have seen, did search for ways to reinstall an ethic of sacrifice in the American public and delivered sobering sermons about limits and constraints. The same cannot be said for President Reagan. Just as his invocation of the traditional domestic symbols of family and God disguised a message of national self-indulgence (except, of course, for the poor), so too did his rhetoric about a world democratic revolution ask very little of the American people. That was the meaning of his Martin Treptow homily, and it set the tone for the ensuing eight years: pride and confidence without sacrifice. According to Reagan, false limits had been imposed on Americans by an obtrusive federal government, which constrained individual freedom, and naysaying experts, who had lost faith in the American dream.

The nation had, of course, for most of the post-1945 era demonstrated a disturbing reluctance to pay for what it wanted. Harry Truman, for example, faced a public that simultaneously demanded military demobilization and a vigorous assault on international communism. NSC-68 had squared this circle by reassuring him that economic growth, rather than increased taxation, could finance much higher defense spending. But what had previously been done sporadically, Ronald Reagan institutionalized by tolerating enormous budget deficits that eventually became a structural feature of the U.S. economy. Moreover, by banishing words like *decline, limits,* and even *solvency* from contemporary political discourse, Reagan repeatedly refused to confront the public with an honest appraisal of America's true global position.[156] Reagan sated the public's understandable desire to "feel good" and thus facilitated a cultural consensus that involved a large dose of illusion.

But not even the irrepressibly optimistic Ronald Reagan could claim to have reconstructed a *procedural* foreign policy consensus. Most observers agreed that he left executive-legislative relations in at least as much disarray as he had found them in 1981. In one of his valedictory addresses he blamed Congress for "on-again, off-again indecisiveness on resisting Sandinista tyranny and aggression" that "left Central America a region of continuing danger." Moreover, Reagan suggested that some congressional actions in foreign affairs—for example, the War Powers Resolution and attempts to restrict the president's power to implement treaties (that is, ABM)—had institutionalized an "adversarial relationship." These and other legislative intrusions had weakened the "strength and resiliency of the presidency."[157] His words echoed those of Oliver North, who eighteen months before had indicted Congress for its "fickle, vacillating, unpredictable, on-again, off-again policy toward the Nicaraguan democratic resistance."[158] At least some members of Congress agreed with Reagan's diagnosis. Two prominent senators, David L. Boren (D-OK) and John C. Danforth (R-MO), after surveying two decades of congressional activism in foreign affairs, deemed much of it "incessant and irrelevant meddling."[159] Thus, members of Congress "take almost limitless opportunities to specify everything from the maximum allowable height above sea level of embassies to the precise manner of deployment of U.S. forces in the Persian Gulf."[160] Or to cite another example, a task force appointed by the House Foreign Affairs Committee to review Congress's role in foreign aid programs and cochaired by Lee Hamilton (D-IN) and Benjamin Gilman (R-NY) concluded that "foreign assistance is vital to promoting U.S. foreign policy and domestic interests, but the program is hamstrung by too many conflicting objectives, legislative conditions, earmarks, and bureaucratic red tape."[161] One scholar, after interviewing substantial numbers of congressional members and staffers, found that most of the Republicans and perhaps half of the Democrats believed that Congress intervened too directly in the conduct of foreign policy, was too involved in policy formulation, and that its deliberative function had consequently suffered.[162]

But some of Reagan's most exuberant admirers blamed the president for allowing Congress to gain this allegedly disproportionate influence over foreign policy. According to this reasoning, Reagan had erred in failing to force an up-or-down vote by Congress that would have established clear responsibility if the *contras* were defeated. Moreover, instead of permitting Attorney General Edwin Meese to treat Iran-*contra* as a possible crime, the president should have told the American people immediately that while the diversion of profits had not been authorized, it was consistent with his policy of using the White House to support the FDN. But rather than claim executive supremacy, he invoked the "ignorance" defense and thus nearly paralyzed the presidency for his remaining two years in office.[163] As George Bush prepared to enter the White House, op-ed pages and policy journals brimmed with urgent advice about the need to restore "bipartisanship."[164]

No doubt pervasive congressional intrusions into the technical minutiae of foreign policy had frequently degenerated into absurdity, and some of the proposals for procedural reform would have helped eliminate these sorts of roadblocks and detours. Yet the causes of presidential-congressional frustrations went deeper. Many of these disputes, as we have previously noted in our discussion of the Nixon and Carter years, reflected genuine *policy* disagreements about the requirements of U.S. security and America's role in the world, and they continued to characterize executive-legislative conflicts during the Reagan administration. Nor can this turmoil be attributed primarily to "mere" partisanship, though with the House under Democratic control for Reagan's entire tenure and the Senate as well after 1986, this factor surely played a role. But the Democratic Party itself continued to suffer from the ideological tensions that had marked its foreign policy outlook since the mid-1960s. During the Reagan administration it contained at least three identifiable foreign policy factions that, although all subscribing to a vague vision of internationalism, differed sharply on several important issues involving, for example, aid to the *contras,* funding for SDI, free trade, and South African sanctions. Indeed, Dukakis's virtual silence on foreign policy during the 1988 campaign stemmed form his need to keep the Sam Nunn–Chuck Robb wing and the Jesse Jackson wing from open warfare. And while many observers believed that Bush was politically vulnerable on the *contra* issue, Dukakis could not raise it because he and his chosen running mate, Lloyd Bentsen (D-TX), took opposing sides on the funding question.

But if some congressional Democrats relied on procedural devices to obstruct administration policies, Ronald Reagan's reluctance to reassert boldly claims of presidential supremacy in foreign affairs demonstrated the continuing relevance of the Vietnam legacy. To be sure, he grumbled about the Boland amendments, challenged the constitutionality of the War Powers

Resolution, argued against stronger South African sanctions, and denounced Senate efforts to compel a strict interpretation of the ABM Treaty. Yet in the end he compromised or surrendered on all these issues. And he did so because, his rhetoric notwithstanding, he appreciate the limits imposed on presidential prerogatives by the public's collective memory of Vietnam.

Notes

1. See Jeffrey B. Abramson, F. Christopher Atherton, and Garry R. Orren, *The Electronic Commonwealth: The Impact of New Media Technologies on Democratic Politics.*

2. Alonzo M. Hamby, *Liberalism and Its Challengers: F.D.R. to Reagan,* p. 350.

3. Hugh Heclo, "Reaganism and the Search for a Public Philosophy," p. 39.

4. Craig Allen Smith, "Mister Reagan's Neighborhood: Rhetoric and National Unity," pp. 220–21.

5. Ronald Reagan, "Address before a Joint Session of the Congress on the State of the Union," January 25, 1983.

6. Ronald Reagan, "Inaugural Address," January 20, 1981.

7. William K. Muir Jr., "Ronald Reagan: The Primacy of Rhetoric," p. 271.

8. Ronald Reagan, "Address to the Nation on the Economy," February 5, 1981.

9. Ronald Reagan, "Address to the Nation on the Economy," October 13, 1982.

10. Reagan, "Economy Address," February 5, 1981; Reagan, "Address on Economy," October 13, 1982.

11. Ronald Reagan, "Address before a Joint Session of the Congress on the State of the Union," January 25, 1984.

12. Heclo, "Reaganism," pp. 39–40.

13. Quoted in ibid., p. 43.

14. Ibid.

15. Ibid., p. 46.

16. Ronald Reagan, "Remarks at the Annual Convention of the American Bar Association," July 8, 1985.

17. William Greider, "The Education of David Stockman," pp. 40–45.

18. Ronald Reagan, "Address to Members of the British Parliament."

19. Samuel P. Huntington, "The Defense Policy of the Reagan Administration, 1981–1982," p. 92.

20. Ibid., p. 94.

21. William P. Clark, "National Security Strategy," May 21, 1982.

22. Ibid.

23. Huntington, "Defense Policy," p. 98.

24. Ibid., p. 101.

25. *New York Times,* June 26, 1981, p. 11; *New York Times,* May 30, 1982, pp. 1 and 12. Caspar W. Weinberger, *Annual Report to the Congress Fiscal Year 1983,* pp. 1–16.

26. Jeane J. Kirkpatrick, "Dictatorships and Double Standards," pp. 34–45. In this article Kirkpatrick castigated the Carter administration for its harsh public criticism of friendly dictators such as Anastazio Somoza for human rights violations, while largely ignoring the supposedly much more serious transgressions of totalitarian regimes. This strategy had played into Moscow's hands, she argued, by destabilizing these dictatorships and bringing to power unreformable totalitarians.

27. *New York Times,* June 1, 1986, p. 6.

28. Gaddis, *Strategies of Containment,* pp. 227–28.

29. Barry Blechman with Ethan Gutmann, "A $100 Billion Understanding," p. 74.

30. Terry L. Deibel, "Reagan's Mixed Legacy," p. 55.

31. Coral Bell, "From Carter to Reagan," p. 496.

32. Peter M. Benda and Charles H. Levine, "Reagan and the Bureaucracy: The Bequest, the Promise, and the Legacy," p. 136.

33. Muir, "The Primacy of Rhetoric," pp. 289, 291, and 290.

34. Alexander M. Haig Jr., "Relationship of Foreign and Defense Policies."

35. Alexander M. Haig Jr., "American Power and American Purpose."

36. Ronald Reagan, "Remarks at the Annual Washington Conference of the American Legion," February 22, 1983.

37. Ronald Reagan, "Question-and-Answer Session with High School Students on Domestic and Foreign Policy Issues," January 21, 1983.

38. Ronald Reagan, "Excerpts from an Interview with Walter Cronkite of CBS News," March 3, 1981.

39. Ronald Reagan, "Address to the National Republican Convention in Dallas, Texas," August 23, 1984.

40. Ronald Reagan, "Address to the Nation on National Defense and National Security," March 23, 1983.

41. Ronald Reagan, "Question-and-Answer with Reporters on Domestic and Foreign Policy Issues," May 4, 1983.

42. Ronald Reagan, "Address Before a Joint Session of the Congress on Central America," April 27, 1983.

43. See Ronald Reagan, "Interview with Representatives of NHK Television in Tokyo, Japan," November 11, 1983.

44. Haig, "Relationship of Policies."

45. Ronald Reagan, "Address to Members of the British Parliament."

46. Ronald Reagan, "Paths toward Peace: Deterrence and Arms Control," November 22, 1982.

47. Jeane J. Kirkpatrick, "The Atlantic Alliance and the American National Interest." Emphasis added.

48. *New York Times,* August 19, 1980, p. D17.

49. *New York Times,* February 21, 1982, p. 2 (IV).

50. Ronald Reagan, "Remarks on Presenting the Medal of Honor to Master Sergeant Roy P. Benavidez," February 24, 1981.

51. Ronald Reagan, "The President's News Conference," March 6, 1981.

52. Ronald Reagan, "The President's News Conference," April 18, 1985.

53. Ronald Reagan, "Remarks to the Corps of Cadets at the U.S. Military Academy," October 28, 1987.

54. Ronald Reagan, "Remarks to the World Affairs Council of Western Massachusetts in Springfield, Massachusetts," April 21, 1988.

55. Ronald Reagan, "Remarks and a Question-and-Answer Session with Students and Guests at the University of Virginia in Charlottesville, Virginia," December 16, 1988.

56. Ronald Reagan, "Farewell Address to the Nation," January 11, 1989.

57. I.M. Destler, "The Evolution of Reagan Foreign Policy," pp. 130–31.

58. Bell, "From Carter to Reagan," p. 492.

59. Ronald Reagan, "Address at Commencement Exercises at the U.S. Military Academy," May 21, 1981.

60. John Lewis Gaddis, "Remarks at Panel on the Reagan Foreign Policy Legacy."

61. See, for example, Michael Krepon, *Strategic Stalemate: Nuclear Weapons and Arms Control in American Politics.*

62. Ronald Reagan, "Address to the Nation on the Iran Arms and *Contra* Aid Controversy," November 13, 1986.

63. CBS/*New York Times* Poll, September 10, 1986, and November 13, 1986.

64. Background interviews, May 1988.

65. Ronald Reagan, "Address Before a Joint Session of the Congress on the State of the Union," February 6, 1985.

66. Ibid.

67. Ibid.

68. Ronald Reagan, "Remarks on the Caribbean Basin Initiative to the Permanent Council of the Organization of American States," February 24, 1982.

69. Ronald Reagan, "Radio Address to the Nation on Central America," February 14, 1985.

70. Lewis Tambs, ed., The Committee of Santa Fe, *A New Inter-American Policy for the Eighties*, p. 52.

71. Ibid.

72. Ibid.

73. Ibid., p. 26.

74. Sally A. Shelton, *Hearing before the Subcommittee on Inter-American Affairs of the Committee on Foreign Affairs,* "United States Policy toward Grenada" p. 56.

75. *Washington Post,* July 6, 1979, A1.

76. Caleb Rossiter, "The Financial Hit List," p. 4.

77. Ibid.

78. Ibid.

79. *Washington Post,* February 27, 1983, p. A1.

80. *Transafrica Forum,* November–December 1983, p. 7.

81. *Washington Post,* February 27, 1983, p. A1.

82. *Transafrica Forum,* November–December 1983, p. 7.

83. U.S. Congress, House, *Hearing on Grenada, 1982,* p. 31.

84. Ronald Reagan, "Remarks at Bridgetown, Barbados," April 9, 1982.

85. Ronald Reagan, "Central America and El Salvador at the Annual Meeting of the National Association of Manufacturers," March 10, 1983.

86. Ronald Reagan, "Address to the Nation on Defense and National Security," March 23, 1983.

87. *Washington Post,* February 27, 1983, p. A1.

88. *Congressional Record,* October 28, 1983, S14884.

89. *Washington Post,* June 8, 1983, p. A10; New York Times, June 10, 1983, p. 8.

90. Ronald Reagan, "Remarks of the President and Prime Minister Eugenia Charles of Dominica Announcing the Deployment of United States Forces in Grenada," October 25, 1983.

91. For a fuller analysis, see Kai P. Schoenhals and Richard A. Melanson, *Revolution and Intervention in Grenada: The New Jewel Movement, the United States, and the Caribbean,* pp. 139–47.

92. Background interviews, Washington, D.C., Summer 1984.

93. *New York Times,* November 7, 1983, p. 12.

94. "Ambassador Kirkpatrick's Statement, United Nations Security Council," October 27, 1983.

95. Ronald Reagan, "Address to the Nation on Events in Lebanon and Grenada," October 27, 1983.

96. *Congressional Record,* October 25, 1983, H8580.

97. *Congressional Record,* October 25, 1983, H8582.

98. *Congressional Record,* October 26, 1983, S14694.

99. *Congressional Record,* October 26, 1983, S14695.
100. *Congressional Record,* October 26, 1983, H8639.
101. *Congressional Record,* October 26, 1983, H8640.
102. *Congressional Record,* October 26, 1983, H8644.
103. *Congressional Record,* October 26, 1983, H8646.
104. *Congressional Record,* October 26, 1983, H8691.
105. *Congressional Record,* October 27, 1983, H8703.
106. *Congressional Record,* October 27, 1983, H8706.
107. *Congressional Record,* October 28, 1983, H8846.
108. *Congressional Record,* October 28, 1983, S14870.
109. *New York Times,* June 21, 1989, p. C22.
110. Until the very eve of the Sandinista takeover, the administration pursued its search for a "moderate" alternative to Somoza and the *Frente Sandinista de Liberacion National (FSLN).*
111. Robert A. Pastor, *Condemned to Repetition: The United States and Nicaragua,* p. 236.
112. Ibid.
113. Roy Gutman, *Banana Diplomacy: The Making of American Policy in Nicaragua, 1981–1987,* p. 78.
114. Ibid.
115. Pastor, *Condemned to Repetition,* p. 237.
116. Testimony of Alexander M. Haig Jr., *Hearings before the Committee on Foreign Relations,* U.S. Senate, "Commitments, Consensus, and U.S. Foreign Policy," pp. 233–34, 242–43.
117. Alexander M. Haig Jr., *Caveat: Realism, Reagan, and Foreign Policy,* pp. 127–28.
118. Cynthia Arnson, "The Reagan Administration, Congress, and Central America: The Search for Consensus," p. 46.
119. Fred Barnes, "Reagan's Last Stand," p. 10.
120. *Economist,* February 13, 1982, p. 26.
121. George Shultz, "The Meaning of Vietnam," April 25, 1985.
122. Ronald Reagan, "Remarks at the Annual Dinner of the Conservative Political Action Conference," March 1, 1985.
123. U.S. National Bipartisan Commission on Central America, "Report of the National Bipartisan Commission on Central America," pp. 4 and 93.
124. Ronnie Dugger, *On Reagan: The Man and His Presidency,* p. 360.
125. *New York Times,* June 24, 1989, p. A9.
126. Gutman, *Banana Diplomacy,* p. 59.
127. Richard Sobel, "Public Opinion toward U.S. Involvement in Central America," pp. 2–11.
128. Background interviews, Spring 1989.
129. Sobel, "Public Opinion," p. 2.
130. Ibid., pp. 13–14.
131. Pastor, *Condemned to Repetition,* p. 260.
132. Reagan, "University of Virginia Address."
133. Reagan, "Farewell Address."
134. Ibid.
135. James Chace, "Is a Foreign-Policy Consensus Possible?" pp. 1–16.
136. Henry Kissinger and Cyrus Vance, "Bipartisan Objectives for Foreign Policy," pp. 899–921.
137. Harold Brown, "Building a New Consensus," p. 1.

138. The ATS project conducted twelve sets of interviews between October 1987 and December 1988 with the assistance of Market Opinion Research, Marttila & Kiley, Inc., and the Daniel Yankelovich Group, Inc. The PAC/Brown study involved exposing nearly 1,000 eligible voters to some three hours of discussion focused on four alternative futures of U.S.–Soviet relations.

139. Ronald Brownstein, "The New Politics of National Security," p. 18.

140. John Marttila, "American Public Opinion: Evolving Definitions of American Security," pp. 280, 270, and 291.

141. Daniel Yankelovich and Richard Smoke, "America's 'New Thinking,' " p. 2.

142. Brownstein, "The New Politics," p. 19.

143. Martilla, "American Public Opinion," p. 313.

144. Brownstein, "The New Politics," p. 19.

145. Simon Serfaty, *After Reagan: False Starts, Missed Opportunities and New Beginnings*, p. 4.

146. Robert W. Tucker, "Reagan's Foreign Policy," p. 10.

147. Ibid., p. 24.

148. ATS surveys.

149. ATS, no. 12, p. 33.

150. Yankelovich and Smoke, "America's 'New Thinking,' " p. 1.

151. ATS, no. 12, p. 11; Marttila, "American Public Opinion," p. 272.

152. Marttila, "American Public Opinion," pp. 265–66.

153. Ibid., p. 315.

154. Ronald Reagan, "Inaugural Address," January 20, 1981.

155. George Shultz, "Power and Diplomacy in the 1980s," April 3, 1984.

156. Tucker, "Reagan's Foreign Policy," p. 27.

157. Quoted in L. Gordon Crovitz, "How Ronald Reagan Weakened the Presidency," p. 28.

158. Reagan, "University of Virginia Address."

159. Quoted in Jay Winik, "Restoring Bipartisanship," p. 111.

160. Ibid.

161. Quoted in Bernard E. Brown, "The Structural Weaknesses of United States Foreign Policy," p. 8.

162. Ibid.

163. Crovitz, "How Ronald Reagan," pp. 27 and 28.

164. For example, the symposium "Building a New Consensus: Congress and Foreign Policy," pp. 1–72; and David L. Boren, "Speaking with a Single Voice: Bipartisanship in Foreign Policy," pp. 51–64.

Part Three

American Foreign Policy Since the Cold War

5

The Bush Administration

The Procedural President

In 1988 Ronald Reagan remained the most popular political figure in America and, if not constitutionally barred from seeking a third term, could undoubtedly have won reelection. After stumbling badly because of the Iran-*contra* scandal that began to unfold in late 1986, President Reagan's standing rose again as he rapidly concluded agreement after agreement with Mikhail Gorbachev. In October 1988 Reagan declared that the Cold War was essentially over.

The irony was that neither Vice-President George Bush, who otherwise tried to wrap himself in the Reagan mantle, nor Michael Dukakis, his Democratic opponent in 1988, would acknowledge Reagan's claim. Indeed, this was the last campaign of the Cold War[1]—backward-looking, cautious, issueless, and filled with the symbols of patriotism, crime, and race. Neither candidate explored the potential opportunities awaiting post–Cold War America. Dukakis, fearful of being branded "just another tax-and-spend liberal" and virtually devoid of any foreign policy experience, tried to campaign as a technocratic problem-solver. George Bush, seventeen points behind Dukakis after the July Democratic convention, was strongly advised by aides Lee Atwater and Roger Ailes to go on the attack. Branding Dukakis a "risk" and "out of the mainstream," Bush castigated him for vetoing as unconstitutional a Massachusetts law requiring public school teachers to lead their students in the Pledge of Allegiance and for maintaining membership in the American Civil Liberties Union. In time, Bush's supporters unveiled a devastating and sinister television ad informing viewers that Governor Dukakis had furloughed (black) convict Willie Horton just prior to a deadly crime spree. Dukakis, evidently surprised by the viciousness of the attacks, seemed paralyzed. His most visible effort to respond—in this case to Bush's claim that Dukakis was a Carter Democrat weak on defense—backfired as the usually dignified governor rode around a Michigan field in a battle tank looking thoroughly ridiculous. Finally, in the last two weeks of the campaign, the now desperate Dukakis abandoned his technocratic "ice man" image and accused Reagan and Bush of impoverishing average working Americans with their "supply side, trickledown" economic policies. This class-warfare theme helped narrow Bush's lead, but in the end Dukakis could capture only ten states and 46 percent of the popular vote.

Yet few, including the victor, believed that Bush had won an electoral mandate. A *Doonesbury* cartoon from early 1989 exaggerated only slightly in having the newly inaugurated president exclaim, "So far today I've said the Pledge and I haven't furloughed any murderers. I've delivered on my entire mandate and it isn't even lunch yet." In fact, George Bush entered the White House with "limited political capital, few political advantages, a weak strategic position" and the need "to compete for authority with congressional Democrats."[2]

But the real problem was not the size of Bush's victory but the difficulty in discerning his domestic priorities. Some observers expected a third Reagan administration. After all, Vice-President Bush had served loyally for eight years, supervised Reagan's deregulation efforts, and sometimes reached out to the Christian evangelical wing of the Republican Party. He was seen by many as Reagan's rightful heir, and his Clint Eastwood dare to Congress at the 1988 Republican convention—"Read my lips, no new taxes"—smacked of pure Reaganism. Furthermore, unlike Eisenhower, who had kept great distance from *his* vice-president in 1960, Reagan warmly endorsed Bush, even at one point raising questions about the mental stability of Michael Dukakis.

Yet some conservatives openly questioned the ideological fitness of George Bush. During the 1988 campaign Bush sought to allay these fears by self-consciously embracing the symbols of conservative populism, proclaimed his love of pork rinds, and emphasized his Texas roots. But in many ways he was by background, training, and temperament a product of the old foreign policy establishment—the Wise Men who had forty years earlier enshrined the internationalist consensus. Born in Massachusetts the son of Prescott Bush, a Wall Street tycoon and moderate senator from Connecticut, George was sent to Phillips Andover Academy and Yale University, where he starred in baseball and achieved membership in the ultra-secret Skull and Bones Society. Like many of his establishment brothers, he compiled a distinguished record in World War II and emerged a genuine hero. But in 1947, after receiving a $300,000 stake from his father, George

Bush moved to west Texas to sell oil-drilling equipment. Yet he continued to summer at the family retreat in Kennebunkport, Maine, and evinced a number of liberal-to-moderate social positions including membership in Planned Parenthood. By the early 1960s he was chair of the moribund Harris County (Houston) Republican Party and trying hard to open its doors to newcomers. He had also become a member of the Council on Foreign Relations. In 1964 he ran for public office—something very few of the Wise Men would have considered. His campaign for the Senate against liberal Democrat Ralph Yarborough proved exceedingly opportunistic, and after his defeat he confided to his pastor,"You know, John, I took some of the far right positions to get elected. I hope I never do it again. I regret it."[3] Two years later, running as a moderate from a prosperous Houston district, Bush was elected to the House, where he served two terms and earned the nickname "Rubbers" from Wilbur Mills (D-AR) for his enthusiastic promotion of world population programs. In 1970 he tried for the Senate again, this time running to the left of Democrat Lloyd Bentsen and hoping to pick up the votes of Yarborough loyalists. But this strategy fizzled when President Nixon and Vice-President Agnew, campaigning for Bush on hard "law and order" themes, drove many Democrats back to Bentsen.

It will be recalled from chapter 1 that the Wise Men of an older generation had usually shunned the messiness of electoral politics for appointive posts in the executive branch. George Bush, in so many ways the presumptive heir of these architects of containment, spent the 1970s loyally serving Nixon and Ford as ambassador to the United Nations, U.S. representative in Beijing, and director of Central Intelligence.[4] Again, like the proudly nonpartisan Wise Men, Bush would have been pleased to remain as CIA chief in the Carter administration and even traveled to Plains to lobby the president-elect for the position.

But George Bush was also an ambitious politician. Declaring his candidacy for the 1980 Republican nomination for president, he tried, at first, to run as a Ford-like moderate. In another era Bush would have been a comfortable part of the eastern, internationalist wing of the party. His famous denunciation of Reagan's tax cut plan as "voodoo economics" reflected his aversion to federal budget deficits. But when conservatives during the early 1980 primaries criticized him as a liberal elitist, he quickly resigned from the Council on Foreign Relations and the Trilateral Commission. In a further attempt to placate the Republican right, Bush appeared to abandon his long-standing positions on population and women's rights issues.[5] It was then, perhaps, not surprising that Bush eagerly accepted Reagan's invitation to be his running mate or that Bush would dutifully and almost invisibly serve as vice-president for eight years.

In sum, George Bush's widely noted "thick résumé" gave few clues about his presidency's priorities, for the unifying theme of his long public career had been loyalty, not convictions.[6] In a general way he evidently favored lower taxes and smaller government, but he had been repeatedly pressured by distrustful conservatives to demonstrate his ideological commitment.

Reluctant to make his "no new taxes" pledge, his convention call for a "kinder, gentler America" formed the core of his "emerging suburban" electoral strategy to appeal to fiscally conservative, socially moderate voters.[7] Yet Bush had simultaneously exploited many of Reaganism's cultural symbols.

What ensued, in the words of one White House adviser, was "a battle for George Bush's mind right from the beginning of his administration."[8] On one side were ideological activists who clustered around an "empowerment agenda" and who were animated by the "new paradigm," an approach to domestic policy articulated by White House staffer James Pinkerton in a February 1990 speech to the World Federalist Society. There Pinkerton claimed that the old New Deal–Great Society "paradigm" was shifting to a new model of socioeconomic policy featuring five elements:

1. Governments were increasingly subject to market forces.
2. Individual citizens desired more choices.
3. Public policies should seek to empower people to make choices themselves.
4. Decentralized public policies are more effective.
5. Public policies should emphasize what works.[9]

Pinkerton and his allies in the Bush administration wanted to center the president's domestic agenda on the empowerment paradigm by providing programmatic content for a "kinder, gentler America." For one of its leading promoters, Charles Kolb, a presidential deputy assistant, "in contrast to Ronald Reagan's *elimination* of programs, the New Paradigm would redefine government in terms of working *for* and *with* people to restore independence and self-sufficiency."[10]

Accordingly, a dozen or so activists in the cabinet, White House, and Congress repeatedly urged the administration to emphasize such empowerment items as educational choice, homeownership and expanded tenant management in public housing, job training, lower capital gains tax rates, enterprise zones, welfare reform, family-support measures, and Small Business Administration loans to promote entrepreneurial capitalism.[11] Economic growth, individual opportunity, and institutional reform became their mantra, but they also pressed President Bush to confront and provoke the Democratically controlled Congress by implementing the line-item veto without prior Court approval; by indexing the capital gains tax to inflation through executive rulemaking; by making recess appointments; and by demanding that Congress reform itself.[12]

While Bush was loath to challenge Congress in these ways, he did occasionally include much of the New Paradigm agenda in his speeches. For example, in his first address to Congress on February 9, 1989, and in an accompanying 193-page document entitled "Building a Better America," President Bush appeared to embrace much of the empowerment agenda, though he deleted the phrase "I am a reformer," that Pinkerton had inserted because it "strained credulity."[13] From early 1989 through the 1992 election campaign Bush would sometimes, though irregularly, pay lip service to empowerment initiatives. But the New Paradigmers were constantly disappointed by what they saw as the president's "failure to follow through on his rhetoric, to prioritize his goals, and to marshal his resources for a big drive on Congress."[14] Even on the morrow of the Gulf War, when his approval ratings had soared to an incredible 90 percent, Bush asked nothing more of Congress than its passage of transportation and crime bills. Ultimately activists such as Kolb, Pinkerton, Housing and Development Secretary Jack Kemp, Drug Czar William Bennett, and Congressman Vin Weber (R-MN) were appalled by Bush's failure to appreciate "how ideas could be deployed as part of an agenda to bolster, sustain, and advance"[15] a coherent Republican approach to domestic policy. To them, "when it came to ideological questions, Bush understood the words but not the music."[16]

Arrayed on the other side in the battle for Bush's mind were such process pragmatists as Chief of Staff John Sununu, Office of Budget and Management (OMB) Director Richard Darman, and Domestic Policy Council Director Roger Porter, variously disparaged by the New Paradigmers as foxes (as opposed to big-thinking hedgehogs), bean counters, technocrats, empiricists, and "gnomish gnostics." Indeed, they seemed to hold few convictions about domestic policy apart from a deep concern about the corrosive effects of the large and growing federal budget deficit. The New Paradigmers confidently predicted that "just as we had forced the collapse of communism, we would have grown our way out of the budget deficit,"[17] but most economists had concluded that it had to be significantly cut. Darman and Treasury Secretary Nicholas Brady agreed with the economists, and both worked hard to convince Bush to renounce his "read my lips" pledge.

For the first eighteenth months of the administration, however, the deficit issue appeared to serve Bush's purposes, for it allowed him to propose programs for education, the environment, crime, poverty, and drug control

and to challenge Congress to fund them.[18] The 1987 Deficit Reduction Act
("Gramm-Rudman-Hollings") had set mandatory spending targets that, if
exceeded, would trigger indiscriminate, across-the-board cuts. To avoid
these draconian steps the Bush administration during 1989 negotiated with
congressional Democrats a budget agreement purporting to meet the
Gramm–Rudman 1990 deficit target of $100 billion. But the plan relied on
highly optimistic economic assumptions, one-time savings, and various accounting gimmicks. It simply postponed the hard choices.

As the economy slowed in late 1989 and early 1990, OMB, warning of a
resulting decline in revenues, repeatedly raised its estimate for the fiscal
1991 budget shortfall. The next Gramm–Rudman mandatory target was $64
billion, yet by July 1990 the deficit estimate had soared to $231 billion.
Bush, aware that Reagan had been able to blame congressional Democrats
for tax increases during his administration, tried the same tactic by calling
for bipartisan budget negotiations. But this time Senate Majority Leader
George Mitchell (D-ME) and House Speaker Thomas Foley (D-WA) demanded that Bush first renounce his famous pledge. The president, under
strong pressure from Darman and Brady, reluctantly did so and promptly
triggered a revolt among House Republicans led by Minority Whip Newt
Gingrich (R-GA). To them and to the New Paradigmers in his administration, Bush's action constituted an act of betrayal, his "single biggest mistake as president, [and] led directly to the unraveling of the Reagan
coalition."[19] They had lost the battle for Bush's mind, and they dismissed
his subsequent spurning of this budget deal in March 1992 as a cynical act
of desperation.

To understand why Bush would risk the destruction of the Reagan coalition we need to consider his somewhat peculiar approach to governance, for
it, in large measure, constituted his real domestic priority. Or, to put it
slightly differently, the flow of current events largely determined Bush's
domestic and foreign policy priorities. As he saw it, his challenge was to
react to these events by the consistent application of appropriate procedures.
Favorable policy outcomes would flow from this approach.

Ronald Reagan had brought to the White House a clear set of substantive
convictions and priorities enshrined years earlier in "The Speech." Aides to
Bush had no comparable statement to guide them, but they were issued a
list of "golden rules" that the president expected them to follow:

1. Think big.
2. Challenge the system.
3. Adhere to the highest ethical standards.
4. Be on the record as much as possible.

5. Be frank.
6. Fight hard for your position.
7. When I make a call, we work as a team.
8. Work with Congress.
9. Represent the United States with dignity.[20]

In fact, this curious list neatly captured Bush's fear of disorder and unpre-
dictability, his "Tory" sense of the fragility of institutions, and the importance he attached to good manners in building consensus.[21] For Bush,
political visionaries threatened the social order by unleashing uncontrollable
passions—hence his disparagement of the "vision thing." By establishing
personal relationships resting on reciprocity and loyalty, and by working
quietly with fellow insiders—whether members of Congress or foreign
leaders—George Bush hoped to create effective policy coalitions. Periodically, of course, it might be necessary to abandon this "governing mode" for
the rhetorical nastiness of the "campaign mode," but Bush perceived himself as an unwilling campaigner and was confident that the electorate, like
himself, could distinguish between these activities.[22] Usually cautious in
the governing mode and skeptical of new ideas, he was inclined to accept
the conventional wisdom of experts unless obvious contrary facts arose.
And if events did force change, Bush would typically react incrementally
and reluctantly.

This "process Toryism," then, not only helps to explain why he agreed to
new taxes in 1990—the experts told him the deficit was out of control—but
also why he sent Darman and Sununu to negotiate in secret with Democratic leaders—agreement among insiders was essential. It also sheds light
on Bush's extreme slowness in offering initiatives to counter the stubborn
economic recession. After all, most professional economists expected a
"soft landing" for the economy, a mild slowdown in growth, and then a
rapid recovery. Very few experts anticipated the prolonged, "double dip"
recession that mired the economy until late in Bush's term.

In sum, the essence of governing for George Bush involved the reliance
on insider networks to construct coalitions designed to resolve problems.
Enhancing the *process* was his overriding purpose, for if it worked
smoothly, the social fabric would be preserved and strengthened. Ironically,
in view of Dukakis's claim that the 1988 election would be about "competence,"Bush shared the Massachusetts governor's commitment to managerial excellence. And like his opponent, Bush, too, would be vulnerable to
the charge that he lacked compassion and convictions.

Perhaps because of this emphasis on process, President Bush found it
difficult to relate his domestic priorities and approach to governance to his

foreign policy objectives. The White House New Paradigmers repeatedly urged him to link their "empowerment" agenda to the dramatic changes occurring in Eastern Europe and the Soviet Union by asserting that his domestic mission of enhancing individual freedom rested on the same principles that had inspired the revolutions of 1989.[23] Bush mostly ignored this advice until quite late in his term, largely because he feared the destabilizing potential of these revolutions. His reluctance to demonstrate that his domestic and foreign policy objectives were mutually reinforcing had unfortunate consequences, for by late 1991 the public began to feel that Bush's international activities were actually hurting his ability to handle the economy.

From Containment to the New World Order

It became quickly evident that George Bush would be both a post-Vietnam and a post–Cold War president. From July to December 1989 Poland, Hungary, East Germany, Czechoslovakia, Bulgaria, and Romania overthrew communist dictators and replaced them with leaders apparently committed to democratic politics and market economies. In 1990 the process of German reunification began, and by the end of the following year the Soviet Union itself had ceased to exist. Presidents from Eisenhower to Reagan had formulated their strategic objectives against the backdrop of a divided Europe and a hostile Soviet Union. Even post-Vietnam presidents, as Jimmy Carter discovered, could hardly afford to ignore the eastern bloc. George Bush, whose outlook, skills, and political constituency were products of the Cold War, had inherited a grand design that was four decades old, grounded in the precepts of the Truman Doctrine and expressed in the strategy of containment.

The Bush administration would have been comfortable in continuing this tradition. Its "process Tory" preferences were well suited to manage the Cold War, where cautious, prudent reactions to Soviet provocations had always been at a premium. The president, proud of his credentials and determined to make foreign policy his principal activity, created an inner circle of largely like-minded "professional buddies"—Secretary of State James Baker, National Security Adviser Brent Scowcroft and his deputy (later CIA director) Robert Gates, and Defense Secretary Richard Cheney. None of them initially shared Ronald Reagan's enthusiasm for Mikhail Gorbachev or Reagan's belief that the Cold War had ended. They entered office fully prepared to contain the Soviet Union.

Scowcroft, in particular, viewed some of Reagan's arms control proposals as reckless and myopic. Firm advocates of deterrence, the Bush team rejected Reagan's nuclear abolitionism—most evident at the 1986 Iceland summit—and worried that the momentum of START could, if not slowed, produce a treaty that denuclearized U.S. defenses. Furthermore, these officials wished to shorten the wild swings that had allegedly characterized the American public's approach to East-West relations since the early 1970s. They believed that Reagan had exacerbated this tendency by first helping to initiate a second Cold War and then prematurely announcing its demise. The Bush administration desired instead a superpower relationship immune to exaggerated fears and unfulfilled hopes.

Yet this task was made even more difficult by the ongoing drama in the Soviet Union and Eastern Europe. Not since Harry Truman had anyone assumed the presidency at a time of comparable international flux, and Bush's first challenge was simply to make sense out of these upheavals. But by late 1989 a host of questions still needed to be answered: What kind of Soviet Union would Gorbachev's pursuit of *glasnost* and *perestroika* produce? Should the United States wish him well? How attainable were his goals? What would be the new status of Eastern Europe? Could and should NATO survive if the Soviet threat disappeared or was drastically diminished? What would be the role of the United States in a post–Cold War environment? Could a domestic foreign policy consensus be fashioned in the absence of a Soviet threat?

Senior administration officials, comfortable with the verities of the Cold War, were hard pressed to discern Gorbachev's motives, predict the results of his reforms, or evaluate the implications for Soviet-American relations. Placed on the defensive by Gorbachev's enormous international popularity ("Gorby fever"), the administration seemed almost annoyed with the Soviet leader as, for example, in May 1989, when a frustrated White House Press Secretary Marlin Fitzwater dismissed him as a "drugstore cowboy" presumably dispensing phony elixirs to a gullible public. But this outburst reflected the confusion felt by the Bush inner circle. When in April 1989 Richard Cheney "guessed" that Gorbachev would fail in his reform efforts and be replaced by a reactionary, Bush publicly disagreed with his defense secretary.

In part to slow down the momentum begun by the Reagan–Gorbachev rapprochement and in part to buy time, President-elect Bush had ordered a top-level strategic policy review. By April 1989 this review had yielded a thirty-page document designed to "insure compatibility among . . . commitments, capabilities, and resources" and recommended an approach to the Soviet Union called "status quo plus," provisionally concluding that the process of change in the Soviet Union was likely to continue for several years, even if Gorbachev were replaced.[24] It counseled the president to broaden the superpower dialogue carefully to include such regional issues as Africa, as well as functional topics such as terrorism and chemical weapons. At least some administration officials, however, were disappointed in the results, and one observed that "the vision ... is not articulated very strongly, there are plenty of caveats and what-ifs in there."[25]

The Bush team spent most of 1989 attempting to shape a strategy for a world turning upside down. The imminent end of the Cold War era proved positively unsettling to some old hands, who had grown almost fond of its predictability. In September Deputy Secretary of State Lawrence Eagleburger voiced these sentiments in a Georgetown University address suggesting that "the process of reform in the Soviet bloc and the relaxation of Soviet control over Eastern Europe" were "bringing long-suppressed ethnic antagonisms and national rivalries to the surface, and putting the German question back on the international agenda." The waning of the Soviet-American duopoly had produced a nascent multipolar world that would not necessarily be "a safer place than the Cold War era ... given the existence and proliferation of weapons of mass destruction."[26]

But building pressure on Bush from Western European governments and congressional Democrats to engage Gorbachev seriously forced the administration to move beyond "status quo plus." Borrowing a phrase from Michael Dukakis, Baker privately argued that "testing Gorbachev" sounded appropriately skeptical and hard-headed to American ears,[27] and the inner circle agreed that regional conflicts from Afghanistan through Angola to Central America would provide a good "test." Gorbachev, though apparently offended by the condescending tone of the phrase, moved to end Soviet support for several Third World clients, including Cuba. Nevertheless, only a few weeks before the fall of the Berlin Wall, Brent Scowcroft told senior official that "it would be dumb if we decided the Cold War is over, or that the Soviets aren't a threat anymore, or that we don't need NATO and we can use our defense budget to straighten out our domestic economic order."[28]

Certainly the administration's response to the pro-democracy movement in China smacked of Cold War geopolitics. As student demonstrations mounted in size and intensity during the spring of 1989 the Bush team openly worried about the stability of the Chinese government. Fearing the removal of a strategic counterweight to Moscow (the old "China card"), but at a time when the Soviet empire was collapsing, President Bush pursued a policy that seemed a parody of triangular diplomacy. When Chinese troops brutally crushed the Tiananmen Square demonstrators, Bush cited the importance of the Sino-American "relationship" and merely "deplored" the massacre. His secret dispatch of Scowcroft and Eagleburger to Beijing in December, so reminiscent of Kissinger's 1971 trip, provoked an angry congressional response. But Bush remained undeterred, vetoing a bill designed to grant permanent residency to Chinese students studying in the United States and extending China's Most Favored Nation (MFN) trading status into 1991.

Secretary Baker, in particular, however, believed that Gorbachev had passed his "tests" and that it was now time to improve the relationship further. He urged Bush to meet Gorbachev soon. The president, who had been avoiding such a meeting for almost a year, reluctantly agreed but insisted that it not be called a "summit." In fact, their "nonsummit" in Malta in early December 1989 proved pivotal in inaugurating the final phase of Soviet-American relations, one that Baker soon referred to as a "partnership." According to Michael Beschloss and Strobe Talbott, Bush decided at Malta that Gorbachev would be a reliable partner. He seemed almost like a Western European politician to the president, and Bush sympathized with Gorbachev's domestic political predicament.[29]

From then until the abortive coup in August 1991 the Bush administration attempted to realize five strategic objectives designed to ease the transition to a post–Cold War world: (1) to encourage Gorbachev on the path of political and economic reforms; (2) to "lock in" arms control agreements favorable to the United States in case Gorbachev fell to hardliners; (3) to maintain the territorial and administrative integrity of the Soviet Union; (4) to insist that a reunified Germany be a member of NATO and the EC; and (5) to achieve a stable and democratic Eastern Europe.

Some senior Bush officials, among them Robert Gates and Vice-President Dan Quayle, worried that an economically and politically reformed Soviet Union might still pose a threat to the United States, especially if its military capabilities remained intact. Consequently they were not sure that they wanted Gorbachev to succeed, and even Baker, perhaps the administration's biggest fan of Gorbachev, opposed direct economic assistance to Moscow for fear that it would be wasted and might even be used to prop up the Soviet military-industrial complex. Gorbachev denied any interest in "charity," but his increasingly desperate domestic situation intensified his pleas for loans and for admittance to the G-7, IMF, and World Bank on the grounds that membership would mollify his opponents. Bush, who had experienced Gorbachev's economic illiteracy firsthand at Malta, resisted this pressure, though steps were taken to grant the Soviets observer status in these institutions. Furthermore, the administration made MFN for the Soviets dependent on their passage of liberal emigration laws and refused to waive the old Jackson–Vanik restrictions and approve credit guarantees for $1 billion in agricultural purchases until December 1990. Even then the commodity credits were delayed for months, MFN status was further postponed, and Gorbachev was actively discouraged from attending the July 1991 G-7 summit in London.

This balancing act of wishing Gorbachev well while refusing to provide much material help was pursued, in part, because of the situation in the Baltics. The United States had never officially recognized the Soviet absorption of these three republics in 1940, and when Lithuania declared its independence in March 1990 followed by Latvia two months later, Bush came under considerable domestic pressure to acknowledge their sovereignty. During the remainder of 1990 the Soviets tried to intimidate these new governments, and in January 1991 their troops seized parliamentary buildings in Vilnius and fired on civilians there and in Riga. President Bush repeatedly warned Gorbachev to find a peaceful solution but declined to do more for fear of provoking the violent disintegration of the Soviet Union. While Lithuanian leaders publicly accused the United States of "appeasement," Gorbachev implored Bush to understand his exceedingly fragile domestic predicament. Faced with a choice between Lithuanian self-determination and Soviet stability, Bush opted for the latter and delayed recognition until September 1991,[30] although he continued to chastise Gorbachev for his heavy-handedness.

Yet the administration's refusal to offer significant economic assistance to Gorbachev went deeper than the Baltics dispute because, finally, it could never abandon its suspicion that aid would be, at best, squandered. This understandable fear explains Bush's antipathy toward the "Grand Bargain," a scheme devised by Grigori Yavlinsky, a former deputy prime minister of the Russian Republic, and a small group of Harvard academics led by Graham Allison, dean of the Kennedy School of Government. It proposed that the G-7 offer, in specific phases, several kinds of economic assistance, beginning with food, medicine, and technical help, and ultimately progressing to the financing of infrastructure reconstruction. The aid, to be disbursed between 1991 and 1993, would have totaled as much as $60 billion. Allison, working at Harvard through a former Bush NSC staffer, Robert Blackwill, attempted to enlist the support of Undersecretary of State Robert Zoellick. But senior Bush officials found the plan risky and expensive, and the Soviet government hesitated to commit to the prescribed reforms. The Bush team decided to confine its support for Gorbachev to largely symbolic actions.

On December 25, 1991, the Soviet Union officially disbanded, although Russian President Boris Yeltsin had for some time acted as the region's dominant political figure. Yeltsin appeared to be more serious about economic reform than Gorbachev, but the administration remained hesitant to provide much assistance. In March 1992 Richard Nixon publicly lambasted

Bush's aid program as "a pathetically inadequate response in light of the opportunities and dangers" presented by the crisis in the former Soviet Union.[31] In a memorandum circulated among foreign policy analysts Nixon recalled that the "hot-button issue in the 1950s was 'Who lost China?' If Yeltsin goes down, the question, 'Who lost Russia?' will be an infinitely more devastating issue in the 1990s." The former president concluded that "the bottom line is that Yeltsin is the most pro-Western leader in Russia in history," and the West must help his government in six ways: (1) by providing humanitarian, food, and medical aid until the reforms began to work; (2) by creating a "free-enterprise corps" that would send thousands of Western managers to Russia to educate new enterprises in the ways of capitalism; (3) by rescheduling debts incurred under Gorbachev and deferring interest payments until a market economy took hold; (4) by allowing Russian exports greater access to Western markets; (5) by providing tens of billions of dollars through the IMF for currency stabilization as soon as Russia controlled its money supply; and (6) by creating a single Marshall Plan type of organization to coordinate private and public assistance. If Yeltsin failed, Nixon warned, "war could break out in the former Soviet Union as the new despots use force to restore the 'historical borders' of Russia"; the "new East European democracies would be imperiled ... , China's totalitarians would breathe a sigh of relief," and the new Russian leaders—in collaboration with Iraq, Syria, Libya, and North Korea—would threaten American interests "in hot spots around the world."[32]

The White House protested that it had previously proposed the addition of $645 million in aid to the former Soviet Union to supplement the $1.5 billion announced in late 1991 and blamed Congress for stalling on a $12 billion request to replenish the IMF. Stung by Nixon's characterization of his assistance program as "penny ante," President Bush argued that "there are certain fiscal financial constraints on what we can do, but we have a huge stake in the success of democracy in Russia and in the other CIS [Commonwealth of Independent States] countries."[33]

The White House feared that any serious effort to increase assistance would further alienate a public whose historic animosity to foreign aid had recently grown even more pronounced and who already saw Bush as a president excessively interested in foreign policy. A 1989 survey, for example, found that fully half of the American public believed that foreign aid constituted the single largest item in the federal budget![34] Nevertheless, in the wake of Nixon's criticisms, a surprising number of senators and congressmen, including conservatives Jesse Helms (R-NC) and Strom Thurmond (R-SC), strongly urged the White House to provide more leadership on this issue. According to Representative David Obey (D-WI), "the

White House has been so rattled by Pat Buchanan that they're bobbing and weaving on many issues, including this."[35] In the end the domestic political vagaries of 1992 whipsawed the administration and exposed significant divisions within the Republican Party on Russo-American relations.

Second, President Bush tried to "lock in" arms control agreements with Gorbachev (and later Yeltsin) in case hardliners came to power in Moscow. During the Nixon, Ford, Carter, and Reagan administrations arms control negotiations had been at the core of Soviet-American relations. Protracted wrangling over seemingly arcane minutiae was common, symbolic of the reality that neither side really trusted the other. Even when agreements had occasionally been reached, American critics routinely claimed that the Soviets would subvert them anyway.

Although initially reluctant to unveil an arms control strategy, domestic pressure, as well as Gorbachev's penchant for announcing unilateral reductions, forced a reconsideration. The pace of two interminable negotiations quickened—Conventional Armed Forces in Europe (CFE) and Strategic Arms Reduction (START)—especially after Malta. By the time Bush left office in January 1993 CFE and START agreements had been reached with Gorbachev and a START II pact had been concluded with Yeltsin. Together these treaties effectively ended the East-West military confrontation of almost a half-century. Yet because of the dizzying speed of political and economic change in the East, they were widely seen as little more than footnotes to the disintegration of the Warsaw Pact, the demoralization of the Red Army, and the disappearance of the Soviet Union. These agreements, however, were significant, for taken together they dramatically reduced conventional force sizes from the Urals to the Atlantic and ultimately diminished the number of strategic nuclear warheads from about 30,000 to fewer than 7,000. Moreover, the Bush administration eliminated long-standing United States manpower and weapons disadvantages with these understandings, although, to reiterate, they may in any event have soon disappeared. Finally, the decision to move quickly in 1990 and 1991 was partially vindicated by subsequent Soviet foot-dragging over treaty interpretation and implementation made worse by the August 1991 coup.

Third, as described by George F. Kennan in 1947, the goal of containment was to cause either the mellowing or collapse of the Soviet Union, but few American strategists had taken this possibility seriously. To the contrary, as the Cold War became an apparently permanent condition, U.S. policymakers focused on the more immediate problem of deterring a Soviet nuclear attack. Although the Nixon–Kissinger strategy of détente sought to modify Soviet behavior by enmeshing Moscow in a web of linked agreements and dependencies, even it did not envision a world without the Soviet

Union. Some Reagan officials claimed retrospectively that their strategy had aimed to implode the Soviet empire, but even if true, there is little evidence to suggest that they had thought through the consequences of success. Gorbachev's political reforms, however, unleashed such powerful centrifugal forces that the Bush administration was forced to confront the likelihood of Soviet collapse. It decided to do what it could to prevent the violent breakup of the old adversary. In early 1991 Brent Scowcroft summarized the administration's strategic objective at an NSC meeting: "Our policy has to be based on our own national interest, and we have an interest in the stability of the Soviet Union. The instability of the USSR would be a threat to us. To peck away at the legitimacy of the regime . . . would not . . . promote stability."[36] In particular, senior Bush officials worried that the excesses of "romantic nationalism" could lead to civil war, which in turn could undermine the security of the Soviet nuclear arsenal. Or, to put the Bush strategy in the syntax of Kennan: it wanted Moscow to mellow without collapsing.

But apart from offering reassuring words to Gorbachev, the administration could (or would) do little to prevent disintegration. On August 1, 1991, Bush tried to help in a speech delivered to the Supreme Soviet of the Republic of the Ukraine. Bush had not been eager to visit the capital of an outlying republic, fearing his presence would undermine Gorbachev's efforts to maintain the unity of the Soviet Union, but the administration was under considerable domestic pressure to support the principle of national self-determination. With the onset of the 1992 presidential campaign only five months away, senior advisers convinced Bush to make a "gesture" toward the republics.[37] But the "gesture" seemed designed primarily to bolster Gorbachev, for the president referred to his Kiev audience as "Soviet citizens," warmly praised Gorbachev's vision of the Soviet future, and made clear his lack of enthusiasm for Ukrainian secession.[38] Promptly dubbed the "Chicken Kiev" speech by *New York Times* conservative columnist William Safire and widely adopted by other commentators, Bush's remarks were, however, wholly consistent with his desire to preserve the Soviet Union.

Gorbachev, squeezed between communist centralizers and secession-minded republics, wobbled back and forth. His offer of a "Union Treaty," granting significant power to the periphery, precipitated the hardline coup that almost toppled him in August 1991. Soon afterward, Bush and most of his inner circle resigned themselves to the collapse of the Soviet Union but still hoped that the breakup would be peaceful. The administration now began to work with Yeltsin and the leaders of the other republics with nuclear weapons (Ukraine, Belarus, and Kazakhstan) to ensure the safety of their arsenals. In the end, Bush's goal of a reformed Soviet Union proved an oxymoron, and it was forced to confront the prospect of resurgent nationalism and pandemic instability in Eurasia.

Interestingly, in pursuing its fourth interim strategic objective, the administration showed no hesitancy in supporting *German* national self-determination, probably because it believed that reunification would lead to greater European stability. For decades, American (declaratory) policy had encouraged the creation of a unified German state as long as it remained closely tied to the West, but as the Cold War glacier froze Central Europe, United States strategists largely stopped considering that prospect and quietly hoped for a perpetuation of the status quo. Even as East Germany collapsed in late 1989, with thousands of its citizens voting with their feet against a divided state, it seemed inconceivable that the nation would soon be reunified. These events surprised the administration and worried London and Paris. Instead of placing obstacles in the path of German reunification, however, the United States devised a negotiating framework designed to keep the new Germany anchored in NATO and the EC. Under this arrangement, the two Germanies first agreed on the terms of reunification after which the four occupying powers—Britain, France, the Soviet Union, and the United States—accepted the results. The administration worked to reassure Margaret Thatcher and François Mitterrand that they need not fear this Germany and pressed Moscow to acquiesce in NATO membership for it. Bush's strategic objective was achieved in July 1990 when Helmut Kohl promised significant economic assistance to Moscow in exchange for Gorbachev's surrender on NATO.

The administration pursued its final transitional strategic objective—the nurturing of democratic governments in Eastern Europe—with considerably less boldness and creativity than it had demonstrated in handling German reunification. Nevertheless, it surely passed the modest test it set for itself: to do no damage. As Michael Mandlebaum observed, the Bush administration could have erred in two directions. On the one hand, it could have loudly and ostentatiously celebrated the demise of the Warsaw Pact, thus embarrassing Gorbachev and perhaps endangering the remarkable peacefulness of the East European revolutions. At the other extreme, it might have negotiated the future of those nations with the Soviet Union out of fear that Gorbachev would otherwise use force to preserve the Pact. But by constantly reassuring Moscow that these revolutions need not imperil legitimate Soviet interests, the Bush administration helped events in Eastern Europe run their course.[39]

Yet in the aftermath of the incredible revolutions of 1989, as these fledgling democracies struggled to build viable political institutions and market economies, the administration's interest in them appeared to wane. In part, of course, the Persian Gulf crisis diverted its attention for several months. Furthermore, the ongoing drama in the Soviet Union preoccupied it. Nonetheless, as Terry Deibel rightly noted in late 1991, Bush and his advisers failed to appreciate that these East European experiments might indicate whether a successful transformation from command to market economies was possible.[40] Consequently, it offered only meager amounts of assistance to these governments, and even after Congress raised the total to $500 million, this aid still represented less than .5 percent of the Marshall Plan in 1990 dollars. Instead, the administration encouraged the European Community to shoulder the aid burden.

From 1989 to 1991, the bipolar structure of the international system was transformed. Democratic institutions and market economies, in various forms, emerged in Eastern Europe, parts of the former Soviet Union, and almost all of Latin America. The victory over Iraq in the 100-hour Persian Gulf War in February 1991 confirmed the United States as the "world's sole, remaining superpower." Even the normally cautious and incremental George Bush proclaimed in September 1990 that a "new world order" was imminent and that Iraqi aggression constituted its first challenge. Critics claimed that Bush had used this phrase merely to gain legitimacy for Operation Desert Storm by rebutting charges that oil was the sole reason for American action. In fact, Bush had previewed his new world order just prior to the invasion of Kuwait. With Margaret Thatcher at his side in Aspen, Colorado, on August 2, 1990, he proposed an active and ambitious role for America in an allegedly unpredictable world. In this speech, which had been gestating in Bush's inner circle for months, the president acknowledged that the recent changes in Eastern Europe and the Soviet Union had "transformed our security environment" and greatly lessened "an immediate threat to Europe and the danger of global war." Yet the United States remained "a pivotal factor for peaceful change" with "important interests in Europe and the Pacific, in the Mediterranean and in the Persian Gulf. . . ."[41] The world, Bush warned, was still "dangerous, with . . . various threats . . . wholly unrelated to the earlier patterns of the U.S.-Soviet relationship . . . [which] can arise suddenly, unpredictably, and from unexpected quarters." The president argued that "terrorism, hostagetaking, renegade regimes with unpredictable rulers, new sources of instability—all require a strong and engaged America" with military "forces able to respond to threats in whatever corner of the globe they may occur."[42]

Surprisingly, Bush had not included aggression among the threats he anticipated in the wake of the Cold War. Nevertheless, Iraq's invasion of Kuwait on the day of the Aspen speech validated for senior administration officials the essential correctness of their analysis, much as North Korea's attack in June 1950 had confirmed the predictions of NSC-68 for Harry Truman. When Bush first spoke explicitly of the new world order on September 11, 1990, he now made resistance to aggression the litmus test of global stability.

In part, circumstances dictated this change in rhetoric. The disparate international coalition that Bush organized against Iraq shared but one characteristic: all its members claimed to be independent states. Since the eighteenth century, most states had agreed that an unprovoked attack by one against another constituted aggression and justified both unilateral and collective armed resistance. More recently, both the League of Nations and the United Nations had sought to enforce this principle formally. All victims of aggression, irrespective of their size or internal characteristics, had the right to collective protection. The United States had occasionally argued that only "democracies" could invoke this principle, as in the Reagan Doctrine, but this claim had never gained the status of international law.

To sustain the international coalition and to avoid undermining Saudi Arabia and the exiled Kuwaiti government, Bush could hardly allow "democracy" to be at stake in the Gulf, nor could "national self-determination" be at issue for fear of fueling Palestinian claims against Israel. Neither, for obvious reasons, could "defense of the free world" or "resistance to communism" be cited by Bush. Deprived of many of the arguments and symbols used by Cold War presidents to inspire domestic support, Bush relied on World War II metaphors and referred to Kuwait as a victim of Nazi-like aggression.

But neither the fragility of the international coalition nor the undemocratic nature of the Kuwaiti government can fully explain Bush's decision to place the punishment of "aggression" at the center of his new world order. This choice accurately reflected the administration's conservative understanding of world politics, its preference for stability to reform, and its identification of stability with the status quo. Lawrence Eagleburger's wistful reminiscences in 1989 about the orderliness of the Cold War captured this outlook. It also accounted for Bush's decisions to terminate the Gulf War without removing Saddam Hussein and to discourage attempts by Kurds and Shiites to break Iraq apart.

The Bush administration's willingness to use force to protect interests and its recognition that conflict remained an integral feature of world politics put it firmly in the tradition of Alexander Hamilton, Henry Cabot Lodge, and Henry Kissinger. But as Robert W. Tucker and David Hendrickson observed, Bush's post–Cold War grand design—the new world order—also departed from that tradition, for although the global balance of power was no longer threatened, the administration behaved as if

American security was still seriously at risk. Freed from the necessity of containing the Soviet Union, Bush implied that America could now serve as the guarantor of international law and order. Bush, the erstwhile "process Tory," agreed with Woodrow Wilson that America could play this role because it alone had sufficient "moral standing."[43] But whereas Wilson wished to renounce military force in favor of world public opinion and economic sanctions to enforce the democratic peace, Bush embraced the instruments of the "old diplomacy" to ward off international anarchy.[44]

In effect, Bush's America was to function as a kind of benevolent hegemon, protecting the growing "zone of democratic peace" against regional outlaws, terrorists, nuclear proliferators, and other threats to order. It would do so in concert with others, if possible, and unilaterally, if necessary. This vision married the universalist aspirations of Wilson's liberal internationalism to the military instruments of Lodge's nationalism. At the same time, it also made more explicit the outlook enveloped by the Cold War chrysalis.

As the 1992 presidential campaign approached and as the public evinced a growing concern about the domestic economy, George Bush showed a reticence to elaborate his potentially controversial grand design further. He had originally scheduled four foreign policy speeches for June 1991 in which he was expected to address the new world order but then decided to use these occasions to attack the Great Society programs of the 1960s, condemn "political correctness" on college campuses, and malign Congress for allegedly practicing partisanship in foreign affairs. According to David Gergen, the president's staff feared "that public debate over a new world order was spinning beyond control."[45] And so, to stifle that debate, George Bush rarely spoke of a new world order after the summer of 1991 and confined his foreign policy statements to rhetorical celebrations of the Gulf victory.

Yet within the administration, especially in the office of the undersecretary of defense for policy, work proceeded to operationalize the new world order. These efforts had begun shortly after the Gulf War ended as small Pentagon study groups examined alternative strategic objectives, tried to identify the regional implications of the Cold War's demise, and reevaluated the size and composition of the American nuclear arsenal as well as the appropriate conventional "base force."[46] The early fruits of these labors were leaked to the New York Times in February and March 1992 in the form of drafts of two planning documents. In the first, the Pentagon argued that United States military forces in the post–Cold War era required funding sufficient to allow it to fight at least two major regional conflicts (MRCs) simultaneously, while standing ready to repel an attack on Europe by a resurgent Russia. The document listed seven "illustrative scenarios" that the United States should be prepared to deter or resolve: (1) an Iraqi invasion of

Kuwait and Saudi Arabia; (2) a North Korea attack on South Korea; (3) the simultaneous occurrence of both; (4) a Russian assault on Lithuania through Poland with the help of Belarus; (5) a coup in the Philippines threatening 5,000 American residents; (6) a Panamanian coup endangering access to the Panama Canal; and (7) the emergence of a new expansionist superpower. An accompanying memorandum instructed the three service secretaries to use these scenarios in planning budget requests from 1994 to 1999. This document appeared to envision a base force at mid-decade considerably larger than the one suggested by President Bush in his 1992 State of the Union address, but perhaps appropriate for the expansiveness of the new world order.[47]

A related series of studies, coordinated primarily by Zalmay Khalilzad, assistant deputy undersecretary for policy planning, produced a second (leaked) document. Khalilzad's group focused explicitly on America's role in the post–Cold War world and tried to be deliberately provocative.[48] It examined and rejected three strategic options for the United States: isolationism, collective security, and balance of power. It did so because isolationism failed to acknowledge America's vital overseas interests; because collective security entrusted the protection of this nation's interests to others; and because balance-of-power systems historically had always resulted in major war. This planning group instead preferred "global leadership," an option that appeared to capture much of Bush's new world order. "Global leadership" presumed America's continuing international preeminence and argued that it should actively prevent the emergence of a bipolar or multipolar world. By using existing security arrangements to ensure the safety of its allies, the United States would view as potentially hostile any state with sufficient human and technological resources to dominate Europe, East Asia, or the Middle East. This strategy recognized that by early in the next century Germany and Russia might threaten Europe; Japan, Russia, and eventually China might threaten East Asia; and the domination of either region would consequently imperil the Middle East. Yet its architects did not consider the strategy to be anti-German or anti-Japanese. While they did fear the emergence of an unstable "Weimar Russia," Khalilzad and his colleagues argued that the United States could preserve German and Japanese friendship by nurturing existing security arrangements. Thus these two states would presumably have no incentive to challenge American preeminence, for their interests would be cared for by Washington. Notably missing from the global leadership strategy was any significant role for the United Nations.

Despite its apparent fidelity to Bush's new world order, this document, "Defense Planning Guidance, 1994–1999" (DPG), deeply embarrassed the administration. Senior Pentagon officials quickly disavowed it, even though Undersecretary for Policy Paul Wolfowitz and probably Richard Cheney had known of it for some time. They did so because it offended important U.S. allies and threatened to unleash a potentially divisive domestic debate about America's role in the post–Cold War world. A revised version of the DPG, leaked to the press in May 1992, appeared to support a strategy more seriously committed to multilateral institutions, but even its authors thought the changes were largely cosmetic.[49]

The new world order also featured a foreign economic component, and responsibility for its articulation largely fell to the Office of the Undersecretary of State for Economic Affairs, Robert Zoellick. It had done so because senior Treasury and Commerce officials tended to eschew grand strategy in favor of a case-by-case approach, while Zoellick, who enjoyed the full confidence of Secretary Baker, had earned a reputation as one of the administration's few genuine conceptualizers. Like the DPG, Zoellick's strategy began with the assumption of American global preeminence and noted that this nation's economy accounted for 22 percent of the world's gross product. He enunciated this view in an April 1992 speech in which he observed that

> the United States is the only nation in the world today that ranks at the top of political, military, and economic power. Over the course of the past few years—in Europe, the Gulf, and elsewhere—we have once again demonstrated our political and military leadership. But it is also vital that we remain in the forefront of international economic policy.
>
> We've taken important steps in this direction. The US is the largest exporter in the world. Nearly one-third of our growth in GDP from 1986 to 1991 is due to our increased exports. The US worker is the most productive in the world, 31% above Japan, 26% above the western states of Germany. During the 1980s, the productivity of our manufacturing workers grew an average of 3.6% per year.[50]

From Zoellick's perspective, the United States could best serve its economic interest by acting as the primary catalyst for a series of integrative economic structures that would substantially increase global prosperity. By spurring economic growth, these structures would encourage further democratization of political systems, which in turn would bring to (or keep in) power leaders committed to even greater regional economic integration. The United States could play a key role in sustaining this accelerating cycle of trade liberalization, democratization, and economic integration. For Zoellick, "America's message should be that it wants to reduce barriers to trade and investment with all, but will proceed with those countries that are willing."[51] From these precepts he and his colleagues developed a "new world order of trade" strategy designed to link American economic and geopolitical goals and interests. First, it sought to deepen the institutionalized economic and security interaction between the United States and its major traditional allies—Western Europe and Japan. Through a variety of bilateral, regional, and global trade agreements these long-standing relationships would be further solidified. Economic liberalization between the United States and the European Union, for example, would proceed apace with NATO's evolution.

Second, the United States would reach out to a second tier of potential "partners" in Latin America, East Asia, and Eastern Europe to develop increasingly dense institutional linkages. Devices such as the North American Free Trade Association (involving the United States, Canada, and Mexico), the Enterprise for the Americas Initiative (which envisioned a hemispheric free trade zone), and the Asia-Pacific Economic Cooperation (APEC) forum (largely a "talking shop" but possessing institutional possibilities) represented obvious examples of this notion. These developing institutions would gradually develop habits of cooperation among their members that could, in times of crisis, "be drawn on to build ad hoc security coalitions *under American leadership.*"[52] They might also prove useful in helping to settle regional issues as, for example, Argentina's decision to stop the purchase of Iranian missiles and to sign a nuclear nonproliferation agreement with Brazil. While the Bush administration did not regard these arrangements as "trading blocs," it did recognize that they could serve as useful levers to encourage states in other regions to liberalize their trade policies or to increase pressure for concessions in the GATT negotiations.[53] Finally, Zoellick and others understood that such multiple liberalization efforts could help President Bush rally congressional support for free trade by seizing the initiative from protectionists who had benefited from the deadlock in the Uruguay Round.

And third, even farther on the periphery, loomed Russia, China, and the Middle East. Zoellick advised that "over time we should seek to demonstrate to them the benefits of their peaceful integration into the system as well."[54]

Like its Defense Department counterpart, the administration's foreign economic strategy asserted the indispensability of American global leadership. It strongly supported the voluntary creation of a series of regional economic integrative institutions (within the GATT framework) in which the United States would act as the common linchpin. In Zoellick's strategy, as in Khalilzad's, all roads ultimately led to Washington.

President Bush did little more to define his grand design until after the November election. He had decided to run on his record and to celebrate the

Persian Gulf War victory rather than offer a potentially controversial foreign policy blueprint. Then, in two valedictory speeches, at Texas A&M University in December 1992 and at West Point in January 1993, he spoke more directly about America's role in the post–Cold War world and suggested several guidelines for the use of U.S. troops abroad. Except for the greater emphasis Bush placed on "collective action," his Manichaean description of the emerging international system, his identification of American security with world order, and his expansive definition of this nation's global responsibilities, all bore striking resemblance to the Truman Doctrine of 1947.

President Truman had seen a world riven by two "ways of life"—one free and the other repressive—in which free people were threatened by outside pressure and subverted by armed minorities. He claimed that "totalitarian regimes imposed upon free peoples, by direct or indirect aggression, undermine the foundations of international peace and hence the security of the United States." Truman concluded that "it must be the policy of the United States to support free peoples who are resisting attempted subjugation by armed minorities or by outside pressures."[55] With these words he had created the intellectual foundation for the strategy of global containment.

In his Texas A&M speech George Bush described a similarly divided world: "The alternative to democracy . . . is authoritarianism: regimes that can be repressive, xenophobic, aggressive, and violent." But unlike 1947, when free institutions teetered, Bush suggested that "the community of democratic nations is more robust than ever, and it will gain strength as it grows." But, he warned, "the collapse of the democratic revolutions could pose a direct threat to the safety of every single American . . . [and] the new world could, in time, be as menacing as the old." A failure of the United States to lead, Bush predicted, would result in "not more security for our citizens but less, not the flourishing of American principles but their isolation in a world actively hostile to them."[56] In short, a democratic world order resting on this nation's leadership, Bush claimed, was essential to the security of the United States. It was this equation of global order and national security that above all linked the analyses of Harry Truman and George Bush, despite the obvious fact that in 1992 the United States no longer faced a global threat.

In contrast to Truman, who had placed no apparent limits of the instruments the United States would employ to help free people defend themselves, in his January 1993 West Point speech President Bush tried to define more rigorously America's military role in the post–Cold War world. Speaking against the backdrop of the recent Somali humanitarian intervention, Bush sought to distinguish "leadership" from "unilateralism" and "universalism." He noted that "there is no support abroad or at home for us to play this role [of world policeman] nor should there be. We would exhaust ourselves in the process." On the other hand, the president observed that as the "only remaining superpower, it is the role of the United States to marshal its moral and material resources to promote a democratic peace. . . . There is no one else." And while "we need not respond by ourselves to each and every outrage of violence. . . , [at] times real leadership requires a willingness to use military force." Unfortunately, however, "in the complex new world we are entering, there can be no single or simple set of fixed rules for using force. . . . Each and every case is unique." Nor could "the relative importance of an interest [serve as] a guide." Nevertheless, Bush suggested some "principles to inform our decisions:

> Using military force makes sense as a policy where the stakes warrant, where and when force can be effective, where no other policies are likely to prove effective, where its application can be limited in scope and time, and where the potential benefits justify the potential costs and sacrifice.[57]

He further argued that whenever possible the United States should lead international coalitions and contribute to them "in a manner commensurate with our wealth . . . and strength." But other nations with a stake in the outcome should also help militarily and economically. At the same time, "a desire for international support must not become a prerequisite for acting. Sometimes a great power has to act alone," as for example, in Panama. But, President Bush concluded, "in every case involving the use of force, it will be essential to have a clear and achievable mission, a realistic plan for accomplishing the mission, and criteria no less realistic for withdrawing U.S. forces once the mission is accomplished.[58]

Taken together these farewell addresses carried a decidedly mixed message. In the Texas A&M speech Bush embraced the Truman Doctrine's identification of world order with American security. The end of the Cold War, he inferred, had not reduced this nation's very demanding security requirements: Americans could feel safe only in a democratic world. Here Bush spoke as an unreconstructed Wilsonian. His West Point address, however, strongly echoed the Weinberger Doctrine in its attempt to provide criteria for United States military interventions. While Bush's "principles" were not quite as restrictive as Weinberger's six "tests," they served a similar purpose—to reassure the public that blood and treasure would not be recklessly risked. In doing so he inverted a traditional relationship by suggesting that, in deciding whether to intervene, the *tactical* military "doability" of the mission might receive priority over the *strategic* importance of the interest involved. This was a curious way for a great power to conduct its affairs, but it was testimony to the continuing pull of the Vietnam legacy despite Bush's protestations.

As we have seen, the Bush foreign policy passed through three major phases. During the first, which lasted for most of 1989, the administration clung to a largely inherited Cold War outlook to test Gorbachev's commitment to domestic reforms and genuinely different Soviet international behavior. In the middle phase, roughly 1990 and 1991, the Bush inner circle attempted to achieve several transitional strategic objectives amid fundamental change in the Soviet Union and Eastern Europe without yet having developed a post–Cold War grand design. The third phase began during the Persian Gulf crisis and thus partly overlapped the second. It involved the incomplete articulation of a post–Cold War grand design—the new world order—accompanied by an ambitious (and partly disavowed) global strategy called variously "global leadership" and "collective engagement." Yet throughout these phases the administration's tactics remained rather constant and simple and very similar to those used to promote its domestic agenda.

George Bush placed an enormous emphasis on personal diplomacy. His reliance on the telephone to converse with other heads of state quickly earned him the sobriquet of the "rolodex president." This practice reflected his belief that warm personal relations among leaders was essential to the successful conduct of diplomacy. His Tory instincts attracted him to established leaders of established states—Brian Mulroney, François Mitterrand, Helmut Kohl, Margaret Thatcher, John Major—and he liked to nurture these budding friendships by playing the gracious host at Kennebunkport. Much more wary of unknowns and upstarts—Gorbachev and Yeltsin, at first, Poland's Lech Walesa, Vytautas Landsbergis of Lithuania—Bush welcomed them to his inner circle only if they proved their "soundness." If, however, foreign leaders misbehaved, they would quickly earn the president's personal animosity. Thus Bush quite characteristically ostracized Manuel Noriega and Saddam Hussein and attacked their character (as well as their policies). But for those who followed the rules benefits invariably followed in the form of personal notes, presidential visits, and joint news conferences.[59]

The administration's need to interpret the enormous changes unfolding on the international landscape and to craft appropriate responses could have deeply divided the foreign policy agencies. After all, Nixon and Kissinger had essentially subverted the bureaucratic apparatus in order to frame and implement their grand design, and both the Carter and Reagan administrations had been plagued by highly publicized disputes among senior foreign policy advisers. Yet it proved surprisingly easy to legitimate the Bush foreign policy within the bureaucracy.

In contrast to his domestic policy advisory system, where "empowerment" conservatives repeatedly clashed with process technocrats, Bush's foreign policy inner circle was notably free of ideological cleavages. Inevitably, disagreements over specific policy alternatives occurred, but President Bush and his senior advisers shared an internationalist outlook that provided them with a set of broadly similar convictions. Moreover, most of the inner circle had worked together during the Ford administration where they had directly experienced assaults on the détente strategy from both the political right and left. Brent Scowcroft, national security adviser in both administrations, deliberately maintained a low public profile, shunning the media in favor of Bush, Baker, Cheney, and JCS Chairman General Colin Powell. Scowcroft viewed his role as integrative, believing that the NSC should coordinate, rather than make, policy. James Baker, who relied on a handful of intimates for advice—Eagleburger, Zoellick, Dennis Ross, Margaret Tutweiler, Robert Kimmitt, and Janet Mullins—did isolate himself from the middle levels of the State Department. Furthermore, he focused on a handful of issues that he believed had the potential for major payoffs.[60] By so doing he often ignored or misunderstood administration policy on other issues such as its approach to Iraq in the months before the invasion of Kuwait.[61] Baker's operating style sometimes confused those in the State Department charged with policy implementation, but it triggered no rebellion. The Defense Department, despite post–Cold War "downsizing," trusted Bush to maintain American military strength while avoiding imprudent overseas interventions. At the same time, however, the Pentagon showed an eagerness to articulate its very expansive understanding of the new world order, in part to ensure that American policy remain globally engaged. Perhaps the greatest amount of bureaucratic infighting occurred between the State and Treasury departments over control of foreign economic policy—a struggle probably exacerbated by the fact that both secretaries, Baker and Brady, considered themselves close friends of the president. Yet even here, the disputes centered more on "turf" issues than any fundamental disagreement over strategy.

The Bush administration's public legitimation efforts involved four elements: (1) the daily demonstration of foreign policy competence to achieve the perception of what we have termed "cognitive legitimacy"; (2) a declaratory history that attempted to link the Cold War and post–Cold War eras by emphasizing the indispensability of American leadership during both periods; (3) the repeated warning that the renewed threats of isolationism and protectionism endangered the global status of the United States; and (4) an increasing reliance on the concept of a "democratic peace" to achieve "normative legitimacy" for a post–Cold War foreign policy.

Unlike Reagan, who relied heavily on rhetoric to engage the public, George Bush hated making speeches. He was, however, extremely proud of his foreign policy accomplishments and confident in his ability to understand international relations. He genuinely enjoyed diplomacy, especially its interpersonal side—foreign travels, state banquets, telephone chats with foreign leaders, and weekend têtes-à-têtes at Kennebunkport. Given these self-perceived strengths, Bush simply assumed that the public would be impressed by the administration's cool professionalism. In many respects, it *was* impressed by the Bush team's foreign policy competence, particularly during the Persian Gulf crisis. The president's creation and maintenance of the unwieldy anti-Iraq international coalition; his adroit use of the United Nations to increase pressure on Saddam Hussein; and his careful orchestration of domestic public opinion were masterful displays of proficiency. While the failure to destroy Iraq's best troops, to remove Saddam Hussein from power, and to immediately assist Kurdish rebels until public pressure forced his hand tarnished Bush's overall performance, the president's popularity nevertheless reached unprecedented heights by the late winter of 1991. Despite rather belated Democratic attempts to criticize the administration's "appeasement" of Saddam Hussein before the invasion of Kuwait, to link Vice-President Bush to the Iran *contra* scandal, and to claim that the president lacked a compelling global vision, the public never seriously questioned the foreign policy *competence* of the Bush administration

Bush encountered trouble at the end of 1991, however, when he tried to show that he "cared" about the economy by appearing to blame the recession on Japanese trade practices. He had originally planned to cap a "grand tour" of East Asia with a visit to Japan to confirm that region's central importance in the emerging post–Cold War order. But the upset victory of Democrat Harris Wofford running as a health care reformer in a special Senate race in Pennsylvania over former Attorney General Richard Thornburgh panicked the White House. Bush's domestic political advisers convinced him to postpone the trip and to repackage it as a "jobs summit." With leading American business leaders in tow, Bush then descended on Tokyo to pry open the Japanese economy to U.S. exports.

This ill-conceived venture smacked not of statesmanship but of political opportunism. Surrounded by the CEOs of some of this nation's least efficient corporate giants, President Bush, the architect of the new world order, seemed more like an undignified huckster hawking American automobiles. The resulting fiasco, which included the president becoming ill at a state dinner, undermined the public perception that he could smoothly handle foreign policy.

Second, although he personally had little interest in reading history, President Bush nevertheless extensively employed a declaratory history of American foreign relations. This narrative was simple, seamless, and designed to show that he personally embodied a half century of foreign policy wisdom and continuity. During the 1988 campaign, for example, Bush portrayed himself as the rightful heir to the Kennan-Truman-Eisenhower bipartisan internationalist tradition and Michael Dukakis as the offspring of neoisolationist McGovern Democrats who feared to exercise American power. Charging that the Massachusetts governor's foreign policy views amounted to a "repudiation of the Truman Doctrine and the vision of John Kennedy," Bush claimed that there had been a bipartisan consensus since World War II based on an "effective deterrent, unsurpassed military force and the demonstrated will to use it." In praising Truman's boldness in defeating the Berlin blockade and Kennedy's firmness during the Cuban missile crisis, Bush asked, "Do today's liberals understand what it means to stand up to a challenge and meet our commitments? I guarantee I will."[62] In running against Bill Clinton four years later, he again placed himself within the internationalist mainstream while raising questions about his opponent's patriotism. During the lead-up to the Gulf War, Bush employed a similar technique against Saddam Hussein, comparing the Iraqi leader with Hitler and inferring that his own actions were much like Churchill's and FDR's.

Yet the administration's declaratory history could also serve less partisan purposes. During much of 1989, for example, he spoke frequently and approvingly of the containment strategy. This declaratory history surprisingly ignored the Reagan Doctrine and instead portrayed his predecessor as a faithful servant of containment. This account did substantial damage to the actual historical record, yet it seemed somehow appropriate that George Bush, whose background and credentials would in an earlier day have made him a leader of the old establishment, chose to extol that group's major contribution to postwar foreign policy. And perhaps Bush believed that in order to move "beyond containment," as he put it in 1989, it was first necessary to pay homage to its original architects and to argue for the essential continuity of American foreign relations.

As the Cold War ended, Bush's declaratory history included a new theme. Now he argued that at least since 1947 the exercise of American political, military, and moral power had been, and would continue to be, indispensable for global peace and prosperity.[63] Interestingly, he did not claim that the Reagan arms buildup had caused the Soviet collapse: "in the end, Soviet communism was destroyed by its own internal contradictions,"[64] just as, he might have added, Kennan had predicted. But whereas Kennan had anticipated a post–Cold War world built on a traditional multipolar balance, Bush foresaw an era remarkably similar—except for the absence of the USSR—to that of the Cold War. American global involvement remained essential: "It doesn't mean bearing the world's burdens all alone. But it does mean leadership, economic, political, and, yes, military, when our interests are at risk, and where we can make a difference."[65]

In sum, President Bush used the history of the Cold War to vindicate his vision of the future. The Vietnam War played no explicit part in this selective account, though his admonitions against "reckless, expensive crusades" surely pointed toward it. Nevertheless, the war's legacy weighed heavily on the administration and influenced military decisions taken in the Gulf, Somalia, and Bosnia. And although the president, on the conclusion of Operation Desert Storm, proclaimed, "By God, we've kicked the Vietnam syndrome once and for all," his senior advisers found this boast premature at best.[66] They recognized that that war's continuing legacy would complicate American efforts to bring order to the post–Cold War world.

Third, President Bush tried to legitimate his foreign policy by claiming that the alleged alternatives—neoisolationism, Pax Americana, and protectionism—were wholly unacceptable. Here he walked a well-trod path, for since the Truman administration presidents had fended off critics from both the left and the right by claiming that their foreign policies avoided the twin disasters of withdrawal and overinvolvement. Representing yet another dimension of the Vietnam legacy, since the late 1960s liberals had frequently warned of the dangers of a Pax Americana, while conservatives had evinced fears that this nation's foreign policy had turned dangerously inward. Consensus-building presidents had typically moved to occupy the political center by simultaneously claiming that the United States had global responsibilities and denying that it had any desire to act as the "world's policeman." These clearly constituted attempts to reassure a wary public that America could pursue an internationalist course without risking additional Vietnams. Despite his claim that the Vietnam syndrome had been buried in the sands of Iraq, George Bush felt obliged to continue this rhetorical tradition. Like his predecessors, he never explicitly defined the contents of a "neoisolationist" or "world policeman" foreign policy, because he too employed these terms as slogans designed to worry the public. But he inferred that the first alternative would lead to global disorder, while the second would produce reckless crusades. By offering the public these unpalatable choices, the administration hoped the American people would support the "middle way"—its policy of "collective engagement."[67]

For more than two decades, the U.S. economy had been growing more dependent on foreign markets, and the end of the Cold War promised to accelerate this trend. The Bush administration attempted to craft a foreign economic policy appropriate to this environment, but some commentators and politicians, as we see later in this chapter, argued vociferously that alleged Japanese violation of international trading rules had taken American jobs. In response, President Bush accused these critics of "protectionism" while pledging to continue working for the opening of global markets through GATT and other agreements. He argued that free markets, free trade, and global economic integration would eventually benefit the entire American economy. Conversely, the administration asserted that "fair trade" policies would protect inefficient domestic industries and raise prices for all consumers. In effect, it attempted to extend a long-standing *elite* free trade consensus to a public largely uninterested in the issue but willing to impose tariffs to "protect jobs." It did so, in part, by linking "protectionism" to "neoisolationism" and claiming (with questionable logic) that the first policy would necessarily beget the second.

Finally, George Bush attempted to achieve "normative legitimacy" for his new world order. Like a neo-Wilsonian he alluded to a rising tide of democratic revolutions, an expanding zone of democratic peace, and a future without war as long as the United States remained a world leader. He also spoke glowingly of a community of cooperation centered in the United Nations. The administration had promoted (with varying enthusiasm) free elections, under UN supervision, in Afghanistan, Angola, Cambodia, El Salvador, Namibia, and Nicaragua as alternatives to power sharing and as a means to legitimate the outcome. Their success in terminating civil wars proved very uneven, but Bush frequently used these elections as evidence of a global democratic trend. Yet, unlike Wilson, he showed little willingness to rely on economic sanctions and the force of world public opinion to deter and defeat aggression. Ultimately, Bush relied on American arms to do so. At the same time, however, the prospect of endless military interventions clearly worried the public and in the wake of Somalia forced Bush to offer his limiting "principles." In short, George Bush presented himself as a "prudent Wilsonian," devoted to a capitalist, democratic world, but careful not to overreach in pursuing it. Yet it remained unclear whether this persona was genuine or one crafted merely to win public support.

A Post–Cold War Foreign Policy Consensus?

To a remarkable degree the Bush administration attempted to re-create the Cold War policy consensus without the Cold War.[68] In chapter 1 I identified seven axioms that lay at the core of that earlier policy consensus and suggested that all had enjoyed substantial public and elite support from the late 1940s to the late 1960s. The Bush administration embraced four of these precepts and slightly modified the other three to try and forge a "new" domestic foreign policy consensus. Did it succeed? Let us consider these axioms and the public's reaction to them.

1. *Alone among the world's nations the United States has both the material power and the moral responsibility to create a just and stable international order.* Senior administration officials worried that after the Cold War the public would once again be tempted to turn inward, as it had allegedly done in the wake of other great conflicts.[69] To keep the public engaged internationally the Bush administration repeatedly emphasized America's indispensability in creating and maintaining a stable and just world, and it reminded the nation that past failures to assert global leadership had always brought on disaster.

Polls from the early 1990s suggested, however, that these fears may have been unwarranted, for internationalist sentiment continued at the same high levels as the 1980s—about 70 percent—with roughly one-quarter of the public resisting an active role for the United States. The evaporation of the Soviet threat had not notably amplified isolationist sentiments. If the *structure* of public opinion remained largely unchanged, so too did the *salience* of its attitudes, for issues of economic security such as "protecting the jobs of American workers" and "assuring adequate energy supplies" dominated both the public's global and domestic priorities after the Cold War as they had after Vietnam.

On the other hand, the relatively mild, if persistent, "double dip" recession of 1990 and 1991 helped to put the public in a surprisingly sour and fretful mood. Most Americans had concluded (incorrectly) that Japan possessed the world's largest and most powerful economy and constituted the single greatest threat to this nation's security. Despite the smashing military victory over Iraq, the public evinced concern that the United States was "in decline." These worries, rather than any new fondness for isolationism, may explain why a large majority by late 1991 felt that President Bush was devoting excessive time to foreign policy. Conservative columnist Patrick Buchanan, in challenging Bush for renomination in 1992, tried to exploit these concerns. During the New Hampshire primary campaign, for example, he argued that Bush "would put America's wealth and power at the service of some vague new world order. We put America first." Yet his cultural attacks on Bush for such transgressions as federal funding of "pornography" through the National Endowment for the Arts may have been more effective than his isolationist platform.

2. *In view of the interdependent nature of the world, American security*

interests must necessarily be global. During the Cold War this axiom meant, in reality, that American interests were global because of the presumably universal nature of the Soviet threat. This reasoning lay at the heart of the global containment strategy. The Bush administration tried to sustain the precept in the absence of a Soviet threat by offering three arguments. First, it suggested that the post–Cold War world was intrinsically highly interdependent, especially economically, and that American prosperity was directly linked to the health of the global economy. Second, it claimed that, if left unchallenged, regional despots and aggressors, by encouraging imitators, could wreak global disorder. Stopping Saddam Hussein thus became a "litmus test" for the new world order and, of course, American will. Finally, the administration asserted that because this nation's security depended on the creation of a democratic world, its interests could not be artificially delimited.

These sweeping claims received a mixed response from the public. It accepted the administration's rather commonplace observation about growing interdependence and believed that the United States had no choice but to participate in the world economy. It also shared to a degree the administration's concerns about regional outlaws with nuclear weapons but preferred that the United Nations take the initiative in taming them. But the public showed little enthusiasm for fostering democracy abroad and implicitly rejected the administration's assertion that American security required a democratic world. In fact, as we have seen, Bush and his advisers, despite their rhetoric, placed tight economic and military limits on what it would do to sustain the "democratic revolution."

3. *Nondemocratic powers intent on dominating critical regions constitute the primary threat to world peace.* This revised axiom, which replaced the Cold War focus on "communist aggression and subversion," formed the core of the January 1993 Department of Defense document entitled "Defense Strategy for the 1990s: The Regional Defense Strategy." Moreover, the administration based its response to Iraq's invasion of Kuwait on this precept. Unlike its Cold War counterpart, which had identified only leftist security threats, the new version included all nondemocratic regimes as potential concerns. In so doing the administration embraced an academic argument of, most notably, Princeton political scientist Michael Doyle. Doyle and others had recently "discovered," after a review of the historical record, that for a variety of reasons, democracies did not go to war against one another.[70] Here was apparent empirical proof for a key Wilsonian (and Kantian and Jeffersonian) contention, and the administration made it the basis for its "zone of democratic peace" concept. If, it argued, this still fragile zone was to flourish, miscreant nondemocratic states had to be stopped and punished.

Though increasingly popular in academic circles,[71] the public seemed little moved by these syllogisms. It did worry about the prospect of nuclear weapons in the hands of such nations as Iraq, Iran, and North Korea. It did support the administration's claims that American economic security had been threatened by Saddam Hussein. But political elites seemed more impressed than the public about ideological distinctions between democratic and nondemocratic states.[72]

4. *The strategy of collective engagement represents the best way to deter regional aggression.* By 1992, the administration had settled on "collective engagement" as the preferred description of its post–Cold War strategy. By substituting this phrase for "containment" and "regional aggression" for "Soviet and Soviet-inspired expansion," the Bush inner circle hoped to create the basis for a new domestic foreign policy consensus. Yet, as we earlier observed, President Bush did not wish to risk a grand national debate about post–Cold War American foreign policy in the midst of his reelection effort. While Baker and Cheney, in early 1992 congressional testimony, did try to spark discussion, the president, already under attack for allegedly ignoring domestic affairs, waited until after the election to spell out the new strategy. To reiterate, "collective engagement," while emphasizing the centrality of multilateral institutions and denying any "global policeman" intentions, nevertheless bore a close resemblance to the leaked (and discredited) "Defense Planning Guidance" of March 1992.

George Bush left office before "collective engagement" had any chance to achieve the status of a policy axiom, though, as we discover in the next chapter, it did anticipate in several ways the Clinton administration's strategy of "engagement and enlargement." Democrats picked at the specifics of the Bush foreign policy record—Haiti, Bosnia, Russia, and defense spending, for example. But they failed to offer a consistent strategic alternative apart from arguing that the nation's domestic economic base needed first to be strengthened. Republican Pat Buchanan offered isolationism as an appropriate course in a postcommunist, neomercantilist world, but this strategy found only limited public support and almost no elite enthusiasm.

5. *The United States must possess sufficient military power to discourage potential aggressors.* This axiom's Cold War counterpart had specified that "the United States must possess nuclear weapons in order to deter a Soviet attack on it and its allies," but with the virtual disappearance of the Soviet nuclear threat, the Bush administration sought a broader formulation. On the surface, this revised precept appeared to command widespread public support. Most Americans had rejoiced over the triumph of their forces in the Persian Gulf War and extended to General Norman Schwartzkopf and his troops an extraordinary outpouring of gratitude. Nor did polls indicate

that the public, despite some congressional pressure for a "peace dividend," wished to reduce defense spending drastically. Finally, there was no evidence that the public wanted the United States to destroy the rest of its nuclear arsenal, although it supported the administration's efforts to cut deeply into it in tandem with the Soviet Union.

At the same time, however, the American people remained wary of employing this nation's vast military resources unless they could be persuaded that important, tangible national interests were at risk. "Stopping aggression," "restoring democracy," or "feeding the hungry" as general rationales for military intervention received only modest public support. Yet some observers correctly noted that as long as interventions cost little in blood and treasure, the public would acquiesce. This tendency to "go with success" helps explain, for example, the favorable public reaction to Operation Just Cause in December 1989 in which Panamanian leader Manuel Noriega was quickly deposed and imprisoned. It also accounts for the initial public toleration of Operation Restore Hope three years later when it appeared that starving Somalis could be fed at minimum risk to American troops. During Operation Desert Shield/Storm, the Bush administration mobilized public support by cleverly combining several arguments: (1) the economic security of the West (and American jobs) was threatened; (2) Iraq's aggression had violated international law and the UN Charter; (3) Saddam Hussein was a latter-day Hitler intent on acquiring nuclear weapons;[73] (4) the entire international community supported U.S. policy; (5) Iraq would obliterate Kuwait before economic sanctions could prove effective; (6) large international contributions greatly alleviated the American financial burden; and (7) if war came, it would not be another Vietnam. The Iraqi military collapsed so quickly that the resiliency of these arguments was never tested, though some prewar polls suggested that public support would have waned rapidly in the face of rising American casualties.[74]

This post–Cold War "axiom," then, while perhaps appealing as an abstract proposition, proved difficult for the administration to operationalize. The president, for example, repeatedly refused to answer "hypothetical" questions designed to determine if the United States would stop future aggressions that did not involve oil. Ironically, some liberal internationalist elites, who had shown extreme reluctance to use military power since Vietnam, now began to countenance it, not primarily to stop aggression, but to alleviate humanitarian disasters, to restore democratic governments, and to punish human rights violations.[75]

6. *A stable, open world economy requires American leadership.* This axiom had survived the tumult of Vietnam and remained fundamental to American foreign policy in the post–Cold War era. The Bush administration

viewed it as an integral and increasingly critical component of its strategy of collective engagement. As we have seen, the administration undertook several efforts to promote global and regional trade liberalization, including the Uruguay Round of GATT, NAFTA, and the Enterprise of the Americas Initiative. Like every administration since FDR's, it took as an article of faith the assumption that free trade and world peace were causally linked.

At the same time, however, the ending of the Cold War seemed to expose the structure of the American economy to heightened scrutiny. Some observers noted lagging productivity, a stagnant standard of living, low savings rates, and a stubborn trade imbalance with Japan as reasons for concern. They also argued that with the disappearance of the Soviet threat the United States had no obligation to give its allies a "free ride" by subsidizing their security costs while they increased their economic competitiveness. Most professional economists remained committed to free trade. A number of "trade strategists," led by Clyde Prestowitz, a former Reagan official in the Commerce Department, now claimed, however, that since this nation's Asian trading partners presumably rejected the laissez-faire approach to markets and trade, the United States could no longer afford to play by the old rules. Like its competitors, the U.S. government should identify and nurture promising technologies with export potential while protecting the home market from unfair foreign assaults. These strategists suggested that many of America's domestic economic weaknesses could be alleviated through a "fair trade" policy.[76]

Whether or not this analysis was correct, it seemed to reflect a mood apparent among a public historically much less committed to free trade than political elites. As surveys taken for the Chicago Council on Foreign Relations from 1975 to 1991 made clear, the public primarily worried about protecting American jobs and paid little attention to abstract arguments about the benefits of free trade. It would support whatever policy best preserved personal economic security—free, fair, or otherwise.

In the light of these long-standing concerns, as well as the additional pain seemingly caused by the "Bush recession," it was not surprising that free trade critics crowded the early 1992 presidential field. Democratic Senators Tom Harkin of Iowa and Bob Kerrey of Nebraska, conservative Republican commentator Pat Buchanan, and independent business executive Ross Perot all suggested that American workers needed protection against unfair foreign competitors. Even President Bush, as we have seen, felt compelled to transform his January 1992 visit to Japan into a trade mission, and Governor Bill Clinton of Arkansas withheld full support from NAFTA until late in the election campaign. Nevertheless, voters did not reward those who ran as protectionists, and a fragile free trade national consensus appeared to survive the end of the Cold War. But "fair traders," intent on "leveling the playing field" had emerged as significant forces in future debates about foreign economic policy.

7. *The United States must assume leadership in organizations like the United Nations.* Throughout the Cold War, public support for the United Nations remained consistently high despite the belief that, on balance, the organization's performance was "poor."[77] Since the emergence of a Third World voting majority in the General Assembly in the early 1970s, the United States generally refused to submit important security issues to it or to the veto-bound Security Council. The Nixon and Reagan administrations, in particular, expressed open contempt for the UN's anti-American ideological orthodoxy. To protest its displeasure this nation had routinely withheld its full payment of dues and had even withdrawn from two specialized agencies—UNESCO and the International Labor Organization.

The end of the Cold War changed many features on the international landscape but none more so than the role of the United Nations. By making it the centerpiece of the efforts to isolate Saddam Hussein, the Bush administration returned the organization to a prominence it had not enjoyed in American foreign policy since the late 1940s. Bush's decision to approach the UN instead of Congress to gain immediate legitimacy for Operation Desert Shield closely mirrored Truman's actions after North Korea's invasion in 1950.

In the aftermath of the Persian Gulf War the United Nations achieved "a uniquely favored place in the public's perception."[78] Seventy-eight percent of the American people in the fall of 1991 approved of the job it was doing. More significantly, perhaps, polls indicated that "when faced with future problems of aggression," as many as 85 percent wanted the United Nations, not the United States, to "take the lead."[79]

The Bush administration, however, appeared considerably less willing to grant that kind of authority to the United Nations. By 1992 the post–Cold War world showed signs of considerable disorder: humanitarian disasters in Africa, the violent disintegration of Yugoslavia, ethnic unrest in parts of the former Soviet Union, the potential development of nuclear weapons by North Korea and Iran, and the Haitian refugee crisis, for example. The administration's devotion to the United Nations, however, had strict limits, and, if anything, it sought to dampen public euphoria for the organization. It would use the Security Council to enforce postwar sanctions against Iraq, but it would resist Secretary General Boutras Boutras-Ghali's calls for ambitious UN "peacemaking" responsibilities.[80]

In sum, the Bush administration's sometimes half-hearted efforts to resurrect, with some modifications, the policy axioms of the Cold War proved only modestly successful. It apparently recognized that as least some of these precepts would prove controversial with both public and elites, for it declined to open a grand national debate on America's post–Cold War role. If given a second term in office, the administration may well have moved to mobilize support for these axioms. To do so, however, would have required it to be more explicit about the "benevolent hegemon" role it wished America to play in the new world order. Instead, the administration attempted to place operational, not strategic, limits on the scope of this nation's international activities. It did so because it sensed a public desire for relief from the demands of the Cold War, and because it remained, finally, an administration of cautious "process Tories."

As we noted in the previous chapter, Ronald Reagan clearly failed to create a new procedural foreign policy consensus, and he left executive-legislative relations in at least as much disarray as he had found them in 1981. Did George Bush, who so valued "right process," achieve greater success than his more ideological predecessor?

He tried, in his Inaugural Address, to set a more positive tone:

> We need a new engagement . . . between the Executive and the Congress. We must ensure that America stands before the world united, strong, at peace, and fiscally sound. We need to compromise; we've had dissension. We need harmony; we've had a chorus of discordant voices.
>
> It's been this way since Vietnam. That war cleaves us still. But, friends, that war began in earnest a quarter of a century ago, and surely the statute of limitations has been reached. This is a fact: The final lesson of Vietnam is that no great nation can long afford to be sundered by a memory. A new breeze is blowing, and the old bipartisanship must be made new again.[81]

In late March 1989 the administration announced a bipartisan accord on Central America that aimed to remove Central America as a source of presidential-congressional conflict. Under the terms of the accord the United States promised to provide $4.5 million a month to the *contras* for food, clothing, shelter, and medical supplies until the Nicaraguan elections scheduled for February 1990. But these funds would cease after November 1989 unless approved by four separate congressional committees.[82] The bitterest criticism of this unusual arrangement came from White House legal counsel C. Boyden Gray, who condemned it as an unconstitutional abrogation of executive power in foreign affairs. Gray, in turn, received an equally surprising public rebuke from Marlin Fitzwater, who praised the agreement for ending "years of dissension between the executive and legislative branch."[83] Yet as the February 1990 Nicaraguan elections approached, new disputes arose. The vice-president predicted that the Sandinistas would never allow free elections. When the administration asked Congress for money to supervise the balloting and to aid opposition parties, some Democrats argued that neither the CIA nor the National Endowment for Democracy—the administration's choices—should play a role in the process. On the other hand, some conservatives claimed that any American aid would legitimate inevitably unfair elections that would elect the Sandinistas. Violetta Chamorro's stunning upset of Daniel Ortega surprised the White House and many in Congress, but Bush's efforts to obtain emergency aid for the new Nicaraguan and Panamanian governments were blocked. A majority wished to make such assistance conditional on a drastic cut in aid to El Salvador to punish that regime for failing to prosecute those responsible for murdering several leading university clerics in 1989.

The aftermath of the failed Panamanian coup of October 1989 also produced a good deal of bickering. Bush, Baker, and other senior administration officials had frequently called on Panamanians to overthrow Noriega and establish democracy. But when mid-level officers in the Panamanian Defense Force (PDF), with the apparent knowledge of the Bush administration, attempted to oust the general, Washington did very little to help the rebels. Its failure provoked a public squabble between David Boren (D-OK), chairman of the Senate Select Committee on Intelligence, and Brent Scowcroft. When Boren ridiculed the administration's failure to coordinate planning with the PDF rebels, Scowcroft complained that Boren's own committee had previously placed crippling restrictions on potential American involvement in coups.[84] In contrast, congressional support for the invasion of Panama and the arrest of Noriega in December 1989 rivaled that given to the Grenada "rescue mission" once its success became apparent.

But at least some in the White House remained annoyed with what they saw as congressional meddling in foreign policy. In May 1990, in a public exchange with journalist Theodore Draper, a top aide to C. Boyden Gray complained of a "legislative usurpation of executive power" and a "virtual constitutional *coup d'état*" since the early 1970s. This "antifederalist counterrevolution," the official concluded, resulted in "imperial and highly partisan congressional foreign policy micromanagement."[85]

A year later, in the wake of the Persian Gulf War, President Bush echoed these complaints. Speaking at Princeton University in May 1991 he noted that "while Congress necessarily adopts the views of its constituents, . . . the President and the Vice President are the only officials elected to serve the entire Nation. It is the President who is responsible for guiding and directing the Nation's foreign policy, . . . 'with secrecy and dispatch' when necessary."[86] And though claiming to have "great respect for Congress," Bush, like Reagan, bemoaned "congressional oversight" that had "grown exponentially." He proudly reminded his audience that he had vetoed six bills that would have weakened presidential powers and had repeatedly "stated that statutory provisions that violate the Constitution have no binding legal force."[87]

These rather extravagant claims prompted at least one constitutional scholar to accuse Bush of creating a "semi-sovereign presidency" largely immune from legislative oversight.[88] Whether true or not, Bush's treatment of Congress during the Persian Gulf crisis struck some observers as highhanded. Fearful of defeat in Congress the president relied on the UN Security Council to apply increasing pressure on Iraq. His late October 1990 decision to double American troop strength in the region made war much more likely, yet Bush declined to inform Congress of this action until immediately *after* the midterm elections. He did eventually ask for congressional support on the eve of Operation Desert Storm, but he insisted that he already had the authority to use force regardless of the vote in Congress. As it turned out, large Democratic majorities in both houses opposed the president, but the resolutions nevertheless squeaked through.[89]

Yet despite this emotional and potentially divisive episode and despite Bush's inclination to conduct foreign policy as a Cold War president, executive-legislative relations generally improved from the Reagan years. Nuclear and conventional arms agreements sailed through Congress, a bipartisan military base closing procedure was created, and while funding for SDI and a few other weapons systems remained contentious, the overall atmosphere appeared less charged than in the 1970s and 1980s. Potentially disruptive post–Cold War disputes over humanitarian interventions, aid to Russia, "ethnic cleansing" in Bosnia, the expansion of NATO, the creation of NAFTA, the trade deficit with Japan, and the restoration of Haitian democracy certainly loomed, but the removal of communism and the Soviet Union as hot-button issues in American politics at least helped to rearrange the old presidential-congressional fault lines.

But the end of the Cold War did nothing to dampen the "cultural wars" that had been wracking the nation since the late 1960s. If anything, the defeat of communism abroad appeared to intensify social conflict at home. The social, sexual, and racial revolutions that largely coincided with the Vietnam War had provoked powerful, antagonistic reactions that, as we have seen, both Richard Nixon and Ronald Reagan had exploited in somewhat different ways. George Bush's call for "a kinder, gentler America" in his 1988 nomination acceptance speech constituted a veiled plea for a truce in this cultural combat. He then promptly violated the cease-fire by relying on extremely divisive symbols during the ensuing campaign.

Once elected, Bush largely cast these symbols aside in favor of others more appropriate for the "governing mode." He attempted to build cultural support for his foreign policy by linking its goals to the values of the World War II generation he wished to personify. By stressing such themes as patriotism, respect for the military, the promise of democracy abroad, and the ever-present danger of global disorder, President Bush generally ignored the ongoing cultural wars in favor of an older—and, perhaps, fictitious—social unity. He rested his new world order on a venerable cultural base: the new experts, like the old establishment, would run foreign policy smoothly, coolly, and in the "national interest."

But as the 1992 election approached George Bush again took up the arms of cultural warfare. In March, under great pressure from Pat Buchanan, he fired his NEA director for having approved federal grants for "pornography." Then, in exchange for an endorsement from Buchanan, he allowed the Republican convention to be controlled by the party's right wing. It used the Houston meeting to declare war on America's domestic enemies. In a widely watched prime-time speech Buchanan set the tone by observing that

> there is a religious war going on in this country for the soul of America. It is a cultural war, as critical to the kind of nation we shall be as the Cold War itself, for this war is for the soul of America. And in that struggle for the soul of America, Clinton & Clinton are on the other side, and George Bush is on our side.[90]

Hailing the soldiers who had retaken south central Los Angeles during the May 1992 race riots, Buchanan closed by asserting that so too "we must take back *our* cities, and take back *our* culture, and take back *our* country.[91]
Pat Robertson, the televangelist, directly connected foreign policy to domestic culture: "The people of Eastern Europe got rid of their left wingers; it is time that we in America got rid of our left wingers." He noted that although international communism had fallen, centralized government in the United States was "a more benign but equally insidious plague . . . [and] the carrier of this plague is the Democratic Party."[92] Senator Phil Gram of Texas likened liberal Democrats to North Korean and Cuban communists in their devotion to big government.[93] Second Lady Marilyn Quayle, a corporate lawyer, nevertheless suggested that women who stay at home to raise a family were "closer to their essential natures" than those who did not.[94] Throughout the convention, Republicans claimed that while they stood for "family values," the Democrats presumably embraced gays, pornographers, abortionists, atheists, and other perverts. They appeared to nominate the Bush *family* to run against *Hillary* and Bill Clinton.

Unlike Richard Nixon, who unleashed a *Kulturkampf* as part of his "new majority" governing strategy, George Bush mostly confined it to his "campaign mode." In building cultural support for a post–Cold War foreign policy, he ignored the widespread sociocultural changes that the nation had undergone since the 1960s—for example, changes in family structure, the effects of large-scale immigration, and the changed status of women and blacks. By reaching back to World War II and the early Cold War for unifying symbols he implicitly acknowledged a fundamental problem facing post–Cold War America: the apparent lack of legitimate, contemporary symbols in an increasingly balkanized political culture. It was difficult to anchor a new grand design in this soil.

Notes

1. This term was coined by Sidney Blumenthal in his book *Pledging Allegiance: The Last Campaign of the Cold War.*
2. Charles O. Jones, "Meeting Low Expectations: Strategy and Prospects of the Bush Presidency," p. 63.
3. Garry Wills, "The Hostage," p. 22.
4. Bush also served, at Nixon's request, as chairman of the Republican National Committee.
5. He also bowed to pressure from the right when, as CIA director, he ordered a second analysis of Soviet military spending and packed the study group (Team B) with very hawkish experts.
6. Blumenthal, *Pledging Allegiance,* p. 54.
7. John Podhoretz, *Hell of a Ride: Backstage at the White House Follies, 1989–1993,* p. 161.
8. Charles Kolb, *White House Daze: The Unmaking of Domestic Policy in the Bush Years,* p. 8.
9. Ibid., p. 187.
10. Ibid.
11. Ibid., p. 204.
12. Ibid., p. 340.
13. Ibid., p. 8.
14. Ibid., p. 234.
15. Ibid., p. 347.
16. Podhoretz, *Hell of a Ride,* p. 167.
17. Kolb, *White House Daze,* p. 86.
18. Representative Charles Schumer (D-NY), quoted in Barbara Sinclair, "Governing Unheroically (and Sometimes Unappetizingly): Bush and the 101st Congress," p. 164.
19. Kolb, *White House Daze,* p. 56.
20. Ibid., p. 6.
21. Kerry Mullins and Aaron Wildavsky, "The Procedural Presidency of George Bush," p. 39.
22. Blumenthal, *Pledging Allegiance,* p. 319.
23. Kolb, *White House Daze,* p. 243.
24. *New York Times,* April 9, 1989, p. 1.
25. *New York Times,* April 9, 1989, p. 1.
26. *New York Times,* September 16, 1989, p. 1.

27. Michael R. Beschloss and Strobe Talbott, *At the Highest Levels: The Inside Story of the End of the Cold War*, p. 56.

28. Ibid., p. 123.

29. Ibid., p. 167.

30. He had wanted Gorbachev to extend recognition first but finally lost patience. Gorbachev followed four days later with recognition.

31. *New York Times,* March 10, 1992, p. A10.

32. *New York Times,* March 10, 1992, p. A10.

33. *New York Times,* March 11, 1992, p. A12.

34. Cited by David Gergen, "America's Missed Opportunities," p. 9.

35. *New York Times,* March 14, 1992, p. A10.

36. Beschloss and Talbott, *At the Highest Levels,* p. 346.

37. Ibid., p. 408.

38. Ibid., p. 418.

39. Michael Mandelbaum, "The Bush Foreign Policy," pp. 6–7.

40. Terry L. Deibel, "Bush's Foreign Policy: Mastery and Inaction," p. 13.

41. George Bush, "Remarks at the Aspen Institute Symposium in Aspen, Colorado," August 2, 1990, pp. 1190, 1191.

42. Ibid., p. 1192.

43. Robert W. Tucker and David C. Hendrickson, *The Imperial Temptation: The New World Order and America's Purpose,* p. 57.

44. Ibid., p. 58.

45. Gergen, "America's Missed Opportunities," p. 12.

46. Interview with Zalmay Khalilzad, Washington, DC, November 21, 1994.

47. *New York Times,* February 17, 1992, pp. A1, A8.

48. Interview with Khalilzad.

49. *New York Times,* May 24, 1992, p. 1.

50. Robert B. Zoellick, "The North American FTA: The New World Order Takes Shape In the Western Hemisphere."

51. Robert B. Zoellick, "Project for the Republican Future: Is There a 'Republican' Foreign Policy?" p. 3.

52. Interview with Robert B. Zoellick, Washington, DC, January 27, 1995.

53. Ibid.

54. Zoellick, "Is There a 'Republican' Foreign Policy?" p. 2.

55. Reprinted in Thomas G. Paterson, ed., *Major Problems in American Foreign Policy, Volume II: Since 1914,* p. 298.

56. George Bush, "Remarks at Texas A&M University in College Station, Texas," December 15, 1992, pp. 2191, 2192.

57. George Bush, "Remarks at the United States Military Academy in West Point, New York," January 5, 1993, p. 2229.

58. Bush, "Remarks at West Point," pp. 2230, 2231.

59. Mullins and Wildavsky, "The Procedural Presidency," pp. 40–43.

60. Interviews with State Department officials.

61. Ibid.

62. *New York Times,* August 5, 1988, pp. A12, A1.

63. Bush, "Remarks at Texas A&M," p. 2190.

64. Ibid.

65. Ibid., p. 2192.

66. Interview with Bush NSC official.

67. This represented the administration's final attempt to name its strategy.

68. Tucker and Hendrickson, *The Imperial Temptation,* p. 190.

69. Interview with Richard Haass, Washington, DC, December 8, 1994.

70. See, for example, Michael Doyle, "Liberalism and World Politics"; and Bruce Russett, *Controlling the Sword: The Democratic Governance of National Security.*

71. Not everyone accepted this thesis. See, for example, Christopher Layne, "Kant or Cant: The Myth of the Democratic Peace"; and David E. Spiro, "The Insignificance of the Liberal Peace."

72. Evidence to this effect was uncovered by Bruce Jentleson in his "The Pretty Prudent Public: Post Post-Vietnam American Opinion on the Use of Military Force."

73. Focus groups convened by administration pollsters during the crisis indicated that people were most concerned about the dangers of a nuclear Iraq. As a result, Bush's statements began to emphasize this factor more than previously.

74. See, for example, the results of a *Washington Post* poll reported in that newspaper on January 8, 1991.

75. Charles Krauthammer, "How the Hawks Became Doves."

76. See, for example, Clyde V. Prestowitz Jr., "Beyond Laissez Faire."

77. Jeffrey Laurenti, *American Public Opinion and the United Nations, 1992: Evolving Perceptions of a Changing World.*

78. *Americans Talk Issues, Survey no. 16,* "The Emerging World Order," p. 12.

79. Laurenti, *American Public Opinion,* p. 23.

80. *An Agenda for Peace: Preventive Diplomacy, Peacemaking and Peace-keeping.* Boutros-Ghali's recommendations are nicely summarized in his "Empowering the United Nations."

81. George Bush, "Inaugural Address," January 20, 1989, pp. 2–3.

82. George Bush, "US Support for Democracy and Peace in Central America."

83. *New York Times,* March 28, 1989, p. 8.

84. *New York Times,* October 12, 1989, p. 8, p. 1.

85. George Bush, "The Constitution in Danger: An Exchange."

86. George Bush, "Remarks Upon Receiving an Honorary Degree From Princeton University in Princeton, New Jersey," May 10, 1991, p. 590.

87. Ibid., p. 591.

88. Charles Tiefer, *The Semi-Sovereign Presidency.*

89. In the Senate, Republicans voted in favor of the resolution 43–2, while Democrats opposed it 45–9. Partisan splits in the House were only slightly less dramatic.

90. Quoted in Garry Wills, "The Born-Again Republicans," p. 9.

91. Ibid.

92. Ibid.

93. Ibid.

94. Ibid., p. 13.

6

The Clinton Administration:
An Early Appraisal

By winning 43 percent of the vote in a three-candidate field Bill Clinton entered the White House in 1993 with an ambiguous mandate for "change." The five-term Democratic governor of Arkansas had succeeded in turning the 1992 election into a referendum on George Bush's handling of the economy. Relying heavily on the ideas of Robert Reich, a Harvard political scientist and certifiable "Friend of Bill" (FOB) since Oxford,[1] Clinton argued that the "trickle down" economic policies of Bush and Reagan had badly hurt middle-class Americans who "work hard and play by the rules." He portrayed the 1980s as a "decade of greed" when good jobs had been shipped abroad; when America had lost its comparative edge and become the world's biggest debtor; and when myopic policies had caused the domestic infrastructure to decay. The "Bush recession," Governor Clinton claimed, was the inevitable result of the failure to invest in the future of the American workforce. Again and again Clinton emphasized the need for "change" and, in the course of a very long campaign made many promises: to make health care more affordable and accessible; to reform welfare "as we know it"; to cut the taxes of the middle class; to overhaul lobbying practices and campaign financing; to cut the federal deficit in half by 1997; and to "invest" in education, national service, job retraining, environmental technology, defense conversion, and several other programs.[2] But above all he "focused like a laser" on the allegedly sad state of the American economy.

In August 1991 George Bush and his political advisers,[3] to capitalize on the president's unprecedented popularity, decided to conduct a cautious, traditional campaign in which the incumbent would run on his record.[4] After all, Bush's approval rating stood ten full points above Reagan's at the same time in his term, and most of the strongest potential Democratic candidates had already bailed out of the 1992 race. But by early 1992 the economy seemed to be "double-dipping," Pat Buchanan had challenged Bush for renomination from the right, and Texas billionaire Ross Perot was threatening a third-party run. Bush's aura of invincibility had been pierced, yet he remained extremely confident. Perot, who had campaigned as a "deficit hawk," suddenly withdrew from the race immediately after Clinton received his party's nomination in July and gave him a critical boost by hailing the "revitalization" of the Democratic Party.[5] In fact, the quixotic Perot had quit largely because of his inability to offer a politically appealing balanced budget proposal.[6] When he reentered the campaign on October 1, Clinton had moved comfortably ahead of Bush. Although Perot won no states in the election, his 19 percent total was more than any third party candidate since Theodore Roosevelt in 1912. His antiestablishment, semi-isolationist message of fiscal conservatism had obviously attracted a very large following.

Bill Clinton's character had been an issue since before the New Hampshire primary as the press raised questions about his draft record, his marital infidelity, and his use of marijuana. Yet President Bush, still confident of victory, largely avoided "going negative" until late in the campaign, when he questioned Clinton's patriotism in organizing anti-Vietnam War demonstrations while a Rhodes scholar and in making a trip to Moscow in 1969. These insinuations would have been devastating during the Cold War, but in 1992 they had little impact, especially after it was revealed that the State Department had undertaken a search of Clinton's passport file on the administration's behalf.

Nevertheless, the "character issue" plagued Clinton throughout the campaign. It had heavily influenced his decision to stay out of the 1988 presidential race, and it had made him vulnerable in the 1992 primaries, particularly after former California governor Jerry Brown pinned the "slick Willie" sobriquet on him.[7] Clinton's staff worked feverishly to manufacture a positive, countervailing persona. When Clinton, despite being battered by stories about a long affair with Gennifer Flowers, finished second in the New Hampshire primary, he quickly dubbed himself the "Comeback Kid." Then, on the basis of intense focus-group research conducted by pollster Stanley Greenberg, Clinton was reinvented at the Democratic convention as "the Man from Hope."[8]

The campaign staff took two additional steps to defuse attacks on Clinton's character, record, and policy positions. First, in order to respond instantly to criticism (as Dukakis had failed to do in 1988), it set up a "war room" in Little Rock under the direction of political operatives James Carville and Paul Begala. Second, in order to personalize himself and to create the illusion of intimacy in an electronic age, Clinton made frequent appearances on talk shows, including Arsenio Hall's, where he wore dark glasses and played the saxophone, and on MTV.[9] By thus going over the heads of the press, he tried to convince a cynical electorate that he was willing to submit his character to direct examination.[10]

Foreign policy issues virtually disappeared in this first post–Cold War campaign. George Bush, the quintessential foreign policy president, was largely robbed of his strongest suit by a public demanding that he devote more time to domestic matters. While he repeatedly trumpeted his role in defeating Iraq and winning the Cold War, disparaged Clinton's utter lack of international experience, and questioned the Arkansas governor's allegiance to America, President Bush nevertheless promised to give domestic issues top priority in a second term. Ross Perot condemned the administration's foreign economic policy as a jobs giveaway to Mexico and Japan and relentlessly needled Bush for his alleged role in the Iran-*contra* scandal. In three major addresses Clinton closely aligned himself with Bush on most foreign policy issues, agreeing that American global leadership remained indispensable in a still dangerous post–Cold War world. But he lambasted the administration for failing to provide an adequate domestic base to support its international strategy and complained that it had betrayed American ideals by "coddling" foreign dictators. Bush, he claimed, had forgotten that "global economic competition is the hallmark of this new age":

> This has been the administration's most glaring foreign policy failure. An anemic, debt laden economy; the developed world's highest rates of crime and poverty; an archaic education system; decaying roads, ports, and cities; all these undermine our diplomacy, make it harder for us to secure favorable trade agreements and compromise our ability to finance essential military actions. Mr. Bush's economic neglect literally has invited foreign pity.[11]

Furthermore, emphasizing a theme reminiscent of Jimmy Carter in 1976, Clinton cited the administration's alleged reluctance to support democrats "from the Baltics to Beijing, from Sarajevo to South Africa." Instead, "George Bush sided with the status quo rather than democratic change—with familiar tyrants rather than those who would overthrow them."[12] Clinton demanded that the administration cease repatriating Haitian refugees and pressure China to respect human rights. Perhaps more surprising, given the post-Vietnam proclivities of the Democratic Party, he also urged the administration to consider the use of air power to protect Bosnian Muslims against Serbian aggression. Indeed, all three demands would come back to haunt President Clinton in 1993.[13]

"A New Kind of Democrat"

In the aftermath of the 1994 midterm elections, Representative Dave McCurdy (D-OK), chair of the centrist Democratic Leadership Council

(DLC) and recently defeated in a Senate race, blamed his party's disastrous showing directly on Bill Clinton. After running and winning in 1992 as a New Democrat, Clinton, McCurdy charged, had then governed like a traditional big-government liberal.[14] The electorate quite predictably rebelled two years later against this perversion of "change" and gave Republicans control of Congress for the first time in forty years. McCurdy's analysis, while quite seductive, ignored the complexities (and occasional contradictions) of Bill Clinton's gubernatorial record, presidential campaign, domestic priorities, and approach to governance.

We need not dwell on Clinton's early years—rural Arkansas, Georgetown University, Rhodes scholar, Yale Law School—except to note an abiding interest in politics and policy and a long-standing desire to move the Democratic Party beyond the nostrums of the New Deal.[15] Narrowly defeated in a bid for a House seat in 1974 and elected Arkansas attorney general two years later, in 1978 Clinton became the nation's youngest governor in three decades. His performance in Little Rock foreshadowed that of his presidency in both style and content.

During his first gubernatorial campaign Clinton made fifty-three specific promises, many of them based on ideas that he and his wife, Hillary Rodham, had collected from progressive policy thinkers from around the country. These included pledges to create energy and economic development departments, to expand the rural health care system, to reorganize local school districts, and to reorder the entire state education system—all in two years. But Clinton also wished to preempt criticism that he was just another "tax and spend liberal," and so he asked Dick Morris, his pollster, to survey voters about their program preferences. According to Morris, the young governor, "like a kid in a candy store, . . . wanted to do it all," but he finally decided to choose one issue to define his administration: road improvements.[16] To fund these projects Clinton proposed to raise vehicle license fees based on the value of the car or truck. When the state's powerful trucking and poultry industries voiced strong opposition, Clinton suggested a compromise—tying the fee to the vehicle's weight—that angered all sides, including low income drivers of heavy old jalopies and pickups.

Furthermore, the governor's management style left much to be desired. Refusing to appoint a chief of staff, he relied instead on three executive assistants—young, hairy, and very liberal—who soon became known as the "Three Beards."[17] They failed to discipline a governor with outsized appetites and a penchant for tardiness. When he was swept from office in the 1980 Reagan landslide, Clinton became the youngest governor in American history to be defeated.[18]

Elected again in 1982 (as well as 1984, 1986, and 1990) Clinton, chastened and angered by his loss, developed a "survival plan" to succeed based on three axioms.[19] First, he began to recognize the importance of blending policy ends and political means to rebut charges that he was an intellectual out of touch with the real Arkansas. Second, he vowed never again to rely on the "free media" to define his programs and accomplishments. Morris's polls indicated that in 1980 voters could remember only that he had increased license fees, so in the second term Clinton turned to paid media, commercials, and grassroots mailings to "spin" his message. Finally, he and Morris decided to survey voters continuously, using the results to shape the substance and the rhetoric of the ensuing policies. According to David Maraniss, Clinton "sang from a political score that he and the voters had jointly composed."[20]

By the mid-1980s Bill Clinton had begun to gain national visibility as "the education governor." Forced to devise reforms because of an Arkansas Supreme Court ruling that directed the state to find a more equitable formula to finance education, he had appointed his wife chair of an Educational Standards Commission to develop proposals. To fund the suggested programs Clinton asked the legislature to increase the state sales tax—a regressive levy but one that needed only a majority vote for passage. Then, largely to counter polls that showed Clinton perceived by many as a tool of liberal interest groups, he threw in a last-minute idea—teacher competency testing—that ironically became the symbolic heart of the entire program.[21]

Clinton now had a clear (if somewhat unintentional) identity, and, in a speech at the 1984 Democratic convention, he used it to anticipate many of his later themes. In it he decried the nation's sagging productivity growth, its eroding national competitiveness, the soaring federal budget deficit, increasingly unaffordable health care, and the miserable state of primary and secondary education. After the 1984 election, Governor Clinton began to ground his reform proposals in the broader theme of "opportunity and responsibility," which he recognized as a way to justify change without alienating the middle class.[22] As chair of the National Governors Association, he offered suggestions for making welfare payments contingent on work, education, and child care. Clinton's claim to represent the mainstream appeared fully justified by his election to the chair of the DLC in 1991, a position previously occupied by Sam Nunn (D-GA) and Charles Robb (D-VA), both southern moderates.

Yet, as John Judis observed, Bill Clinton's 1992 presidential campaign themes and promises were composed of a complex and potentially contradictory mix of forty parts liberal populism, thirty parts Perotist economic nationalism, and thirty parts DLC New Democrat.[23] For example, Clinton's stump speeches variously described Republicans as fronts for rich special interests and potential coalition partners for his administration; condemned excessive corporate pay and drug price gouging; pleaded for more individual responsibility; belatedly endorsed NAFTA; and demanded legislation to punish unfair trade competitors. In part, Clinton's rhetoric stemmed from the need to hold traditional Democratic constituencies, win back conservative Reagan Democrats, and appeal to potential Perot voters. But it also reflected an ideological battle among his advisers for control of Clinton's message and helped make the drafting of *Putting People First,* the basic campaign document, an exercise in chaos and anger.[24] Moreover, it foreshadowed a struggle during the first part of the Clinton presidency over the definition and sequencing of the domestic agenda.

Bill Clinton came to Washington armed with an enormously ambitious policy agenda and determined to make government work for the average citizen. At a mid-February 1993 Camp David meeting with his staff and cabinet, he set his priorities *for the first year.* They included (1) an economic stimulus package to create jobs rapidly; (2) a deficit reduction program; (3) shifting government spending into more productive "investments"; (4) a bill to reform campaign financing and lobbying rules; (5) a national service act; (6) welfare reform; (7) a comprehensive overhaul of the health care system; (8) trade initiatives designed to address the realities of other nations' practices; and (9) a variety of government proposals to deal with the environment, work apprenticeships, illiteracy, and the homeless.[25] Notably missing from this long list was the promised middle-class tax cut, an issue that had figured prominently in the Clinton campaign, especially as a weapon against deficit hawk Paul Tsongas during the early primaries.

Even before his inauguration, Clinton had decided to abandon the tax cut. In December 1993 Federal Reserve Bank Chairman Alan Greenspan had begun to convince Clinton of the paramount danger of high interest rates caused by the deficit. He argued that Clinton's economic plan had to "play" in the bond market. Serious deficit reduction, Greenspan suggested, would lower long-term rates without threatening inflation, spur economic growth by making borrowing easier, increase employment, and thus improve the prospects of the middle class. Lower rates would, in effect, constitute a tax cut without inflation. To the dismay of his more liberal advisers, Clinton more or less accepted this "financial markets strategy" designed to eventually help Main Street by first reassuring Wall Street. Furthermore, although deficit reduction had not played a major role in Clinton's campaign rhetoric, to win the support of Perot voters, the new president recognized that the issue needed to be addressed. Moreover, in early January 1993 outgoing OMB director Richard Darman significantly increased his five-year deficit projection and forced Clinton—much as he had forced Bush in 1990—to make some hard budget choices. Finally, Stanley Greenberg's ongoing focus-group research had shown that voters wanted to make some sacrifices to lower the deficit and did not even remember Clinton's promise of a tax cut.[26]

We need not retell the ugly and convoluted story of the administration's efforts to win congressional approval for its economic plan, but several observations can be offered. First, even before unveiling the program in mid-February, a series of early blunders, including the mishandling of several appointments and the gays in the military issue, raised questions about Clinton's judgment. Second, his first presidential actions involved issuing executive orders dealing with abortion funding, fetal research, and family planning. While designed to repeal the most controversial parts of the Reagan–Bush social agenda, these actions made it easier for Republicans to castigate Clinton as a typical liberal beholden to Democratic constituent groups.[27] Third, in order to win the support of Democratic congressional leaders for his economic plan, Clinton quickly abandoned his promises to back campaign financing reform, the overhaul of lobbying rules, and the line-item veto. In so doing, he failed to appreciate pervasive public disgust with Congress, especially among the Perot voters he so wanted to woo. Fourth, President Clinton's economic plan proved to be an extraordinarily unwieldy potpourri of deficit reduction, new "investments," and tax increases. While it raised gasoline taxes 4.3 cents per gallon, hiked the income taxes of only the most affluent, and cut the deficit by nearly $500 billion over five years, Clinton's failure to articulate his program's purpose clearly and consistently allowed Republicans rather unfairly to brand it as a "tax and spend" disaster. In the end, not a single Republican in either House voted for the package. Finally, throughout the entire process serious disagreements among Clinton's advisers continually erupted and exposed significant ideological rifts within the administration. In general, a coalition composed of the political consultants—Begala, Carville, Greenberg, and Mandy Grunwald—viewed themselves as "empowerment populists" committed to improving the lot of middle-class workers. This group supported Clinton's stimulus proposal, investments in education and apprenticeships, comprehensive health care reform, and efforts to clean up Congress. At the urging of Hillary Clinton they attempted to craft a coherent, understandable "story" for the president to tell the public that would integrate Clinton's many initiatives.[28] Arrayed against the consultants was the president's economic team—Treasury Secretary Lloyd Bentsen, National Economic Council Director Robert Rubin, OMB Director Leon Panetta, and Panetta's deputy, Alice Rivlin. These deficit hawks—derisively dubbed the "pod people" by Grunwald—embraced the financial markets strategy, worried about the costs of health care and welfare reform, wanted to cooperate with Congress, and rejected what they saw as the consultants' focus on "class warfare" issues.[29] This group was often supported by Vice-President Al Gore, Chief of Staff Thomas ("Mac") McClarty, and Laura D'Andrea Tyson, chair of the Council of Economic Advisers. Influential White House aides George Stephanopoulos and Gene Sperling were frequently caught in the middle of these debates—along with, significantly, President Clinton.

Unlike George Bush, primarily a foreign policy president, Bill Clinton cared passionately, even obsessively, about domestic policy. A true "wonk," he was exceptionally well versed in the details as well as the general outlines of a host of domestic programs. He could thus appreciate the complexity of issues, but this reinforced his almost congenital aversion to making decisions in a timely manner. Undisciplined, interminable, often inconclusive staff meetings characterized the White House, whether debating domestic or foreign policy, and conveyed to the media and the public an aura of confusion, disarray, and inconsistency.

Yet despite all these difficulties Clinton ended 1993 with a substantial list of legislative accomplishments. They included large parts of his economic plan, NAFTA, national service (Americorps), a direct student loan program, handgun registration (the Brady bill), increased aid to Russia, family leave, and "motor voter" registration. Furthermore, a "reinventing government" (REGO) effort under the leadership of Vice-President Gore had been launched with the intent of making the federal government slimmer, more efficient, and "user friendly." Health and welfare proposals were pushed back to 1994, and early that year the administration decided to make crime legislation a second-year priority.

During the 1992 campaign Clinton had emphasized the growing unaffordability of health care for the middle class, yet when the administration finally unveiled its reform program in January 1994, the aim of extending coverage to all Americans—potentially very expensive—had seemingly taken precedence over the goal of cost containment. This shift in emphasis, as well as the mind-boggling complexity of the plan, allowed Republicans to condemn it as a vast, government-run redistribution scheme.

Its ultimate defeat in Congress threatened to destroy the Clinton presidency, but the entire episode provided several insights into Bill Clinton's approach to governance. First, Clinton genuinely believed in the ability of government to do "good works." While he also wished to make it more efficient and responsive, he nevertheless maintained a New Dealish faith in government's potential to improve the well-being of ordinary citizens.

Clinton's package of "investments," including health care reform, were all designed to "give people the chance to help themselves," as he often put it, with a boost from the government. Second, Clinton approached governance not as a manager but as a seminar leader. He gave virtually no thought to how he should organize the White House staff, despite the complexity of his policy agenda. This almost perverse disregard of process resulted in a slew of gaffes, missteps, and delays, including the long postponement of the health care initiative. The situation improved slightly with the installation of Leon Panetta as chief of staff in mid-1994 and somewhat more with the subsequent appointment of Erskine Bowles, a management specialist, as one of his deputies. Access to the president was restricted, meetings became more focused and productive, and Clinton's congenital tardiness grew less obvious. But the appointment process remained embarrassingly amateurish. Third, Clinton aspired to be a very personal president, even by contemporary standards. One of his most frequently used (and satirized) phrases—"I feel your pain"—typified his approach. He relied on town meetings, talk-show appearances, and other populist devices to push a variety of initiatives and again appeared on MTV. Yet these efforts at electronic intimacy, which had apparently been effective during the campaign, threatened to demean the dignity of the presidency in ways reminiscent of Jimmy Carter.[30] Indeed, opinion polls indicated that the public wished for Clinton to act more "presidential." Fourth, Bill Clinton understood governance as a seamless extension of campaigning. Since his second term as governor of Arkansas, Clinton had maintained a "permanent campaign." Polling and focus-group research helped to define, refine, and even provide the wording for virtually the entire Clinton agenda, including health care. His political consultants gained remarkable access to the White House. Planning for the 1996 election began before the first term had commenced. In this age of cynicism such activities could hardly inspire public trust, but they reflected a trend that had long been evident in national politics. Finally, at especially difficult junctures, President Clinton often sought counsel from outside experts to gain insights into more effective governance. He periodically conferred with presidential scholars, other historians and political scientists, theologians, psychologists, and even such "positive thinking" gurus as Anthony Robbins. Such behavior tended to confirm the perception of Clinton as restless, intellectually inquisitive, and willing to adjust course as necessary. But it also suggested a certain desperation as he sought to bolster his sagging fortunes.

In the light of Clinton's obvious desire to emphasize his domestic agenda, one might expect to find little relationship between it and his foreign policy.

On one level, at least, that would be an accurate assessment, for he treated a trio of inherited international problems largely as distractions from his main business. Indeed, he dealt fitfully and reluctantly with Bosnia, Somalia, and Haiti.

Yet, on another level, the administration maintained a close, though generally overlooked, connection between the domestic and foreign realms. What engaged Clinton most, after all, was the economy, and he and his advisers, to a greater degree than Cold War administrations, appreciated the intimate relationship between the domestic and the international economy. As governor of Arkansas, Clinton had viewed his state as an essentially underdeveloped economy that could benefit from foreign investments and export markets. He had long harbored free trade proclivities and had delayed endorsing NAFTA largely for fear of alienating labor and environmentalists—two traditional Democratic constituencies. As president he threw himself into the effort to win its passage with an intensity not evident in his handling of Bosnia, Somalia, or Haiti. Clinton's near obsession with "national competitiveness" accounted for his "lifelong learning" investments, his creation of a national economic council, his tireless promotion of American exporters, and his elevation of the Commerce Department to a foreign policy stature not seen since the 1920s. This administration equated economic policy with security policy to an almost unprecedented degree.

Much as George Bush reached back to the Ford administration for many of his senior foreign policy appointments, Bill Clinton drew several of his top advisers from the Carter foreign policy team.

Secretary of State Warren Christopher had served as deputy to Cyrus Vance and Edmund Muskie and had been instrumental in negotiating the release of hostages in Iran. A lawyer by training and temperament, Christopher appeared to lack firm convictions apart from a general commitment to the "peace process" whether in the Middle East or elsewhere.[31] Anthony ("Tony") Lake, who had headed the State Department's Policy Planning Staff during the Carter years, had been candidate Clinton's chief foreign policy adviser and thus mainly responsible for the campaign's ambitious, activist rhetoric. Lake had previously demonstrated an extreme reluctance to employ military force for fear of producing a new Vietnam, but his campaign advice to Clinton indicated that in the post–Cold War era he would be considerably less inhibited. Lake's deputy was Samuel R. ("Sandy") Berger, another Democratic insider who had also served at Policy Planning during the Carter years. Clinton appointed Madeleine Albright to the now highly visible post of UN Ambassador. Albright, daughter of a Czech political refugee and student of Zbigniew Brzezinski, had been a member of the Carter NSC staff, where she had grown critical of the president's aversion to force.[32] Yet she had opposed Operation Desert Storm, arguing that economic sanctions had been prematurely abandoned. Clinton went to Congress to find his secretary of defense, Les Aspin, the rather hawkish former chair of the House Armed Services Committee and an original "whiz kid" from Robert McNamara's Pentagon. Aspin had largely supported the use of force in Central America and the Gulf, yet as secretary of defense (for a year) he would oppose military intervention in Haiti and Bosnia. Clinton's other major foreign policy appointment, though it was not viewed as such at the time, was Ron Brown as secretary of commerce. Brown, a lawyer, lobbyist, and chairman of the Democratic Party, would quickly become the most influential Commerce secretary since Herbert Hoover.

Three Early Dilemmas

As members of the Carter administration, Christopher, Lake, Albright, and Berger had agonized over whether to send troops to Nicaragua, Iran, and the Horn of Africa. Fifteen years later, they agonized over whether to send troops to Bosnia and Haiti or, in the case of Somalia, reinforcements. Yet international circumstances had changed dramatically. In the 1970s the Soviet-American struggle had presumably imparted enormous urgency and potential danger to the question of intervention. But in the 1990s, with the Cold War ended, the Clinton administration seemed to perceive Bosnia, Somalia, and Haiti more as inconvenient public relations problems than as genuine security dilemmas. Nevertheless, these changed circumstances did not make the administration's task noticeably easier.

The United States had supported the territorial integrity and political unity of multiethnic Yugoslavia since World War II. Marshal Tito's secession from the Soviet empire in the late 1940s served American interests, and so Washington consistently overlooked his often repressive rule. Tito's death in 1980 put his fragile and complex political edifice in jeopardy, yet Yugoslavia limped along for another decade. Then, prompted in part by the revolutionary examples rife in Eastern Europe, it began to disintegrate violently. In the fall of 1990 the Bush administration notified NATO of an impending crisis there, but, distracted by events in the Gulf, it deferred to its European allies' wish to handle the Yugoslav problem. Though Secretary Baker, in a well-publicized speech in Belgrade in the spring of 1991, pleaded for Yugoslavian unity, he seemed to be aiming his remarks primarily at the Soviet republics. Moreover, he also acknowledged at about the same time that "we don't have a dog in this [i.e., Yugoslav] fight." In June 1991 Slovenia and Croatia declared their independence, but ethnic Serbs, trapped in Croatia, with assistance from elements of the largely Serbian Yugoslav army command in Belgrade, took up arms against the new Zagreb government. A ghastly ethnic war ensued. In December Germany formally recognized both governments. The European Union and the United States soon followed. Meanwhile, Macedonia had seceded from the federation, and, after holding a referendum that was boycotted by ethnic Serbs, Bosnia-Herzegovina withdrew in February 1992. The Bush administration—no longer constrained by events in the now defunct Soviet Union—quickly recognized the new Muslim-dominated Sarajevo government. War now engulfed Bosnia as Serbs, Croats, and Muslims battled one another in the most vicious fighting in Europe since World War II. The Bush administration, the United Nations, and the European Union applied economic sanctions against Belgrade for its support of the Bosnian Serbs; provided humanitarian assistance to the Muslims; and instituted an arms embargo against all the combatants. Washington also lent tacit support to a Bosnian peace plan devised by Cyrus Vance and former British Foreign Secretary David Owen (representing the United Nations and the European Union respectively) that would have broken Bosnia into ten semiautonomous ethnic enclaves. But the Bush administration refused to contribute American troops to a large UN "peacekeeping" force, and placed Bosnian air operations under the joint control of NATO and the Security Council, thus seriously undermining American moral and military authority.[33] Moreover, it appeared uninterested in reports that the Bosnian Serbs had committed atrocities as part of their "ethnic cleansing" program.

Into this fray rode candidate Bill Clinton. Suggesting that the United States had a moral responsibility to punish Serbian transgressions, in early August 1992 he recommended the use of air power "to try to restore the basic conditions of humanity."[34] In mid-October he remarked that as president he would consider lifting the arms embargo against the Bosnian government because "they are in no way in a fair fight."[35] This activist rhetoric continued into the first weeks of the Clinton administration. On February 4, 1993, the new president reaffirmed his reservations about the Vance–Owen plan, suggesting that it unduly penalized the Bosnian Muslims. Shortly thereafter, he registered his opposition to the "terrible principle of ethnic cleansing." Secretary Christopher added that "beyond these humanitarian interests, we have strategic concerns as well," citing a "river" of refugees flooding Europe and describing Bosnia as a test of how the world "will address the concerns of ethnic and religious minorities in the post–Cold War world."[36] Administration officials also expressed worries about the potential spread of the conflict to Macedonia, Kosovo, and perhaps even parts of the former Soviet Union.

But rather than act decisively, Clinton and his senior advisers engaged in protracted agonizing. As Serb artillery relentlessly pounded a half-dozen Muslim-held cities, the administration continued to debate the "lift and strike" option. Pollster Stanley Greenberg reported to Clinton that while Bosnia was a subject on which public opinion could be shaped, there would be little support for unilateral action by the United States. This information reinforced the multilateral inclinations of administration officials, who feared the "quagmire" potential of Bosnia. One participant described these endless meetings as "group therapy—an existential debate over what is the role of America."[37] This near-paralysis led to a revolt of several mid-level foreign service officers working this issue who, in a letter to Christopher, demanded military action. Five of them eventually resigned, marking the largest such exodus since Vietnam.[38]

Throughout 1993 and 1994 Bosnia policy frequently seemed driven largely by television coverage of the slaughter of civilians. This pattern emerged in April 1993 when gruesome pictures from the besieged town of Srebrenica (coupled with an emotional visit to the new Holocaust Museum in Washington) apparently pushed Clinton to adopt the "lift and strike" option. But Defense Department officials expressed great reluctance to become involved in what senior military leaders and Secretary Aspin viewed as an intractable civil war. Recognizing that unilateral American action was out of the question, Clinton, in early May, dispatched Christopher to Europe to ask for NATO support. Yet both he and the secretary seemed almost relieved when the Europeans rejected these tentative overtures. The British and the French argued that the "lift and strike" option would escalate the war and endanger their peacekeepers. They also suggested that Washington's refusal to contribute to the UN force in Bosnia undercut the credibility of the administration's arguments. Another pattern was thus set.

We need not recount the tortuous path of the administration's policy in detail. Washington's unwillingness to act alone or to exert pressure on NATO; its reluctance to confront Russia, a traditional patron of Serbia; its insistence that the United Nations be involved in any punitive actions against the Serbs; its inability to decide whether a civil war or aggression was under way in Bosnia; and its refusal to shape public and congressional opinion combined to place strict limits on the available options. The United States subsequently air-dropped supplies to several besieged Muslim-held cities; led an international effort to declare Sarajevo a "safe haven" from Serb attacks; brokered a political confederation of Bosnian Muslims and Croats; and supported a peace plan that would have given Muslims control of 51 percent of Bosnian territory (presumably to defend the principle of national self-determination). Yet throughout this sad and complex episode the Clinton administration continually worsened its situation by creating a chasm between its often maximalist rhetoric and its rather minimalist actions. It spoke with a loud voice and wielded a small stick.

In December 1992 President Bush announced that he had ordered 28,000 U.S. troops to southern Somalia in order to facilitate the feeding of the starving population so graphically pictured on television. Once the recipient of substantial American military and economic aid during the Cold War—after switching sides in the late 1970s—Somalia had descended into civil war and chaos. Warring clans manipulated meager food supplies to reward friends and punish enemies. Notwithstanding the largely political roots of the famine, in announcing Operation Restore Hope President Bush described it as a purely humanitarian mission to feed the hungry. That Bush, in so many ways a practitioner of *Realpolitik,* would have intervened in an area now wholly devoid of strategic significance, appeared to expand considerably the meaning of his "new world order." He did so in large part to compensate for the frustrations the administration had experienced in Bosnia, where it had deferred to the Europeans. In Somalia Bush was given a second chance to help a suffering Muslim nation. President-elect Clinton welcomed the action, CNN crews televised the marine landing, and the public offered strong initial support.[39]

Yet potential difficulties loomed. Despite the rapid opening of roads to outlying towns and villages, Bush administration officials recognized that this first, rather benign phase would be followed by a longer one during which UN forces, assisted by some remaining Americans, attempted to prevent a new famine. Thus, from the beginning, Operation Restore Hope anticipated the eventual rebuilding of Somali political and security institutions.[40]

Tensions quickly developed between UN Secretary-General Boutros Boutros-Ghali and the Bush administration. American envoy Robert Oakley wished to have completed by Inauguration Day an agreement setting a date for the "hand off" from U.S. to UN command. But the secretary general postponed a decision for months, in part because of the difficulty in persuading other nations to contribute peacekeepers, and in part because he wanted the United States to disarm the warring factions before the transition to UN command occurred. While Washington declined to undertake large operations to seize or destroy weapons, American diplomats in Mogadishu, the Somali capital, did attempt to persuade the clans to mothball their "technicals" (vans and jeeps with mounted machine guns) for later use by a new national army. Furthermore, U.S. troops, even while Bush was president, often raided suspected arms depots as the Mogadishu defense perimeter was extended outward.[41]

In sum, the mission had begun to "creep" even before Clinton took office, for it became practically impossible to conduct a purely humanitarian operation. The famine's political roots could not be ignored, and neither Bush nor Clinton was inclined to simply deliver food and then allow the horror to resume.

Thus Bill Clinton inherited a deceptively fluid and ambiguous situation from President Bush. In March 1993, with the famine clearly easing, the new administration strongly supported a Security Council resolution formally enabling the United Nations to help rebuild Somalia's "national and regional institutions and civil administration." This action directly threatened those clan leaders who aspired to rule the nation, especially Mohammed Farah Aidid, who had used the famine to strengthen his power base. A month after command was turned over to a Turkish general in early May, twenty-four Pakistani peacekeepers were killed in an ambush. The Security Council, with American backing, demanded the arrest of those responsible for the attack. As a result, Jonathan Howe, a retired admiral and former senior Bush NSC official, now serving as Boutros-Ghali's personal representative in Somalia, directed a hunt for Aidid, the chief suspect. He offered a $25,000 reward and requested that Washington send Rangers and Delta-force commandos to capture or kill the warlord.

Though skeptical of the secretary general's obsession with Aidid, senior Clinton officials nevertheless agreed to support a UN resolution authorizing the dispatch of these forces. Ambassador Albright publicly proclaimed that nothing less than the fate of Somalia as a "failed state" or "an emerging democracy" was at issue and asserted an American responsibility to persevere.

On October 3, 1993, after nearly two months of searching in vain for Aidid, American troops fought a bloody street battle with his supporters, killing several hundred, but suffering eighteen dead. Television pictures showed Somalis dragging the body of an American soldier through Mogadishu as well as a badly wounded, captured helicopter pilot. The effect on the public, especially those who had seen these pictures, was instantaneous. Support for Operation Restore Hope evaporated, many in Congress demanded an immediate withdrawal, and many observers compared the reaction to that of Beirut in 1983 after the marine massacre. Unlike Reagan, who benefited from the near-simultaneous invasion of Grenada, Clinton was soon saddled with another embarrassment as Haitian gangs prevented the landing of American training troops in Port-au-Prince. In a nationwide address—his first on foreign policy—Clinton delivered a speech in some ways reminiscent of some of Nixon's Vietnam statements. Asserting that there was a right and a wrong way to withdraw from Somalia, he argued that a hasty exit would make a new famine inevitable; severely damage America's credibility with its friends and allies; undermine this nation's ability to provide global leadership; and encourage "aggressors, thugs, and terrorists" to declare an "open season on Americans."[42] The president then announced that the 5,000 U.S. troops still in Somalia would be supplemented by an additional 1,700 soldiers, plus 3,600 marines deployed offshore. Clinton described the mission: (1) to protect American troops and bases; (2) to ensure the continued delivery of food supplies; (3) "to keep the pressure on those who cut off relief supplies and attacked our people . . . to prevent a return to anarchy"; and (4) to help make it possible for Somalis to settle their disputes and "survive when we leave." He also announced that Ambassador Oakley would try again to negotiate an end to the clan internecine warfare. But Clinton promised that an orderly withdrawal of all but a few hundred noncombat support personnel would be completed by March 31, 1994. Even so, the administration barely beat back a congressional attempt to advance this date by two months.[43]

What had begun as a popular humanitarian intervention thus ended in disappointment and disillusionment. Neither American arms nor diplomacy could reknit Somalia. The troops left on schedule. A year later, the final withdrawal of all remaining UN contingents took place. Clan warfare continued. But the experience severely dampened the administration's early enthusiasm for "assertive multilateralism" under UN control. When a genocidal reign of ethnic violence erupted in Rwanda in March 1994, the United States refused to support the dispatch of "peacekeepers." After repeated delays and thousands of more deaths from disease, the administration did send 478 troops to provide humanitarian assistance to refugees fleeing into Burundi, yet it wanted no part in helping to rebuild Rwanda.

Furthermore, although candidate Clinton had offered support for a standing UN force to fight terrorism and ethnic violence, Somalia forced the administration to reassess its thinking. When it finally released its long-delayed document on reforming multilateral peace operations (PDD-25) in May 1994, the contrast with its early rhetoric was striking. The administration now rejected the idea of a permanent UN army, endorsed multilateral missions only if they served American interests, and warned that strict conditions would have to be met before the United States would support any peacekeeping initiative. The new policy described peacekeeping as merely one tool and not a central conceptual feature of American strategy.[44] Yet despite this significant retreat, U.S. involvement in UN operations remained a volatile domestic issue. In early 1995 the Republican-controlled House of Representatives attempted to deduct American financial contributions to peacekeeping missions from its overall annual budgetary obligations notwithstanding Clinton's threat to veto this part of the "Contract with America."[45]

Haiti also proved to be an enormous distraction and frequent embarrassment for the administration, with policy largely driven by the demands of domestic politics. It also constituted the third unresolved international problem with the potential for military intervention that Bill Clinton inherited from George Bush.

In December 1990, under close international supervision, Haiti held the first genuinely honest election in its grim and bloody history. Jean-Bertrand Aristide, a leftist priest despised by much of the Haitian establishment, became the new president. His efforts to overhaul the army and undertake social and economic reforms provoked a violent coup less than eight months into his term and sent Aristide into exile in the United States. If Aristide's overthrow had occurred during the Cold War, Washington would doubtless have recognized General Raul Cedras, the coup's leader, as an anticommunist patriot.[46] But the Bush administration unequivocally condemned the military government, supported a series of Security Council resolutions imposing increasingly tight economic sanctions on Haiti, and welcomed the mission of Dante Caputo, Boutros-Ghali's personal representative, to negotiate Aristide's restoration to power. This unprecedented intrusion of the United Nations into Western Hemispheric relations would have been unthinkable during the Cold War and indicated the organization's new stature in world politics.

Pressured by domestic concerns about illegal immigration, however, the Bush administration refused to treat fleeing Haitian "boat people" as potential political refugees. As the sanctions crippled the Haitian economy, and as Cedras's government continued murdering Aristide supporters, the tide of boat people swelled enormously. Candidate Bill Clinton criticized the Bush administration for intercepting refugees before they reached the United States and then either returning them to Haiti or holding them, without a hearing, at the Guantanamo naval base in Cuba. He vowed, if elected, to change that policy, but even before taking office, he reversed himself and continued Bush's approach, largely because he feared another *Mariel*-type crisis.[47] This action also pleased the governor of Florida, a Democrat seeking reelection in 1994.

But the Clinton administration faced countervailing domestic pressure from the Congressional Black Caucus and its leader, Kwasi Nfume (D-MD). This group argued that the United States had an obligation to help restore Haitian democracy, by force if necessary. Unlike Bush, who could afford to keep his distance from this group, Clinton needed its members' votes for his domestic program. Indeed, they periodically held his legislation hostage to Haitian policy, as, for example, his crime bill in the late summer of 1994. Randall Robinson, the head of Transafrica, a lobby that had played an important role in persuading Congress to apply sanctions against South Africa in the 1980s, undertook a hunger strike in the spring of 1994 that proved decisive in altering administration policy.[48] Arguing that the return of Haitian refugees without asylum smacked of racism and contrasted sharply with the treatment afforded Cuban boat people, Robinson threatened to fast until Clinton blinked. The president did so on May 8, acceding to Robinson's demands and appointing William H. Gray III, former Democratic congressman and chair of the Black Caucus as his special envoy to Haiti. The pressure on Cedras to step aside now increased palpably as Clinton officials began to speak openly of an invasion as a virtual inevitability.

Observers noted that the administration's credibility now seemed at stake. In June 1993, after all, it had sponsored a Security Council resolution that imposed an arms and oil embargo on Haiti. The following month it had helped broker the "Governor's Island accord," in which General Cedras had reluctantly agreed to resign by October 30 in favor of President Aristide. But on October 11, to the profound embarrassment of Washington, armed thugs in Port-au-Prince prevented the docking of the *Harlan County*, carrying 200 American troops sent to retrain the Haitian army. Senate Minority Leader Robert Dole (R-KS), claiming that Aristide's return was not worth a single American life, introduced legislation barring an invasion in the absence of national security interests. The Senate passed a version of Dole's initiative in August 1994 in the wake of an administration-sponsored Security Council resolution authorizing the use of force as a last resort to oust Cedras. George Bush, James Baker, and Richard Cheney, claiming that no important interests were at stake, all warned against an invasion, while many liberals who had opposed the Gulf War now urged military action in Haiti.

The Clinton administration had backed itself into a corner. Whipsawed by conflicting domestic pressures, increasingly trapped by its own bellicose rhetoric, facing a public notably unenthusiastic about invading Haiti, and internally divided between a very skeptical Defense Department and officials such as Lake, Albright, and Berger who saw in Haiti a wonderful opportunity to use force in support of moral principle, the administration wobbled through the summer of 1994. It publicly set a deadline for Cedras's resignation, but the junta remained defiant. With many observers predicting a bloody invasion and prolonged occupation—the most recent had lasted from 1915 to 1934—Jimmy Carter unexpectedly came to the rescue and offered his diplomatic services to Clinton. Accompanied to Port-au-Prince by Colin Powell and Senator Sam Nunn (D-GA), Carter cajoled and flattered the military rulers into quitting, though the imminent threat of the 82nd Airborne in Haiti surely helped them decide. On September 19 American forces began an unopposed landing. Less than a month later,

Aristide returned to the island as president, promising to hold new elections in 1996 and to step down thereafter.

On the eve of Operation Restore Hope Clinton explained the reasons for the action in a nationwide address. After the obligatory denial that the United States harbored any "world policeman" ambitions, the president emphasized the multinational character of the expeditionary force (though, in fact, it would be overwhelmingly American). He then offered four main rationales for ousting Cedras and his colleagues. First, Clinton cited human rights atrocities perpetrated by the military rulers and their recent expulsion of the international observers who had exposed these violations. Second, he raised "the threat of a mass exodus of refugees and its constant threat to stability in our region and control of our borders," reminding his audience that the United States had already spent "millions and millions" of dollars to sustain those fleeing Haiti. Third, the president, echoing the claims made by the Bush administration, asserted that "democracies . . . are more likely to keep the peace, . . . to create free markets and economic opportunity and to become strong, reliable trading partners." Thus "restoring Haiti's democratic government will help lead to more stability and prosperity in our region, just as our actions in Panama and Grenada did." And fourth, Clinton rather cryptically suggested that "the United States also has strong interests in not letting dictators, especially in our own region, break their word to the United States and the United Nations."[49] Perhaps Clinton was making veiled threats to Iraq and North Korea. In any event, in emphasizing that the mission was achievable, limited in time, and supported by the international community, he repeated the assurances offered by George Bush at the outset of Operation Restore Hope.

But the administration was determined to avoid another Somalia. American troops did confiscate almost 10,000 guns from the Haitian army and spent $1.8 million to buy back thousands of guns and grenades from the wider populace. They did not, however, undertake aggressive weapons searches or seek to disarm the paramilitary thugs previously shielded by the army.[50] Ambassador Albright promised there would be no "mission creep" and contrasted the situations in Haiti and Somalia: "You don't have warlords; it's a different political climate."[51] Indeed, the United States suffered but a single combat death from the time of the landing in September until the "hand off" to the United Nations on March 31, 1995.

Yet it was too early to be sure that democracy could be "restored" to a country utterly lacking the rudiments of civil society. Deeply riven by class animosities and extremely skewed income distributions, bereft of a legal tradition or civilian control of the military, Haiti presented the United Nations with enormous challenges. But in the short run, at least, Clinton had quieted those domestic critics who had warned of a Haitian bloodbath.

In late October 1994 Anthony Lake traveled to Harvard University to deliver an important address in which he invited a "national debate on the critical questions of where, when and how to use military force."[52] Recalling that in Vietnam "the relationship between means and ends in fighting limited wars was never satisfactorily defined," Lake essentially accepted George Bush's rather restrictive guidelines for *using* force as outlined in his speeches at Texas A&M and West Point. But Lake wished to be more explicit about defining those interests that might warrant a military response in the first place. He listed seven, "in general, if not perfect, order of priority":

- To defend against direct attacks on the United States, its citizens at home and abroad, and its allies.
- To counter aggression, which is central to preserving a peaceful world.
- To defend our most important economic interests, because it is here that Americans see their most immediate personal stake in our international engagement.
- To preserve, promote and defend democracy, which in turn enhances our security and the spread of our values.
- To prevent the dangerous proliferation of nuclear weapons and other weapons of mass destruction; to prevent acts of terrorism and to combat the deadly flow of drugs.
- To maintain our reliability. When the U.S. makes commitments to other nations, we must keep our promises.
- And for humanitarian purposes, such as combating famine and other natural disasters and in cases of overwhelming violations of human rights.[53]

The national security adviser noted that "none of the interests in this general hierarchy—with the certain exception of attacks on our nation and its allies and the possible exception of aggression elsewhere—should automatically lead to the use of force."[54] He explained that the case for intervention in Haiti had been "compelling" because "we saw democracy denied, our borders threatened, our reliability on the line, and a reign of terror of brutality so close to our own shores." [55] While acknowledging that television could distort public reactions to violence, Lake applauded the American people for supporting the use of force "if classic interests like security in Europe or Asia or the Middle East are in question."[56] Here he implicitly referred to the Gulf War and suggested that public enthusiasm for military action to defend less traditional interests might be difficult to sustain. He ended this rather candid address by inviting Congress to amend the War Powers Resolution as a way to achieve a new foreign policy (procedural) consensus.[57] He surely did not anticipate a Republican takeover of Congress in November 1994, an event that would substantially heighten executive-legislative conflict over a range of foreign policy issues including the United Nations, foreign aid, Russia, and even Mexico.

Lake's taxonomy of interventions was surprisingly inclusive and suggested that military action was at least possible in a wide variety of situations. Ethnic conflict did not make the list and humanitarian interventions were relegated to the bottom rung of the ladder, yet many possible *casus belli* remained. Yet when combined with Lake's caveats about the actual mechanics of deploying force—for example, a clear, doable mission that would not "creep," an exit strategy, international support in most cases, and public enthusiasm for the enterprise—the Clinton administration appeared to embrace the cost-conscious realism practiced, if not always preached, by George Bush after the Gulf War.

A Strategy of Engagement and Enlargement

In retrospect, Bosnia, Somalia, and Haiti constituted distracting sideshows that muddied the Clinton administration's more fundamental strategic objectives: (1) the containment of a handful of "backlash" states deemed threats to regional stability; and (2) nurturing Russia into a "normal state." Both represented essentially continuations of policies pursued during the post–Cold War phase of the Bush administration.

The Clinton team identified five "outlaw" or "backlash" states that allegedly shared the intention, if not yet the capability, to damage America's desire for a democratic, capitalist, and peaceful world. These states—Iraq, Iran, Libya, North Korea, and Cuba—allegedly possessed several common characteristics including coercive rulers, radical ideologies, a record of human rights abuses, an antipathy to democratic institutions, an inability to engage constructively with the outside world, and a siege mentality resulting in the desire for weapons of mass destruction.[58] Furthermore, the Clinton administration asserted a "special [American] responsibility . . . to neutralize, contain, and, through selective pressure, perhaps eventually transform these backlash states . . . into constructive members of the international community."[59]

Central to this ambitious strategy was the "dual containment" of Iraq and Iran. During the 1980s the United States, in order to isolate Iran, had, in effect, tilted toward Iraq, in the hope of bolstering it against its stronger and presumably more threatening neighbor. Saddam Hussein's invasion of Kuwait had, of course, discredited that approach and made a new strategy inevitable. Indeed, the Bush administration had inaugurated dual containment through its postwar pursuit of strict economic sanctions against Baghdad and the simultaneous isolation of Iran. Clinton officials worked hard to prevent France and Russia from diluting the Security Council's anti-Iraq resolutions, ordered air strikes against Baghdad in June 1993 in retaliation for an alleged assassination plot against George Bush, and deployed thousands of additional American troops in the Gulf region a year later when Saddam Hussein again appeared to menace Kuwait. Despite some early rhetoric to the contrary, Clinton reiterated his predecessor's assertion that normal relations with Iraq were impossible as long as Saddam Hussein remained in power.

While protesting that it did not oppose Islamic governments as such, the administration branded Iran an "extremist" regime and tried to build an international consensus against it comparable to the one against Iraq. In early 1995 it forbade Conoco, a petroleum unit of DuPont, from concluding an exploration contract with Teheran but found it very difficult to prevent Chinese missile exports and the transfer of Russian nuclear technology to Iran. On April 30, 1995 Clinton considerably escalated tensions by announcing a total economic embargo of Iran, in part to pressure Moscow to halt its impending nuclear sale, and in part to preempt congressional Republicans from legislating a secondary boycott of the country as well. But several observers warned that dual containment risked driving Iraq and Iran closer together.[60]

The United States had treated Libya as a pariah since the 1970s, but since the 1986 air attacks on General Khadaffi's headquarters, his regime had apparently grown more cautious in sponsoring terrorism. Nevertheless, Khaddafi refused to extradite two men accused of bombing an American passenger jet over Scotland in 1988, so the Clinton administration sponsored Security Council sanctions aimed at depriving Libyan planes of international landing rights. Yet enforcement proved difficult as even Saudi Arabia, a close American ally, refused to cooperate fully.

Of the five designated "backlash" states, the administration appeared to worry most about North Korea. In 1994 new Secretary of Defense William Perry claimed that "in many ways Korea poses the greatest security threat to the United States and the world today." It did so because of its apparent intention to develop nuclear weapons and the possibility that it already had built one or two. We need not detail the torturous cat-and-mouse game that Pyongyang played with the International Atomic Energy Agency and American negotiators, but a few points deserve mention. First, the Clinton administration considered the North Korean government to be among the world's most isolated and least predictable, and it openly acknowledged its inability to determine the purposes of this nuclear program. Some suspected that North Korea—desperately poor and bereft of allies since the end of the Cold War—saw nuclear weapons as bargaining chips to win economic assistance from the United States, Japan, and South Korea. But other officials feared that Kim Il Sung (who died in July 1994) or his successors would use an atomic bomb to blackmail Seoul and escalate tensions in East Asia. At the least, a nuclear North Korea might well drive Japan and South Korea to acquire their own capability, yet there was no guarantee that Pyongyang would thereby be deterred. Second, President Clinton's public vow of November 1993 to prevent North Korea from going nuclear (when Les Aspin had concluded that it may have already done so) significantly increased the pressure on Washington to act forcefully. But while some domestic critics demanded preemptive air strikes against Pyongyang's nuclear facilities, American military planners doubted their effectiveness, and Japan and China strongly opposed such action.[61] Finally, the unlikely and unofficial intrusion of Jimmy Carter into this growing crisis in June 1994 helped to start bilateral negotiations that produced a complicated agreement in late October. According to its terms, North Korea pledged to freeze and then dismantle its nuclear program in return for the international construction of two light water reactors deemed unlikely to be a source of nuclear weapons material. The United States agreed to normalize trade and diplomatic relations gradually with the North by, for example, providing oil to meet its interim energy needs. The IAEA decided to postpone its inspection of two North Korean nuclear waste sites for five or six years, thereby violating its own procedures. Not surprisingly, some of those who had been urging military action condemned this arrangement as "appeasement."[62] The North Koreans delayed its implementation, and by mid-1995 the Clinton administration continued to worry about the issue's impact on its overall counterproliferation efforts.[63]

The decision to put Cuba on the "backlash list" must be attributed almost wholly to the pressures of domestic political lobbies. Castro may well have once posed a genuine threat to America's core interests; by the 1990s, he ruled a beleaguered, bankrupt, and discredited regime. Nevertheless, largely because of the impressive political influence of Jorge Mas Canosa and his Cuban American National Foundation, neither the Bush nor the Clinton administration dared to alter Washington's ancient policy toward Castro.[64] Indeed, as the United States moved to normalize relations with Vietnam and North Korea, the Cuban Democracy Act of 1992 tightened the economic embargo that had been in place for three decades. This legislation, offered by Congressman Robert Toricelli (D-NJ) and strongly supported by Mas Canosa, banned foreign subsidiary trade with Cuba and urged the president to impose sanctions on third countries that aided Cuba.[65] The Bush administration initially quietly resisted the bill, but it jumped on board after Bill Clinton, while campaigning in Miami's Little Havana, declared, "I like it."[66] As president, Clinton resolutely refused to open a dialogue with Castro—despite the urging of other Cuban-American groups—and placed the regime on the short list of "backlash" states. In so doing he did significant damage to the coherence of this concept.[67]

In May 1995, however, the administration began to alter its Cuba policy. It announced that in the future the United States would routinely return Cuban "boat people" to their island, and it strongly denounced pending legislation cosponsored by senators Jesse Helms (R-NC) and Dan Coats (R-IN) that would have further tightened the economic embargo. Whether these steps indicated a desire to begin a "dialogue" with Castro remained unclear, but they seemed to signal that Cuba had at least partly been removed from the "backlash" list.

In each of his three major foreign policy campaign speeches in 1992 Bill Clinton criticized President Bush's handling of relations with Russia. He castigated his opponent for remaining overly loyal to the unelected Gorbachev at the expense of the democratically chosen Yeltsin; he implied that the Republicans appeared more committed to Russian stability than democracy, thus echoing the charge made by, among others, his close friend Strobe Talbott in an influential *Foreign Affairs* article; and he chastised Bush for failing to provide adequate aid to Russia and the newly independent states (NIS) of the former Soviet Union (FSU), while being careful not to commit himself to expensive new assistance packages.[68]

In contrast to his rather off-handed treatment of several other foreign policy issues, President Clinton immediately demonstrated considerable interest in the Russian relationship. He assembled an unusually talented team of advisers to focus on this issue, including Thomas Pickering as ambassador to Moscow, Undersecretary of the Treasury Lawrence Summers, NSC official Toby Gati, and Special Ambassador (later Deputy Secretary of State) Strobe Talbott. During his first three months in office Clinton devoted nearly half of his foreign policy time to Russia, and by early 1994 had already met with Yeltsin on three occasions. Clinton soon began to characterize the relationship as a "strategic alliance" and a "new democratic partnership."[69]

Secretary Christopher, who would later devote the bulk of his energies to the Middle East "peace process," delivered an important and highly detailed speech on Russia and the NIS in late March 1993. He argued that the

United States in the post–Cold War era had three priorities: to strengthen the domestic economy, to modernize the military within budgetary constraints, and to extend democracy in the world. If America failed to encourage Russia to become a pluralistic, market society, it would probably revert to its authoritarian and imperialist traditions. And if Russia did regress, Christopher warned, all three American priorities would be imperiled, for the United States would be forced to devote enormous resources to containing this renewed threat.[70]

The Clinton administration soon identified five interconnected reasons for focusing on Russo-American relations. First, although the United States could hardly guarantee success, if it failed to encourage increased international lending, private investment, and technical assistance, Russian reforms would almost certainly fail. Second, the United States, in order to help smooth the transition from Soviet empire to self-determined republics, should nurture constructive relations among these new states through economic incentives, political mediation, and constant reassurance. Third, Russia still maintained significant nuclear capabilities, and political turmoil in the FSU could endanger the integrity of command and control systems. Furthermore, economic chaos in Russia and Ukraine could tempt their governments to export nuclear technology to raise cash, while their unemployed scientists and engineers might sell their services to the highest international bidder. Fourth, Russia remained an important power and, if democratic and secure, could serve as a barrier against threats from the Eurasian "heartland," as a "secular dam" against Islamic radicalism, and as an international stabilizing force in general. Finally, increased tensions with an autocratic, ambitious Russia would provide American conservatives with a political opening to derail President Clinton's domestic initiatives and foreign economic strategy by increasing the defense budget.[71]

For an administration routinely accused of foreign policy incoherence as it lurched from crisis to crisis in Bosnia, Somalia, and Haiti, its approach to Russia appeared quite consistent and even sophisticated. Unlike the Carter administration, whose Soviet policy was, in the memorable phrase of Stanley Hoffmann, "the hole in the [strategic] doughnut," Clinton understood the continuing significance of Russia and its potential impact on other administration priorities. But a series of disturbing developments there inevitably raised questions about the wisdom of Clinton's approach. During 1993, for example, the Russian economy teetered on the edge of collapse; renegade legislators occupied the parliament building only to be forcibly removed by troops loyal to Yeltsin; and in December elections brought to parliament large numbers of radical nationalists, including the bizarre Vladimir Zhirinovsky. Meanwhile, Russian foreign policy grew more confrontational as Moscow tilted strongly toward Serbia, complained about

American plans to grant certain East European states associate membership in NATO through the "Partnership for Peace" program, and by early 1995 appeared determined to sell Iran large nuclear reactors (but very similar to the ones that the administration had promised North Korea). Most disturbing, perhaps, were Russian efforts to reassert influence (or even control) over the "near abroad." Indeed, it appeared to claim a unilateral right to intervene in these borderland republics. Yeltsin's bloody and disastrous war against the breakaway republic of Chechnya, begun in late 1994, shocked the West and nearly scuttled the May 1995 Russo-American summit.

These events prompted critics to raise questions about the premises of Clinton's Russian policy. As early as February 1994 Senator Richard Lugar (R-IN) characterized the relationship as a "tough rivalry" rather than a partnership. Several Republicans claimed that the administration had shown excessive optimism about the democratic potential of Russia, had granted Yeltsin too many concessions, and had been oblivious to the justified East European fears of Russian imperialism. Zbigniew Brzezinski urged Clinton to extend security guarantees to the NIS to demonstrate his commitment to the principle of self-determination.[72] On the eve of the May 1995 summit, the influential liberal columnist Thomas L. Friedman referred approvingly to current Russo-American relations as a "Cold Peace."[73]

In fact, the Clinton administration had already begun to deromanticize relations with Yeltsin by emphasizing their limits as well as their possibilities. For instance, in March 1994 Secretary Perry acknowledged that Russia's interests would inevitably diverge from America's. While Washington continued to encourage foreign investment and pressured the IMF to approve a $1.5 billion loan, the tone of the relationship did change perceptibly. When Clinton met Yeltsin in Moscow to commemorate V-E Day, he persuaded the Russian leader to cancel part of the nuclear deal with Iran, submit the rest of it to a bilateral commission, and to agree eventually to join the "Partnership for Peace." He evidently also criticized Yeltsin in strong terms for the war in Chechnya. Nevertheless, Republican opponents continued to belittle the administration's Russia policy as naive.

The notion of America as a "commercial republic" antedated even the War of Independence and was central to the thinking of several of the leading Founders. Indeed, the idea had driven American foreign policy for much of its history until the Great Depression, World War II, and Cold War largely submerged it. But with the collapse of Soviet communism and the triumph of capitalism in both the developed and much of the developing world, the concept of the "commercial republic" as a linchpin of American foreign policy reemerged with a vengeance.

We saw in the previous chapter that Robert Zoellick had begun to develop for the Bush administration a foreign economic policy to support the "new world order." To a remarkable degree the Clinton administration accepted Zoellick's recommendations and, by elaborating and refining them, formulated a "big emerging markets" (BEM) strategy that constituted the central organizing concept of its grand design. According to its chief architect, Jeffrey E. Garten, undersecretary of commerce for international trade, "We are entering an era when foreign policy and national security will increasingly revolve around our commercial interests, and when economic diplomacy will be essential to resolving the great issues of our time."[74] Under Garten's tutelage, and that of Secretary Ron Brown, the Commerce Department shaped American foreign policy more than at any time since Herbert Hoover's tenure.

The BEM strategy identified ten current "regional economic drivers" at present committed to trade-led economic growth and reasonably amicable relations with the United States. The ten included China (plus Hong Kong and Taiwan), India, Indonesia, South Korea, Mexico, Brazil, Argentina, Poland, Turkey, and South Africa—states whose expansion could benefit neighboring markets as well. By the year 2000, Clinton officials projected that American trade with these BEMs would exceed that with either Japan or Europe and that in another decade would be greater than the combined trade with those two markets.[75] Thus this nation's domestic economic success would become increasingly dependent on deepening its engagement with the BEMs.

Garten articulated this strategy in a September 1993 report to Congress and in two largely unnoticed speeches in early 1994.[76] He suggested that the BEMs possessed enormous potential for the expansion of U.S. trade in goods and services because they bought heavily in economic sectors at present dominated by America: information technology, health and medical equipment, telecommunications, financial services, environmental technology, transportation, and power generation. By stimulating exports in these key areas, Garten predicted, millions of high-quality jobs in the United States could be created, productivity enhanced, inflation restrained, and both trade and federal budget deficits reduced. The public would also be more likely to support a foreign economic strategy that had brought it such obvious, tangible benefits.[77] Thus the administration's "intermestic" approach assumed tight and positive links between global economic interdependence, an American comparative advantage in several "big emerging sectors," and an electorate increasingly engaged by the prospect of greater economic security.

Yet this strategy rested on a potentially shaky foundation. First, it required close and growing convergences of interest between the United States and the BEMs. At a minimum, the BEM governments needed to sustain their commitment to export-led growth and ever-greater market access. Yet their political institutions remained in many cases fragile at best. Indeed, BEMs such as China were serious violators of human rights. President Clinton's May 1994 decision, after much public hand-wringing, to sever the tie between human rights and MFN status for China rested on the comfortable assumption that economic growth would eventually encourage political reforms. Yet it also risked subordinating important national values to the lure of commercial benefits. Moreover, China's continuing desire to export advanced weapons and nuclear technology to "backlash" states such as Iran directly challenged other administration strategic objectives. In sum, the rosy assumption that deepening commercial relations foster converging political interests may yet prove to be mere liberal capitalist cant.

Second, as the Mexican peso crisis of 1994–95 so vividly demonstrated, economic interdependence, particularly among states at dramatically different levels of development, may inevitably entail significant and unwanted political commitments by the strong to the weak. Even if Mexico did, in fact, represent a unique case because of its size, prosperity, and diasporic potential, the Clinton administration's rush to stabilize the peso, in spite of congressional and public skepticism, was enormously instructive. It demonstrated, above all, that in the post–Cold War world, future "quagmires" may well lurk not in tropical jungles but in the fragile financial institutions of BEMs such as Mexico.

Finally, this strategy prescribed no obvious roles for Japan, the European Union, or Russia, for it possessed a clear developing world focus in which all roads led to Washington. The administration did not consider Russia to qualify at present as a BEM, though if its internal reforms succeeded, it could, in principle, eventually join that club. In the meantime, Russia constituted primarily a threat to the BEM strategy, for if it reverted to aggressive authoritarianism, it would force the United States to expend resources on a new containment policy. The Clinton strategy implicitly viewed Japan as a competitor—even rival—in its plans to tap the Asian BEMs, and Tokyo's mercantilist tendencies inevitably challenged the administration's free trade goals. Some observers even suggested that Clinton's highly visible pressure on Japan to open its domestic market to American automobiles and automobile parts was designed to make it easier to sell free trade to a public that may see it only as a threat to their jobs.[78] In this sense, Japan became a useful pawn in the BEM strategy. Other observers urged the administration to propose a Transatlantic Free Trade Agreement (TAFTA) since, in contrast to the more closed capitalism of Asia, the United States and Europe possessed similar, relatively open economic systems.[79] Yet to do so might have undermined the gist of the BEM strategy: to exploit the rapidly growing markets of the leading developing economies.

Overall, the tactics employed by the administration to support its grand design and strategic objectives were unexceptional, but those used to implement the BEM strategy deserve special mention. Three elements, in particular, stood out. First, the president enhanced the stature of the secretary of commerce by increasing the responsibilities of the interagency Trade Promotion Coordinating Committee (TPCC) and by naming Ron Brown as chair. Brown announced his intention to make high-profile visits to each of the ten BEMs. Second, in November 1993 Clinton created another cabinet-level coordinating body with a focus of foreign economic strategy, the National Science and Technology Council, whose functions included reforming export control policies and finding ways to accelerate research and development in the "big, emerging export sectors."[80] Most important, Garten helped establish an "advocacy center" or "economic war room" to directly assist American companies in winning huge contracts for infrastructure projects in the BEMs. To do so this center coordinated the efforts of several agencies, including Commerce, State, Energy, the Export-Import Bank, the CIA, and the Overseas Private Investment Corporation. Frequently President Clinton himself lobbied foreign governments on behalf of such corporations as Enron, General Electric, and Bechtel. According to Joan Spero, undersecretary of state for economic affairs, these tactics represented a "big conceptual change" from previous administrations: "there is a recognition now that promoting private investment and trade abroad is a primary interest of our policy."[81] These significant tactical innovations may well become permanent central features of post–Cold War American foreign policy and, at the least, force a redefinition of the "national security state."

How did Bill Clinton attempt to legitimize a foreign policy rather grandly described by the White House as "A Strategy of Engagement and Enlargement?" Unlike some of its post-Vietnam predecessors the administration remained generally free of paralyzing feuds and disagreements among its senior foreign affairs officials. It was true that the White House was rather embarrassingly forced to postpone for several months the publication of its national security strategy (as required by Congress) because of uncertainty particularly about the role of the United Nations.[82] And Undersecretary of State for Political Affairs Peter Tarnoff (yet another Carter veteran) caused a stir by suggesting off-the-record that the United States would be forced to retrench and turn over some responsibilities to multilateral organizations. When word leaked out, Christopher was obliged to rebuke Tarnoff publicly and disavow his remarks.[83] But relations with the Defense Department, and especially the uniformed services, constituted by far the president's main internal legitimation problem. Bluntly put, significant parts of the military distrusted and even disliked Clinton for a combination of personal and policy reasons. His anti-Vietnam War activities while at Oxford as well as the widely shared suspicion that he had dodged the draft lay at the root of the difficulty. But President Clinton worsened his situation by immediately announcing his intention to lift the ban on gays in the military. Soon stories circulated that Clinton still harbored antimilitary feelings, and much was made of an unfortunate incident in which a young White House staffer informed a visiting army general that she did not speak to people in uniform.

At the policy level the administration's evident early desire to expand the traditional role of the U.S. military into such areas as multinational humanitarian and "peacemaking" missions further raised tensions. A battle raged for months within the administration over this issue. Finally, in May 1994 the belated release of PDD-25 indicated the degree to which the Defense Department had successfully diluted the White House's initial ambitions.

President Clinton quickly became aware of these misgivings and tried to reassure the military that he valued and respected it. White House aides arranged high-visibility visits to military and naval facilities, and when Clinton was heckled by veterans at the Vietnam Memorial in May 1993, General Colin Powell publicly jumped to the president's defense. But despite these efforts, relations remained strained and stood in stark contrast to the very high esteem in which the military held Reagan and Bush.

Despite his justifiable claim to be the first wholly post–Cold War president, Bill Clinton's attempts to legitimate *publicly* his grand design, strategic objectives, and foreign policy tactics broke little new ground. He relied on most of the same devices as his predecessors, although, because he defined himself primarily as a domestic president, Clinton devoted less time to these activities than his Cold War and post-Vietnam counterparts.

Clinton, of course, loved to talk, but he gave relatively few speeches about foreign affairs as traditionally understood. During his first two-plus years in office he addressed the nation on television only twice on the subject—Somalia in October 1993 and Haiti in September 1994—but in both instances the focus was narrow, the remarks brief, and the speeches reacted to specific crises. President Clinton did develop a practice early in his administration that he employed with surprising consistency: to deliver speeches immediately before attending overseas meetings, conferences, and summits in which he sought to define the agenda and explain the administration's objectives. But Clinton typically offered these remarks to small and specialized audiences and aimed them more at foreign leaders than the American public.

He did, however, speak a great deal about foreign economic policy—NAFTA, GATT, the Japanese market, national competitiveness—and sought to show how it affected average American workers. By emphasizing these "intermestic" issues, President Clinton tried to demonstrate the connections between a well-educated, well-paid workforce and the success of the United States in the world economy.

Yet the public gave Clinton remarkably little credit for the exceptionally strong performance of the economy. He remained unpopular even as the economy boomed. The media, in seeking to unravel this mystery, focused on the "angry white men" phenomenon, in which younger, less educated "victims" of an increasingly high-tech economy and liberal social policies lashed out at Clinton and the Democratic Party.

On another level, however, the public questioned the *competence* of the Clinton foreign policy team. The administration may have considered Russia and the BEMs to be at the heart of its strategy, but the public and the media focused on the disarray evident in its Bosnia, Somalia, and Haiti policies. This failure to achieve *cognitive* legitimacy plagued the Clinton administration, especially in 1993, and damaged its *normative* efforts.

Furthermore, Bill Clinton's personal history made it more difficult to offer a *declaratory* history of American foreign relations. His record of antiwar protest and possible draft evasion seriously tainted his ability to narrate an inspiring, patriotic account of America's historical role, despite the public's overwhelmingly negative collective memory of Vietnam. Some Republicans, such as Robert Dornan (R-CA), publicly accused Clinton of providing "aid and comfort to the enemy." The President's chief political rival in early 1995, Robert Dole, had been a genuine hero in World War II. Moreover, because 1994 and 1995 were years that marked the fiftieth anniversary of a host of that war's most memorable events, Clinton was naturally obliged to participate in many of the ceremonies. Yet his presence at them inevitably angered a significant portion of the American public.

Finally, like all the presidents discussed in this book, Clinton tried to achieve *normative* legitimacy by placing his foreign policy firmly between the reviled poles of "isolationism" and "world policeman." Clinton understood that while most of the public desired that the United States play an active role in the world (65 percent in the 1995 Chicago Council on Foreign Relations poll), it strongly preferred to coordinate that activity with other nations and international organizations. In short, unilateral behavior risked acting like a "world policeman," which in turn could bring on another Vietnam. On the other hand, because two-thirds of the public and 98 percent of the opinion leaders held internationalist views, Clinton, like his predecessors, relied on the "isolationist" shibboleth to besmirch his opponents. Clinton and Anthony Lake employed this device more frequently after the 1994 elections when many Republicans spoke out against the United Nations and foreign aid. In response, Republicans accused the administration of eroding American sovereignty by allegedly subordinating its foreign policy to the United Nations. In so doing, both sides continued a discourse at least as old as the one between Woodrow Wilson and Henry Cabot Lodge.

Notes

1. See, for example, Robert Reich, *The Work of Nations: Preparing Ourselves for 21st Century Capitalism.*
2. Bill Clinton, *Putting People First: A National Economic Strategy for America.*
3. Betty Glad, "How George Bush Lost the Presidential Election of 1992," p. 12.
4. Ibid., p. 19.
5. Ibid.
6. Ibid., p. 20.
7. After Clinton's gubernatorial defeat in 1980 Brown had invited him to serve as his chief of staff in California! David Maraniss, *First in His Class: A Biography of Bill Clinton,* p. 389.
8. W. Lance Bennett, "The Cueless Public: Bill Clinton Meets the New American Voter in Campaign '92," p. 109.
9. Ibid., p. 99.
10. Ibid., p. 105.
11. Bill Clinton, Speech to the World Affairs Council, Los Angeles, August 13, 1992.
12. Ibid.
13. Ibid. In the words of David C. Hendrickson, "Clinton's strategy in the game of political poker he played with Bush was to see all bets the incumbent had placed and then raise him" ("The Recovery of Internationalism," p. 27). This high-risk strategy placed the Clinton administration in an extremely uncomfortable predicament early on.
14. Quoted in John B. Judis, "From Hell: The New Democrat Delusion," p. 14.
15. Maraniss, *First in His Class,* p. 416.
16. Ibid., pp. 360 and 361.
17. Ibid., p. 364.
18. Ibid., p. 387.
19. Ibid., p. 407.
20. Ibid., p. 408.
21. Ibid., pp. 411–12.
22. Ibid., p. 417.
23. Judis, "From Hell," p. 16.
24. Bob Woodward, *The Agenda: Inside the Clinton White House,* p. 41.
25. Elizabeth Drew, *On the Edge: The Clinton Presidency,* p. 52.
26. Woodward, *The Agenda,* pp. 70, 79, and 78.
27. Drew, *On the Edge,* p. 42.
28. They were given extraordinary access to the president. One "story line" emphasized Clinton's commitment to "lifelong learning," while another focused on "economic

security." Clinton tried out the latter formulation in an October 1993 speech at the University of North Carolina but dropped it quickly.

29. Woodward, *The Agenda*, p. 241.

30. Drew, *On the Edge*, p. 233.

31. Other Carter veterans included Lynn Davis, undersecretary of state for arms control and international affairs, and Peter Tarnoff, undersecretary of state for political affairs.

32. See chapter 3 for evidence of this outlook.

33. Michael Kelly, "Surrender and Blame," p. 46.

34. Quoted in ibid., p. 47.

35. Ibid.

36. Drew, *On the Edge*, p. 147.

37. Ibid., p. 150.

38. Lake, of course, had been among the earlier group of protesters.

39. Support for the Somalia mission peaked at about 70 percent.

40. *Christian Science Monitor*, November 29, 1993, p. 12.

41. Ibid. ·

42. Bill Clinton, "Address to the Nation on Somalia," October 7, 1993.

43. Ibid.

44. "The Clinton Administration's Policy on Reforming Multilateral Peace Operations," p. 4.

45. It remained unclear if the Senate would acquiesce.

46. Gaddis Smith, "Haiti: From Intervention to Intervasion," p. 57.

47. Clinton blamed his 1980 defeat on the uprising of some of these exiles at Fort Chafee, Arkansas, and the negative public reaction to it.

48. Robinson, it will be recalled from chapter 4, had tried very hard to prevent the invasion of Grenada in 1983.

49. *New York Times*, September 16, 1994, p. A10.

50. *Wall Street Journal*, January 16, 1995, p. A10.

51. *Washington Post*, January 3, 1995, p. A15.

52. Anthony Lake, "Warren and Anita Manshel Lecture," October 21, 1994.

53. Ibid.

54. Ibid.

55. Ibid.

56. Ibid.

57. Ibid.

58. Anthony Lake, "Confronting Backlash States," p. 46.

59. Ibid.

60. See, for example, F. Gregory Gause III, "The Illogic of Dual Containment."

61. *Washington Post*, April 13, 1995, p. A27.

62. David Hendrickson effectively criticizes such views in "The Recovery of Internationalism: Salvaging Clinton's Foreign Policy."

63. *Washington Post*, April 22, 1995, p. A19.

64. Carla Anne Robbins, "Dateline Washington: Cuban-American Clout," p. 163.

65. Ibid., p. 167.

66. Ibid.

67. As early as the summer of 1994, however, there was evidence that the administration may have begun to rethink its Cuban policy in the aftermath of another wave of "boat people."

68. Clinton cleverly exploited Richard Nixon's criticisms of the Bush policy for his own advantage.

69. Clinton offered these formulations in March and April 1993, respectively.

70. Michael Cox, "The Necessary Partnership? The Clinton Presidency and post-Soviet Russia," pp. 641–42.

71. Ibid., pp. 643–46.

72. Ibid., p. 654.

73. *New York Times,* April 20, 1995, p. A25.

74. John Stremlau, "Clinton's Dollar Diplomacy," p. 18.

75. Ibid., p. 19.

76. U.S. Department of Commerce, *Toward a National Export Strategy;* Jeffrey E. Garten, "The Big Emerging Markets: Changing American Interests in the Global Economy"; and idem., "Trade, Foreign Policy, and National Security: Reflections on Economic Diplomacy."

77. Stremlau, "Clinton's Dollar Diplomacy," p. 23.

78. *New York Times,* May 8, 1995, p. D2.

79. *Business Week,* May 8, 1995, p. 122.

80. Stremlau, "Clinton's Dollar Diplomacy," p. 26.

81. *New York Times,* February 19, 1995, p. 3:1.

82. The document "A National Security Strategy of Engagement and Enlargement" appeared in July 1994. The second annual report, with the same title but with some subtle changes that indicated a backing away from "assertive multilateralism," was released on time in February 1995.

83. Tarnoff had been a close adviser to Cyrus Vance in the Carter administration.

Part Four

Conclusions

7

American Foreign Policy
Since Nixon

The past twenty-five years of American foreign policy might very well be viewed as a "lump," wherein unifying themes, recurrent patterns, and over-arching generalizations gave to these decades a certain degree of predictability. Conversely, a chronicler of these years could perhaps just as easily look for evidence of discontinuity, idiosyncrasy, and happenstance in order to explain American grand strategy.[1]

By employing the method of structured, focused comparison, this book has attempted to identify concepts, approaches, behaviors, and goals that have both united and separated the foreign policies and domestic legitimation efforts of Presidents Nixon, Ford, Carter, Reagan, Bush, and Clinton. To this end we posed an identical set of questions to each of these administrations:[2]

1. What were their domestic priorities?
2. How did these presidents perceive the problem of governance?
3. What were the relationships of questions 1 and 2 to their foreign policies?
4. What were the grand designs, strategic objectives, and tactics of the Nixon (Ford), Carter, Reagan, Bush, and Clinton foreign policies?
5. How did these presidents attempt to legitimate their foreign policies to the bureaucracy and the public?
6. Did any of them succeed in reconstructing the substantive, cultural, and procedural components of a domestic foreign policy consensus?

Detailed answers to these questions were offered in earlier chapters. Tables 7.1 through 7.6 provide handy summaries of those conclusions.

Table 7.1

Domestic Priorities

Nixon	Carter	Reagan	Bush	Clinton
Molding a post–New Deal "new majority" that tapped the resentments of those opposed to Great Society "excesses," federal social engineering, the youthful "counterculture," and anti-Vietnam protesters	Restoring the trust of the American people in government after Watergate and Vietnam by personally embodying the values of the public, offering comprehensive, "fair" responses to complex, long-standing national problems such as energy, health care, tax structure, and welfare	Restoring the American economy through tax and federal social spending cuts	Few substantive goals apart from smoothing hard edges of the "Reagan Revolution"	Enormously ambitious agenda including economic stimulus package, deficit reduction, public "investments" in "lifelong learning," health care and welfare reform, national service corps, and "reinventing government" initiatives
Replacing the "failed" leadership of the liberal establishment—with Main Street loyalists	Emphasizing the limits of the federal government's capacity to solve problems	Returning collective political and economic power to "we the people" from federal social engineers	Tepid and inconsistent embrace of an "empowerment agenda"	
Returning to the states such services as education, job training, and public health, while enlarging the federal role in areas such as welfare, energy, and the environment		Undertaking a massive defense buildup to make up for the "decade of neglect"	Desire to reduce federal deficit balanced by fear of inflaming conservatives	

Table 7.2

Approaches to Governance

Nixon	Carter	Reagan	Bush	Clinton
Government as the legitimate expression of the "new majority's" values and aspirations	Problem-solving competence	Presidential rhetoric as national motivator	Effort to divorce "governing mode" from "campaign mode"	Faith in federal government to do "good works"
"Hardball" politics employed to expose and dislodge liberal elites from power and influence	Presidential responsibility to transcend "politics" in the name of the national interest	Government as the "problem" to be tamed by decentralization, voluntarism, and the free market	Belief that good governance results from application of appropriate procedures rather than the "vision thing"	President as national policy "seminar leader" unconcerned with process
President as fearless leader determined to do the "right," not the "easy," thing	President as a flawed average citizen drawing strength from the people	President as but another "extraordinary, ordinary American"	Preference in working with fellow insiders to create policy coalitions	President as highly personal empathizer with average citizen
				Governing and campaigning a seamless web requiring same kinds of advice

Table 7.3

Relationship of Foreign Policy to Domestic Priorities and Approaches to Governance

Nixon	Carter	Reagan	Bush	Clinton
Little direct relationship: Nixon hoped that "silent majority" would tolerate phased withdrawal from Vietnam and that "new majority" would allow the pursuit of a largely amoral foreign policy	Very close relationship: human rights, the management of détente, and the resolution of regional and transnational disputes would support Carter's domestic themes of competence and moralism	Very close relationship: emphasis on free markets, individual liberty, and democratic community at home to be reflected in the rising tide of democratic revolution and the defeat of "big" government abroad	Very little direct relationship apart from common commitment to "good process" in both arenas	Little obvious connection for a "domestic" president occasionally distracted by foreign policy
			Growing public perception that preference for foreign policy detracted from domestic performance	On another level, a close relationship between foreign economic policy and domestic economic priorities

Table 7.4

Grand Designs, Strategic Objectives, and Tactics

Nixon	Carter	Reagan	Bush	Clinton
Grand Design Stable, multipolar equilibrium guided primarily by the United States, misleadingly described by Nixon as a "stable structure of peace"	***Grand Design*** (1977–78): stable, just world featuring an increasingly cooperative superpower relationship, a mutually beneficial North–South "dialogue," and a "mature" United States adapting to change and leading by example (1979–80): Same essential vision, but the realization that its achievement would be indefinitely delayed because of the "shocks" of 1979	***Grand Design*** A gradually articulated vision of a fully demo-cratic world reflective of American (and universally shared) values	***Grand Design*** Initial acceptance of Cold War paradigm replaced by poorly articulated new world order with America as a "benevolent hegemon"	***Grand Design*** America as the world's paramount "commercial republic" committed to the enlargement of "zone of the democratic peace"

(continued)

Table 7.4 (continued)

Nixon	Carter	Reagan	Bush	Clinton
Strategic Objectives Superpower détente designed to (self-)contain the Soviet Union through the deft management of incentives, threats, and proscriptions and the conclusion of arms control agreements	***Strategic Objectives*** (1977–78): Effective U.S. Management of "complex interdependence" through adroit manipulation of shifting global coalitions	***Strategic Objectives*** Initial "prevailing with pride" strategy involving economic warfare against the Soviet Union, avoidance of superpower arms control agreements, nuclear and conventional force modernization facilitating "horizontal escalation," an information offensive, and support for Third World anticommunist "freedom fighters"	***Strategic Objectives*** Pursuit of five strategic objectives during 1990 and 1991 designed to ease transition to post–Cold War world	***Strategic Objectives*** Containment and/or isolation of "backlash states"
Gradual withdrawal from Vietnam intended to preserve U.S. credibility and thus contribute to the emerging international equilibrium	Restoration of a balance between commitments and resources by reducing commitments, shifting burdens to allies, and accommodating rivals		These objectives largely supplanted by NWO goals of regional stability, nonproliferation, and resistance to aggression	Encouragement of Russia's evolution into a "normal country"
"Peripheral" strategy embodied in Nixon Doctrine that would avoid future Vietnams by relying on local resistance to	Achievement of Brzezinski's ten goals	A personal presidential commitment to nuclear abolition through SDI and arms reduction agreements		BEM strategy to support its grand design
	(1979–80): Return to containment in order to punish Soviet aggression in Afghanistan and			

aggression and sub-version and/or collaborating with Moscow to resolve regional disputes

Normalization of relations with the PRC designed to complicate Moscow's security dilemma, facilitate an honorable withdrawal from Vietnam, and encourage the growth of a multipolar balance

to deter it from further expansion

The determination—expressed in Carter Doctrine—to defend the Persian Gulf as a vital interest

Tactics
Radical centralization of power in White House to formulate and implement strategy

Emphasis on speed, dexterity, manipulation and geopolitical ruthlessness.

Tactics
(1977–78): explicit rejection of Nixon–Kissinger approach in favor of openness, honesty, and public participation in foreign policymaking

(1979–80): Renewed emphasis on strong presidential leadership at a time of "crisis"

Tactics
Declaratory signaling aimed at intimidating the Soviet Union and later focused on lending rhetorical support to "democratic revolutions"

Reliance on presidential character to reflect values of "ordinary, extraordinary Americans"

Tactics
Reliance on personal diplomacy conducted primarily with leaders of established states

Tactics
President as active salesmen for American business

Use of an "economic war room" to help win international contracts for U.S. exporters

Table 7.5

Legitimation Strategies

Nixon	Carter	Reagan	Bush	Clinton
A laudatory declaratory history of post–World War II American foreign policy	(1977–78): a rather critical account of American foreign policy since 1945	A declaratory history condemning U.S. foreign policy in the 1930s and 1970s and extolling the record of the 1940s, 1950s, and 1980s	Daily demonstration of foreign policy competence	Presidential speeches designed to set agendas for upcoming international meetings
An explanation of the ways the world had changed since 1947 and how his policies appropriately addressed those changes	The claim that the world had changed decisively in the past three decades	The reassurance that recent foreign policy setbacks were self-inflicted and easily reversible	A declaratory history that linked the indispensability of American leadership in Cold War to requirements of post–Cold War world	Attempt to demonstrate relevance of "intermestic" issues to average American workers
An effort to castigate domestic critics as isolationists who would abandon U.S. world leadership	The assertion that his foreign policy reflected the character, values, experiences, and aspirations of the American people	A description of the contemporary world that stressed continuity with the past	Repeated warnings of a post–Cold War resurgence of isolationism and protectionism	President's personal history made articulation of a declaratory history of U.S. foreign policy difficult
Surprises and televised spectaculars designed to demonstrate Nixon's indispensability	A description of his foreign policy as courageously and comprehensively responding to complexity	The assertion that his foreign policy was well equipped to fight evil in the world	Increasing reliance on concept of the "demo-cratic peace" as guarantee of global stability	Attempt to portray domestic opponents as isolationists and protectionists

A Wilsonian promise of a "full generation of peace"

The warning that "peace with honor" in Vietnam would produce a world to challenge the character, will, and spiritual strength of the American people

The assurance that America could afford to be generous and cooperative

The promise of an emergent, cooperative global community

(1979–80): a laudatory declaratory history stressing the continuities and wisdom of the foreign policy record

A predominately negative portrayal of international change

A description of a complex, turbulent world requiring a strong American economic and military foundation

The assurance that the U.S. had regained its military superiority

Theatrical exercises designed to demonstrate his determination to confront a world in "crisis"

The claim that both America and the world possessed very similar political "neighborhoods"

The increasingly confident promise of a fully democratic world as a result of his policies

Table 7.6

Success in Achieving Domestic Foreign Policy Consensus

	Nixon	Carter	Reagan	Bush	Clinton
Policy Consensus	Short-lived consensus about the promise of détente	Largely unsuccessful in achieving consensus for either world order initiatives or neocontainment	Substantial success except for Central American policy	Modest success in resurrecting and modifying policy axioms of the Cold War undercut by refusal to publicly debate merits of the new world order	
Cultural Consensus	Goal was *Kulturkampf*, not consensus, and was largely successful in that regard	Unsuccessful in reinstilling an ethic of sacrifice	Mostly successful in instilling an ethic of national greatness through self-indulgence	Attempt to exploit domestic cultural chasms while in "campaign mode" damaged other efforts to ignore these rifts while "governing"	
Procedural Consensus	Heightened dissensus	Largely failed to work out new "codetermination" arrangements	Largely unsuccessful in either reasserting primacy of president or reaching agreement about proper congressional role	Executive-legislative relations improved from Reagan years as a result of removal of communism and the Soviet Union as hot button, ideological issues	

The Nixon Administration

If Richard Nixon had been elected in 1960 instead of 1968 he probably would have pursued a policy of anticommunist global containment largely indistinguishable from that of Truman and Eisenhower. Furthermore, his efforts would have been sustained by a broad domestic consensus regarding the interests, goals, and instruments of American foreign policy. But by 1968 deep, angry cleavages among elites and the wider public produced mostly, though not solely, by the Vietnam War, had shattered the consensus and threatened to paralyze U.S. foreign policy. Many observers feared that the country lay on the edge of civil war.

The Nixon–Kissinger foreign policy reformulation and their attempts to achieve "peace with honor" in Vietnam constituted largely improvised responses to both domestic dissensus and a series of unwelcome international changes that had begun to erode America's preeminent global position. Because the American people, in the aftermath of the Tet offensive in early 1968, opposed further increases in U.S. ground troop strength, Nixon reluctantly decided to rely primarily on American air power and "Vietnamization" to preserve a noncommunist South Vietnam. He did little to mobilize a domestic consensus for this policy of phased withdrawal. Instead, Nixon tried to build majority support by unleashing a provocative and divisive *Kulturkampf* against "effete snobs," "isolationists," "campus bums," "nattering nabobs of negativism" (an Agnew contribution), and other miscreants who allegedly sought defeat and disgrace in Vietnam. Against these liberal elitist "appeasers" Nixon juxtaposed the "silent" or "new" majority—patriotic, "Main Street" Americans who resented the perceived excesses of the Great Society fully as much as they desired "peace with honor" in Southeast Asia. In this way Nixon attempted to build a post–New Deal conservative *social* coalition that, among other things, would provide majority support for his Vietnam policy.

On the other hand, Nixon's pursuit of superpower détente at a time of growing Soviet strength risked condemnation by the "new majority" as dangerously retreatist. Moreover, Nixon and Kissinger made détente even more vulnerable to conservative criticism by professing to be unconcerned with Soviet *domestic* practices as long as its foreign policy demonstrated prudence and responsibility. Aware of these potential domestic difficulties, Nixon tried to disguise the "European" character of his détente behind a Wilsonian promise of a "full generation of peace," a promise that could be fulfilled, he asserted, only if "peace with honor" were achieved in Vietnam. And, for a brief moment in 1972 and 1973, Nixon did enjoy something approaching consensual support for his strategy of détente.

Yet even without the Watergate scandal it appears unlikely that Nixon could have built a lasting consensus on this version of détente. First, the *promises* Nixon made on behalf of this strategy—arms control, regional stability, Soviet adherence to a superpower code of conduct—were perceived by many Americans (led by neoconservative elites) as much greater than the rather meager results of détente. According to this view, SALT had granted numerical superiority to Soviet strategic weapons; the 1973 Middle East war had demonstrated Moscow's determination to expand recklessly its influence in a volatile region; and its massive arms buildup proved its commitment to military superiority, not stable parity. Second, Nixon's (and Ford's) subsequent efforts to emphasize the "tough" side of détente—the "sticks"—by threatening to intervene militarily in regional disputes in Africa and the Middle East to maintain American credibility were undermined by a public and a Congress that above all feared another Vietnam. Indeed, the Nixon Doctrine had *obscured* rather than defined those interests in defense of which the United States would employ military force. Nixon and Kissinger had hoped to preempt the issue of American intervention on the periphery by improving superpower relations, but renewed Soviet activity in the Third World forced Nixon and Ford to appeal to a public now extremely leery of military action. Furthermore, it seems doubtful that Nixon—even without Watergate—could have persuaded Congress to authorize a reintervention in Vietnam, in part because of the deep animosities previously planted by Nixon in his war against the liberal establishment.

Still, despite these significant failures, Nixon and Kissinger were responsible for some solid foreign policy accomplishments. First, by implicitly acknowledging that American power had finite limits, they sought ways to accommodate a new world no longer wholly susceptible to U.S. hegemonic fiat. Though, as, for example, in Chile, they found it difficult to live with the consequences of their insights, the overall impact of their reformulation resulted in a modest "deideologization" of American foreign policy. "Stability" now vied with "mission" as a national priority. Second, by recognizing that simple anticommunism could no longer serve as the *sole* basis of American foreign policy, Nixon and Kissinger searched for alternative definitions of the national interest, notions that included the necessity of working with the Soviet Union. Third, by placing nuclear arms control on the superpower agenda, Nixon and Kissinger at least raised the possibility that an uncontrolled arms race could be regulated in mutually beneficial ways. Fourth, in moving to normalize relations with China, Nixon and Kissinger signaled a willingness to manipulate the international status quo in order to encourage the growth of a stable equilibrium.

Yet notwithstanding these admirable efforts to achieve a "philosophical deepening" of American foreign policy, the Nixon–Kissinger reformulation ultimately failed the test of domestic politics, for both liberals and conservatives condemned the search for a "stable equilibrium" as the abandonment of traditional American values and principles.

The Carter Administration

Members of the Carter administration shared the perception that the American people, traumatized by Vietnam and Watergate and frightened by inflation and the energy crisis, had lost faith in themselves and their institutions. Fearing that this widespread disillusionment could create demands for an isolationist foreign policy, Carter attempted to reestablish the global "relevance" of the United States by "getting on the right side of change" and by emphasizing his dedication to human rights. America's new task would be the adroit management of "complex interdependence" in an era of increasingly diffused power. Carter hoped that the competence and courage that he displayed in pursuit of a moral, humane, and mature foreign policy would help restore national self-confidence.

Occasionally this approach bore fruit as, for example, in the Panama Canal treaties and the Camp David Accords. And, if he had faced the reform-minded Mikhail Gorbachev, instead of the intransigent Leonid Brezhnev, Soviet-American détente might have been strengthened and expanded. But Carter's early efforts to portray the Soviet Union as a largely satisfied power that could positively contribute to world order appeared increasingly at odds with Moscow's actual behavior. Furthermore, Carter's inability to tame domestic inflation or to manage Third World crises in Iran and Nicaragua raised disturbing questions about his competence and "toughness." Neoconservative and conservative commentators and politicians relentlessly attacked Carter as both incompetent and ideologically misguided. They argued persuasively that at the core of Carter's "mature" foreign policy lay retreatism, appeasement, and hypocrisy.

Confronted with this acute domestic challenge as the 1980 election drew closer, Carter tried to placate these critics by embracing a more traditional, Soviet-centered, foreign policy approach. Now he claimed—at Brzezinski's urging—that the American people had so "overlearned" the lessons of Vietnam that the use of U.S. military power in *any* circumstance had wrongly been proscribed. In place of his earlier efforts at retrenchment and burden sharing, President Carter enunciated a Persian Gulf "doctrine" that appeared to expand the vital interests of the United States. Yet opinion polls indicated that although the public wanted America to reassert its "global leadership," there remained widespread resistance to the employment of military power abroad. In sum, the ambiguous and divisive legacy of Vietnam haunted U.S. foreign policy at the end of the 1970s just as the reality of that war had deepened domestic dissensus at the beginning of that decade.

The Reagan Administration

Ronald Reagan shared Jimmy Carter's conviction about the necessity for restoring national self-confidence. But whereas his predecessor had initially offered a complex program of unfocused moralism, managerial incompetence, and world order initiatives to achieve this goal, Reagan resurrected the priorities of Cold War presidents: a high-growth, low-inflation economy, a powerful national defense, and a strident anticommunist rhetoric. Reagan and his advisers may have harbored the vague hope that the patient pursuit of these goals might *eventually* result in the moderation or capitulation of the Soviet Union, but in the early 1980s they anticipated a long, "twilight struggle" comparable in intensity to the high Cold War. The administration's early "prevailing with pride" strategy neatly captured this pugnacious outlook.

Yet Reagan faced a public that, while eager to reassert American global leadership after the national embarrassments of the late 1970s, simultaneously feared both superpower nuclear war and another Vietnam quagmire. These public pressures severely constrained Reagan's foreign policy options by forcing him to enunciate an arms control program and to renounce any intention of direct intervention in Central America. The result was that Reagan—the "Great Communicator"—unveiled a foreign policy distinguished by heavy declaratory signaling to overseas adversaries and the American public. By ridiculing rival governments and lavishing praise on the American people, Reagan was able to pursue an essentially cautious foreign policy that largely replaced deeds with words. At the same time, the partial restoration of the national economy enabled Reagan's rhetoric to find a receptive domestic audience.

Indeed, it was *rhetoric* that united the otherwise quite distinct foreign policies of Reagan's first and second terms, for if the early years witnessed a heavily stylized new Cold War that featured evil empires and similar dragons, the late 1980s were alleged by Reagan to be a new era of "democratic revolutions" sweeping away the last vestiges of authoritarian rule. If nothing else, Reagan had succeeded in persuading the American people of the revitalized global relevance of the American dream.

The Bush Administration

George Bush, by background, training, and temperament very comfortable with the verities of the Cold War, would have preferred to pursue a strategy of anticommunist containment. Indeed, he spent much of 1989 attempting to slow down the momentum of the Reagan–Gorbachev express. But at the Malta "nonsummit" in December of that year Bush finally concluded that he could do business with Gorbachev and proceeded to pursue a set of strategic objectives designed to ease the transition to a post–Cold War world. Among these goals was German reunification, and the administration orchestrated that process with adroitness, patience, imagination, and aplomb.

After continuing Ronald Reagan's policy of détente with Iraq in an effort to balance the power of Iran, Saddam Hussein startled and initially confused Bush by invading Kuwait in August 1990. Yet by first creating and leading an unlikely international coalition and then carefully cultivating domestic support for military action in the Persian Gulf, Bush performed masterfully, and a grateful American public made him the most popular president since approval polls existed.

But from this pinnacle reached in early 1991 Bush stumbled badly. Instead of risking a national debate over America's role in his new world order, he retreated into merely celebrating and recelebrating the victory in Desert Storm. Furthermore, the administration ceded leadership in the Yugoslavian cauldron to the European Union, shrank from doing much to assist the new postcommunist governments in Eastern Europe, and appeared reluctant genuinely to assist Boris Yeltsin.

In large part this timidity was driven by the exigencies of the 1992 presidential campaign. Dogged by the widespread perception that he cared little for domestic issues and plagued by a recession that refused to end, George Bush came to regard his foreign policy accomplishments and aspirations as significant impediments to his reelection chances.

Nevertheless, this transitional president bequeathed to his immediate successors a set of global priorities for the world's sole, remaining superpower. That agenda featured efforts to retard the proliferation of weapons of mass destruction; the further expansion of free trade areas with the United States as the fulcrum; the continuing reliance on American military power to provide "regional stability," especially in East Asia and the Middle East; the formal obligation to involve international organizations in this nation's foreign policy initiatives; and the public reassurance that the "democratic peace" required American global leadership. In all these ways George Bush "set the table" for his post–Cold War successors.

The Clinton Administration

This first wholly post–Cold War president possessed a vast factual knowledge of the details of domestic policy and tried to withdraw as much as possible from most international issues save for Russia and foreign economic policy. Yet Clinton was repeatedly distracted by a series of annoying, frustrating, largely inherited foreign policy problems including Bosnia, North Korea, Haiti, Cuba, and Somalia.

The administration had entered office determined to exploit the United Nations as a potential fulcrum of post–Cold War international security. It recognized the American public's preference for multinational initiatives in the wake of Operation Desert Storm and simultaneously hoped that an assertive United Nations could relieve America of some of the more onerous global leadership burdens. But the October 1993 disaster in Somalia as well as the long-running embarrassment in Bosnia provoked an acute, and negative, domestic reaction and forced Clinton to trim his multinational sails. Yet he resisted congressional Republican legislation that would have, in effect, prohibited future American participation in UN peacekeeping activities.

President Clinton did, however, steadfastly emphasize the significance of a "normal" Russia to the stability of the post–Cold War world. Despite growing Republican demands that he "get tough" with Yeltsin, Clinton continued to treat the Russian president largely as a potential partner. By mid-1995 several obstacles to better relations had emerged, but the administration had grown more optimistic about the future prospects of the Russian economy.

But what gave to this first post–Cold War presidency its distinctiveness was neither its confusion about the conditions that warranted military action nor its focus on Russia. Indeed, as we have seen, these themes had been hallmarks of every administration since Nixon's. Instead, it was Clinton's resurrection of America as a commercial republic that defined his grand design and accounted for the centrality of his BEM strategy. In so doing Clinton sought to return American foreign policy to a tradition interrupted but not extinguished by the national security priorities of the Cold War. But whether it would form the conceptual basis for a new domestic foreign policy consensus remained to be seen.

Notes

1. These terms are employed by John Lewis Gaddis in his classic work, *Strategies of Containment.*

2. To repeat, it is premature to evaluate Clinton's efforts to build a post–Cold War domestic foreign policy consensus.

Bibliography

Books

Abramson, Jeffrey B.; Atherton, F. Christopher; and Orren, Garry R. *The Electronic Commonwealth: The Impact of New Media Technologies on Democratic Politics.* New York: Basic Books, 1988.

Almond, Gabriel A. *The American People and Foreign Policy.* New York: Harcourt Brace, 1950.

Ambrose, Stephen E. *Nixon: The Triumph of a Politician, 1962–1972.* New York: Simon and Schuster, 1989.

Americans Talk Issues: Serial National Surveys of Americans on Public Policy Issues. Winchester, MA, 1991–92.

Americans Talk Security: A Series of Surveys of American Voters: Attitudes Concerning National Security Issues. Winchester, MA, 1988–90.

America's Place in the World: An Investigation of the Attitudes of American Opinion Leaders and the American Public about International Affairs. Washington, DC: Times Mirror Center for the People and the Press, November 1993.

Anderson, Martin. *Revolution.* New York: Harcourt Brace Jovanovich, 1988.

Arnson, Cynthia J. *Crossroads: Congress, the Reagan Administration, and Central America.* New York: Pantheon Books, 1989.

Bell, Coral. *The Reagan Paradox: U.S. Foreign Policy in the 1980's.* New Brunswick: Rutgers University Press, 1990.

Beschloss, Michael R., and Talbott, Strobe. *At the Highest Levels: The Inside Story of the End of the Cold War.* Boston: Little, Brown, 1993.

Bill, James A. *The Eagle and the Lion: The Tragedy of American-Iranian Relations.* New Haven: Yale University Press, 1988.

Blumenthal, Sidney. *Pledging Allegiance: The Last Campaign of the Cold War.* New York: HarperCollins, 1990.

Boutros-Ghali, Boutros, *An Agenda for Peace: Preventive Diplomacy, Peacemaking, and Peace-keeping.* New York: United Nations Department of Public Information, 1992.

Brandon, Henry. *The Retreat of American Power.* Garden City, NY: Doubleday, 1973.

Brown, Harold. *Thinking about National Security: Defense and Foreign Policy in a Dangerous World.* Boulder, CO: Westview Press, 1983.

Brzezinski, Zbigniew. *Power and Principle: Memoirs of the National Security Advisor, 1977–1981.* New York: Farrar, Straus and Giroux, 1983.

Cannon, Lou. *Reagan.* New York: Putnam, 1982.

Carter, Jimmy. *Keeping Faith: Memoirs of a President.* New York: Bantam, 1982.

———. *Why Not the Best?* Nashville: Broadman Press, 1975.

Christopher, Warren; Saunders, Harold H.; Sick, Gary; et al. *American Hostages in Iran: The Conduct of a Crisis.* New Haven: Yale University Press, 1985.

Clinton, Bill. *Putting People First: A National Economic Strategy for America.* Little Rock: The Clinton for President Committee, n.d.

Crabb, Cecil, Jr., and Holt, Pat. *Invitation to Struggle: Congress, the President, and Foreign Policy.* 3rd ed. Washington, DC: CQ Press, 1989.

Dallek, Robert A. *Ronald Reagan: The Politics of Symbolism.* Cambridge: Harvard University Press, 1984.

Destler, I.M.; Gelb, Leslie H.; and Lake, Anthony. *Our Own Worst Enemy: The Unmaking of American Foreign Policy.* New York: Simon and Schuster, 1984.

Drew, Elizabeth. *On the Edge: Inside the Clinton White House.* New York: Simon and Schuster, 1994.

Dugger, Ronnie. *On Reagan: The Man and His Presidency.* New York: McGraw-Hill, 1983.

Edsall, Thomas, and Blumenthal, Sidney, eds. *The Reagan Legacy.* New York: Pantheon Books, 1988.

Feinberg, Richard E. *The Intemperate Zone: The Third World Challenge to U.S. Foreign Policy.* New York: Norton, 1983.

Ford, Gerald R. *A Time to Heal: The Autobiography of Gerald R. Ford.* New York: Harper & Row, 1979.

Fossedal, Gregory. *The Democratic Imperative: Exporting the American Revolution.* A *New Republic* Book. New York: Basic Books, 1989.

Franck, Thomas M., and Weisband, Edward. *Foreign Policy by Congress.* New York: Oxford University Press, 1979.

Gaddis, John Lewis. *The Long Peace: Inquiries into the History of the Cold War.* New York: Oxford University Press, 1987.

———. *Strategies of Containment: A Critical Appraisal of Postwar American National Security Policy.* New York: Oxford University Press, 1982.

Gallup Opinion Index 92 (February 1973).

Gallup Opinion Index (June 1974).

Gallup Opinion Index 71 (September 1980).

*The Gallup Poll, Public Opinion 1935–1971.*Vols. 1–3. New York: Random House, 1972.

Gardner, Lloyd. *The Great Nixon Turnaround.* New York: New Viewpoints, 1973.

Garthoff, Raymond L. *Detente and Confrontation: American-Soviet Relations from Nixon to Reagan.* Washington, DC: Brookings Institution, 1985.

Gelb, Leslie H., with Betts, Richard K. *The Irony of Vietnam: The System Worked.* Washington, DC: Brookings Institution, 1978.

George, Alexander M., and Smoke, Richard. *Deterrence in American Foreign Policy: Theory and Practice.* New York: Columbia University Press, 1974.

Gibbons, William Conrad. *The U.S. Government and the Vietnam War: Executive and Legislative Roles and Relationships.* Parts 1–3. Princeton: Princeton University Press, 1986 and 1989.

Glad, Betty. *Jimmy Carter: In Search of the Great White House.* New York: Norton, 1980.

Greenstein, Fred I., ed. *Leadership in the Modern Presidency.* Cambridge: Harvard University Press, 1988.

———, ed. *The Reagan Presidency: An Early Assessment.* Baltimore: Johns Hopkins University Press, 1982.

Gutman, Roy. *Banana Diplomacy: The Making of American Policy in Nicaragua, 1981–1987.* New York: Simon and Schuster, 1988.

Hagstrom, Jerry. *Beyond Reagan: The New Landscape of American Politics.* New York: Norton, 1988.

Haig, Alexander M., Jr. *Caveat: Realism, Reagan, and Foreign Policy.* New York: Macmillan, 1984.

Haldeman, H.R. *The Haldeman Diaries: Inside the Nixon White House.* New York: Putnam, 1994.

Hamby, Alonzo L. *Liberalism and Its Challengers: F.D.R. to Reagan.* New York: Oxford University Press, 1985.

Hamilton, Edward K., ed. *America's Global Interests: A New Agenda.* New York: Norton, 1989.

Hamilton, Nora; Frieden, Jeffry A.; Fuller, Linda; and Pastor, Manuel, Jr. *Crisis in Central America: Regional Dynamics and U.S. Policy in the 1980s.* Boulder, CO: Westview Press, 1988.

Hargrove, Erwin C. *Jimmy Carter as President: Leadership and the Politics of the Public Good.* Baton Rouge: Louisiana State University Press, 1988.

Hart, Roderick P. *The Sound Leadership: Presidential Communication in the Modern Age.* Chicago: University of Chicago Press, 1987.

Hersh, Seymour. *The Price of Power: Kissinger in the White House.* New York: Summit Books, 1993.

Hoffmann, Stanley. *Primacy or World Order: American Foreign Policy Since the Cold War.* New York: McGraw-Hill, 1978.

Hogan, J. Michael. *The Panama Canal in American Politics: Domestic Advocacy and the Evolution of Policy.* Carbondale, IL: Southern Illinois University Press, 1986.

Holsti, Ole R., and Rosenau, James N. *American Leadership in World Affairs: Vietnam and the Breakdown of Consensus.* Boston: Allen and Unwin, 1984.

Holsti, Ole R.; Siverson, Randolph M.; and George, Alexander M., eds. *Change in the International System.* Boulder, CO: Westview Press, 1980.

Hyland, William G. *Mortal Rivals: Understanding the Pattern of Soviet-American Conflict.* New York: Random House, 1987.

Isaacson, Walter, and Thomas, Evan. *The Wise Men: Six Friends and the World They Made.* New York: Simon and Schuster, 1986.

Johnson, Haynes. *In the Absence of Power: Governing America.* New York: Viking Press, 1980.

Jones, Charles O. *The Trusteeship Presidency: Jimmy Carter and the United States Congress.* Baton Rouge: Louisiana State University Press, 1988.

———, ed. *The Reagan Legacy: Promise and Performance.* Chatham, NJ: Chatham House, 1988.

Jordan, Hamilton. *Crisis: The Last Year of the Carter Presidency.* New York: Putnam, 1982.

Kissinger, Henry A. *American Foreign Policy.* Expanded ed. New York: Norton, 1974.

———. *Diplomacy.* New York: Simon and Schuster, 1994

———. *White House Years.* Boston: Little, Brown, 1979.

———. *A World Restored: The Politics of Conservatism in a Revolutionary Era.* London: Victor Gollancz, 1977.

———. *Years of Upheaval.* Boston: Little, Brown, 1982.

Kolb, Charles. *White House Daze: The Unmaking of Domestic Policy in the Bush Years.* New York: Free Press, 1994.

Krepon, Michael. *Strategic Stalemate: Nuclear Weapons and Arms Control in American Politics.* New York: St. Martin's Press, 1984.

Krieger, Joel. *Reagan, Thatcher, and the Politics of Decline.* New York: Oxford University Press, 1986.

Kymlicka, B.B., and Matthews, Jean, eds. *The Reagan Revolution?* Chicago: Dorsey Press, 1988.

Lake, W. Anthony, ed. *The Legacy of Vietnam.* New York: New York University Press, 1976.

Larson, Deborah Welch. *Origins of Containment: A Psychological Explanation.* Princeton: Princeton University Press, 1985.

Laurenti, Jeffrey. *American Public Opinion and the United Nations, 1992: Evolving Perceptions of a Changing World.* New York: United Nations Association of the USA, 1992.

Leigh, Michael. *Mobilizing Consent: Public Opinion and American Foreign Policy.* Westport, CT: Greenwood Press, 1976.

Lippmann, Walter. *Public Opinion.* New York: Macmillan, 1922.

Litwak, Robert. *Détente and the Nixon Doctrine: American Foreign Policy and the Pursuit of Stability, 1969–1976.* New York: Cambridge University, 1984.

Lowi, Theodore J. *The Personal President: Power Invested, Promise Unfulfilled.* Ithaca: Cornell University Press, 1985.

Luttwak, Edward. *The Endangered American Dream.* New York: Simon and Schuster, 1994.

McLellan, David S. *Cyrus Vance.* Totowa, NJ: Rowman and Allenfield, 1985.

Maraniss, David. *First in His Class: A Biography of Bill Clinton.* New York: Simon and Schuster, 1995.

May, Ernest R. *Lessons of the Past: The Use and Misuse of History in American Foreign Policy.* New York: Oxford University Press, 1973.

Mayers, David. *Cracking the Monolith: U.S. Policy against the Sino-Soviet Alliance, 1949–1955.* Baton Rouge: Louisiana State University Press, 1986.

———. *George Kennan and the Dilemmas of American Foreign Policy.* New York: Oxford University Press, 1988.

Melanson, Richard A., and Thompson, Kenneth W., eds. *Foreign Policy and Domestic Consensus.* Lanham, MD: University Press of America, 1985.

———. *Writing History and Making Policy: The Cold War, Vietnam, and Revisionism.* Lanham, MD: University Press of America, 1983.

Morris, Roger. *Richard Milhouse Nixon: The Rise of an American Politician.* New York: Henry Holt, 1989.

———. *Uncertain Greatness: Henry Kissinger and American Foreign Policy.* New York: Harper & Row, 1977.

Mower, A. Glenn, Jr. *Human Rights and American Foreign Policy: The Carter and Reagan Experiences.* Westport, CT: Greenwood Press, 1987.

Muravchik, Joshua. *The Uncertain Crusade: Jimmy Carter and the Dilemmas of Human Rights.* Lanham, MD: University Press of America, 1986.

Nathan, Richard P. *The Plot That Failed: Nixon and the Administrative Presidency.* New York: Wiley, 1975.

Newhouse, John. *Cold Dawn: The Story of SALT.* New York: Holt, Rinehart, and Winston, 1973.

Newsome, David D. *The Soviet Combat Brigade in Cuba: A Study in Political Diplomacy.* Bloomington: Indiana University Press, 1987.

Nixon, Richard M. *RN: The Memoirs of Richard Nixon.* New York: Grosset and Dunlop, 1978.

Noonan, Peggy. *What I Saw at the Reagan Revolution: A Political Life in the Reagan Era.* New York: Random House, 1990.

Nye, Joseph S., Jr., ed. *The Making of America's Soviet Policy*. New Haven: Yale University Press, 1984.

Oye, Kenneth A.; Rothchild, Donald; and Lieber, Robert J., eds. *Eagle Defiant: United States Foreign Policy in the 1980s*. Boston: Little, Brown, 1983.

———. *Eagle Entangled: U.S. Foreign Policy in a Complex World*. New York: Longman, 1979.

———. *Eagle Resurgent? The Reagan Era in American Foreign Policy in the 1980s*. Boston: Little, Brown, 1987.

Palmer, John L., ed. *Perspectives on the Reagan Years*. Washington, DC: The Urban Institute, 1986.

Pastor, Robert A. *Condemned to Repetition: The United States and Nicaragua*. Princeton: Princeton University Press, 1987.

Phillips, Kevin. *The Emerging Republican Majority*. New Rochelle: Arlington House, 1969.

Podhoretz, John. *Hell of a Ride: Backstage at the White House Follies, 1989–1993*. New York: Simon and Schuster, 1993.

Posen, Barry R. *The Sources of Military Doctrine: France, Britain, and Germany between the World Wars*. Ithaca, NY: Cornell University Press, 1984.

Powell, Jody. *The Other Side of the Story*. New York: Morrow, 1984.

Quandt, William B. *Camp David: Politics and Peacemaking*. Washington, DC: Brookings Institution, 1986.

Ranney, Austin, ed. *The American Elections of 1980*. Washington, DC: American Enterprise Institute, 1980.

Reagan, Ronald. *An American Life*. New York: Simon and Schuster, 1990.

Regan, Donald T. *For the Record: From Wall Street to Washington*. New York: Harcourt Brace Jovanovich, 1988.

Reich, Robert. *The Work of Nations: Preparing Ourselves for 21st Century Capitalism*. New York: Vintage Books, 1992.

Reichley, A. James. *Conservatives in an Age of Change: The Nixon and Ford Administrations*. Washington, DC: Brookings Institution, 1981.

Rielly, John E., ed. *American Public Opinion and U.S. Foreign Policy 1995*. Chicago: Chicago Council on Foreign Relations, 1995.

———. *American Public Opinion and U.S. Foreign Policy 1991*. Chicago: Chicago Council on Foreign Relations, 1991.

———. *American Public Opinion and U.S. Foreign Policy 1987*. Chicago: Chicago Council on Foreign Relations, 1987.

———. *American Public Opinion and U.S. Foreign Policy 1983*. Chicago: Chicago Council on Foreign Relations, 1983.

———. *American Public Opinion and U.S. Foreign Policy 1979*. Chicago: Chicago Council on Foreign Relations, 1979.

———. *American Public Opinion and U.S. Foreign Policy 1975*. Chicago: Chicago Council on Foreign Relations, 1975.

Rosati, Jerel A. *The Carter Administration's Quest for World Community: Beliefs and Their Impact on Behavior*. Columbia: University of South Carolina Press, 1987.

Rosecrance, Richard, ed. *America as an Ordinary Country: US Foreign Policy and the Future*. London: Cornell University Press, 1976.

Rubin, Barry. *Paved with Good Intentions: The American Experience and Iran*. New York: Oxford University Press, 1980.

Russett, Bruce. *Controlling the Sword: The Democratic Governance of National Security*. Cambridge: Harvard University Press, 1990.

Safire, William. *Before the Fall: An Inside View of the Pre-Watergate White House*. Garden City, NY: Doubleday, 1975.

Sanders, Jerry W. *Peddlers of Crisis: The Committee on the Present Danger and the Politics of Containment.* Boston: South End Press, 1983.

Scammon, Richard M., and Wattenberg, Ben J. *The Real Majority.* New York: Coward-McCann, 1970.

Schoenhals, Kai P., and Melanson, Richard A. *Revolution and Intervention in Grenada: The New Jewel Movement, the United States, and the Caribbean.* Boulder, CO: Westview Press, 1985.

Schoultz, Lars. *National Security and United States Policy toward Latin America.* Princeton: Princeton University Press, 1987.

Schram, Martin. *Running for President: A Journal of the Carter Campaign.* New York: Simon and Schuster, 1977

Schulzinger, Robert D. *The Wise Men of Foreign Affairs: The History of the Council on Foreign Relations.* New York: Columbia University Press, 1984.

Serfaty, Simon. *After Reagan: False Starts, Missed Opportunities and New Beginnings.* Foreign Policy Institute Papers in International Affairs. Lanham, MD: University Press of America, 1988.

Shultz, George P. *Turmoil and Triumph: My Years as Secretary of State.* New York: Scribner's, 1993.

Sick, Gary. *All Fall Down: America's Tragic Encounter with Iran.* New York: Random House, 1985.

Smith, Gaddis. *Morality, Reason, and Power: American Diplomacy in the Carter Years.* New York: Hill and Wang, 1986.

Smith, Hedrick. *The Power Game: How Washington Works.* New York: Random House, 1988.

Smoke, Richard. *War: Controlling Escalation.* Cambridge, MA: Harvard University Press, 1977.

Spanier, John, and Nogee, Joseph, eds. *Congress, the Presidency, and Foreign Policy.* New York: Pergamon Press, 1981.

Szulc, Tad. *The Illusion of Peace.* New York: Viking Press, 1978.

Talbott, Strobe. *End Game: The Inside Story of SALT II.* New York: Harper & Row, 1979.

———. *The Master of the Game: Paul Nitze and the Nuclear Peace.* New York: Knopf, 1988.

Tambs, Lewis, ed. The Committee of Santa Fe. *A New Inter-American Policy for the Eighties.* Washington, DC: Council for Inter-American Security, 1980.

Tiefer, Charles. *The Semi-Sovereign Presidency: The Bush Administration's Strategy for Governing without Congress.* Boulder, CO: Westview Press, 1994.

Tucker, Robert W. *Nation or Empire? The Debate over American Foreign Policy.* Baltimore: Johns Hopkins University Press, 1968.

Tucker, Robert W., and Hendrickson, David C. *The Imperial Temptation: The New World Order and America's Purpose.* New York: Council on Foreign Relations, 1992.

Tulis, Jeffrey K. *The Rhetorical Presidency.* Princeton: Princeton University Press, 1987.

Vance, Cyrus. *Hard Choices: Critical Years in America's Foreign Policy.* New York: Simon and Schuster, 1983.

Walt, Stephen M. *The Origins of Alliances.* Ithaca, NY: Cornell University Press, 1987.

Warburg, Gerald F. *Conflict and Consensus: The Struggle between Congress and the President over Foreign Policymaking.* New York: Harper & Row, 1989.

Weinberger, Caspar. *Fighting for Peace: Seven Critical Years in the Pentagon.* New York: Warner Books, 1990.

White, John Kenneth. *The New Politics of Old Values.* Hanover, NH: University Press of New England, 1988.

Wills, Garry. *Reagan's America: Innocents at Home.* Garden City, NY: Doubleday, 1987.

Witcover, Jules. *Marathon: The Pursuit of the Presidency, 1972–1976.* New York: New American Library, 1977.

Wittkopf, Eugene R. *Faces of Internationalism: American Public Opinion and Foreign Policy.* Durham: Duke University Press, 1990.

Woodward, Bob. *The Agenda: Inside the Clinton White House.* New York: Simon and Schuster, 1994.

———. *Veil: The Secret Wars of the CIA 1981–1987.* New York: Simon and Schuster, 1987.

Wooten, James. *Dasher.* New York: Summit Books, 1978.

Yankelovich, Daniel, and Harmon, Sidney. *Starting with the People.* Boston: Houghton Mifflin, 1988.

Articles

Allison, Graham; May, Ernest; and Yarmolinsky, Adam. "U.S. Military Policy: Limits to Intervention." *Foreign Affairs* 48 (January 1970).

Barnes, Fred. "Reagan's Last Stand." *New Republic, April* 11, 1988.

Bell, Coral. "From Carter to Reagan." *Foreign Affairs, America and the World, 1984* 63 (1985).

Bell, Daniel. "The End of American Exceptionalism." *Public Interest* 41 (1975).

Bennett, W. Lance. "The Cueless Public: Bill Clinton Meets the New American Voter in Campaign '92." In *The Clinton Presidency: Campaigning, Governing, and the Psychology of Leadership,* ed. Stanley A. Renshon. Boulder, CO: Westview Press, 1995.

Blechman, Barry, with Gutmann, Ethan. "A $100 Billion Understanding." *SAIS Review* 9 (1989).

Boren, David L. "Speaking with a Single Voice: Bipartisanship in Foreign Policy." *SAIS Review* 9 (1989).

Brown, Bernard E. "The Structural Weaknesses of United States Foreign Policy." *American Foreign Policy Newsletter* 12 (1989).

Brown, Harold. "Building a New Consensus." SAIS Review 9 (1989).

Brownstein, Ronald. "The New Politics of National Security." *Public Opinion* 11 (1988).

Califano, Joseph A., Jr. "Imperial Congress." *New York Times Magazine,* January 29, 1994.

Carlson, Allan C. "Foreign Policy and 'the American Way': The Rise and Fall of the Post–World War II Consensus." *This World* 5 (1983).

Chace, James. "Is a Foreign Policy Consensus Possible?" *Foreign Affairs* 57 (Fall 1978).

Citrin, Jack; Haas, Ernst B.; and Muste, Christopher. "Is American Nationalism Changing? Implications for Foreign Policy." *International Studies Quarterly* 38 (1994).

"The Constitution in Danger: An Exchange." *New York Review of Books,* May 17, 1990.

Clarke, Jonathan. "America, Know Thyself." *National Interest* 34 (Winter 1993/94).

Clinton, Bill. "President-Elect Clinton's Foreign Policy Positions." *Foreign Policy Bulletin* 3 (November/December 1992).

Cox, Michael. "The Necessary Partnership? The Clinton Presidency and post-Soviet Russia." *International Affairs* 70 (October 1994).

Crovitz, L. Gordon. "How Ronald Reagan Weakened the Presidency." *Commentary* 86 (September 1988).

Deibel, Terry L. "Bush's Foreign Policy: Mastery and Inaction." *Foreign Policy* 84 (1991).

———. "Reagan's Mixed Legacy." *Foreign Policy* 75 (1989).

Drew, Elizabeth. "Letter from Washington." *New Yorker,* August 28, 1989.

Falk, Richard A. "Lifting the Curse of Bipartisanship." *World Policy Journal* 1 (1983).

Fallows, James. "The Passionless Presidency." *Atlantic Monthly,* May 1979.

Gause, F. Gregory, III. "The Illogic of Dual Containment." *Foreign Affairs* 73 (March/April 1994).

George, Alexander M. "Case Studies and Theory Development: The Method of Structured, Focused Comparison." In *Diplomacy: New Approaches in History, Theory, and Policy,* ed. Paul Gordon Lauren. New York: Free Press, 1977.

Gergen, David, "America's Missed Opportunities." *Foreign Affairs, America and the World 1991/92* (1992).

Gershman, Carl. "The Rise and Fall of the New Foreign-Policy Establishment." *Commentary* 24 (July 1980).

Glad, Betty. "How George Bush Lost the Presidential Election of 1992." In Renshon, ed., *The Clinton Presidency.*

Greider, William. "The Education of David Stockman." *Atlantic Monthly,* December 1981.

Griffith, E.S.; Plamenatz, John; and Pennock, J. Roland. "Cultural Prerequisites to a Successfully Functioning Democracy: Symposium." *American Political Science Review* 50 (1956).

Harries, Owen. "Between Paradigms." *National Interest* 17 (1989).

Harwood, Richard. "Ruling Class Journalists." *Washington Post,* October 30, 1993.

Hassner, Pierre. "The State of Nixon's World (3): Pragmatic Conservatism in the White House." *Foreign Policy* 3 (Summer 1971).

Hendrickson, David C. "The Recovery of Internationalism: Salvaging Clinton's Foreign Policy." *Foreign Affairs* 73 (September/October 1994).

Hertzberg, Hendrik. "At Watergate." *New Republic,* July 3, 1989.

Hodgson, Godfrey. "The Establishment." *Foreign Policy 10* (1973).

Hoffmann, Stanley. "Will the Balance Balance at Home?" *Foreign Policy* 7 (1972).

Holsti, Ole R. "Public Opinion and Containment." In *Containment: Concept and Policy,* ed. Terry L. Deibel and John Lewis Gaddis. Washington, DC: National Defense University Press, 1986.

Hughes, Thomas R. "The Crack Up," *Foreign Policy* 40 (1980).

Huntington, Samuel P. "The Clash of Civilizations." *Foreign Affairs* 70 (Spring 1993).

Jentleson, Bruce W. "The Pretty Prudent Public: Post Post-Vietnam American Opinion on the Use of Military Force." *International Studies Quarterly* 36 (Spring 1992).

Jones, Charles O., "Meeting Low Expectations: Strategy and Prospects of the Bush Presidency." In *The Bush Presidency: First Appraisals,* ed. Colin Campbell and Bert A Rockman. Chatham, NJ: Chatham House, 1991.

Judis, John B. "From Hell: The New Democrat Delusion." *New Republic,* December 19, 1994.

Kegley, Charles W., Jr. "The Bush Administration and the Future of American Foreign Policy: Pragmatism or Procrastination?" *Presidential Studies Quarterly* 19 (1989).

Kelly, Michael. "The Game." *New York Times Magazine,* October 31, 1993.

———. "Letter from Washington, DC: Shame and Surrender." *New Yorker,* December 19, 1994.

———. "Letter from Washington: Surrender and Blame." *New Yorker,* December 19, 1994.

Kennan, George F. "The Sources of Soviet Conduct." In *The Cold War*, ed. Walter Lippmann. New York: Harper & Row, 1972.

Kirkpatrick, Jeane J. "Dictatorships and Double Standards." *Commentary*, November 1979.

Kissinger, Henry. "Domestic Structure and Foreign Policy." *Daedalus* 95 (Spring 1966).

Kissinger, Henry, and Vance, Cyrus. "Bipartisan Objectives for Foreign Policy." *Foreign Affairs* 66 (Summer 1988).

Krauthammer, Charles. "Beyond the Cold War." *New Republic*, December 19, 1988.

———. "How the Doves Became Hawks." *Time*, May 17, 1993.

———. "The Unipolar Moment." *Foreign Affairs: America and the World 1990/91* 70 (1991).

Lake, Anthony. "Confronting Backlash States." *Foreign Affairs* 73 (March/April 1994).

Layne, Christopher. "Kant or Cant: The Myth of the Democratic Peace." *International Security* 19 (Fall 1994).

Lipset, Seymour Martin. "Some Further Comments on 'The End of Ideology.' " *American Political Science Review* 60 (1966).

McCormick, James M., and Wittkopf, Eugene R. "Bush and Bipartisanship: The Past as Prologue?" *Washington Quarterly* 13 (1990).

May, Elaine Tyler. "Cold War–Warm Hearth: Politics and the Family in Postwar America." In *The Rise and Fall of the New Deal Order, 1930–1980*, ed. Steve Fraser and Gary Berstle. Princeton: Princeton University Press, 1989.

Melanson, Richard A. "Action History, Declaratory History, and the Reagan Years." *SAIS Review* 9 (1989).

———. "The Social and Political Thought of William Appleman Williams." *Western Political Quarterly* 31 (1978).

Miller, Warren E. "Misreading the Public Pulse," *Public Opinion* 2 *(1979)*.

———. "Opinion Roundup," *Public Opinion* 2 (1979).

Mullins, Kerry, and Wildavsky, Aaron. "The Procedural Presidency of George Bush." *Political Science Quarterly* 107 (1992).

Nixon, Richard M. "Asia after Vietnam." *Foreign Affairs* 46 (October 1967).

"Of Rifts and Drifts: A Symposium on Beliefs, Opinions, and American Foreign Policy." *International Studies Quarterly* 89 (1974).

Phillips, Kevin. "Did We Elect Another Carter?" *New York Times*, February 9, 1989.

Polsby, Nelson W. "Foreign Policy Establishment: Toward Professionalism and Centrism." In *The Domestic Sources of American Foreign Policy: Insights and Evidence*, ed. Eugene R. Wittkopf. 2nd ed. New York: St. Martin's Press, 1994.

Prestowitz, Clyde V., Jr. "Beyond Laissez Faire." *Foreign Policy* 87 (1992).

Roskin, Michael. "From Pearl Harbor to Vietnam: Shifting Generational Paradigms and Foreign Policy." *Political Science Quarterly* 89 (1974).

Robbins, Carla Anne. "Dateline Washington, DC: Cuban-American Clout." *Foreign Policy* 88 (1992).

Rossiter, Caleb. "The Financial Hit List." *International Policy Report* (February 1984).

Sanders, Jerry W. "Empire at Bay: Containment Strategies and American Politics at the Crossroads." World Policy Paper No. 25. New York: World Policy Institute, 1983.

Schneider, William. "The Public and Foreign Policy." *Wall Street Journal*, November 7, 1979.

Shils, Edward. "The Concept of Consensus." In *International Encyclopedia of the Social Sciences*, ed. David L. Sills. New York: Crowell, Collier, and Macmillan, 1968.

Sinclair, Barbara. "Governing Unheroically (and Sometimes Unappetizingly): Bush and the 101st Congress." In *The Bush Presidency: First Appraisals*, ed. Colin Campbell and Bert A. Rockman. Chatham, NJ: Chatham House, 1991.

Smith, Craig Allen. "Mister Reagan's Neighborhood: Rhetoric and National Unity." *Southern Speech Communication Journal* 52 (1987).

Smith, Gaddis. "Haiti: From Intervention to Intervasion." *Current History,* February 1995.
Spiro, David E. "The Insignificance of the Liberal Peace." *International Security* 19 (Fall 1994).
Stremlau, John. "Clinton's Dollar Diplomacy." *Foreign Policy* 97 (1994/95).
Tannanbaum, Duane L. "The Bricker Amendment Controversy: Its Origins and Eisenhower's *Role." Diplomatic History* 9 (1985).
Trout, Thomas B. "Rhetoric Revisited: Political Legitimation and the Cold War." *International Studies Quarterly* 19 (1975).
Tucker, Robert W. "Reagan's Foreign Policy." *Foreign Affairs, America and the World, 1988/89* 68 (1989).
Wills, Garry. "The Born-Again Republicans." *New York Review of Books,* September 24, 1992.
———. "The Hostage." *New York Review of Books,* August 13, 1992.
Winik, Jay. "Restoring Bipartisanship." *Washington Quarterly* 12 (1989).
Wittkopf, Eugene R. "On the Foreign Policy Beliefs of the American People: A Critique and Some Evidence." *International Studies Quarterly* 30 (1986).
Yankelovich, Daniel, and Smoke, Richard. "America's 'New Thinking'." *Foreign Affairs* 67 (Fall 1988).

Unpublished Works

Balzano, Michael P., Jr. "The Silent Majority: Support for the President." *Richard Nixon: A Retrospective on His Presidency,* Hofstra University, Hempstead, NY, November 20, 1987.
Chittick, William O.; Billingsley, Keith R.; and Travis, Rick. "Discovering the Structure of Foreign Policy Beliefs: From Flatland to Spaceland." Paper, 1994.
Clark, William P. "National Security Strategy." Address. Center for Strategic and International Studies, Georgetown University, Washington, DC, May 21, 1982.
Colson, Charles W. "The Silent Majority: Support for the President." *Richard Nixon: A Retrospective on His Presidency,* Hofstra University, Hempstead, NY, November 20, 1987.
Gaddis, John Lewis. "Remarks at Panel on the Reagan Foreign Policy Legacy." Midwest meeting of the International Studies Association, Columbus, OH, November 11, 1988.
Garten, Jeffrey E. "The Big Emerging Markets: Changing American Interests in the Global Economy." Address before the Foreign Policy Association, New York, NY, January 20, 1994.
———. "Trade, Foreign Policy and National Security: Reflections on Economic Diplomacy." Address at the U.S. Military Academy, West Point, NY, May 4, 1994.
Grayden, Margaret M. "Foreign Policy Legitimation: A Preliminary Framework for Analysis." Paper presented to the annual meeting of the American Political Science Association, Chicago, IL, September 2–5, 1987.
Hult, Karen M., and Walcott, Charles. "Writing for the President: Evolution of an Organizational Function." Paper presented at the annual meeting of the American Political Science Association, Washington, DC, September 1–4, 1988.
Katz, Andrew Z. "Public Opinion, Congress, President Nixon and the Termination of the Vietnam War." Ph.D. diss., Johns Hopkins University, Baltimore, MD, 1987.
Lake, Anthony. "American Power and American Diplomacy." Warren and Anita Manshel Lecture at Harvard University, Cambridge, MA, October 21, 1994.
———. "From Containment to Enlargement." Remarks at the Johns Hopkins School of Advanced International Studies, Washington, DC, September 21, 1993.

Levering, Ralph B. "Public Opinion, Foreign Policy, and American Politics Since the 1960s." Paper presented at the annual Baker Peace Conference, Ohio University, Athens, Ohio, April 1988.

Morris, Roger. "The Foreign Policy Process." *Richard Nixon: A Retrospective on His Presidency,* Hofstra University, Hempstead, NY, November 20, 1987.

Organski, A.F.K., and Tammen, Ronald. "The New Open Door Policy: U.S. Strategy in the Post Cold War World." Paper, 1994.

Rodgers, Donald F. "The Silent Majority: Support for the President." *Richard Nixon: A Retrospective on His Presidency,* Hofstra University, Hempstead, NY, November 20, 1987.

Rosati, Jerel A., and Creed, John. "Clarifying Concepts of Consensus and Dissensus: Evolution of Public Beliefs in U.S. Foreign Policy." Paper presented at the annual meeting of the International Studies Association, St. Louis, MO, March 29–April 2, 1988.

Skidmore, David G. "The Politics of Decline: International Adjustment versus Domestic Legitimacy during the Carter Administration." Essay, 1989.

Sobel, Richard. "Public Opinion toward U.S. Involvement in Central America." Paper presented to the annual meeting of the American Political Science Association, Chicago, IL, September 2–5, 1987.

Trout, B. Thomas. "Legitimating Post Cold War Foreign Policy." Paper presented to the annual meeting of the American Political Science Association, Chicago, IL, September 1992.

Wittkopf, Eugene R., and McCormick, James M. "Was There Ever a Foreign Policy Consensus?" Paper presented at the annual meeting of the American Political Science Association, Washington, DC, September 1–4, 1988.

Zoellick, Robert B. "Project for the Republican Future: Is There a Republican Foreign Policy?" Address in Washington, DC, December 20, 1994.

Government Documents

Cheney, Dick, Secretary of Defense. *Defense Strategy for the 1990s: The Regional Defense Strategy.* Washington DC: Government Printing Office, January 1993.

The Clinton Administration's Policy on Reforming Multilateral Peace Operations. U.S. Department of State, Publication 10161, May 1994.

Congressional Record. Washington, DC, October 1983.

Haig, Alexander M., Jr. "American Power and American Purpose," *Current Policy,* no. 279. U.S. Department of State, April 27, 1982.

———. "Relationship of Foreign and Defense Policies." *Current Policy,* no. 308. U.S. Department of State, July 30, 1981.

———. Testimony. U.S. Congress. Senate. *Hearings before the Committee on Foreign Relations* 99th Cong., 1st sess., February 7, 1985, "Commitments, Consensus, and U.S. Foreign Policy."

Kirkpatrick, Jeane J. "Ambassador Kirkpatrick's Statement, UN Security Council, October 27, 1983." *Department of State Bulletin,* U.S. Department of State, December 1983.

———. "The Atlantic Alliance and the American National Interest." *Current Policy,* no. 581. U.S. Department of State, April 30, 1984.

Lake, W. Anthony. "Pragmatism and Principle in U.S. Foreign Policy." Address to the Boston Council of World Affairs, June 13, 1977. *Current Policy,* no. 213. U.S. Department of State, 1977.

National Security Strategy of the United States. Washington, DC: Government Printing Office, March 1990, January 1993, July 1994, February 1995.

President's Special Review Board (The Tower Commission Report). Washington, DC: Government Printing Office, 1987.

Public Papers of the Presidents of the United States: Richard Nixon, 1969–1973. Washington, DC: Government Printing Office, 1971–75.

Public Papers of the Presidents of the United States: Gerald R. Ford, 1974. Washington, DC: Government Printing Office, 1975.

Public Papers of the Presidents of the United States: Jimmy Carter, 1977–1981. Washington, DC: Government Printing Office, 1978–83.

Public Papers of the Presidents of the United States: Ronald Reagan, 1981–1987. Washington, DC: Government Printing Office, 1983–89.

Public Papers of the Presidents of the United States: George Bush, 1989–1993. Washington, DC: Government Printing Office, 1990–94.

Reagan, Ronald. "Paths toward Peace: Deterrence and Arms Control." *Current Policy,* no. 435. U.S. Department of State, November 22, 1982.

Report of the Congressional Committees Investigating the Iran-Contra Affair. Washington, DC: Government Printing Office, 1987.

Shelton, Sally A. U.S. Congress. House. *Hearing before the Subcommittee on Inter-American Affairs of the Committee on Foreign Affairs.* 97th Cong., 2nd sess., June 15, 1982, "United States Policy toward Grenada."

Shultz, George. "The Meaning of Vietnam." *Current Policy,* no. 269. U.S. Department of State, April 25, 1985.

———. "Power and Diplomacy in the 1980s," *Current Policy,* no. 561. U.S. Department of State, April 3, 1984.

U.S. Congress. House. *Hearing on Grenada.* 97th Cong., 2nd sess., June 15, 1982.

U.S. Congress. Senate. *Nomination of Henry A. Kissinger to be Secretary of State.* 2 parts. 93rd Cong., 1st sess., 1973.

U.S. Congress. Senate. *Hearings Before the Committee on Foreign Relations. Détente.* 93rd Cong., 2nd sess., August 1–5, 20, and 21, September 10, 12, 18, 19, 24, and 25, and October 1 and 8, 1974.

U.S. Department of Commerce. Trade Promotion Coordinating Committee. *Toward a National Export Strategy.* Report to the U.S. Congress, September 30, 1993.

U.S. Department of State, Bureau of Public Affairs. *Current Policy,* 1977–91.

U.S. National Bipartisan Commission on Central America, "Report of the National Bipartisan Commission on Central America." U.S. Department of State, 1984.

U.S. President. *US Foreign Policy for the 1970s: A New Strategy for Peace.* Report to the Congress by Richard M. Nixon, President of the United States, February 18, 1970. Washington, DC: Government Printing Office, 1970.

———. *US Foreign Policy for the 1970s: Building for Peace.* Report to the Congress by Richard M. Nixon, President of the United States, February 25, 1971. Washington, DC: Government Printing Office, 1971.

———. *US Foreign Policy for the 1970s: The Emerging Structure of Peace.* Report to the Congress by Richard M. Nixon, President of the United States, February 9, 1972. Washington, DC: Government Printing Office, 1973.

———. *US Foreign Policy for the 1970s: Shaping a Durable Peace.* Report to the Congress by Richard M. Nixon, President of the United States, May 3, 1973. Washington, DC: Government Printing Office, 1973.

U.S. President. *Weekly Compilation of Presidential Documents,* 1969–95. Washington. DC: Government Printing Office, 1969–95.

"U.S. Support for Democracy and Peace in Central America." *Selected Documents,* no. 36. U.S. Department of State, n.d.

Vance, Cyrus. "Meeting the Challenges of a Changing World." Address before the Chicago Council on Foreign Relations, June 1, 1979. U.S. Department of State, *Current Policy,* no. 501.

Weinberger, Caspar W. *Annual Report to the Congress Fiscal Year 1983.* Washington, DC: Government Printing Office, 1982.

Index

Horton, Willie, 203
House, Edwin, 15
Howe, Jonathan, 260
Human rights, 33, 99, 101–2, 107,
    120, 121–22, 160, 164, 191, 273,
    295
Humphrey, Hubert, 97
Huntington, Samuel, 29, 98
Hussein, Saddam, 227, 229, 230,
    266–67, 297

IAEC. *See* International Atomic
    Energy Commission
IMF. *See* International Monetary Fund
Individual liberties, 11
INF treaty. *See* Intermediate Nuclear
    Forces treaty
Institute for International Economics,
    30
Institutional confidence, 89–90
Interest-group liberalism, 93
Intermediate Nuclear Forces (INF)
    treaty, 145, 159
"Intermestic" issues, 28
International Atomic Energy
    Commission (IAEC), 267–68
Internationalism, 6–7, 10, 233
  and foreign policy establishment,
    15–16
  post–Cold War, 27
  types of, 18–19
International Labor Organization, 238
International Monetary Fund (IMF), 9
International Trade Organization, 9
Intolerance, 10–11
Iowa caucuses, 89
Iran, 159–60, 179, 195, 203, 266–67
Iraq, 219–20, 229, 236, 266–67, 297
*Irony of Vietnam: The System Worked,
    The* (Gelb), 103
Islamic Conference, 114
Isolationism, 6, 18, 64, 101, 222, 233,
    235
  and Nixon, 71–72

Jackson, Henry, 78–79, 128
Japan, 222, 233, 268, 273
Johnson, Lyndon, 14, 43, 56, 64

Johnson, Lyndon *(continued)*
  declaratory history of, 36
Joint resolutions, 14, 21, 83
Jones, Charles O., 90
Jordan, Hamilton, 90
Judis, John, 250

Kemp, Jack, 207
Kennan, George F., 7, 8, 11–12, 35,
    143, 216, 231
Kennedy, John F., 36–37, 56, 148
Kerrey, Bob, 237
Khalilzad, Zalmay, 222
Khrushchev, Nikita, 11
Kim Il Sung, 268
Kirkpatrick, Jeane, 148, 155, 160,
    169–71, 180
Kissinger, Henry, 29, 43, 53–54, 57,
    64, 186
  Carter's criticism of, 95–96
  foreign policy under Ford, 79–80
  foreign policy under Nixon, 72–74,
    78–79, 81, 293–94
  and human rights, 101
Kissinger Commission, 182
"Kitchen debate," 11
Kohl, Helmut, 218
Kolb, Charles, 206, 207
Korean War, 8, 13, 14
  and UN support, 10
Krauthammer, Charles, 29
Kreisberg, Paul, 109, 112
Kristol, Irving, 123
Kurds (people), 229
Kuwait, 220, 236, 297

Laird, Melvin, 57
Lake, W. Anthony, 101, 255, 265–66,
    277
Lance, Bert, 122
Larrabee, F. Stephen, 110
Latin America, 163
Latvia, 214
Leach, Jim, 173
League Covenant, 4
League of Nations, 220
Lebanon, 172
LeFevre, Ernest, 160

About the Author

Richard A. Melanson is professor of international security studies at the National Defense University in Washington, D.C. He is the author of *Writing History and Making Policy: The Cold War, Vietnam, and Revisionism* (1983) and the coeditor (with Kenneth W. Thompson) of *Foreign Policy and Domestic Consensus* (1985).